THE ORCHID MURDER

Untangling a Web
of
Unsolved Murders and Legal Malpractice

Christine Hurt
Isa. 30. 18

RIGHT LINE PUBLISHING

ISBN-13: 978-0-9844395-5-3
ISBN-10: 0-9844395-5-2

Library of Congress Control Number: 2012911359

BISAC Subject Codes:

TRU002000	TRUE CRIME / Murder / General
LAW064000	LAW / Litigation
LAW095000	LAW / Malpractice
BIO020000	BIOGRAPHY & AUTOBIOGRAPHY / Lawyers & Judges
HIS036090	HISTORY / United States / State & Local / Midwest

DISCLAIMER: Statements made by legal experts as well as any and all other legal advice contained within this work, whether in private conversation or as pretrial or trial proceeding, are reprinted here only as matters of historical record in the context of their influence upon this case and are in no way to be assumed, interpreted, or mistaken as or presumed to be legal advice for any other matter in any regard.

Cover design: www.KitFosterDesign.com

10 9 8 7 6 5 4 3 2

Printed in the U.S.A.

AUTHOR'S NOTES

Quotations, actions, and personal conversations described herein were gleaned from documents of public record including trial transcripts and evidence, sworn affidavits and depositions, sworn video depositions, documentation of private conversations subsequently made public (usually by subpoena), notes within attorney files, or were recreated from personal recollections gathered during interviews with the author.

Portions of the 1994 trial transcript were unavailable for review including large portions of Plaintiff's experts' testimony and of Defense polygraph expert, Charles Yeshke.

DEDICATION

to those who understand the need for relationship,
and to those who choose to stand for justice

A fiduciary —

someone who has undertaken to act for and on behalf of another in circumstances which give rise to a relationship of trust and confidence —one who holds a relationship of trust[1]

Fiduciary Duty —

an obligation to act in the best interest of another party[2]

Breach of Fiduciary Duty Law and Legal Definition

A fiduciary obligation exists whenever the relationship with the client involves a special trust, confidence, and reliance on the fiduciary to exercise his discretion or expertise in acting for the client.

When one person does agree to act for another in a fiduciary relationship, the law forbids the fiduciary from acting in any manner adverse or contrary to the interests of the client. The client is entitled to the best efforts of the fiduciary on his behalf and the fiduciary must exercise all of the skill, care, and diligence at his disposal when acting on behalf of the client.

A person acting in a fiduciary capacity is held to a high standard of honesty and full disclosure in regard to the client and must not obtain a personal benefit at the expense of the client.[3]

> "Never leave a client in a worse position than where you found him."
> – Jerry Snider

---

1. *Bristol and West Building Society v. Mothew* [1998] Ch 1 at 18.
2. http://www.lectlaw.com/def/f026.htm. 10-22-2010.
3. http://definitions.uslegal.com/b/breach-of-fiduciary-duty/. 10-22-2010. Abridged.

DRAMATIS PERSONAE

<u>NON-LEGAL PERSONS INVOLVED in *The Orchid Murder*</u>

- Clayman, Butch and Connie – life-long friends of the Wartnicks

- Evers, Tom – former employee, B and B Wholesale Florists

- Friedman, Zola – sold the original key-man insurance policy to Midwest Floral Supply

- Hurkos, Peter – popular entertainer known for performing psychic feats; worked as psychic detective on cases such as the Boston Strangler and the Sharon Tate murder

- Krueger, Russell – former Minneapolis police detective, served as primary investigator in the murder of Bob Nachtsheim

- Kreuser, Dennis – ex-convict (juvenile) and former fiancée of Angie Nachtsheim

- Mentes, Alan – former employee, B and B Wholesale Florists; Mentes and employee Larry Kramlinger discovered the fatally wounded Bob Nachtsheim after the 1973 shooting

- The Nachtsheim Family
  o Angie – younger daughter of the victim
  o Betty – Bob's wife; remarried, became Prokosh
  o Bob – former employee of Midwest Floral Supply; left to form B and B Wholesale Florist, August 1972; murdered May 24, 1973
  o Bobby – oldest son of the victim
  o Debbie (nee Feist) – Bobby's wife
  o John – youngest son of the victim
  o Terry – older daughter of the victim; married name, Peters

- Nordstrom, Roger – ex-convict and close friend of Bobby Nachtsheim

- Strehlow, Larry – close friend of Dennis Kreuser; murdered in the cemetery near the burial site of Bob Nachtsheim

- The Wartnick Family
  o Babe – Norm's wife
  o Jack – Norm's brother

o   Norm – ran Midwest Floral Supply; in 1986 a jury found him responsible for the 1973 wrongful death of Bob Nachtsheim

ATTORNEYS WITHIN *The Orchid Murder*

- Duffy, Walter – Faegre attorney brought in to handle settlement negotiations during 1994 trial
- Friedberg, Joe – 2011 President of the American Board of Criminal Lawyers, member of the American Board of Trial Advocates, and a Fellow in the American College of Trial Lawyers; named to the Minnesota Legal Hall of Fame by *Minnesota Law & Politics* as one of the 100 most influential lawyers in the history of Minnesota; listed in all editions of *The Best Lawyers in America*
- Gainsley, Phillip – Norm Wartnick's attorney during the 1970s and 1980s
- Lerner, Jane – friend and former law partner of Phil Gainsley; married name is McTaggert though, for clarity, maiden name used throughout
- Liberko, Dan – law clerk with Faegre; did major portion of investigation for Wartnick case
- Mason, Jack – partner at Dorsey & Whitney; hired by Moss & Barnett to represent them and Gainsley in defending against the attorney malpractice lawsuit
- Magarian, Ed – Dorsey & Whitney attorney; assisted Jack Mason with Gainsley's defense
- Meshbesher, Ron – one of the most well-known and well-respected lawyers in Minnesota; represented the Nachtsheim family interests in pursuit of Norm Wartnick for responsibility in Bob Nachtsheim's death, throughout the subsequent Wartnick proceedings against Gainsley, and in the collection of moneys to settle the judgment against Wartnick
- Oliver, Bob - an amalgam of those Faegre partners who opposed Wartnick's pursuit of Gainsley
- Severson, Steve – associate then partner with Faegre; assisted Snider with the Wartnick case
- Snider, Jerry – Fellow of the American College of Trial Lawyers, one of *Lawdragon*'s 500 Leading Litigators in America, and listed as one of The Best Lawyers in America in Commercial Litigation; named one of the top 40 business litigators in Minnesota by *Minnesota Law & Politics*
- Thomson, Doug – friend and former law partner of Joe Friedberg; cited by the *Minneapolis Star Tribune* as "a criminal defense attorney in some

of the biggest trials in the last half of the 20th century in Minnesota"; named to Minnesota's Legal Hall of Fame as one of the state's 100 Most Influential Lawyers of All Time

- Webber, Chuck – attorney for Faegre & Benson; a Fellow of the American College of Trial Lawyers

JUDGES WITHIN *The Orchid Murder*

- Davis, Michael – presided over the 1988 trial of the attorney malpractice suit against Phil Gainsley; currently (2012) Chief Judge, U. S. District Court, District of Minnesota

- McCarr, Henry – presided over the original, 1986 wrongful death trial in which Norm Wartnick was found responsible for the death of Bob Nachtsheim

- Schiefelbein, Robert – presided over the 1990 attorney malpractice litigation

- Stanoch, John – presided over the 1994 attorney malpractice litigation

Individuals who appear with an asterick (*) following the first occurrence of their name have had their name changed.

ॐॐ

Did you have any expectations
of how a lawyer would defend you
in relation to being accused of murder?

~ Joe Friedberg

CHAPTER 1

Bob Nachtsheim arrived at B and B Wholesale Florists to continue a routine that had varied little for nearly two decades. He exhaled a cloud of cigarette smoke and ground the butt into the sidewalk with the heel of his shoe, unlocked the front door, switched on the lights, plugged in the coffee pot, and headed for the walk-in coolers that kept fresh a bulk inventory of flowers. Eight months earlier Bob had left the employ of Midwest Floral Supply to start a company of his own. His loyal customers had supported the move. Bob had taken their business away from Midwest Floral and was now responsible not only for the freshness of the flowers but also for paying the bills. Otherwise, everything was the same.

Nachtsheim unlocked the stainless steel cooler door, flipped on the light, and stepped into the damp chill. Customer satisfaction always came first, thus his habitual early check to verify the day's flowers met his standards.

Flower distributors use a variety of techniques to check for freshness. They want the flowers to be "crisp, not soft." A firm response of the delicate petals to a florist's touch indicates many days of life left in that flower. Some florists use the back of their hand, some brush their fingers lightly across the petal tips; most have different ways for different type flowers. Bob had developed a unique way to check carnations—with his chin.

Bob Nachtsheim's first item of routine was to set out the orchids; they must warm or will be too brittle to work with, so Bob lifted the flat of orchids and stepped back into the shop.

A sawed-off shotgun roared into the silence. The blast exploded bird shot into Bob Nachtsheim's head, pinged against the cooler door, and pock-marked surrounding walls. The assailant bolted out the back door. He left behind an overturned flat of orchids and a spreading pool of blood.

CHAPTER 2

Despite Betty Nachtsheim's intense and, some would say, extreme efforts, her husband's murder remained unsolved. Now Betty concluded that Bob's former employer, Norm Wartnick of Midwest Floral Supply, had unfairly benefited from Bob's death and therefore must be guilty of the crime.

Wartnick had motive; that was known since the day of the shooting. At that time, Midwest held a key-man insurance policy on the former employee, had renewed it mere weeks before the shooting—and had received proceeds of one-hundred thousand dollars. Unfortunately for Betty, motive alone is insufficient for a formal allegation and the Hennepin County Attorney found no basis for charges against Wartnick—no grand jury, no arrest, never even taken in for questioning. Wartnick could not be connected to Bob Nachtsheim's shooting in any way.

But that did not stop Betty. She badgered Twin Cities' attorney Ron Meshbesher to do something, pushed and pled for him to prove Wartnick responsible for her husband's death. If Meshbesher could prove Wartnick's culpability, Betty said she could find closure. Yielding to her pressure, in October of 1976 Meshbesher filed a cobbled-together unjust enrichment complaint.

And it sat there. Meshbesher agreed to allow Wartnick and his attorney, Phil Gainsley, to delay answering Betty's complaint, to await solid evidence against Wartnick. None materialized.

Through 1977 and 1978, Betty's lawsuit lay dormant. Then, in 1979, *Nachtsheim v. Wartnick* cycled to the top of Meshbesher's tickler file. He decided to depose Wartnick and bring the suit to a close.

FRIDAY, FEBRUARY 16, 1979

Wartnick was duly sworn in. Meshbesher began the questioning. "Now, you've been sitting here through the deposition of Mrs. Nachtsheim, so you know the way it's conducted. Isn't that correct?"

"Yes, that's correct."

"Now, if you do not understand any of my questions, please advise me and I'll try to rephrase it so that it will be more understandable to you. Do you follow me?"

"Yes."

"What is your employment?"

"I'm a wholesale florist."

"Are you affiliated with any company?"

"Midwest Floral Supply."

"What is your relationship to that company?"

"At the present time I'm the primary stockholder and president of the corporation."

"How much stock did you own in that company at the time of the shooting?"

"Twenty-five percent of fifty percent—No, excuse me, twelve percent of fifty percent. There were two major stockholders and at the time they were fifty-fifty stockholders. My father didn't have a will, so probate divided the stock equally among the three children and his wife, so I was really twelve-and-a-half percent or thereabouts of the fifty percent."

"Well, in 1970 did you own fifty percent of the stock?"

"No."

"Did you ever tell anyone from the retail credit company that you owned fifty percent of the stock and Mr. Benjamin Stoller the other half?"

His attorney's subtle movement caught Wartnick's attention. Wartnick thought he was mistaken, then Gainsley leaned over and whispered, "Read the card."

Wartnick was confused. What did this have to do with anything? But he paid Gainsley to be the lawyer because Wartnick knew he could not do it himself, so he pulled a note card from his shirt pocket and read, "On the advice of my counsel I respectfully refuse to answer that question on the grounds that to do so may violate my rights under the Fifth Amendment of the United States Constitution."

Meshbesher glanced quickly from Gainsley to client, then continued the questioning without breaking his rhythm. "When did you purchase your late father's interest in the company?"

Wartnick noticed Gainsley's gaze was fixed somewhere beyond the conference room ceiling. He dropped the note card to the table. "I never purchased it."

"You never purchased it?"

Wartnick shook his head.

"What happened to his interest?"

"You mean my father's interest?"

"Yes."

"Well, my sister has multiple sclerosis and is in a nursing home, and her percentage of stock was transferred to me. My mother, on her retirement in June of, I believe, 1977 or '76, thereabouts, transferred her stock to me, and my brother maintains his stock."

"Did you know—let me put it this way: It's true, is it not, that Bob Nachtsheim was employed by Midwest Floral Supply?"

Gainsley motioned.

Wartnick winced, shifted in his chair, and fumbled for the note card. "On the advice of my counsel I respectfully refuse to answer that question on the grounds that to do so may violate my rights under the Fifth Amendment of the United States Constitution."

Meshbesher continued without pause. "Isn't it a fact that Midwest Floral had a so-called key-man or key-personnel insurance policy covering the life of Bob Nachtsheim?"

"On the advice of my counsel I respectfully refuse to answer that question on the grounds that to do so may violate my rights under the Fifth Amendment of the United States Constitution."

"Isn't it a fact you refused to take a polygraph examination after requested by the Minneapolis Police Department in connection with the investigation of the homicide of Bob Nachtsheim?"

Wartnick sighed. "On the advice of my counsel I respectfully refuse to answer that question on the grounds that to do so may violate my rights under the Fifth Amendment of the United States Constitution."

This time Meshbesher paused before the next question, inhaled, and continued. "Mr. Wartnick, isn't it a fact that when the psychic or clairvoyant, Peter Hurkos, came to your store you refused to talk with him?"

Wartnick flushed. "On—on the advice of my counsel I respectfully refuse to answer that question on the grounds that to do so may violate my rights under the Fifth Amendment of the United States Constitution."

"Can you state whether or not you, personally, shot and killed Bob Nachtsheim?"

Wartnick looked to Gainsley but could not catch his attention. His advocate leaned back in his chair, hands clasped behind his head, and continued to stare off to somewhere outside the four walls of the conference room. Wartnick exhaled slowly and his shoulders sagged as he again read from the card.

"Off the record, please." Meshbesher removed his reading glasses and looked incredulously at defendant's counsel. "Mr. Gainsley, is your client going to continue repeating his Fifth Amendment rights to every question?"

"I have instructed him to do so until I tell him otherwise."

Meshbesher shook his head and struggled to maintain a poker face. "Then let's continue." He cleared his throat, returned his glasses to his nose, and nodded to the court reporter. "Back on the record. Now then, Mr. Wartnick, where were you between the times of six-thirty and seven o'clock on the morning of Thursday, May 24, 1973?"

Wartnick glanced sideways at Gainsley then read, "On the advice of my counsel I respectfully refuse to answer that question...."

The following Monday, Meshbesher instructed his law clerk to prepare and to file an amendment to their complaint. The new allegation: Wartnick was responsible for the death of Bob Nachtsheim.

In criminal litigation, a defendant is free to assert his Fifth Amendment right—to refuse to testify without creating any assumption the testimony might be incriminating. But in *civil* litigation, if a defendant asserts his Fifth Amendment right, the court and the jury are allowed to draw an *adverse inference*: they can reasonably assume the defendant's answer would incriminate him in some way. Wartnick's declaration of Fifth Amendment rights gave Meshbesher all he needed to take Wartnick to trial.

SEVEN YEARS LATER

THURSDAY, APRIL 24, 1986 - *NACHTSHEIM V. WARTNICK* TRIAL DAY FOUR

Meshbesher's silver hair gleamed under the courtroom's harsh lighting; his reading glasses were perched half-way down his aquiline nose. Meshbesher had Norm Wartnick on the witness stand and was in the midst of proving his case that "Wartnick, acting on behalf of Midwest, caused or procured the murder of Robert Nachtsheim." The six-member jury watched as Meshbesher read his questions from his February 1979 deposition of Wartnick—and Norm Wartnick was required, without clarification or explanation, to read his answers for that jury and for the record.

"Isn't it a fact," Meshbesher continued, "that Midwest Floral had a so-called key-man or key-personnel insurance policy covering the life of Bob Nachtsheim?"

Wartnick cleared his throat then read his previous reply. "On the advice of my counsel I respectfully refuse to answer that question on the grounds that to do so may violate my rights under the Fifth Amendment of the United States Constitution."

"Can you state whether or not you, personally, shot and killed Bob Nachtsheim?"

Scarlet crept up Wartnick's neck and flamed his ears. "On the advice of my counsel," he read, "I respectfully refuse to answer that question on the grounds that to do so may violate my rights under the Fifth Amendment of the United States Constitution."

SATURDAY, APRIL 26, 1986

Jury awards widow $2.35 million in slaying of florist
- Minneapolis Star and Tribune

"A Hennepin County jury ... ordered the former employer of a slain Minneapolis florist to pay the victim's widow, Betty Nachtsheim, $2.35 million in damages after finding that the former employer either killed her husband or caused him to be killed in 1973. ... The award approaches what is thought to be the largest wrongful death [verdict] in Minnesota history. ... No one was ever arrested for the crime. The weapon, a sawed-off shotgun, has never been found. ..."

CHAPTER 3

MID-OCTOBER 1987

Norm Wartnick sat in the waiting area of attorney Joe Friedberg's office, bounced a stuffed manila envelope off his knee and caught it on the rebound, then he stood. The average-sized, sandy-haired Midwesterner preferred to move; sitting aggravated the pain in his lower back.

For over twenty years, Wartnick had spent his days in thirty-eight degree flower coolers and his weeknights on high-school basketball or volleyball courts wearing a striped shirt and blowing a whistle. Wartnick was accustomed to order and routine—equal periods in a game, rules in a guide book with plainly established consequences, flower arrangements carefully built on odd-numbered groupings. To Norm Wartnick there were established rules and schedules for everything. Now, for the first time, it was impossible to blow the whistle in his own life, where it counted most. But he knew he could not quit; he could not accept this new status quo. Norm would not let his family live with this judgment over their heads.

After the April 1986 verdict, Wartnick had allowed his long-time attorney, Phil Gainsley, to represent him in the appeal, but it was doomed faster than Gainsley cashed Wartnick's checks. Wartnick desperately needed an attorney who could extricate him from the disaster. He contacted several; not one gave him a hearing. Then he learned it was possible Joe Friedberg, a criminal attorney with a reputation for grit and honesty, might take an interest.

Friedberg was the man who looked you in the eye and told you the truth, even when he knew it may not be what you wanted to hear. He wore tailored suits and had been a teaching fellow at Stanford University, but he was known for his spunky street-smarts. Born the son of a fabric salesman in Brooklyn, New York, he was awarded the prestigious Order of the Coif at the University of North Carolina School of Law in 1963. Friedberg moved to Minnesota and spent eight years selling encyclopedias door-to-door. In those days he often traveled Minneapolis's poorest neighborhoods where, along with encyclopedias for sale, he offered free legal advice to those in need. Now, in 1987, with two decades of experience since admittance to the Minnesota Bar, Friedberg knew how to choose his battles, knew how to team with investigators, scientists, and other professionals to win complex criminal trials.

Wartnick's early attempts to elicit a sympathetic response from Friedberg had failed. Friedberg's wife and secretary, Carolyn, was an efficient vanguard, but on this chilly October afternoon Carolyn was out of the office and Friedberg was in court. Wartnick knew the high-profile attorney should soon return, so he paced Friedberg's waiting area and instinctively felt the precise, ever-forward progression of the clock on the wall. It was vital he got an audience with this man.

The outer door popped open and Friedberg entered at full stride, saw Wartnick, and kept going. "Get lost," Friedberg called over his shoulder. "Told you the last three times you were in here, I don't sue lawyers."

"But it'll take fifty lifetimes to pay three million dollars." Wartnick followed the attorney through the swinging half-door and stood in the inner-office doorway.

Friedberg hung his suit coat on a brass hook, extracted heirloom cufflinks, shook his head decisively—"Sorry, kid."—and began to turn up French cuffs. "It's not gonna happen."

"But I didn't do it. I did not kill Bob Nachtsheim!"

Friedberg noticed Wartnick was restless, shifted from one foot to the other, yet he did not seem nervous. Friedberg regarded the stuffed manila envelope Wartnick had held straight toward him for well over a minute. "Give me your file. I'll look at it," Friedberg heard himself say. He expected to give it a quick glance then follow-up with a form letter: *Not appropriate for my current case load* or *Not enough information to build a case*. Either way, it would get this guy off his back.

Wartnick started to speak.

Friedberg grabbed the envelope and tossed it to a table. "Now get out of here."

CHAPTER 4

"Norm, no." Babe Wartnick sighed and dropped her hairbrush to the bathroom vanity. "I told you I won't even discuss going through another lawsuit." She retrieved her sweater from its hanger. "I'm through with them. Over. Done."

"You know the judgment's not just going to disappear." Norm caught for her hand, but Babe side-stepped through the doorway.

Norm loped after her toward the kitchen. "And refereeing community league's not going to touch that three mil. No one'll hire someone guilty of murder."

"It was only wrongful death. And you didn't do it!"

"You think people see a difference between wrongful death and murder? Most people don't even know what wrongful—"

"You just couldn't forget Bob, could you?" Babe dropped the hot casserole to the stove top and hip-slammed the oven door. "You had to hang onto him with that ridiculous insurance policy."

"That was fourteen years ago. You think that's going to change anything now?"

She glanced heavenward, muttered, and began to load mixing bowls and measuring cups into the dishwasher.

Norm retrieved a clean spoon and dipped into the creamy chicken mixture topped with tater tots which Midwesterners often call hot dish. "Our name's at stake if nothing else," he said and popped the stolen bite into his mouth. His face reddened; he inhaled sharply and plopped the chicken into his hand. "Th-the children," he spoke carefully to prevent his scorched tongue from touching his teeth. "They've grown up with a father accused of murder. Gainsley had no clue what he was doing."

"Exactly! I told you from the beginning he was incompetent. Shows how you listen."

Norm shook the piece of chicken to cool it while he watched Babe scrub clean a mixing bowl that had been her grandmother's. "I was giving Phil the best chance to prove himself. He still wants to appeal to the state supreme court, you know."

"He plays with his appeals while you have your wages garnished. Just what does all that loyalty get you?"

"It worked well raising the kids and running the business." Norm's voice softened. "And it helped us endure these last years."

She turned to face him, reached for a towel, and began to wipe the bowl dry.

"Right?" He nodded and took a step toward her. "I couldn't have made it without you and the kids."

The front door opened. "We're here!" Butch Clayman called from the foyer. Butch had been Norm's best friend almost since birth and was one of the few who, since the 1986 verdict, still considered Norm a friend.

Norm's focus stayed locked onto Babe's face as he popped the chicken into his mouth, chewed fast, swallowed hard, and called out to Butch, "So you still think Foggie will get his MVP title back this year?"

Babe grinned. "Burn yourself?" she whispered, only inches from his face.

Butch and his wife, Connie, appeared from the front hallway. For almost twenty years the two couples had met every Saturday for dinner and Canasta.

"Think the Gophers'll be smart enough to keep Thompson in the backfield?" Butch replied.

Norm gave Butch a solid thump on the back then led him into the den. He turned the volume knob of the television and the clamor of college football filled the room.

Connie greeted Babe. "Figured out what you're doing for Holly's birthday?"

"Not yet," Babe said. "But I'm sure I'll come up with something to surprise her. I always do." She pulled a serving spoon from a drawer. "Let's eat. I hate lukewarm hot dish."

Connie nodded. "Butch, where'd you put the salad? Never mind—it's by the fridge. You guys have three minutes." No response. "Hey, you two. Dinner's getting cold." Connie put the tips of both little fingers into the corners of her mouth and blasted out a short, yelping whistle.

"Five more minutes." Butch held up a hand, fingers extended. "Game's almost over."

Connie grimaced over her shoulder at Babe. "May as well put it back in the oven. Norm didn't even look up."

Two Weeks Later

"Mr. Wartnick? Joe Friedberg here. I've read your— No, I'm not gonna *do* an appeal." He listened. "Because the case is a mess. But I'll tell you what I *will* do. You let Gainsley shoot his wad. Yes, I know it's your money, but we're gonna see if we can't get some of it back for you. That's right. Let him take it to the supreme court if he thinks he can. No, I don't think he'll make it that far, but when he's done, you call me. Why? Because as soon as you pass a polygraph for me, we're gonna sue him, that's why. For malpractice, Mr. Wartnick. Attorney malpractice."

CHAPTER 5

FIVE MONTHS LATER

Early March 1988

"Judge Devitt,[4] if I could have a word." Joe Friedberg clicked home the latches of his brief case and prepared to exit the courtroom. Friedberg, a criminal litigator, worked solo. To pursue Wartnick's case he needed to team with a civil attorney. Judge Edward J. Devitt had earned national stature, characterized by wisdom, humanity, and commitment to the rule of law. Confident recommendation of a trial lawyer by Judge Devitt would be high praise.

"Sure, Joe. What is it?"

"I'm representing in a new civil action so I need to team with a civil litigator."

"Check with Jerry Snider over at Faegre," Devitt said. "Appeared before me three times in the last year and won jury verdicts. Thoroughly prepared."

Friedberg's legal career was steeped in tragedy; Snider's was steeped in tradition. Jerry Snider was a Southern boy and consummate gentleman, a business trial lawyer with the international silk-stocking firm[5] of Faegre & Benson for eighteen years. Snider's resonant voice and Southern drawl solicited response from listeners, whether he was swapping stories during an intimate dinner party or putting forth facts to a jury.

Snider took Friedberg's call. "My calendar has few openings," Snider said. "And, to be frank, attorney malpractice is the *last* thing I want to litigate. Mr.— Mr. Friedberg. Joe, attorney malpractice is not—. That's *not* the type case—. Even if I was interested—I'm sure you're aware how hard it is to prove a case like that. That's correct, and it'd be a tough sell to the litigation committee. Yes, even *with* significant deviations from normal standards.

---

4. Devitt was a long-time Chief Judge of the U.S. District Court for the District of Minnesota. The Devitt Award, presented annually, honors a judge of Devitt's character: a judge of national stature whose distinguished, life-long career is characterized by decisions which display wisdom, humanity, and commitment to the rule of law; which make clear that bench, bar, and community alike willingly entrust that judge with the most complex cases of the most far-reaching import; and whose activities have improved the administration of justice, advanced the rule of law, or strengthen civic ties within local, national, or international communities. (The American Judicature Society. Accessed Mar 8, 2011.)

5. Representing only large, highly profitable corporations, banks, etc.

"*Instructed* him to take the Fifth?" Snider leaned back in his chair and scratched his chin through a short, dark beard. "And you're sure his story's credible? What's in the file?

"No, that's sufficient. Send it to me. I'll look at it. But, Joe, if I think it's not winnable or if the smallest indication makes me think Wartnick might be guilty, the answer will be 'No.'"

TWO WEEKS LATER

MARCH 1988

"Holy mackerel!" Snider closed the trial transcript for *Nachtsheim v. Wartnick* and dropped it to the desktop. He lifted the handset of his home office telephone and dialed seven digits. Friedberg answered on the fifth ring. "Joe, you've got a case."

Common law reaching back to the 1700s and earlier assumed "it was clear that if the case against him was false the prisoner ought to say so and suggest why, and that if he did not speak that could only be because he was unable to deny the truth of the evidence." In 1975, the U. S. Supreme Court stated that "'[f]ailure to contest an assertion … is considered evidence of acquiescence … if it would have been natural under the circumstances to object to the assertion in question.'"[6]

When Gainsley instructed Wartnick to assert his Fifth Amendment right, the attorney triggered a series of events that directly led to Wartnick being found responsible for Nachtsheim's murder. That Gainsley made the decision rather than allow Wartnick that freedom placed Gainsley in an even more precarious position.

Litigation is the client's case. Whether criminal or civil, it is the client who must make the decisions. An attorney is called *counselor* because that is what he should be—an advisor well-versed in applicable law, someone who knows all the cards and how they can be played. The client, though, makes the decision how to play them.

Evidence showed Gainsley had not understood the implications of having Wartnick plead his Fifth Amendment right—but in spite of Gainsley's actions, pursuit of an attorney would be difficult and risky. In the late 1980s, attorney malpractice was a rarity, an oddity, certainly not potential litigation for a respected firm the size of Faegre. Any quest for justice for Wartnick would require pursuit of another top-five Minnesota firm, Moss and Barnett, for whom Gainsley had worked during the time of the wrongful death trial.

"Not only do you have the Fifth in a civil deposition," Snider told Friedberg during that telephone conversation, "but for Gainsley to mention a polygraph during his opening statement, well, that makes no sense whatsoever."

---

6. Justice Antonin Scalia quoting *United States ex rel. Bilokumsky v. Tod* (1923) as offered in his dissenting opinion in *Mitchell v. United States*. 526 U.S. 314 (1999).

"So," Friedberg finally spoke, "you think an outfit the size of Faegre's going to let you sign on to sue a lawyer for an *individual*—and a broke one at that—on a *contingent* fee case?"

CHAPTER 6

SEVERAL DAYS LATER

"This committee cannot approve this—"Bob Oliver glared, "—embarrassment."

Other Faegre litigation committee members were also concerned. "Jerry, we're looking to you and young partners like you to carry Faegre into the twenty-first century."

"Indeed, to make the last decade of this century our greatest yet."

"Yes," Snider acknowledged. "I understand the import of what you're saying. I also think Faegre has a long history of pursuing justice—"

"This committee," Oliver insisted, "cannot approve—"

Snider turned to managing partner Jim Halls. "Our malpractice insurance carrier is on the other side. I know that's a point against us."

"Not a deciding factor," Halls encouraged. "There's absolutely nothing that says we can't do this."

"It's a good case." Snider straightened to all of his six-feet-one and faced the full committee. "This man had a *right* to speedy, fair justice—to competent representation. Not only did he not get it, he paid heavily. It appears attorney Gainsley never had the police report. He *instructed* Wartnick to take the Fifth Amendment in a civil deposition; no alternatives, no preparation—."

"It's nuts!" Oliver barked.

"I don't see a problem with it." Halls collected the pages in front of him. "I suggest, Jerry, you interview the prospective client and report back. All in favor say 'Aye.'"

The motion carried.

THURSDAY, MARCH 24, 1988

On the twenty-second floor of the Multifoods Building in downtown Minneapolis, Snider and Friedberg sat on one side of a table in a Faegre conference room. Across the wide, mahogany span sat Wartnick, alert and eager but not at ease.

Friedberg slipped a stapled sheaf of papers off a stack in front of him— attorney Gainsley's response to Friedberg's complaint filed the previous January—and passed it down the table. Snider glanced at the pages and addressed his potential client. "Mr. Wartnick, it says here Moss and Barnett

considers this complaint, quote, frivolous and brought in bad faith, end quote."
He spun the document to face Wartnick and slid it across the table.

Wartnick looked up from the pages to meet Snider's steady gaze.

"In fact," Snider continued, "Mr. Gainsley and his employer, Moss and Barnett, state you actually *caused* any damages you sustained. How do you respond to that?"

"I couldn't believe it when Joe showed it to me. I mean, what does Mr. Gainsley think I did besides trust him?"

"Do you remember Phil Gainsley talking about investigation?"

"Only that it was a police job."

"Did he ever show you a police report?"

"Besides the one he got when the trial started?"

Snider's cultivated expression and rhythm did not waver. "Explain that, please. You say he received a police report during the trial?"

"As it was starting, yeah. Someone delivered it as the judge was coming—was it as or before? No, it had to be before because Phil had to sign for it and there wouldn't be time if the judge was already coming in."

"And what did he do with the report?"

"Read it."

"Read it? Immediately?"

"Yeah, the whole time he didn't have something else to do he flipped back and forth."

"Did he perform any other action with it besides reading it?"

Wartnick frowned. "Only when he was trying to get Lieutenant Quinn or other witnesses to talk about it."

Snider had digested the trial transcript for *Nachtsheim v. Wartnick* and knew Wartnick spoke the truth. "When did you first talk to—" he checked notes as a way to assure Wartnick he knew what he was asking, "Lieutenant Krueger, the Minneapolis police detective in charge of the case?"

"The morning after Bob was shot," Wartnick answered.

"Where did that meeting with Lieutenant Krueger occur?"

"He came to Midwest first thing that next morning—after the shooting. Asked me about Bob and Betty, the insurance, everything."

"And what qualms did you have in discussing any of those subjects?"

"You mean did I have a problem talking about it?"

"Exactly."

"No. Why would I?"

+

FRIDAY, MAY 25, 1973

MIDWEST FLORAL SUPPLY—9:00 A.M.

"Lieutenant," Wartnick shook the brawny hand of Detective Russ Krueger who stood, feet splayed, in front of the reception desk. "Just got off the phone with a friend who says you've been asking questions about me," Wartnick said.

Krueger nodded. "I'm interviewing everyone connected, Mr. Wartnick."

"Do I need an attorney?"

"If you want. Tell you what, let's just talk a little off the record." With some effort, Krueger turned his bulk and shuffled toward the open office door. He walked as though the massive arms and shoulders were almost more than his legs could carry. "Just a few questions about the victim, Bob Nachtsheim." Krueger parked himself on the sagging cushions of a couch placed opposite the office window then maneuvered to face Wartnick. "Mr. Wartnick, did you have anything to do with the shooting of Bob Nachtsheim?"

"Are you out of your mind?" Wartnick fired back. He completed the turn around his desk and lowered himself into his chair. "Ben asked me that. I reminded him he knew me better than to ask."

"Ben got a last name?"

"Stoller. Majority stock holder here 'til last year."

"Why would Mr. Stoller ask you that question, Mr. Wartnick?"

"Because you asked *him* that question, Lieutenant. Once you raised it, he wouldn't let it go 'til he heard me deny it."

"So where were you during those early morning hours yesterday?"

"At home. Here. Was a regular work day. Where was I supposed to be?"

"What time did you leave your house?"

"I usually leave about seven forty-five, get here around eight. It was an ordinary day—well, it started out that way."

"Can anyone confirm that?"

"You mean did anybody see me? My wife and kids were in the kitchen when I left, getting ready for school."

Krueger shifted his weight as though he could not find a comfortable position. "And how old are your children?"

"Oldest is seven, youngest is four."

"And your wife's name?"

"Babe. What's all this got to do with Bob?"

Krueger eyed the bus schedule pinned to the bulletin board behind Wartnick's head. "Business doing okay, Mr. Wartnick?"

"Has its ups and downs like everything else. Drought in California or a bus or railway strike can put us in the hole. Is it worth it? I'd say it is, especially since my dad started the business before I was born. Him and my uncle. I grew up learning names of exotic flowers—"

"That don't answer my question." Krueger saw Wartnick's confused expression but continued anyway. "Is it true Midwest held a hundred-thousand dollar insurance policy on Mr. Nachtsheim?"

Wartnick leaned back in his chair. "That's right. A key-man policy. We've had it three years. In fact, I just renewed it. A lot of businesses get them when they've got someone crucial to business operations. That's why it's called 'key man.'"

"When did Mr. Nachtsheim leave Midwest?"

"Last August. Why?"

"Why'd you keep the policy if Nachtsheim no longer worked here?"

"It was already paid for through April and was still in effect for seven months after that. That'd make it, what? Next October? November? Once these policies are issued, they don't just terminate that easy."

"And you renewed it when?"

"End of April, beginning of May. I don't remember exactly."

"It's odd, don't you think—to renew a policy on someone no longer with the company?"

Wartnick popped out of the chair. "Not if you're hoping he'll be back." It took Wartnick three strides to cover the distance to the open safe. Krueger watched him flip through files. "The policy covered loss of business if something happened to Bob, sure, but it was also his retirement package. And he wasn't the only guy here we covered."

He pulled papers from a file and handed them to Krueger. "Bob knew the hundred-thou was his when he turned sixty-five. Incentive, reward, retirement package, whatever you want to call it. Did he leave Midwest? Sure. He wanted to see if he could make a go of it on his own. Did I think he'd make it? Maybe. Maybe not. But I knew if he didn't make it, this policy was leverage for him to consider coming back. To tell you the truth, I was actually thinking about splitting the benefit payment with the family, considering how Bob—," Wartnick inhaled deeply and sat down again, "well …."

Krueger used his pock-marked cheeks to push his glasses up to the bridge of his nose as he fingered the top pages of the policy. "And why would you have to offer an incentive? What was your relationship with Mr. Nachtsheim when he left Midwest? Isn't it true, Mr. Wartnick, you were angry the day he told you he was leaving? So angry you were yelling and cursing not only at Mr. Nachtsheim but also his wife, Betty, and their son, Bobby?"

"Was I upset? You better believe it. Fifty percent of my business was walking out the door. No warning at all. Just walks up, hands me this paper telling me he's leaving. Didn't know it then, but for months he'd been setting up his own place.

"But we talked it out. That's how we do things." Wartnick leaned back in his chair and tried to ease the ache in his low back. "We talked it out, I settled down, and when he left we shook hands and I wished him the best. No hard feelings."

Wartnick thought for a moment then said, "When Betty and Bobby handed in their resignations, all within minutes of each other, mind you—the three of them, I figured they were coming. Was that a disappointment? Don't you believe it for a minute. I kept Betty and Bobby around for Bob's sake. I was glad they were gone. We wouldn't have to listen to any more of their knock-down-drag-outs."

Krueger shifted position to face Wartnick again. "You're saying Bob and Betty argued?"

"Is it something you have to take my word for? No. Ask anybody." Wartnick swept his hand through the air in a gesture that encompassed every employee in the shop. "The two of them had yelling matches right out there; especially Bob and Bobby. Of course, when that happened, Betty nearly always took Bobby's side irregardless. Was amazing the way the three of them'd go after each other. Bob and Bobby'd be getting into it on this side and somehow Betty would sense it from next door, you know, where we sell the glassware, that's what she was in charge of, and she'd come running over—" Wartnick paused at a knock on the open door. "Come on in."

"Sorry to interrupt," Charlie nodded at Wartnick. "California, line two. Take it or keep playing phone tag?"

"Excuse me, Lieutenant. Need to take this one."

"Got a coffee pot?"

"Get him some, would you, Charlie?" Wartnick reached for the telephone. "This is Norm."

Krueger slurped the lukewarm sludge and eyed the floral calendar on the far wall, pretense to study the man behind the desk. Krueger decided he did not like Wartnick. Whether it was the flamboyant gold chains around Wartnick's neck, Wartnick's upbeat, casual confidence about life, the renewed insurance policy, or some other intangible known only to Krueger, everything about Wartnick seemed to yell *suspect* to the detective.

Krueger crushed the empty Styrofoam cup and leveraged himself off the couch. He limped out of the office toward the front of the shop, saw Charlie and held aloft the insurance policy. "Tell him I'm takin' this...."

+

Jerry Snider studied Wartnick's eyes before he asked, "And Lieutenant Krueger was satisfied?"

"He seemed to be. Took the policy with him."

"So he left that day satisfied with what he'd learned in your conversation with him? What signs of distrust or animosity did he show?"

"Everything he did showed he didn't trust nobody. I mean, he's old-school. Bragged his search warrant was a size ten shoe."

Snider referred again to his notes, then leaned back in his chair and studied the drooping shoulders and dogged set of Wartnick's jaw. Snider was ready to note the slightest change in demeanor as he asked, "Then what might explain Mr. Krueger's outburst during the 1986 trial?"

+

Lieutenant Russ Krueger, retired, slouched his bulk against the chair provided in the narrow witness area. He used a fingernail from one hand to slowly scrape under the nails of the other.

Plaintiff's attorney Ron Meshbesher concluded his direct examination of Krueger with the question, "And you and I never had a discussion about your role in this case, other than at the deposition and perhaps passing remarks, is that correct?"

Krueger's fingertips steepled above the food-stained tie fifteen years out of date. "Very few passing remarks," he affirmed.

Meshbesher glanced to Judge McCarr. "I have no further questions of this witness at this time. I may have to recall him later."

Judge McCarr looked up from his notes. "Mr. Gainsley. Your witness."

Gainsley stood behind counsel's table. "Do you recall the content of those passing remarks?"

"We discussed the audacity of Prudential Insurance letting somebody else be the policyholder. That was like a crap shoot in Las Vegas."

"Indeed," Gainsley observed, "that offended you and still offends you?"

Krueger lunged forward in the witness seat. "It's beyond comprehension," he said, his voice became shrill, his face reddened, "that a man can get an insurance policy on another man, and thirteen days later he's shot in the head and killed. And the only man that benefited—" he pointed a thick finger toward Wartnick and shouted, "was that man right there."

+

Wartnick shook his head, glanced first to Snider, then at Friedberg. "I don't think there *is* an explanation. He's Russ Krueger. I hadn't seen him since our talks in '73. And that, that outburst, as you call it, that was so ridiculous. How unprofessional can you get?"

"So in May or June of 1973," Snider said, "there was no animosity that you knew of, between yourself and Lieutenant Krueger."

"None *I* knew of."

"Not even after you called and refused to take the polygraph examination?"

"You mean after Gainsley *told* me not to take the polygraph? No, I never saw Krueger again. Not 'til '86 at the trial."

"And when, prior to the trial, did Mr. Gainsley offer to have you sit for another deposition, this time to freely answer any question Mr. Meshbesher wished to ask?"

"He never did." Crimson began to creep up Wartnick's neck. "He wouldn't, no matter how many times I told him I wanted to. And that's one of the things that convinced me everything would be okay. His confidence—it never seemed to waver."

Snider slid a legal pad toward Friedberg, who glanced at it and nodded. Snider inhaled for the next question. Wartnick spoke first. "Except that Phil told me he took this case with the idea Doug would handle the criminal end of—"

Friedberg straightened. "Doug Who?"

"Thomson. Doug Thomson."

"Gainsley said Thomson would handle the criminal end?" Friedberg shoved the legal pad toward Snider. "You ever talk to Thomson?"

"I met with him twice, I think. Maybe three times. That's the only contact I had with Doug. And I guess I always wondered, why didn't he represent me at trial?"

Friedberg scowled and rocked his chair back and forth in little bursts. "Did Gainsley have reason for him not to?"

"Oh, sure. In fact, I asked him why Doug never came to court. Mr. Gainsley told me that if I brought in a criminal attorney it was as good as admitting I did the crime. To have a criminal attorney sitting next to me in a court room was the same thing as pointing out to the jury, saying hey, he's got to be guilty."

Friedberg blinked, shook his head, and turned to stare at Snider.

Snider's practiced gaze stayed fixed on Wartnick. "Did you, at any time, retain Mr. Thomson to represent you?"

"Oh, sure. It was Doug who got on the phone to Gary Palackny and told Gary to either get back the policy—release it—or file charges." Friedberg and Snider both knew Wartnick meant Gary Flakne, Hennepin County Attorney in the early 1970s.

"Against you," Friedberg said.

Wartnick nodded. "Gary Palackny turned around and released the policy and I was paid. It was Doug who got it released, not Gainsley. But the check was made out to Midwest Floral *and* to Phil Gainsley—or to the Gainsley law firm. His dad was still alive back then. And just before he handed me the check, Phil told me he wanted a third of it."

Snider's bushy eyebrows rose. "Your attorney told you he wanted a third of the insurance proceeds?"

"He wanted one-third." Wartnick nodded. "Even though we'd never discussed fees, just operated by the agreement my dad and his dad made in the '60s. When we got the insurance money, he said he'd written all these letters and things, which wasn't true. If Doug hadn't called, I honestly believe we wouldn't have the money today, still."

"Was a retainer ever paid for Attorney Thomson?"

"Oh, sure. Five-thousand dollars."

Snider jotted three words on the notepad. "Was there any other event of a financial nature between you and Mr. Gainsley? Anything to do with—"

"He told me to sign some letter that authorized opening a checking account between Ron and Betty and me."

"Explain that please. What was the nature of this account?"

"In other words, all the money I received was supposed to go into this account they set up and any time I needed money it had to come out of this account but only with the permission of Meshbesher and Betty."

Friedberg slapped his palm against the table top. "And Gainsley told you to sign this paper?"

"Told me to sign it immediately and send it back to him."

"Did you?" Friedberg snapped.

"Well, my wife had retained an attorney, and we told him about it. He told me and my wife that if we signed it, he'd no longer represent her. I called Mr. Gainsley from that attorney's office and told him what Babe's attorney had told me. And I told him I wouldn't sign the letter. And he said, 'Norm, I didn't even get a chance to read that letter. Give me a few minutes,' or hours or whatever it was, 'and I'll read it and get back to you.' Then we met in Gainsley's office—my wife, her lawyer, and me—and Gainsley said it was a good thing I didn't sign it because he certainly didn't mean for me to sign it."

Snider nodded. "Let's move on, Mr. Wartnick," he said, the Southern drawl slightly more pronounced, "and we're going to change topics, here. I'd like for you to recite, in detail if you would please, all you remember about the exchanges between you and Mr. Gainsley on," again he referred to his notes, "February 16, 1979—the deposition in Ron Meshbesher's offices. Actually prior to that deposition, if you would, please. And Mr. Wartnick, this is the first time I'll have heard the story from you, so please be sure to tell me everything you can remember. Try not to skip anything."

+

Friday, February 16, 1979 — six years after the murder of Bob Nachtsheim

"Thank you, Mrs. Nachtsheim," Phil Gainsley smiled. "I believe those are all the questions I have for you today." He turned to Ron Meshbesher. "What say we take a little break before commencing with your deposition of Mr. Wartnick?"

"Sure." Meshbesher removed his reading glasses and glanced from Gainsley to Wartnick. "Let's meet back here in," a quick glance to the clock above the door, "fifteen minutes?"

Wartnick waited until they had traveled out of ear-shot before he whispered, "What's going on? Why didn't you ask her why she lied about the orchids? About why she made that stupid shotgun statement—that I'm the only one Bob would've let get that close to him with one. You didn't even mention her stopping at the shop on the way to the hospital to look for insurance papers!"

They had arrived, via one short downward flight of stairs, at a lounge area complete with couches, tables, and upholstered arm chairs. The area was deserted except for the two of them. Just outside the door labeled Men, Phil halted, extracted a three-by-five note card from his shirt pocket, and handed it to Wartnick.

Wartnick began to read the card aloud. "'On the advice of my counsel I respectfully refuse to answer that—' What's this?"

Gainsley slouched and his head lolled to the left. "Answer Meshbesher's first questions, your name, address, time at the U of M, and such. Then, when I give you the signal, I want you to read the words on this card in response and continue doing so until I signal you to stop."

"What? Why? There's no reason. I've got absolutely nothing to hide."

"The decision has been made. You must do this."

"I've already answered all their questions."

"I'm your attorney, Norm." Gainsley raised his hand and pushed open the door to the Men's Room. "I am instructing you to read your Fifth Amendment rights in answer to Meshbesher's questions."

The bathroom door closed with a thump.

CHAPTER 7

Friedberg watched Faegre's conference room door whisper close behind Wartnick. "Gainsley misrepresented not only his client but the whole damn profession!" He steered his chair to face Jerry. "Pisses me off to hear Wartnick say he didn't get a criminal lawyer because it'd make people think he's guilty. If Thomson had been asked, he would have advised Wartnick to find a competent *civil* guy!"

Snider rifled through Wartnick's case file spread out in stacks around him.

"Dougie Thomson." Friedberg stewed. He leaned back until the tips of his cap-toed Oxfords barely grazed the carpet. "We were partners back when we should have used old cardboard boxes for filing cabinets. No way he would have let this case get out of hand like it did."

The room was silent except for the shuffle of paper, then Snider spoke as he continued to thumb through documents. "The police report is filled with comments that begged for further investigation, and Wartnick just verified Gainsley didn't even *have* the report. That makes complete sense because I found nothing from the police report in any of Gainsley's motions, briefs, affidavits, nowhere; not until his appellate brief. But something's still bothering me about Gainsley and those insurance proceeds. It's in here somewhere."

"Back before I called you," Friedberg said, "I was already thinking Wartnick didn't have as good a lawyer as he should've had, then I started putting two and two together. Back after this thing went on I was flying to some conference with Meshbesher—Virginia, Carolina, *some*where—and Ron was going on and on about the case he'd just litigated—how arrogant the other guy was, how the other guy would stride back and forth across the front of the courtroom. Ron said all the time he kept thinking, 'Most of this guy's ineptitude won't even show 'cause his arrogance covers his egregious errors.' That other guy was *Phil Gainsley!*"

Still sorting through papers, Snider nodded. "To *never* offer his client the opportunity to get out from under that Fifth Amendment deposition is just…." He shook his head, incredulous that any attorney who had passed the bar could even contemplate doing such a thing, much less consider it reasonable strategy.

Snider plopped one stack of documents on the table, lifted the next stack, and continued his search. "We need Gainsley's time records. I have to be sure. If he didn't do any investigation—"

"You realize there's never gonna be enough money for the hours it'll take."

"Well, I haven't taken it on yet. First I want to see what Gainsley has to say. And I want you to talk with Doug Thomson, see what he remembers."

"Absolutely." Friedberg nodded. "Already set Gainsley's deposition."

"Then we have to find out what the Nachtsheims are willing to settle for; offer them a proposal."

The objective of a malpractice suit against Phil Gainsley would be for relief from the Nachtsheim's judgment against Wartnick. The 1986 jury verdict declared the Nachtsheim family had been injured by Wartnick and, therefore, he owed them what now totaled over three million dollars. After it had been upheld by the appellate court, there was not one thing anyone could do to remove Wartnick's legal obligation to pay Betty. For the rest of his life, and for his estate when he died, Betty virtually controlled Norm Wartnick's purse strings. Wartnick could do nothing in life until that judgment was satisfied.

If a civil complaint against Gainsley and Moss & Barnett was successful, Gainsley and his firm would owe Wartnick just as Wartnick now owed Betty.

To prevail, though, Friedberg and Snider must not only win a jury verdict against Phil Gainsley but Betty Nachtsheim must agree to let the jury's monetary award be sufficient to settle her judgment. If the jury award was too low or if Betty was unwilling to settle, their win against Gainsley would be a loss.

"Gainsley's deposition is two weeks from yesterday. My office." Friedberg sat forward and propped forearms against the table's edge. "That's one of the reasons I called you. I've never taken a deposition before. Never had to, never wanted to. I'm a criminal guy. So I'm gonna need you to instruct on the finer points, organizing questions, things like that."

"Here it is." Snider pulled a single sheet from Gainsley's original correspondence. "A letter from Gainsley demanding payment from Prudential: quote, We are not aware of any reason why the payment of the claim should not have been made long ago, and we must insist upon payment at once, end quote. And get this, Joe. There's a note here at the bottom in Gainsley Senior's handwriting that says, quote, [Insurance] agent Zola Friedman phoned. He had been contacted by Mr. Wartnick after Wartnick received his copy of this letter. Wartnick's message was to the effect that his attorney jumped the gun a bit, end quote."

Snider let the page fall back atop its stack. "Looks as though young Gainsley rather than Wartnick may have been the one to push for payment."[7]

---

7. Additional evidence of this is found in a letter from Gainsley to Doug Thomson dated October 12, 1973. Gainsley wrote, "Consistent with our conference in your office last week, *I* decided that we should not remain silent too long with respect to Midwest's claim against Prudential. I called [name omitted], Supervising Home Office Representative.... He said that Prudential clearly owes someone $100,000, and the company would rather pay it and get it off of its books." [emphasis added]

Friedberg slammed a hand against the arm of his chair. "I want to take that deposition. I want to hear straight from Gainsley's mouth what the hell he was thinking."

CHAPTER 8

WEDNESDAY, APRIL 6, 1988

Friedberg stepped into the conference room at Joseph S. Friedberg, Chartered, and took his seat to Gainsley's right. For most depositions, the one being questioned—the deponent—is seated at one end of the table while attorneys for each side of the case face each other across the plateau. A court reporter is stationed near the deponent so no spoken words are lost.

Today's deponent, Phil Gainsley, slouched at the far end of the table, a video camera at the near end to memorialize his every move. Moss & Barnett attorney Scott Herzog, to Gainsley's left, was set to represent Gainsley. The arrival of Jerry Snider on the case seemed to have made Moss & Barnett sit up and notice Wartnick's action against Gainsley.

Wartnick was seated behind Snider, as far back in the corner as he could lean. Parties in a case have the right to be present during discovery, though they are usually seated away from the deponent and not allowed to interfere or interrupt the proceedings. Wartnick was away from the deponent but could still see the clock on the wall; he habitually counted seconds and minutes just for the mental exercise.

A good attorney instructs his client to show no emotion nor respond to anything the deponent may say—an instruction completely in line with Wartnick's refereeing skills. Such non-verbal cues from a party can speak volumes to opposing counsel. Some attorneys glean best tactics to use or arguments to press based on a party's involuntary responses. And that is the reason for the deposition—facts-gathering. Facts-gathering and the recording of statements made under oath.

Gainsley was sworn in, and Friedberg began with the basics. Wartnick adopted his neutral referee face and let his gaze wander from Friedberg—as restless as Norm felt when stuck in a chair—then to the back of Snider's dark head which could block Gainsley from view if Wartnick leaned far enough to his right.

Friedberg's next question to Gainsley caught Wartnick's attention. "Had you ever, that you can recall, discussed with Mr. Wartnick the *possibility* he might be sued civilly for the death of Mr. Nachtsheim?"

Gainsley's elbows were on the table, one hand clinched, the other hand clasped around it. He rested his mouth against the fist. After several moments with no sound, no movement, he spoke from behind his hands. "I—" he stretched the word into five syllables. "don't think so, before it happened."

"Prior to the first lawsuit in late 1976," Friedberg said, his gravelly voice uncharacteristically calm, "When was the last time you recall doing something in relation to the death of Mr. Nachtsheim?"

"That's a difficult question." Gainsley sighed and slumped backward in his chair. "After we were successful in getting the hundred-thousand dollars, Norm would call me from time to time saying people wanted to talk to him. The only thing I did in response to those calls was to tell him he didn't have to talk to anyone. Advised he *not* talk to anyone."

"Then is it fair to say that between the death of Mr. Nachtsheim in 1973 and the lawsuit in 1976 that you did no investigation into the death of Mr. Nachtsheim?"

"Well, I had my interviews with Krueger. Other than that, I may have had the police reports available to me at that time. I know I had a bad copy of the police report available. I'm not sure if it was between '73 and '76, but, umm," he pursed his lips, "with that understanding."

"Now, you refer to *the* police report. What do you mean?"

"There was a narrative of what was represented to me to be the police report that I think I got from Prudential Insurance Company."

"Was it voluminous, or was it just a couple-of-page narrative?"

"I would say it was quarter-of-an-inch to an inch thick."

"Have you turned it over to us?"

"Yes. Well, I turned it over to Norm. I haven't given you anything in this matter and you haven't requested anything."

Friedberg looked up from his notepad. "I think at this point we can refer to the corporate *us*. If I say 'us,' then—"

"The answer is, Yes, to Mr. Wartnick."

"Let's see if we can detail between 1973 and '76 the number of people you would have talked to concerning the death of Mr. Nachtsheim. You spoke to Mr. Wartnick on a number of occasions, correct?"

"Yes."

"You spoke to Mr. Krueger on at least two occasions. Correct?"

Gainsley's elbows had returned to the table, fingers interlaced. "That's correct," he muttered.

"Who else that would have had information concerning the death of Mr. Nachtsheim did you speak to between '73 and '76?

"Well, I know we spoke to representatives of the Prudential Life Insurance Company." He paused. "I know we spoke to Doug Thomson. I know we spoke to members of the Stoller family." Gainsley paused again. He readjusted the position of his Styrofoam coffee cup upon the table top. "Umm," he nodded, nodded again, and fumbled for the container for a sip of the lukewarm liquid.

"That's all you can recall?"

"That's all I recall," Gainsley said from behind the flimsy, white cup.

"At the time Mr. Wartnick was sued, late '76, did you consult with Doug Thomson?"

"I can't remember."

"Do you remember if after the lawsuit was served you consulted with Mr. Thomson?"

"I'm sure I did."

"Okay." Friedberg said. He leaned toward Gainsley. "Do you remember what you would have talked about?"

"No.

"Can you remember whether it was telephone or personal?"

"I think it was telephone."

"Can you tell us if it was more than ten times or less than ten times?"

"Less than ten times."

"More or less than five times?"

Gainsley cleared his throat. "I think it was once."

"All right. Can you remember the subject matter of the conversation?"

"Simply to tell him that the lawsuit had been commenced."

"And so, still in 1976 when the lawsuit was commenced, you still had in mind that Wartnick had denied any complicity in the death of Mr. Nachtsheim. Is that correct?"

"That's correct. "

"Did you believe him?"

Attorney Herzog raised a finger. "Objection to that as irrelevant. Answer if you want to."

Gainsley reclined head and shoulders toward his advocate. "I don't want to."

Friedberg glanced hard at Gainsley. "Can you tell us *why* you don't want to?"

"I objected that it's irrelevant," Herzog said. "What this man's belief may be as to a criminal act by another is totally irrelevant to the issues framed by this complaint."

"I disagree with that, Mr. Herzog," Friedberg said. "If, in fact, he did not believe Mr. Wartnick, then he had an absolute necessity to convey that to his client."

"If he did not believe—" Herzog tried to interrupt.

"He has an ethical duty," Friedberg insisted, "to convey to his client that he did not believe him, if he didn't."

"I don't know the ethics you're talking about," Herzog said. "Is that from the standpoint of representing a man criminally?"

Gainsley leaned forward. "Let me cut through all that."

Herzog sat back.

"I had two jobs beginning with the commencement of this lawsuit. Two responsibilities to Midwest and to Norm. One was to make sure he wasn't indicted and to keep him out of jail. That's one. And the other was to prevail in the insurance action. To this day, I've accomplished both of those. I told him at the time," Gainsley paused and exhaled, focused up and left, into the distance. "I told him that regardless of what I believed—and I'm not saying I didn't believe him, but the story he told me and the facts were almost literally unbelievable. My procedure, my tactics would have to be that there not be a trial of this insurance action and that we win it as a matter of law, which we ultimately did. I guess if you pushed my back against the wall, I believed Norm. I never had any reason *not* to believe what he told me."

"You said you had a dual responsibility: to keep him out of prison and to get the proceeds for Midwest—"

"No, I didn't say that. It was to prevail in the lawsuit that was brought against him. We had already gotten the proceeds by 1976."

"All right."

"Well, it wasn't so much keeping him out of jail—"

Friedberg restrained a sarcastic chuckle at Gainsley's self-contradiction.

"—I didn't even want him to be indicted. And I always knew that as long as I advised him to remain silent, it would happen."

"You're stating that you knew that as long as—"

"Well, I didn't *know*. I had some judgments I had to make, and I concluded a lawsuit would have to be won as a matter of law."

"When you say one of your two responsibilities was 'protecting,' if we can use that term," Friedberg continued.

"Right, right."

"Was that not the primary responsibility of Mr. Thomson as his criminal lawyer?"

Gainsley hesitated. "It probably was. If I had let Norm go off based upon misadvice, um—. It's true he paid Thomson $5,000 by my recollection—. I would have botched that up, criminally, by telling Norm things other than what I told him."

Friedberg's pen hurried across his note page. He looked up. "Mr. Gainsley, you said that, based on the things you knew about the circumstances surrounding the death of Mr. Nachtsheim, that something was 'unbelievable.' You want to elucidate further on what that was?"

"Sure," Gainsley began, then paused. Silence. An air vent rattled as the heat cycled on. A hallway conversation faded into hearing, then casually faded away. "I think that—um, a lay person—that is to say a non-lawyer—would find it literally unbelievable that Midwest Floral could collect one-hundred-thousand dollars upon the death of not only a person who was a former employee but who became a competitor and who died in the way he did. I think the jury would have a tough time. I think the publicity generated created a tough time. I, as a lawyer, knew Midwest was within its rights in collecting that money and in having the policy in the first instance. It was an unbelievable story."

Silence again.

"Is it—" Friedberg began.

"And as an example of that," Gainsley's words picked up speed. "In one of my motions for a summary judgment, and I made several, one of the judges said, 'You mean to say a competitor can have a policy of life insurance on the life of a competitor and recover?' And I said, 'Yes, Your Honor. That's the law."

"Is it your belief as a lawyer that there was sufficient credible evidence to support the jury's verdict brought in [on the wrongful death]?"

"There clearly was sufficient evidence."

"And what was the evidence?"

"Well, certainly the motive." Gainsley nodded, slowly, several times. "There was also something that was not evidence but there was Norm's demeanor at trial that concerned me throughout—since 1976, frankly—that I was fearful of; but I'm not sure *that* in and of itself resulted—. It was primarily the hundred-thousand, I think, and, um," his pause again filled the room with a tense silence. "Probably a combination of minor things. We had a lot of explaining to do, which is one of the reasons I was concerned that the matter not get to trial."

"Between 1973, the death of Mr. Nachtsheim, and the conclusion of the trial, can you list for me the witnesses or potential witnesses you or someone in your law firm interviewed?"

Gainsley retrieved a yellow sticky note from the middle of the table and began to fold it in half, then in half again. "No."

"Well, tell me the ones you recall."

"Well, in addition to Russ Krueger, there was the people from Prudential; Zola Friedman, who sold the policy in question; Ben Stoller, who operated the business of Midwest. I believe I talked to either a lieutenant or some other officer at the Minneapolis Police Department in addition to Krueger." He shrugged.

"Did you retain an investigator at any point in time?"

"No."

"Would you explain why not?"

"I knew Prudential was in the same boat with us, and they investigated. I knew the case would really hinge on a matter of law, not of fact. And," he shrugged again, "I just had to make some judgments."

"What attempt, if any, in twelve years did you make to find out who *had*, in fact, been responsible for the death of Mr. Nachtsheim?"

Gainsley leaned in, suddenly animated. "My responsibility was to obstruct Mrs. Nachtsheim from showing Norm had done it. It was *not* my responsibility to show who *did* do it."

Friedberg leveled his gaze at Phil. "Did you make *any* attempt to find out who had killed Mr. Nachtsheim?"

Gainsley straightened. His jaw tightened. "Yes," he spit out.

"What did you do in that attempt?"

"I got," Gainsley began. He punctuated each response with a large nod. "I got the police reports. I talked to the police. I read the Prudential file. I made certain conclusions from those attempts."

"You were aware of the fact the police investigation was handled by Lieutenant Krueger?"

"That's correct."

"You were aware of the fact Lieutenant Krueger had an intimate relationship with Mrs. Nachtsheim, the widow?"

"Shortly before I took his deposition."

"Whose deposition?"

"Mr. Krueger's."

Friedberg glanced hard at Gainsley. "That's a deposition the Nachtsheim's attorney, Ron Meshbesher, took."

Gainsley tensed, instinctively pulled away from his accuser. "Well," his lips pursed stiffly. "My recollection is that if Meshbesher hadn't taken it, I would have."

"Mr. Gainsley, in 1982, did you have the police file?"

"Oh." Gainsley glanced sideways at Herzog. "I think so."

A page was marked Gainsley Exhibit 12 and found its way to Gainsley. "Mr. Gainsley, does that indicate whether or not you and Mr. Johnson of Prudential Insurance Company had the complete police file in 1982?"

Gainsley turned away from Friedberg, raised his clenched hands to hide his face, and stayed silent. Herzog intervened. "The document speaks for itself."

Friedberg was undeterred. "Did you have—"

"Yes." He turned his face partially toward Friedberg.

"—the complete police reports—"

"Yes."

"—in 1982?"

"Yes." Gainsley spit out his final affirmation.

Snider made several notes.

"In 1979 the deposition of Norm Wartnick was noted, was it not?" Friedberg continued.

"Yes."

"Prior to the deposition beginning, did you give Mr. Wartnick a card from which he could read?"

"Yes."

"Would it be fair to say that you didn't, then, get involved in any substantive preparation with Mr. Wartnick on matters that would be involved in the deposition?"

"No, that would *not* be fair to say."

"Well, you knew you were going to advise him to take the Fifth Amendment. Correct?"

"That's correct."

"How long before the deposition were you aware of that?"

"That was a process, was a lengthy process, and it was a process that resulted in a lot of judgments that my partners and I had to make. We discussed it with Norm numerous times."

"Did you explain to Mr. Wartnick the ramifications of his taking the Fifth Amendment in the civil litigation?"

"We talked in my office about the distinction between a criminal and a civil matter. I told him it was risky to assert our Fifth Amendment rights because the jury would learn of it. But I thought that when push came to shoves, Norm should not say anything to anyone."[8]

"You did not consult with Doug Thomson any time prior to that deposition?"

"I don't know whether I did or not. It's unlikely. It was a decision I ultimately felt comfortable with, and I take responsibility for."

"And did you explain to Mr. Wartnick prior to the deposition that his taking of the Fifth Amendment was sufficient from a legal standpoint to allow the case to go to the jury?"

"I'm not sure I put it to him in those words. At stake was the hundred-thousand dollars, as far as I was concerned. This was before the wrongful death action. We had succeeded in avoiding an indictment and I just didn't want something to happen where this person would be up against Meshbesher putting questions to him that I thought could lead to some trouble down the pike, criminally. I just had to make those decisions."

"What had Norm said that you believed if stated, in deposition, would incriminate him?"

"I didn't say that. Norm had *not* told me *any*thing that would incriminate him."

"Did you advise him prior to taking the Fifth that he would have to testify at trial?"

"No," Gainsley shook his head. "No, I did not."

---

8. Gainsley was consistent in his determination Wartnick would never say anything. In a letter from Gainsley to Wartnick dated October 21, 1976—two-and-a-half years prior to the fatal deposition—Gainsley said, "I usually prefer to delay interposing an answer until after all of my depositions are taken so that I can more easily define our defenses. The state of the law may be that where we seek affirmative relief from the court, including but not limited to a counterclaim, we may not be able to assert our constitutional right to remain silent in depositions or in trial. That right is crucial in this instance, and our decision with respect to the interposition of a counterclaim will hinge upon our research in this regard."

"Why not?"

"I wanted my options available to me. If I could have Norm testify at trial without affording Meshbesher the luxury of knowing what Norm was going to say at trial, I would have done my job."[9]

"Who made the ultimate decision on whether Norm would take the Fifth Amendment at the deposition?"

"Why? Norm made the ultimate decision, but it was based on the advice I gave him."

"Did you advise him or instruct him?"

Gainsley paused. "It's a blur. It's a blur as to when advice becomes instruction. He relied upon the advice I gave him, and the advice I gave him was to take the Fifth Amendment."

"What ramifications did you give to him regarding taking the Fifth Amendment?"

"I knew if we got to a trial it would not look good to the jury but that hopefully I could cure that by having him testify at a trial."

Friedberg moved on to his next line of questioning. "You wrote a letter to Ron Meshbesher with a conditional offer to let your client be re-deposed, to no longer stand behind the Fifth Amendment. Correct?"

This was the question Wartnick had been waiting for. He had not known that Gainsley ever offered to let him talk until Friedberg showed him Gainsley's 1985 letter to Meshbesher—a copy of which was never sent from Gainsley to Wartnick.

Wartnick fixed his gaze on the back of Snider's head but all his energy focused on hearing Gainsley's reply.

"Well, the letter speaks for itself, but that's essentially correct. I was flirting with the idea of—because now the stakes were greater—now we had a wrongful death action, we had punitive damages, we had a case that I was much more frightened of. I was hoping that what Meshbesher would do would be to say, 'No, you can't have it both ways,' and make his motion accordingly."

"Do you have any reason to believe that if Mr. Wartnick had answered a question about whether he was involved in Mr. Nachtsheim's death that he would've done *anything* but deny his involvement?"

"Why don't you just ask me why I told him to take the Fifth? Isn't that really what you want to know?"

"All right, I'll ask you. Why did you tell him to take the Fifth Amendment, Mr. Gainsley?"

Silence descended as four men awaited Gainsley's response. Herzog leaned back in his chair and exhaled. Friedberg hovered his pen over his notepad and

---

9. Joe would later comment that this answer was "another nonsensical reply by Gainsley ... he had no idea the Fifth could be used against Norm when he gave him the advice to take it and he was trying to think of some reason in retrospect." It is also important to note that the court frowns upon abuse of the discovery process in civil litigation which deprives a plaintiff of discovery of information which could be critical to the outcome of their case.

watched Gainsley's jaw muscles flex and relax. Snider was also watchful but unmoving. Wartnick subconsciously counted the passing seconds.

"There are many things that went into my mind," Gainsley paused again, "and go into my mind when I tell a client to take the Fifth. One of the things is what the client tells you; but another thing I think is very relevant is how well will the client withstand the questioning? Even though what he says may be accurate in black and white, what will his demeanor be? What is the likelihood of him saying something that might be misconstrued?

"We weighed it in our office for hours; I mean hours. Norm's demeanor and potentially argumentative behavior could have been a disservice to him. If a witness and a lawyer get into an argument, the lawyer will always win. Norm was no match for Meshbesher. I knew Ron would do everything he could do to get something out of Wartnick that would be adverse."

"Mr. Gainsley, we're showing you Gainsley Exhibit 16. That's a memorandum 'To Jane from Phil.' Is that the Gainsley firm's associate, Jane Lerner?"

"Yes."

"And 'Phil' is you?"

"Right." Gainsley nodded. "I think this is the memorandum I dictated when I got back from Norm's deposition, after my conversation with Meshbesher." He seemed completely relaxed.

"Why don't you take a minute to review that," Friedberg said.

Gainsley scanned the page, stiffened, and tossed the page to the tabletop.

"Mr. Gainsley, isn't it a fair characterization of this memorandum to say you were asking Jane Lerner to tell you what the ramifications were of your client taking the Fifth Amendment in a civil proceeding?"

Gainsley was motionless.

"Object to—," Herzog began. "The document speaks for itself. You're really asking him to comment on the sentences contained in the document, aren't you?"

"I'm asking him to comment on what he was trying to find out by issuing this memorandum."

"I wasn't trying to find out anything," Gainsley insisted. "I wanted to get myself some law so in the event of trial I could avoid the inferences that could be drawn by his taking the Fifth Amendment."

"Well, then, at the time you either dictated or wrote this memorandum, isn't it fair to say that you *didn't* know what the legal effect was of taking the Fifth Amendment?"

"Oh, indeed I did. Indeed I did."

"Part of what you wrote in the memo is, '[Meshbesher] indicated to me that the law is that when in a civil action one pleads the Fifth Amendment, the jury may be instructed that the probable answer to the question may be adverse to the witness's interest.' Did you believe plaintiff's attorney when he told you that?"

"I guess I kind of knew that to be the case. I mean, I think that's the law. I don't think I formed a belief or non-belief based upon what he told me."

"Well, you indicate in your memorandum that, 'As you know, I instructed Norm Wartnick to plead the Fifth Amendment during the taking of his deposition. How does this affect civil liability? Obviously, I would like your answer to be that it does not.'"

"I wanted to find law to the extent that there would not be that instruction."

"Did you believe such law existed?"

"Yeah, I think there are circumstances where that wouldn't be the case."

"Do you have any research memoranda done prior to the deposition concerning the ramifications of taking the Fifth?"

"Not research memorandum, but I knew that—I knew about another case that was being tried in some court in Minnesota where the issue also arose, coincidentally. I remember reading attorney briefs for those cases. Um, and—" his voice trailed off to silence. He shrugged.

"Did you do that before or after the deposition?"

"Before," Gainsley stated emphatically. "Before. Before."

Friedberg closed his notebook. "I have nothing further. Thank you."

Gainsley leapt from his chair and unclipped the tiny lapel mic. As the others rose, he nodded to Friedberg and Snider. "You must see now that I really did do my job."

Friedberg choked off an angry chortle. "No, Mr. Gainsley. I don't see that at all."

CHAPTER 9

ONE WEEK LATER

Snider strode into his office and greeted the two men waiting for him. "I've officially taken the Wartnick case. The justice of a fair and speedy trial with competent representation—that's what we're after. That's what Wartnick did not get."

Seated near the door was Dan Liberko, a small, mustached French-Canadian who had a friendly word for everyone, yet Snider knew Liberko was a bulldog at digging for truth.

Liberko's undergraduate degree was in law enforcement. In 1988, he worked in Faegre's general litigation department, where he had looked up one day to see Snider hurrying toward him exclaiming, 'You won't believe what I've just come across. This story is incredible!' Liberko had listened to Snider summarize *Wartnick v. Gainsley* and agreed to dig into the Nachtsheim murder. "But if I figure out Wartnick did this," Liberko had said, "we have issues." Liberko could not foresee when he accepted the assignment how dark would be the alleys and how seedy would be the streets he would travel.

Steve Severson, a fair-skinned Norwegian who enjoyed a good laugh, had settled his lanky frame into a chair in front of the plate-glass window twenty floors above the sidewalk. Severson had decided to become a lawyer when, as a child, he had watched the Watergate hearings on television. To date, he had already worked with Snider on several cases, but to Severson the Wartnick case would soon become, and remain, the most notable.

Snider indicated a collection of photocopied pages on the coffee table in the middle of the office. "Joe sent over Ron Meshbesher's analysis of Gainsley's representation of Mr. Wartnick. Copies of it are on the table. There's also a list there of what, from Meshbesher's perspective, needs investigation."

Liberko skimmed Meshbesher's outline, then quoted, "'No evidence of any viable alternative shooter. Nothing linking Wartnick to the crime.'" He glanced up at Snider, who nodded. Liberko continued. "Meshbesher says 'Gainsley, in opening, mentioned that Wartnick gave a full statement to Detective Krueger but then never referred to it again.' Why would he do that?"

Snider lifted his coffee mug from the desktop. "He wanted to completely close off Meshbesher's discovery then have Norm testify at trial. He actually considered that viable strategy."

Severson began to chuckle then quoted from Friedberg's letter. "'Ron also noted several other peculiar things, including Gainsley's advice to have Norm's entire family at court hugging, et cetera, at the front rail; Ron eventually asked the Court to do something about it because it got so obnoxious.'"

Snider's teeth clenched. "Gainsley never allowed Norm to speak freely to Ron Meshbesher, never got Norm out from under the adverse inferences made when he took the Fifth. That, gentlemen, encapsulates a major portion of Gainsley's irresponsibility."

Severson flipped closed his copy of the memorandum. "My picture of your saying, 'Never leave a client worse off,' just got a lot clearer."

Snider acknowledged Steve's compliment with a raise of his eyebrows. "But remember, the burden of proof for attorney malpractice is very hard. We must first win the case within our case—not prove who killed Nachtsheim; prove Wartnick didn't—and that's a very important point. If Wartnick would have lost the trial, anyway, it doesn't matter what Gainsley did or didn't do. So we must prove, first, actual negligence on Gainsley's part, then we must prove that *but for* that negligence there would never have been damages to Wartnick."

"Haven't we already got the negligence part?" Liberko said. "I mean, didn't Gainsley admit he instructed Wartnick to take the Fifth?"

Snider nodded. "He did. And that's a start, but we have a lot of investigation to do on what Gainsley should have uncovered in the original case. That's your bailiwick, Dan. Review discovery materials in the original case. Put together a detailed list of all witnesses who testified at the original trial as well as anyone who *should* have been a witness. Then start interviewing them. We need hard facts, but we also want opinions, characterizations, the works. Let's see what light these individuals can shed.

"Also, after some discussion, Joe and I've decided we'll use an informed consent theory for the attorney malpractice liability. Gainsley failed to explain to Wartnick the consequences of taking the Fifth in his deposition—he denied Wartnick the opportunity to give informed consent. He couldn't because he didn't know those consequences. His smoking-gun memo to Jane Lerner proves it."

"So the only questions will be damages," Liberko said.

"And that, gentlemen," Joe Friedberg whisked into the room, stopped beside Snider's desk, flipped his suit coat back, and placed his fists on his hips, "is going to be a whole lot more difficult than even we expected. The Nachtsheims will not consent to any agreement that benefits Wartnick in any way. The only thing they'll consent to is that they get all the money less attorney's fees. They don't give a squat how many hundreds of thousands Wartnick spent on Gainsley."

Silence hovered for several moments with each man in his own thoughts, then Liberko nodded and said to himself, "People never forget the truth, but they often confuse the lies."

Snider glanced around. "Okay, some good news. What's not mentioned within all these pages is that Ron Meshbesher has agreed to do us a huge favor." He watched for reactions. "He's a close friend with F. Lee Bailey and has agreed to pave our way to have Bailey as an expert witness."

Friedberg chuckled as Severson's eyes got big. "Nice having Meshbesher, huh?"

"We're also looking," Snider continued as he glanced up at Friedberg, "at former Minnesota Chief Justice Robert Sheran as an expert in court procedure."

Friedberg's nod was one of reluctant affirmation.

"Steve," Snider continued, "review the appellate opinions, any relevant correspondence, et cetera, and maybe give Dan a hand with some interviews if you have time. And start lists for us: the information Gainsley should have known that would have benefited Wartnick's defense. Note how one individual's statements contradict the statements of others. Also list any alternative suspects and why you think they could have done it. Use the police report but don't stop there.

"And Steve, it won't be long before we start preparing Norm to testify in deposition and for trial. Gainsley's statement about Norm's," he checked his notes, "'demeanor and potentially argumentative behavior.' Watch and see what he could have meant. He's known Norm since they were boys. I want to know if that's got any basis in fact. That should get us started. Questions?"

"Did you find out why Gainsley didn't want Norm to talk?" Severson said. "To totally muzzle the guy is just crazy."

Friedberg fielded that one. "Gainsley said it was these 'demeanor and argumentative tendencies.' Sounds like something out of right field."

"He says he was concerned Norm would be no match for Meshbesher under oath," Snider added.

"What do you think?" Severson's gaze shifted from Snider to Friedberg and back again. "Is Norm going to fold under pressure?"

Friedberg shrugged. "Gainsley was looking for an excuse." He crossed the room to take a seat in front of Snider's desk. "Jerry and I sand papered Norm pretty hard; we'll do it again to be sure he holds up."

Snider gazed steadily at Severson. "That's why I want you to watch him."

Severson hated the sight of blood, anyone's blood. He was a young lawyer who had intentionally chosen Faegre's Business Litigation Group because it did *business* litigation rather than the sometimes gruesome personal injury or tort cases handled by the general litigation group. To say he was uncomfortable meeting with Norm Wartnick was an understatement. A chill stung him deep inside at the realization he would soon sit across the table from a possible murderer.

CHAPTER 10

SIX WEEKS LATER

LATE MAY 1988

Snider leaned back into his desk chair and waited for Friedberg to answer at the other end of the phone line. Dan Liberko knocked on the open office door just as Friedberg picked up. Snider motioned Liberko into the room.

"Joe? I just got the polygraph analysis. Wartnick's responses confirm he had nothing to do with Nachtsheim's death." Laughter resonated deep in Snider's chest. "Yeah, but it's good to see it in writing. Dan's begun the interviews. He should have notes to you toward the end of the week." He looked toward Liberko and received a nod of confirmation. "Talk to you then." A click and Snider turned full attention to his investigator.

"Two things," Liberko began. "The MPD[10] file confirmed polygraph test results were reported for both Betty and Bobby Kauffman, and on Larry Kramlinger and Tom Evers. All done at the U of M,[11] all assumed cleared of any involvement. My best guess from initial interviews and studing law enforcement—from reading between the lines of Krueger's notes in the police file—I'd say Bobby must've been tanked on Quaaludes in order to pass that poly."

Snider processed the information with a nod.

Liberko placed his Memorandum to File on Snider's desk. "That one you'll want to talk to yourself. Dennis Kreuser. A Nervous Nellie when I started. He really didn't want to talk but eventually warmed up. Good memory and good source for a lot of the missing details."

"Such as?"

"Such as an insider's view of the relationships among the Nachtsheim family, especially between Bob and Bobby. *And* Kreuser was at the drug party the night before the shooting."

"You think there's some significance to that?" Snider reached for the report.

"He says Bobby actually talked about robbing Bob Nachtsheim; drew out floor plans of the florist shop for an ex-con named Roger Nordstrom—" Liberko grunted a chuckle as Snider's bushy eyebrows rose high above wide-open blue eyes. "Yeah, but there's more. Bobby also tried to enlist him, Kreuser,

---

10. Minneapolis Police Department
11. University of Minnesota

to do the driving for this robbery they were planning. Kreuser would have none of it and left."

Snider's surprise ebbed as he mentally slotted Liberko's findings into memory. An air of intense concentration filled the room.

Liberko continued. "Kreuser says he considered Bob a friend. Next thing he hears, Bob's been shot and Bobby's got what he wanted, to run the shop. And Kreuser doesn't particularly care for Bobby, I can tell you that."

Snider flipped through Liberko's detailed report. "Think we could get all these guys together?"

"Only if you want another shoot-out at the O.K. Corral."

An amused smirk flit across Snider's face, then seriousness returned. "Have Steve help you see what some of these guys have to say. And set up a meeting with Kreuser. Let's see if he can keep his story straight. First, though, see what the Marine—" Snider glanced at the report, "Tom Evers, can tell us."

TUESDAY, JUNE 7, 1988, NOON

Liberko knocked on the front door of Tom Evers's 1930s raised bungalow. Evers answered immediately and ushered Liberko into the cozy living room.

"I noticed the Marine Corps flag on your van."

"'Nam. Not back long when I went to work for Bob. Coffee?"

"Sure. Black." Liberko followed him into the kitchen. "Mr. Evers—"

"Tom. Have a seat." He placed a steaming mug of brown syrup near a chair at the kitchen table and stayed standing.

Liberko sat in the offered chair and leaned his briefcase against its leg, but his focus stayed on the Marine. "We're investigating the events surrounding the death of Bob Nachtsheim. Anything you can tell us would be a help."

The lanky man turned to stare through the screen in place over the space left by a patio door slid all the way open. The curtains trembled in a hot breeze. Light glittered from myriad droplets that shot upwards from Evers's lawn sprinkler. Evers sipped from his coffee mug. "You defending Wartnick?"

"No. Actually this time we're pursuing a case on Mr. Wartnick's behalf."

"Against Betty?" He turned to face Liberko.

"No, against his previous attorney, Phil Gainsley. Mrs. Nachtsheim's involved, of course. Anything we win will go toward covering her judgment against our client."

Evers snorted. "Figures."

"Why do you say that, Mr. Evers—Tom?"

"She's a gold digger. I've never met anyone as devious as that woman." He stared again into the backyard. When he spoke, his subdued volume conveyed a quiet, menacing confidence. "The Corps trained me to tear down, reassemble, and operate any weapon you can name. There's not a piece of material or equipment on earth I can't blow up. I'm trained to do three things: blow things up, kill people, and survive, and I have nine decorations to prove

I did my job and took care of my men. You think I'm a little crazy now, wait 'til Bobby or Betty try to walk in there." He nodded toward the backyard then drained his cup of coffee.

Liberko inhaled a slow, deep breath and willed his shoulder muscles to relax.

Evers poured himself another cup and sat down at the table. "Back a few years ago, that woman was calling me in the middle of the night, screaming I murdered her husband. Bob's dad was a friend of mine since I was a kid, and while he was trying to find out who killed his son, twice somebody took shots at him. I saw the bullet holes. One in his foundation and one in his garage door. He was convinced Bobby was involved. Still had the bullet that hit the house—the one that almost got him."

"So you knew the Nachtsheim family growing up. Is that how you got the job at B and B?"

"No, only really knew Grandpa Paul. Bob hired me the week of—"

"Grandpa Paul?"

"Paul Nachtsheim, Bob's dad."

Liberko recorded the facts in a small spiral notebook.

"Bob hired me mid-February '73 just before Hallmark's made-up holiday. Wanda, my wife, was a beautician; used to do Betty's hair. One day Betty mentioned Bob was looking for a salesman and would I like the job." He shrugged. "I was selling motorcycle parts and looking for something different, so when Bob called, I signed on."

"And you've been in the flower business since?"

"Right. Wholesale end."

"Tell me about working at B and B."

"I enjoyed it. Bob and I got along well. Seventy percent of what I know about the business, I learned from Bob."

"Were you familiar with a man named Dennis Kreuser? How did he get along with Bob Nachtsheim?"

"Denny? Good. Why?"

"He's been mentioned as a potential suspect in the shooting."

"I doubt it. He and Bob got along real well—had a mutual respect for each other. Denny and Angie were engaged. Probably would have married if Betty hadn't gotten in the way."

"Angie Nachtsheim? Bob and Betty's daughter?"

"The younger one. Right."

"So you knew that Mr. Kreuser, back in the early '70s, had been in prison in—"

"Reformatory. St. Cloud. Not prison, exactly. He was a juvenile. Ready for another cup?"

"Sure. Thanks."

"Yeah, Denny had been in for something petty," Evers spoke as he moved toward the coffee pot. "B & E.[12] Vandalism. Don't remember exactly. Angie arranged for Bob to provide Denny with employment so he could get early release." Evers set the filled cup back on the table. "That was one reason Denny was so dedicated to Bob, so conscientious about the work he did for him."

"And everyone else at B and B got along with Bob? No troublemakers? Customer problems?"

"Only his family. None of the Nachtsheims got along with each other. Well, except Bob and John, but John was a cool little squirt back then. Not like later. Too bad Bobby raised him instead of Bob."

"Can you elaborate on those relationships within the Nachtsheim family? You say none of them got along?"

Evers seated himself at the table opposite Liberko. "Bobby and Bob would argue about anything. If one of them said it was three minutes after two, the other one would say it's four. More times than not, when Bob and Bobby argued, Betty sided with Bobby. Bob and Betty were worse. They argued about everything under the sun."

"Could you expand on that?"

"Color of the paint, what day it was. It didn't matter. They were at each other's throats."

"Did you ever see any affection between Bob and Betty while you were working there?"

"No. Never. To be fair, part of that could have been because Bob was a workaholic. His flower business was his life, except he even thought more of his customers than he did of his business. Whenever he'd get into a dispute with a supplier about the quality of a product, he'd absorb the costs." Evers smirked. "Probably didn't go over well with a wife who's a gold-digger."

"Can you tell me more about the day of the shooting? Were you at work that day?"

"I was running about half an hour behind. Had the company truck and was at the airport picking up freight, flowers. Had trouble with the truck."

"Did you have the truck here at home, or did you pick it up at the store?"

"Here. Was running about a half hour behind, so I called the shop to tell them I was on the way. Larry Kramlinger, I think, answered and told me what happened."

"That Mr. Nachtsheim had been shot?"

"Right."

"Why were you half an hour late?"

"The choke on the truck stuck."

"So you fixed the truck that morning and—"

"Well, I got it to run. I wouldn't say I fixed it."

12. Breaking and entering

"Right. But you picked up your flowers at the airport and came back to the shop."

Evers nodded. "I arrived a little after seven. Seven-fifteen, maybe."

"What happened then? Who did you talk to?"

"Krueger, the homicide detective, asked me questions. Wanted to know if anything was missing. Normal police stuff."

"And what did you do at B and B that day?"

"Filled orders, preexisting orders. Called customers and explained what had happened."

Liberko hesitated only a moment before asking the next question. "Was there a need for someone to clean up from the shooting?"

"Yeah, there was."

"And did you participate in that?"

Evers stood slowly, noiselessly, and moved again to the patio door. He watched droplets from the sprinkler spatter and spread across the patio. "I cleaned it up. The other guys were—it was a mess, a gruesome mess." He paused and inhaled. "I'd seen a lot worse in the service, so...." His eyes tracked the sprinkler's spray as it retreated.

Liberko gave Evers a chance to collect himself then asked, "Were you familiar with Norm Wartnick then?"

"Yeah. A couple of hours after the shooting Norm came to the shop. He spent the day filling orders."

"Did you ever suspect he might have anything to do with the shooting?"

"No way." Evers scooped his mug off the table and headed for the coffee pot. "When I learned about the key-man policy, I wondered if he might have, but from my limited exposure with him, he was just a nice guy. Hyper, but a nice guy. Someone said he might be taking Valium."

"So it's your opinion there is no way Mr. Wartnick shot Bob Nachtsheim?"

"Plain and simple, Norm's not a trigger man."

"I'd like to read you a portion of Krueger's file." Liberko retrieved pages from his case and mentally assembled his facts. "He states, 'In January of this year Bobby Nachtsheim, son of the victim, quit the company. He said that yesterday his father called him about 4:45 p.m. and asked him if he wanted to come back to work. Apparently he decided against it.' That would be the day before the murder. Do you know anything about that?"

"What a load of crap. Nothing could be further from the truth."

"Did you see or hear anything that would lead you to believe Bobby's statement?"

"I'd say that's purely b.s."

"Based on what?"

"Bob had a strong dislike for his son. They had no ties. Bob wanted no ties, no contact. He was done with his son."

"He told you that?"

"Right." Evers nodded. "Bob had known Bobby was selling drugs, but one day he caught him actually selling out the back door of the shop. Bob was already ready to get rid of him because Bobby had ripped him off, took several thousand dollars from what Bob said, so the drug deal was the last hurrah. Bob told him to get out and never come back."

"Mr. Nachtsheim told you that."

"Correct."

"So, to your knowledge, after Bobby was fired Bob had no contact with him. Correct?"

"Pissed Bob off so bad no way he'd ever ask Bobby back to the shop."

"So the first time you saw him, then, was the day his father was shot?"

"That's correct. He came into the store and took charge."

"And between the time he was fired, some six to nine months before, and the day of the shooting, Bobby was never around?"

"Right. At least not that I saw. He was a chicken without feathers but he wasn't stupid."

"How did the other members of the Nachtsheim family feel about the firing?"

"We never discussed it."

"What can you tell me about them?"

"Well, I already told you Betty's extremely devious, a gold-digger. My impression? Her biggest ambition in life is to be wealthy. And I could name four guys off the top of my head that she was shagging just during the four months I was there."

"Was Bob aware of it?"

"I think he was. We never discussed it."

"What about the daughters?"

"I didn't know much about Angie other than she's engaged to Denny. She and Betty worked the books. I went to school with Terry but didn't know her."

Evers was silent while Liberko jotted down notes, then he surprised Liberko when he said, "Betty Nachtsheim enlisted Peter Hurkos for her shindig, you know."

"The psychic who worked the Boston Strangler murders?"

"Right. She and Krueger flew out to L.A. for a few days and talked with him several times. Then she arranged for Hurkos to stop in the Twin Cities on his way to Chicago. Krueger called me. He wanted me to meet with him, with Hurkos."

"Did you?"

"On my terms. It had to be somewhere public, and if she was going to be there it couldn't be anywhere near me."

"How did it go?"

"Before he even opened his mouth, I told Hurkos I didn't believe the crap psychics came up with and if he even suggested I had anything to do with the murder, I'd mess him up bad."

Liberko's raised eyebrow asked the next question.

Evers laughed. "He handed me a piece of paper and told me to write down two sets of numbers as he gave them to me. I did. Then he told me the first number was the serial number of the .44 magnum I had under my jacket and the second was the odometer reading on my truck."

"And?"

"He was right. Even told me what color my bedroom was. The part that spooked me, though, was when he gave details about experiences in 'Nam that could only have been known by people who'd been dead a long time."

Liberko gulped down the rest of his coffee.

"Hurkos stared into my eyes for a long time. While he was staring, I looked at Betty and said, 'You ever accuse me again of your husband's death, I'll personally see you suffer the most excruciating death possible, and after you're buried I'll piss on your grave.'" Evers solemnly nodded. "Hurkos looked at Betty and told her I had nothing to do with the homicide and I'd do exactly what I'd just said."

"Did she leave you alone?"

"To this day."

"Did Hurkos talk to anyone else while he was here?"

"I heard he tried to talk to Bobby. Went to his house but Bobby bolted the door and ran upstairs to his bedroom.[13] Locked that door, too. He wanted absolutely nothing to do with Hurkos—but that's just hearsay."

Evers leaned back in his chair, stretched his long legs out in front of him, and crossed his arms. "But the most perplexing thing about all this, at least to me? You know about Russ Krueger while Bob was in the hospital? He wanted to start a rumor Bob regained consciousness long enough to identify his attacker. Krueger was just trying to flush out the shooter, but Betty would have nothing to do with it. Squashed that rumor immediately. Now, why in the world would she do that? Why wouldn't she want to know who murdered her husband? Unless, of course, she already knew."

---

13. Betty later used a variation of this story but turned it into Norm Wartnick at his floral shop who ran from Hurkos, a story that could not be substantiated.

CHAPTER 11

"Nachtsheim family's accused us of selling out in order to settle." Friedberg spoke to Snider via telephone. "They're insisting they get to approve any settlement of less than a million-and-a-half."

Snider absorbed the information, then said, "Retaining Justice Sheran plus a damages expert is likely to incur between fifty and a hundred thousand dollars."

"Damage recovery, though, is likely to be, well," Joe paused. "You know liability here's as clear as it's ever gonna get for legal malpractice."

"Have you heard from Moss and Barnett on ALAS[14] coverage?" Snider asked.

"No. I'll give Herzog a call. I did talk with Doug Thomson, though. He mentioned something very interesting. Would you believe Gainsley demanded a third of that five-thousand retainer?"

Silence made the phone connection sound hollow. Friedberg waited. Snider finally spoke. "Did Thomson pay it?"

"Yep. Sixteen hundred sixty-six."

"I must consult with the litigation committee, Joe. Wartnick will never be able to reimburse expenses for this case. What little he has is tied up in garnishment."

"Do that," Friedberg agreed. "Then think about some kind of proposed settlement demand. If we don't resolve the division of fees early, this is gonna turn into a pile of crap."

"It's going to be—" Snider started, then paused. "There are Faegre partners who want this case to dry up and blow away."

"Well, the system's a lot bigger than a judge, a partner, or a bad attorney."

MONDAY, JUNE 20, 1988

Phil Gainsley and Moss & Barnett filed a motion for summary judgment.[15] They said that even if allegations of negligence were taken as true, Wartnick's

---

14. Attorneys' Liability Assurance Society – the legal malpractice insurance carrier. (www.ALAS. com. March 22, 2011).

15. A final decision by a judge, given upon a party's motion, that resolves a lawsuit before there is a trial. The party making the motion marshals all the evidence in its favor, compares it to the

malpractice action failed as a matter of law based on the doctrine of judgmental immunity; that is, they claimed an attorney cannot be held liable for errors in judgment.

Was it possible that any reasonably adept attorney would not understand the inference of having his client claim Fifth Amendment rights during a civil deposition? Snider knew they now had to prove it was not.

Snider turned his attention to drafting opposition to Gainsley's motion for summary judgment. Research of judgmental immunity was assigned to Steve Severson with authority to request summer associates in order to cut costs.

For the second time, Severson sat across the table from Norm Wartnick and questioned, probed, prodded, and pushed. As he shook hands with the man and watched him trudge toward the elevator, Severson knew their client was innocent. There was no way Norm Wartnick could have done any of the things Betty Nachtsheim had accused him of doing.

WEDNESDAY, JUNE 22, 1988

Dan Liberko stood outside the screen door. He studied the gnarled, trembling hands and glazed eyes of the woman who had responded to his knock. "Thank you so much for agreeing to see me, Mrs. Nachtsheim. I'm truly sorry for the loss of your son." There was no response. "Mrs. Nachtsheim? You are Mrs. Paul Nachtsheim, aren't you?"

"Ya-a-a." The word was elongated in her Norwegian accent. "Who are you?"

"My name is Dan Liberko. Tom Evers gave me your name and address."

No light of recognition.

"We talked on the phone yesterday? About your husband, Paul." Still nothing. "About the investigation your husband did into the murder of your son, Bob."

Her eyelids narrowed. A scowl formed across her broad, wrinkled brow.

"If you'd like for me to come back another—"

"I burned *all* dat mess." The light of defiance broke through in her eyes. "I burnt it. Every page I could put my hands on. By St. Olaf, I don't know why he trew away our marriage on such as dat, God rest his soul. Was never my way of doing, I tell you."

"You burned all his investigation work?"

"Da week after I lay him in da ground, God rest his soul. I wanted it out of dis house!" Her knees buckled. She clutched at the doorframe with twisted fingers.

"Mrs. Nachtsheim, are you okay? Do you need something? To sit down?"

---

other side's evidence, and argues that there are no "triable issues of fact." Summary judgment is awarded if the undisputed facts and the law make it clear that it would be impossible for the opposing party to prevail if the matter were to proceed to trial. (Nolo.com. Access Mar 12, 2011.)

"Get out."

"Can I get you a glass of water?"

"Get out. Get out and leave me alone."

WEDNESDAY, JUNE 29, 1988

Phil Gainsley telephoned Doug Thomson regarding the fee-split. Gainsley categorically denied having ever received any monies from Thomson's firm for any reason.

"Phil," Thomson responded. "We sent you sixteen-hundred sixty-six dollars. It's on the books."

Phil Gainsley composed a letter to Doug Thomson and requested a copy of the canceled check, front and back. Thomson sent it to him the next day.

TUESDAY, JULY 5, 1988

Snider sent Friedberg a draft of their Memorandum in Opposition to Defendant's Motion for Summary Judgment and included Gainsley's pattern of requesting unearned funds. He listed both the request for one-third of the insurance proceeds and the splitting of Wartnick's retainer for Doug Thomson as further evidence of Gainsley's failure in his fiduciary duty to his client.

THURSDAY, JULY 7, 1988

Wartnick gave affidavit in support of Snider's memo opposing Gainsley's motion for summary judgment. In paragraph 20, for the first time, Wartnick detailed specifics on Gainsley's demand for one-third of the insurance proceeds from the key-man policy on Nachtsheim, which would have amounted to thirty-eight thousand dollars.

"At no point in time prior to the receipt of these funds did Gainsley discuss with me any contingent fee for services he was providing. To avoid any dispute with Gainsley, I finally consented, over protest, to pay Gainsley, above his normal hourly billings, $14,000 of the insurance proceeds."

Paragraphs 21 and 22 included, "At no point in time was the fee-splitting arrangement discussed with me. I did not even know that any of the $5,000 retainer had been paid to Gainsley until my present attorneys informed me this had occurred."

MONDAY, JULY 11, 1988

Gainsley swore in affidavit to never requesting any fee-split and never receiving any monies.

A hearing was held on Defendant Gainsley's Motion for Summary Judgment before Judge Michael Davis. Gainsley's attorney Scott Herzog's verbal argument included:

"Plaintiffs aren't asking summary judgment be denied because they haven't completed discovery. Apparently they conceded that the discovery is complete and that this matter is ripe for disposition by the Court. ..."

Herzog was saying that since Friedberg and Snider did not say, 'Wait! You can't give them summary judgment yet because we haven't finished digging up all the facts,' then they must have actually finished digging up all the facts they needed; so we must all be ready for you, Judge Davis, to get this show on the road and decide this thing.'

Herzog wanted to put a stick through the spokes of Wartnick's team making further discovery. He insisted, "Indeed, they did have all of Mr. Gainsley's files, all of the Moss and Barnett files. They've reviewed them completely.

"Now," Herzog continued, "I know they've talked to attorneys. They've talked to Doug Thomson, and that's the one part of their response this morning that disgusts me most of all. In their response last Thursday night, they say, 'Oh, by the way, there was fee splitting between Mr. Thomson and Mr. Gainsley way back in 1973, fifteen years ago.' That was not in their complaint, was not in their answers to interrogatories. Mr. Gainsley was not deposed on that item. But, most critically, there's no affidavit from Mr. Thomson. ...

"A malpractice action is a claim brought by someone who loses his case. And if it were allowed, then we're telling *all* civil law attorneys that if you have a difference of opinion and you implement your difference of opinion regarding the liability or the applicability of a statute and you lose, you might get sued for malpractice.

"If this lawsuit is permitted to proceed, we're in effect telling *all* civil litigators, *all* trial attorneys that every time there's a jury verdict that comes in, *some*body's going to get sued. You're going to have one malpractice action for every civil verdict because somebody lost."

Immediately following the hearing, Doug Thomson swore in affidavit that Gainsley had, in fact, requested the fee split. Thomson included copies of his firm's ledger pages as well as the front and back of the check which Gainsley endorsed.

TUESDAY, JULY 19, 1988

Gainsley wrote Judge Davis: "I have an ethical duty to apprise you" that I had nothing to do with any fee-splitting as alleged by Mr. Thomson and Mr. Wartnick.

The matter was now in the capable hands of Judge Michael Davis.

CHAPTER 12

THREE MONTHS LATER

WEDNESDAY, OCTOBER 12, 1988

Snider turned the corner into Faegre's reception area and saw Wartnick drop the new issue of *Time Magazine* onto a coffee table. That particular edition documented squabbles over how some new thing called fiber-optic cable was going to destroy network television. Snider thought Wartnick would probably be content with continued reruns of *Happy Days*.

"Norm. Sorry, I was delayed." Snider offered his hand. Wartnick shook it. "Joe's waiting for us in Conference Room G."

Moments later it was Friedberg's hand that gripped Wartnick's. "Good to see you again. Have a seat." He handed Wartnick a copy of Judge Davis's Order on Gainsley's motion for summary judgment. "The bad news is we can't pursue Phil for his failure to obtain the complete police file."

"Though we can still show," Snider interjected, "that he failed to interview or make adequate investigation into the murder. Can I get either of you something to drink?"

"Cup o' coffee'd be great," Friedberg replied. "And we can pursue Gainsley's prejudicial statement to the jury with that idiotic reference to the lie detector in opening."

"So, wait a minute," Wartnick said. "You're telling me Judge Davis didn't give us the summary judgment."

"No." Snider set a steaming mug in front of Friedberg then seated himself and cracked open the cap on a bottle of water. "We're saying Judge Davis did not give Gainsley *his* motion for summary judgment."

"*We* didn't file for summary judgment." Friedberg tapped the table, palm down, with a wedding-ring clunk for emphasis. "Gainsley did."

"I don't understand." Wartnick stared at Friedberg. "How could he not—. Oh, got it. If Davis had granted the summary judgment, we'd have lost the whole thing."

Snider nodded. "Exactly."

"I've always been on the 'want it' side with Gainsley." Wartnick leaned back in the swivel chair and pulled his copy of the report toward him. "Feels strange. Seemed like every few months he filed another motion requesting summary judgment, or was in court arguing for summary judgment, or he was talking about summary—"

"But ya don't want to file one 'til ya have all the facts," Friedberg said. "And here's a reason why—one more win Judge Davis threw our way." Friedberg leafed through the pages of Davis's Order. "Here. 'Attorney Gainsley did not allow Wartnick to make his own informed decision to assert the Fifth Amendment at his deposition.'" The document fluttered closed. "That makes this case a walkover."

Wartnick's nose was still buried in the judge's Order. "So we can't complain he made Thomson split the retainer I paid Doug, and we can't complain Gainsley didn't have the police file," Wartnick said, "but we can say he didn't investigate like he should've and that I should've been able to answer Meshbesher's questions like I wanted."

Snider nodded. "Exactly."

"And that he was an idiot for raising the polygraph in opening," Friedberg added and reached for his coffee.

Snider's raised eyebrow caught Friedberg's attention. The shorter man grinned a toothy smile and nodded to Wartnick. "Take away that Fifth and they got nothin' on ya."

THREE WEEKS LATER

MONDAY, OCTOBER 31, 1988

Liberko and Severson sat in Snider's office and waited for their boss to get off the phone. His only words were, "I see." "Um-hmm. Unjust enrichment." Pause, then "Expand on that, please." With the handset at last in its cradle, Snider leaned back and dropped his hands to the arms of his chair. "That was Joe. He still believes one of our best arguments, actually equal to the Fifth Amendment instruction, is Gainsley's failure to raise the statute of limitations early on. That, of course, is what enabled Meshbesher to gerrymander around his own mistake."

"And that's where couching his complaint in unjust enrichment comes to play?" Severson looked for and received confirmation. "Meshbesher's ruse to cover his own negligence. How could Gainsley not have seen that?"

Snider nodded. "That's why we're here. Also, Moss and Barnett's taking us more seriously. We've just received notice Jack Mason of Dorsey and Whitney's been retained by Moss and Barnett."

Liberko's eyebrows rose. "'Black Jack' Mason?"

"You know him?" Snider asked.

"Only by reputation," Liberko said. "'Mercurial temper personified.'"

"Aaargh," Severson piped up. "It's Halloween. Be very afraid!"

"Unfortunately it's no laughing matter," Snider said. "Mason will blindside us if we're not prepared."

"We at least have to warn Wartnick how cross-eyed the guy is."

"In time," Snider smiled. "Dan, what've you got?"

"I found the woman Tom Evers mentioned—the one who might have known the girl who was Bobby's fiancée at the time of the shooting."

Snider nodded for him to continue.

"Evers thought she might've been a friend of Anita Lange's, Bobby's fiancée. Turns out the name Anita Lange didn't even ring a bell, but the name Bobby Nachtsheim did. She hadn't seen him since she was about fifteen, but she definitely remembered who he was." Liberko flipped backward in his pocket notebook. "'Well, he was the kind of guy my dad would say, "I don't want to see you going out with him."'—and the only other thing she could recall was it seemed like Bobby was always in trouble."

"Have you contacted Dennis Kreuser?"

"He said it couldn't be a worse time for him, personally; something about the custody of a child. If I remember, his exact words were, 'My life's been absolute turmoil' and the last thing he wants to think about right now is the Nachtsheims, murder or family. I'll give him a call the first of December."

EARLY NOVEMBER 1988

Jane Lerner put through a telephone call to Jack Mason. She had never met the man, personally, but knew of him from her years as a partner in the Gainsley firm. Mason could be a nasty opponent, good at low blows and delay tactics, or at least that is what she had heard.

The ringing stopped abruptly. "Mr. Mason, my name is Jane Lerner. I was a partner in the Gainsley firm back in the '70s. Yes, with Phil Gainsley. Precisely why I called. I would like to offer you my services.

"No, actually," Lerner said. "I got your number from Jerry Snider. Yes, that's right—he questioned whether I had any independent recollection of a February 1979 memo from Phil in which Phil asked me to research Fifth Amendment ramifications.

"No," she answered Mason, "I said only that I needed to see the file. Then he mentioned you were representing Phil's interests." She smiled. "Yes, I thought you would want to talk. I'm no longer in the Cities. I took a partnership in Cincinnati in 1983. Yes, Cincinnati, Ohio—but Phil and I have stayed in touch throughout these years.

"Mr. Mason, I—Well, thank you, Jack. And you must call me Jane. I would be glad to be of service to Phil in any way I'm able. In fact, I'm sure if you would be willing to make my trip to Minneapolis possible—. Yes, an excellent suggestion. It will be such a pleasure to meet you."

CHAPTER 13

TUESDAY, JANUARY 17, 1989

Snider watched the teenage gum-smacker lower a plate of ham and eggs to the table. "Anything else I can get you?" She was gone before he could answer. Dan Liberko shrugged and used his thumbnail to scrape dried egg yolk from his fork.

Dennis Kreuser was halfway through his first stack of plate-sized pancakes. "I never talked to any Mr. Gainsley." He stuffed a forkful of pancakes into his mouth and talked as he chewed. "Never heard of him. Never heard Betty filed suit, either, but it don't surprise me, greedy cat."

"So your relationship with the Nachtsheims was not a good one?" Snider asked.

"Nah, Bob was good to me. I liked working with him." Droplets of greasy syrup quivered from Kreuser's mustache, then dropped into his scraggly beard. "Never had anyone treat me with the kind of respect he did—in fact, I always thought maybe Bob thought I was like the son he never had." He swallowed and stared through a framed photograph of a '54 Chevy on the far wall of the diner. "Angie, she was daddy's girl. Her and me and Bob, we had some laughs, some good times."

With what might have been a sigh, he refocused on his plate. His right leg twitched up and down; the vibration rattled the table top. "Betty, on the other hand, was a witch." He crammed in another forkful. "Her and Bobby was nuts—plain bad news. Always fighting and finding something to complain about. I felt sorry for Bob, being married to her.

"Bobby never had any regular hours that he'd work," Kreuser continued, "just sort of showed up whenever he felt like it. Irritated the hell out of Bob. And they was always yelling at each other. Always. Wouldn't have surprised me to hear someone'd seen them throwing punches.

"Bobby never got along with Betty, either—he argued with her as much as Bob. Then, it was really strange, you know after Bob's death, Betty let Bobby run the shop however he wanted—suddenly they get along fine. Except after about six months Bobby'd run the place into the ground and Betty had to close the doors." A grunt emerged from his massive chest. Snider could not decide—Was that a laugh? "Bobby just plain ran the thing into the ground."

The waitress slopped coffee into Snider's mug and rolled a creamer toward him. It made it almost halfway across the table. Kreuser picked it up and extended it to Snider, who took it but didn't use it.

"And you know, as great as Bob was to me, I gotta admit—the shop was his life. He worked fourteen, eighteen hours a day. Never spent extra time with nobody." Both plates of pancakes were gone and he started on the skillet full of potatoes, eggs, and meat.

"Mr. Kreuser," Snider said. "I understand you were no longer working at B and B after January of 1973. Is that correct?"

Kreuser nodded and chewed. "Something like that. You're talking sixteen years ago."

"I'd like to ask you bluntly: Were you fired because you tried to sell Bob stolen merchandise?"[16]

"What? Who told you that? I was fired 'cause Betty found out Angie was putting her money in my checking account. We was getting married and Angie wanted to be sure her money didn't just happen to disappear. Oh, man, and when Betty found out, she was Mt. St. Helens-ing all over the shop. You'd-a thought I was Adolf Hitler and Jack the Ripper both. Threw such a fit, Bob *had* to fire me. Don't know what I'd-a done in his shoes." He wiped his mouth and sat up as straight as his bulk allowed. "You going to ask me about the party?"

"I would be interested in hearing all you can remember about those two days—the day prior to and the day of the shooting."

"Well, Bobby's girlfriend, Debbie, had a party over at her—"

"Wait. His girlfriend? I thought he was engaged to someone named Anita Lange."

"Yeah, that's what I heard, too. Even heard wedding invitations was sent out and all that crap. But his girlfriend's name was Debbie. Debbie Feist. Never saw anyone named Ann."

"Thank you. Go on."

"It was Debbie's party at her place. The party wasn't our first choice, but I picked up Strehlow and we got there kinda late. Bobby and Al Mentes and Roger Nordstrom," he counted on his fingers, "were there when we got there. May have been one or two others but I don't remember their names; they didn't stay long after we got there. Anyway, Mentes was gone and Strehlow's passed out on the couch, then Bobby starts shooting his mouth off about how he'd get to be some big-time owner of his dad's business if his dad was out of the picture—how easy it'd be to stick up his old man for some cash. Well, Nordstrom took it serious; said, 'Draw me a map.' And Bobby did. Right there."

+

---

16. This statement came from Betty Nachtsheim as made to Russ Krueger and was found within the police report.

Bobby Nachtsheim—twenty, pockmarked, and restless—stabbed a calloused finger against a sketch of his father's business, B and B Wholesale Florist. "Doors 're here and here," he said and glanced to his closest comrade, ex-con Roger Nordstrom, seated upright and fidgety on Bobby's right. "The back one'll be unlocked."

Nordstrom acknowledged the information with an eager nod and chugged the last of a beer.

Bobby squinted through the haze of cigarette and marijuana smoke which hung thick in the stale air of the cheap, two-room apartment. "Denny," he called and watched for movement from the long-haired seventeen-year-old sprawled on the sofa. "Hey, Kreuser, you're drivin'."

Denny Kreuser grunted and shook his head to clear a self-induced stupor. Even semi-conscious Denny did not like what he heard. He forced open his eyelids and glared at Nachtsheim. "Forget it, man. You're crazy." He grabbed the scrawny teen passed out beside him. "Strehlow, get up. Come on, Strehlow." Denny shook the gangly boy then pulled him to a standing position, pointed him toward the door, and propelled him forward. "We're outta here."

Bobby's eyes were dark, lifeless as he watched the teens stumble from the apartment.

+

Kreuser again stared through the '54 Chevy on the restaurant's far wall. This time, though, his expression had hardened. "Had doors and windows and how they were locked. Even told his dad's schedule down almost to the minute. I remember Nordstrom got real excited, kinda jumpy-twitchy, you know? Then Bobby told me I'd be the driver, the getaway driver. Can you believe that? After all Bob done for me? I yanked Strehlow off the couch and we left. I wanted no part of that."

"Were you good friends with Bobby?" Snider asked. "Why would you go to a party of his?"

"We weren't good friends but we weren't bad friends. I was engaged to his sister. We just hung around sometimes, once in a while. Had a few beers, smoked some pot."

"What about Roger Nordstrom? Had you known him before?"

"Seen him at the shop with Bobby once or twice. Never came inside. Nordstrom was a different bird, you know. Real gun freak. Caught up in the drugs and all."

"Can you list for me the occasions when you have seen Mr. Nordstrom since that night?"

"Yeah, easy. None. To this day. And don't want to, neither." By now his twitchy leg rattled the whole table. "I got no idea where he's at. May be out of state for all I care."

"What happened after that?"

Kreuser pulled a package of cigarettes from his shirt pocket and lit up. "I went home. Well, first I dropped off Strehlow. My mom hollered at me when I came in so she'd probably still remember what time I got back. That woman remembers everything. Next I knew, Bob was gone and Krueger was hell-bent to pin it on me."

"Why do you say that?"

"He pounded on me every day—every day, man. Tried to make me confess I had something to do with it."

"How did you get caught selling drugs to the undercover officer?"

"Bobby set me up." Kreuser took a long drag and exhaled smoke. "He gave me this package—said it was pot—I found out later it was crack—ask me to drive it over to St. Paul and meet this guy at this location and he'd give me cash for the package. Well, I didn't make it to meet the guy. I'm not real familiar with the streets over there and I got lost and couldn't find the guy and on and on, so I just came home. I wasn't home ten minutes before the feds busted down my door and tore up the place. I got no doubts Krueger had Bobby set me up 'cause the first one to come see me in jail was him."

"Was Lieutenant Krueger? Interesting."

"Man was shoving pictures of Bob in my face, you know, with him lying there on the floor." Kreuser closed his eyes. "Bragging he had clout and if I told him what he wanted to know he'd work it with the feds to get the charges dropped. But I had nothing to tell him." Kreuser's massive hands went palms up with fingers spread wide, ashes dangling from the stub of the cigarette. "I didn't know anything—and I sure wasn't going to say I shot Bob. That guy was the closest thing to a dad I ever had."

"What happened then?"

Another long drag, then Kreuser's massive hand crushed the cigarette filter into the ash tray. The cigarette package was retrieved and another one lit. "Three years in maximum at Oxford." The smoky haze grew more dense above the table. "Hey, you mind if I get some more 'cakes?"

"No, that's fine." Snider spotted the waitress across the room and lifted his hand to summon her. She disappeared into the kitchen.

"Got another visit from Krueger, too, except this time instead of trying to intimidate me he said Betty was willing to give me five Gs to confess."

"And? Were you tempted to take it?"

"No way in hell I'd touch her money, you kidding me? I'm not covering for Bobby." He dragged deeply on the cigarette, exhaled gray smoke. "I told him to get lost.

"You know," Kreuser continued, "when I got out, I spent months tracking Bobby so I could settle with him for setting me up. I couldn't find him anywhere. Then one morning I woke up and thought to myself, 'This is absolutely crazy.

This Nachtsheim family ain't done nothing but create problems for me since the day I started dating Angie.' I stopped tryin' to find Bobby and decided to try to make something of my life."

The waitress reappeared, glared at Snider, and took the order from the booth next to theirs. "Miss. Miss, we'd like to—" Snider said, but he spoke to her back.

"You want my theory on what happened that day?"

"Please, and you might be more successful at getting her attention."

Kreuser gave the waitress a nod when she turned around. "I don't think they meant to kill Bob. I think they only wanted to scare him. Yeah, another stack of 'cakes, please. Thanks." He crushed the stub into the ash tray. "They only wanted to scare him into giving them money.

"Knowing Bob, he probably looked at Nordstrom and said—'cause, you know, I think Nordstrom probably pulled the trigger—Bobby's a wimp, Nordstrom's got itchy fingers and he was always, well, he struck me as always wanting to please Bobby. Nose up to him, you know?—anyway, Bob probably said something like 'F—'" He stopped, glanced around, and noticed three old ladies chattering at a nearby table, leaned as far toward Liberko as his stomach allowed, and mouthed, "You," before he straightened and continued. "'You want money from me, you'll have to kill me for it.'" Kreuser clutched his coffee mug and drained it.

"Mr. Nachtsheim might have said something to that effect?" Snider asked.

"Oh, yeah. Bob's a tough character. He wasn't taking nothing off nobody."

"And what would Bobby's involvement have been?"

"Everything else. Plans, timing, driving—all that stuff. Bob would've definitely turned his back on Bobby—and he was shot from behind, wasn't he?" Kreuser made it clear he was not asking the question to get information.

"That's the opinion of the investigators."

"Bobby hurries up and marries this Debbie chick so she can't testify against him.'Cause there were only four conscious people at that party who knew what was going on: Roger Nordstrom and Bobby, Debbie Feist, me and Strehlow. Five people. Now Roger's missing, Bobby married Debbie, and then set me up to go to prison. I think he's probably responsible for Strehlow's death, too. You tell me how else that freaky death could happen. Definitely something needing investigating."

"Mr. Strehlow's death was ruled accidental," Liberko said. "They say he was drunk, that he'd been running through that graveyard and fell against the grave marker which fell on top of him."

"Fifteen-hundred pounds? You ain't telling me you're believing that?"

"What do you believe, Mr. Kreuser?" Snider asked.

"Strehlow grew up around that cemetery. He was probably using it as a shortcut to get home; he just lived like six blocks away. And yeah, he told me stories about how he and his friends would get drunk and go knock over grave stones as kids. I can't believe that somebody who was good at something like that like Strehlow was, I mean it was wrong to do, but he did know how the whole thing worked, 'cause that grave stone that fell on—they had to get a truck in there to lift it off him. Strehlow weighed one-eighty soaking wet, and he's going to be able to knock over fifteen-hundred pounds and have it land on his head?"

The pancakes arrived. Kreuser drew circles on the top of the stack with the syrup.

"I tell you, Mr. Snider, I'm real uncomfortable about something."

Snider waited.

"When Krueger retired I was pretty sure the cops wouldn't be investigating Bob's death any more. It was the first time I felt like I didn't have to be looking over my shoulder all the time."

"Why is that?"

He stuffed a bite into his mouth. "If no one's investigating, the pressure's off Bobby and Nordstrom." He swallowed and fixed his gaze on Snider's face. "Now you're bringing it up again. You have no idea who you're dealing with."

"We would prefer that none of the people we're trying to locate know what we're doing or why. If you encounter any problems, please, let me know," Snider said.

Kreuser wiped up the last of the syrup with the last bite of pancakes. "You understand I'm not saying all this stuff on no official record. With my kids and all I can't take that chance." He chewed for a while, then swallowed. "I'd really like to find out who shot Bob. Make him pay for what he did—and not just murdering Bob—'cause he screwed up a lot of people's lives."

That afternoon Dan Liberko began the work required to have subpoenas issued for depositions of Dennis Kreuser, Tom Evers, Russ Krueger, and Alan Mentes.

CHAPTER 14

It had become clear that both Tom Evers and, especially, Dennis Kreuser were strongly hesitant to speak publicly about anything dealing with the Nachtsheims, so Steve Severson called Jack Mason. "Jack, we just want to make sure their identities are protected, their statements are kept confidential until the trial."

Mason's response was to accuse Snider and Severson of merely wanting to assume some tactical advantage. "That's baloney. I've dealt with lawyers who b.s."

"These guys are afraid for their lives, Jack. Since you don't believe me, why don't you call them and *ask* them why they'd rather not have their statements made public."

"No. I don't want to," Mason said. "You're doing this for strategic advantage and bringing an unfounded claim."

"Well," Severson said. "We can appreciate that you think so. We'll just file a motion for protective orders." And he did.

Severson followed up with a letter to Jack Mason:

> Dear Mr. Mason:
>
> This will confirm that I called you today in response to your letter in which you stated that you were 'skeptical about the factual or legal basis for [our] proposed Protective Order.' When I asked you why you were skeptical, you said you thought that even if Witness No. 1 actually had concern for his/her safety that his/her concern was not 'reasonable.' You did not explain why you thought that, but did state that you thought we were using the Protective Order for 'tactical advantage.'
>
> I assured you that we were not using the Protective Order for tactical advantage and that I believed that after you read plaintiff's interrogatory answers you would agree that there is good reason for the Order. I also said that if, after you read the answers, you did not agree there was a sufficient basis for

the Protective Order, you could move the Court to modify or rescind it. You would not agree to this.

I do not know what more I can do or say to change your mind without disclosing the very information which Witness No. 1 has asked us to keep confidential.

I am afraid you leave us with no choice but to bring this matter before the Court.

Very truly yours,

Steve Severson

LATER THAT DAY

Severson note to file:

I returned Jack's call — he called to discuss the depositions — he wants them postponed because he needs our answers to discovery in order to be ready.

Re the Nachtsheims', he'll let us take their depo and will send an associate to cover — but wants the right to redepose them.

Re Kreuser's and others', wants them put off — says he's not paid to redepose them. Basis for his request is a "new" rule which he said he did not know the number of — says "new" rule says we can only take three depositions then must get permission of the court. He refused to tell me the number of the rule saying that since I was the one accusing people of malpractice I should know the rule.

Re Jane Lerner's, says he talked to Lerner — Lerner is willing to come to Minneapolis at her own expense — she says she told Jerry and another lawyer but was told by Faegre people not to come out here and that we would go there.

He asked why depo in Cincinnati — I said I did not know why but assured it was for her convenience. Mason accused me of sloppy practices, saying he thought it was done for strategic reasons.

Severson telephone conversation with Ron Meshbesher:

Terry Nachtsheim is the family counselor — she is contacting Betty and John to arrange them for depositions voluntarily. Ron will call tomorrow with that info.

Bobby is in California — Ron does not want to be seen as setting Bobby up, so he will only try to get us Bobby's telephone no. or address.

Severson also verified with Ron Meshbesher that the senior attorney was appalled that someone might think he would have ever raised the polygraph issue during the original, 1986 trial.

Dear Steve:

This is further to my effort to resolve by agreement the issues raised by your service of eleven (11) deposition notices on January 11, and will supplement my earlier correspondence.

Although the Rule which prohibits noticing or taking depositions in excess of three doesn't explicitly say so, I assume we would be permitted to resolve the scheduling by agreement without taking the time of the Court. The proposal I made in this respect seems to me to be an appropriate compromise, and I hope you will agree to it.

In seeking to resolve the scheduling of depositions, in our phone conversation I asked you why the deposition of Jane Lerner had been scheduled for Cincinnati. You declined to answer, but requested that I put the question to you in writing. I hope you will now answer.

Sincerely,

John M. Mason (signed "Jack")

FRIDAY EVENING, JANUARY 20, 1989

Dear Mr. Mason:

Quite frankly, I am surprised at the position you are taking on these depositions. You apparently want them postponed but have not articulated any basis for that position. …

In addition, we are accommodating your request that we serve our responses prior to the thirty day deadline. … Obviously, had defendants not taken so long in obtaining new counsel in this case and in submitting their discovery requests, they would not have to ask plaintiff to expedite service of his responses.

As you know, the discovery period will end in this case on February 24, 1989. For that reason we feel we must press ahead with our discovery. We are, of course, always willing to try to accommodate any reasonable request you may have with respect to scheduling.

I have been notified by Ronald Meshbesher that Betty, Terry, Angie, and John Nachtsheim will appear for deposition voluntarily without need for subpoena. However, they have requested that the depositions take place in Mr. Meshbesher's office. Enclosed and hereby served upon you, please find Amended Notices of Taking Deposition for the Nachtsheim family members.

Bobby Nachtsheim resides out of state and apparently will not voluntarily appear for deposition in this matter. Therefore, please consider his deposition continued. I will advise you as soon as we have rescheduled that deposition.

You state in your letter that I 'declined' to answer why Jane Lerner was being deposed in Cincinnati. That implies I know why her deposition was scheduled for Cincinnati. As I explained to you, I did not schedule Ms. Lerner's deposition nor have I spoken to her. As I suggested, if you would like her deposition held in Minneapolis and are willing to pay her expenses in having her come to Minneapolis, should she require that, we would be happy to depose her in Minneapolis.

I would hope we could resolve our discovery disputes amicably. In this regard, I again ask you to reconsider your refusal to stipulate to the entry of the proposed Protective Order.

MONDAY, JANUARY 23, 1989

Dear Steve:

Thanks for your letter of Friday, January 20, messenger delivered at 5:10 p.m., in which you again decline to answer why Jane Lerner's deposition was scheduled for Cincinnati, on the grounds that you did not schedule Ms. Lerner's deposition, and that you have not spoken to her. Will you please find out why the deposition of Jane Lerner was scheduled by your office to be taken in Cincinnati, and tell me what the answer is?

Dear Mr. Mason:

Enclosed and hereby served upon you by hand, please find the following:

1. Plaintiff's Answers to Defendants' Interrogatories to Plaintiff, Set Two;

2. Plaintiff's Response to Defendant's First Request for Production of Documents; and

3. Plaintiff's Response to Defendant's Second Request for Production of Documents.

I am serving these discovery responses one week before they are due in order to accommodate your request for expedited response.

I have now had an opportunity to look into the scheduling of Jane Lerner's deposition. Her deposition was scheduled for Cincinnati because that is where she lives and works. The deposition was arranged by our paralegal, Daniel Liberko. He tells me that Ms. Lerner indicated she comes to the Twin Cities from time to time but that she had no plans to be here in early February. Had she been planning to come to Minneapolis, of course we would have scheduled her deposition in town. However, since her deposition must be completed prior to February 24, we could not wait until she would be in Minneapolis to take her deposition.

Ms. Lerner's deposition was scheduled for Cincinnati as a convenience to her and not, as you have implied, for some 'tactical advantage.'

As you know, Rule 30.02(h) of the new Rules of Civil Procedure limits the right of a party to take more than three depositions in a case. The Advisory Committee Notes to the Rule indicate that the parties may agree to permit the taking of more depositions by stipulation. I would hope we could stipulate to the depositions we now have scheduled rather than bother the Court with this issue. Delaying these depositions will only inconvenience the witnesses, many of whom have already been served with subpoenas.

TUESDAY, JANUARY 24, 1989—DELIVERED BY MESSENGER

Dear Mr. Mason:

This will confirm our telephone conversation this morning in which I attempted to resolve our dispute concerning the depositions scheduled for next week. I proposed that we stipulate to allow the depositions to proceed as scheduled and that we further stipulate that plaintiff would not object to defendants redeposing those witnesses at a later date. You declined to respond to that proposal. I then asked you to tell me what your position was on the depositions. Would you agree to permit them to go forward or not? You again declined to answer. You did so despite the fact that I had told you I needed to know your position as soon as possible as several of the witnesses are under subpoena.

Instead of responding to my proposals and questions, you proceeded to make personal attacks against me. Your attacks lasted for at least ten minutes and by those attacks you made it very clear you had no intention of trying to work out our differences.

As I explained to you at the end of the conversation, because of your nonresponsive and belligerent attitude you left me no choice but to contact the Court to schedule a discovery conference.

I will advise you as soon as I have been notified by the Court when it will be able to hold the discovery conference.

Very truly yours,

Steven L. Severson

Later that day, Severson reached his limit on how much of Jack Mason's verbal abuse he was willing to handle. He noted in the file:

I called Jack. We agreed to meet in my office at 3:00 p.m. He will bring an associate.

I asked him not to be unprofessional and rude to me. He claimed I was being rude, called me "piously oily"—"unctuous"—laughed at me sarcastically, but he did confirm he got my letter re conference call with judge.

Also told him I would be filing a motion for protective order.

SEVERAL WEEKS LATER

"I tell you, Jerry, if Mason calls me unctuous one more time—"

"It gets old, doesn't it." Snider smiled sympathetically at Severson. "Consider it desperation on his part. Prepare an affidavit—let the judge know what's happening behind the scenes—and let's focus on the case. Who have you listed as possible alternative suspects?"

"Well, Bobby and Roger Nordstrom, obviously—or one or the other or both."

Liberko nodded his agreement. "Nordstrom's an unguided missile. The moral compass of those guys points due south—and neither one of them has much to lose."

Snider leaned back in his chair. "Anyone else?"

"It could have been someone off the street," Severson continued. "Mention was made in the police report of juveniles seen fleeing the area but no follow-up seems to have been done. And there's always one of the flower hawkers who sold old flowers on street corners—"

"—known or unknown to Mr. Nachtsheim," Snider added.

"Right. Or a flower distributor from Chicago. There's mention of one who had a heated argument with Nachtsheim one or two days before the shooting. And also a couple of Midwest employees who'd had physical confrontations with Nachtsheim while he worked there. They should probably have been questioned. Unfortunately, one of them is now deceased."

"Have you been through the transcripts of Peter Hurkos's taped sessions with Betty Nachtsheim?" Snider asked. "There may be something else in there."[17]

Severson shook his head. "Not yet. There's a long list of things in the police report, even in Paul Nachtsheim's statement that Norm says he never knew."

"Use of the Paul Nachtsheim Statement is tenuous," Snider said. "We might move it be admissible as proof of exculpatory testimony[18]—use it to show there was relevant information available rather than offering it for the truth of his assertions. Can we prove any of it?"

"Some we can," Liberko said. "A lot of evidence was burned by his wife after he died."

"Did you see the report that her house was burglarized about that same time?"

Severson nodded. "I did. It sounds like they really tore up the house looking for something. And I read Tom Evers's statements, again, about the shootings. Paul Nachtsheim was shot at two separate times. You think it's possible Betty or Bobby targeted Evers as Wartnick's alleged accomplice because of his connection to Paul Nachtsheim? Evers said Paul Nachtsheim slept with a gun under his pillow. He was certain someone wanted him dead."

"I think," Snider said, "we could realistically speculate about anything from Bobby taking revenge to some Chicago mob hit. None of that helps our client. We're here to show Mr. Wartnick should not have been penalized as though he had committed that murder, and we're going to do everything in our power, regardless of unspoken traditions or expectations, to do just that."

It soon fell to Dan Liberko to subpoena Bobby Nachtsheim to return to Minnesota for deposition. Within hours of the subpoena, Liberko began to

17. Dennis Kreuser was initially the primary suspect, according to Hurkos, though he later altered his opinion and affirmed that Kreuser only knew much more than he had said to anyone. Hurkos also confirmed several times that Norm Wartnick was not connected with the shooting. Betty would reveal in their conversations that she worried her son, Bobby, was involved. Hurkos agreed. "My first step is to see your son—but don't tell." To which Betty responded, "I can't. Peter, he's going to be ugly and mean."

18. Applied to evidence which may justify or excuse an accused defendant's actions and which will tend to show the defendant is not guilty or has no criminal intent (legal-dictionary. thefreedictionary.com. Mar 22, 2011); in this context, Gainsley should have known and investigated facts given in the Paul Nachtsheim statement which proved Wartnick innocent.

receive late night, threatening phone calls. Then one night, after working late, Liberko came home to a front door standing open and the insistent bleating of his telephone receiver off the hook.

Liberko began to look over his shoulder wherever he went. It was years before he would feel completely safe again.

CHAPTER 15

MONDAY, MAY 22, 1989

The court reporter sat near the deponent so she could hear and record every word. Two days short of the sixteenth anniversary of his father's murder, the court reporter raised her right hand and asked Bobby Nachtsheim to do the same. "Do you swear to tell the truth, the whole truth, and nothing but the truth, so help you God?"

He exuded an air of casual indifference, but self-preservation glinted in the Scandinavian blue eyes. "Yeah." The syllable emerged as compactly as Kauffmann could utter it. His elbows were propped on the arms of the conference room chair. He lazily intertwined his fingers across his mid-section then floated the chair first to his left then to the right, back and forth. His gray tweed jacket was almost new; his mother had dressed him well.

"I'd like the record to also reflect before we get started," Snider began, "that in addition, Mrs. Betty Nachtsheim—and I'm sorry, I don't know your present name."

"Prokosh." She replied with an air of subdued superiority. "P-r-o-k-o-s-h."

"Mrs. Prokosh is also in the room." Betty Nachtsheim-Prokosh would be present during the depositions of each of her children, Bobby, Terry, Angie, and John, as well as the deposition of her daughter-in-law, Debra Feist Nachtsheim. Betty was approved by the court to represent the Nachtsheim family in her case against Norm Wartnick. That made her a plaintiff, and a plaintiff always has the right to attend depositions connected with their case—the link, here, being that if Wartnick won his suit against Gainsley, Betty would receive the money Wartnick was forced to pay to eliminate her judgment against him.

Snider turned to the deponent and spoke in his measured baritone. "Mr. Nachtsheim, it's your task this morning as a witness, to simply answer my questions. If at any time I ask a question that's unclear, please ask me to clarify. I'd also like you to know, in the event you don't know now, that your testimony is under oath. Is that something you're aware of this morning?"

"As I recall you just swore me in." A cocky grin slurred his words.

"Right. Did you understand the significance of that?"

"Yes."

"What is your understanding of it?"

"That I'm under oath. I'm obliged to tell the truth."

"When were you born, Mr. Nachtsheim?"

"1952."

"And where are you currently residing?"

"Los Angeles, California."

"Okay. You went to work at Midwest Floral Supply when you were seventeen?"

"As I recall."

"And what did you do at Midwest Floral?"

"I started as a stock boy."

"Who did you report to?"

"Norm, Ben, whoever was head of the area I was working in."

"When you say Norm, you're talking about Norm Wartnick who is seated next to me?"

"Yes."

"You recognize Mr. Wartnick seated next to me?"

"Yes, I do," Bobby nodded. His gaze shifted to Norm but his face displayed no reaction.

"How long did you work at Midwest Floral?"

"A couple years. Two, maybe—two to three years. I can't recall exactly how long I did. There was a short break there while I spent some time in the military."

"When were you in the military, Mr. Nachtsheim?"

"For a very short time after a lottery, whatever."

"What branch did you serve in?"

"The army."

"What was your rank on leaving the service?"

"I have no idea." There was the smirk again.

"What was your job assignment in the service?"

"Never had one."

"Where did you serve in the army?"

"About two-and-a-half months at Fort Ord and two-and-a-half months at Fort Knox."

"How were you able to complete your military service in five months?"

"My captain and I had an understanding: I didn't want to be there and there was no need *for* me to be there."

"You don't know what kind of discharge you got?"

"It was a general under-honorable, based on the inability to adapt to military service."

"Okay. Why did you leave Midwest Floral?"

"Our family opened a competing business. B and B Wholesale Florist was the name."

"Is it true that your father terminated your services at B and B Wholesale Florist?"

"I would agree with that, yes," Bobby nodded.

"Would you tell me why he terminated you?"

"Him and I weren't getting along, and I was probably making his job harder."

"Why weren't you getting along?"

"I really don't know."

"Did he ever accuse you of dealing drugs out of B and B florist shop?"

Bobby hesitated. When he spoke, the words came slowly. "I would say No."

The pace of Snider's questioning did not change. "Did your father or anyone connected with B and B ever accuse you of using drugs at the B and B florist shop?"

"I can't recall."

"Did you ever steal any money from your father or from his business?"

The smirk hovered at the corners of his mouth. "I don't believe so."

"When were you fired by your father from B and B Wholesalers?"

"I can't recall."

"Sometime before your father's death, obviously. Correct?"

"I think that's obvious."

"Well, how long before that? Give me your best estimate," Snider said.

"Six to nine months, I'd say, probably."

"When did your grandfather, Paul Nachtsheim, die?"

"I don't know."

"Did you go to his funeral?"

Bobby's jaw tightened. "No, I did not."

"After your father was shot, did you tell your grandfather, in any substance or effect, that you didn't give a damn about your old man?"

The hint of a sneer reappeared as he replied. "No."

"Have you seen statements your grandfather gave with regard to your father's death?"

"I really don't care."

"You didn't like your grandfather very much. Is that correct?"

"I didn't dislike the man."

"Do you like your grandmother?"

"I don't know her."

"You've met your grandmother, haven't you?"

"Yes."

"Okay. During this six to nine months that you weren't talking to your dad prior to the time that he died, were you talking to any of your other family members?"

"Not that I recall. No."

"And you didn't talk to your mother during this period of time, either. Is that correct?"

"I can't recall that I did."

"Did you ever come to physical blows with your father?"

The chair stopped. "Did I ever?"

Snider nodded. "Yes, sir."

"No."

"You were never restrained by others at B and B Floral from, in effect, going after your father in a physical way?"

"I don't recall that that happened."

"If there were witnesses who testified to that, would you deny that happened?"

"No, I wouldn't."

"Did it ever come to your attention your grandfather accused you of killing your father?"

"Yes."

"How did that come to your attention?"

"I think my mother."

"What did she say to you?"

Bobby shrugged. "I have no idea."

"She just told you that your granddad was accusing you of killing your father?"

"I would say that's how it came out, in a conversation."

"Did you have conversations from time to time with others about the fact you were in line to inherit your father's business if something happened to him? That you were entitled to fifty-one percent of the business?"

Bobby nodded in a slow, well-defined arc. "I recall that."

"Did you ever visit with your dad about that?"

He laughed. "I would say No."

Snider's composure was constant. "Did you know a Roger Nordstrom?"

"Yes."

"Was he a friend of yours?"

"Yes."

"How did you meet Roger Nordstrom?"

"From high school."

"But you knew him outside of high school as well?"

"After high school, yeah."

"Did Roger Nordstrom ever threaten your father with a shotgun?"

"No."

"Do you have recollection of your father trying to get one of his cars back from you?"

"Of my father *trying*? My father came to the door and simply took the car."

"Was this a car that you had borrowed from your father?"

"This was a car that my father signed for the loan papers on."

"But it was your car?"

"Yes."

"Why did he come pick it up?"

Bobby snorted. "I wasn't making the payments."

"Your grandfather," Snider pressed, "gave a statement to police prior to his death, and in that statement indicated Mr. Nordstrom assisted you in keeping your father from picking up an automobile; that Mr. Nordstrom threatened to shoot your father with a shotgun. Do you know anything about that?"

"No, I don't."

"Did you talk to your father when he came to pick up the car?"

"I seen him face to face."

"Did you talk to him?"

"Very little. He wanted the keys."

"And you gave them to him?"

"I had no option."

"Was that the last time you saw your father before he was killed?"

"I don't recall."

"The police reports indicate that on the night of May 23rd and the morning of May 24th you were at a party. Is that correct?"

"Some acquaintances stopped by our apartment."

"And this was the evening before your father was shot the next morning. Is that correct?"

"Yes."

"And who was there? Who came?"

"Roger Nordstrom was there. As I recall, Kreuser and Strehlow dropped by."

"Larry Strehlow?"

"Yeah, Denny's sidekick."

"What happened that evening? Did you start drinking?"

Bobby nodded and again caused the chair to drift from side to side. "Uh-huh."

"What were you drinking?"

"I don't recall. Beer, I imagine."

"Was there any drug use going on during this time period?"

"There was probably some pot being smoked."

"Do you recall having conversations with Dennis Kreuser at this time? At the party?"

"We had—." Again Bobby stared through narrowed eyelids. "It was a small place. We were sitting around talking."

"So if anybody was talking, everyone could hear what everyone else was saying?"

"Absolutely."

"And isn't it true, Mr. Nachtsheim, that at this party on the evening of the 23rd of May, 1973, and into the early morning hours of May 24th, 1973, you discussed with the participants of that party that you would become part owner of your father's business upon his death?"

"I don't recall that conversation taking place."

"Do you deny that conversation took place?" Snider's tone had developed a harder edge.

"I won't deny it, but I don't recall that conversation taking place."

"But you did testify a few moments ago that you've made such statements."

"Yes."

"In fact, you said you would inherit fifty-one percent of your father's business?"

"That's, at the time, what I felt."

"Okay. Isn't it true that at this party, that you entered into a discussion with the participants, including Mr. Dennis Kreuser, about how easy it would be to stick up your old man?"

"No."

"Do you deny that you made comments like that at the party?"

"I deny I made that comment because I know exactly what was said."

"Tell me exactly what was said, then, please, Mr. Nachtsheim."

"Exactly what was said was that it would be easy to get money from my father simply by waiting 'til nighttime, using a long pole, the bathroom window was always open, the pants were always hanging on the back of the bathroom door with his billfold in it, and in that billfold would be four to five hundred cash money."

"And were you talking about his pants being at the business or at his home?"

"At home," Bobby laughed. "He generally waited until evening to take his pants off."

"So you did have a discussion about a way to get money from your father?"

"Out of his pants pocket," a nod accompanied each assertion, "hanging on the bathroom door, at night, while they were asleep."

"Did you need money at this point in time?"

"I never, ever have had enough of it, really."

"Was Debra Feist at this party?"

"Yes."

"And at the time, she was not your wife but you were living with her. Is that correct?"

"That's correct."

"Okay. Were you engaged to Anita Lange in 1973?"

"Yes."

"During what period of time?"

"I don't recall. It was springtime."

"The *springtime* of 1973?" Snider had him.

The chair stopped. "No." Nachtsheim squinted as though it was painful to look at Snider. "It was after that."

Liberko's chronology, pieced together from police reports and various testimonies, indicated Bobby Nachtsheim had broken off his engagement to Anita Lange and married Debbie Feist soon after his father's murder—a time line supported by Snider's discussion with Dennis Kreuser and, later, by Terry Nachtsheim-Peters's deposition testimony.

Debra Feist was present at the gathering where Nachtsheim and Nordstrom discussed robbing Nachtsheim's father. The police reports revealed Feist's statements to police changed—they had all gone out for pizza after Kreuser left; then Feist stated she, Nordstrom, and a fourth man had gone out for pizza and left Nachtsheim asleep on the couch; then, later in Krueger's investigation, her testimony and Nachtsheim's matched: they had gone to bed together and slept all night.

A wife cannot be forced to testify against her husband. Were they married as cover for Nachtsheim? All the facts taken together along with Nachtsheim's statement, 'It was springtime,' then his denial of the same seemed to confirm that assumption.

"It was *after* that?" Snider's expression betrayed nothing.

"Uh-huh." The squint had become a scowl.

"You were engaged to her prior to the time your father was killed. Is that correct?"

"No, it was after that."

"It was after that?"

Nachtsheim nodded.

"Were you dating Anita Lange prior to the time your father was killed?"

"I don't think so."

"Did you know her prior to that time?"

"I don't think so."

"What was the reason for breaking your engagement with Anita Lange?"

"I had stronger feelings for Debbie."

"Have you ever sold drugs?"

Again Nachtsheim hesitated. "By drugs, what do you mean?"

"Well, I'm talking about any controlled substance."

"I sold some marijuana."

"Anything else?"

"No."

Questions continued on how Bobby had prepared for the deposition, who he had talked with about it. Snider included Roger Nordstrom in that question. Bobby stated he absolutely had not had any contact with Roger Nordstrom since shortly after the shooting.

"But Mr. Nordstrom was at the party—"

"Yes."

"—the night before your father was killed. You've testified to that. And he left town right after your father was killed, did he not?"

"Shortly thereafter," Bobby acknowledged slowly. The deponent had stilled, pushed backward, and turned his head ever-so slightly away from his interrogator. His gaze fixed on Snider, unblinking, like a rattlesnake caught sunning himself and now must decide whether to slither back under his rock. "As I recall."

"And do you know where he went?"

"I don't know for sure, no. I was told—somebody said he went to Texas."

"Did Mr. Nordstrom have a gun collection?"

"Not that I ever seen."

"Did he have a shotgun?"

"Not that I can recall, No."

"Okay," Snider said, then inhaled and paused. "Let's talk about Lieutenant Krueger for just a bit. He was the police officer assigned to investigate the killing of your father. Is that correct?"

"My understanding, yes. He was the one always around asking questions."

"Did you tell Lieutenant Krueger you had not spoken to your father for six to nine months? Did he ever ask you that?"

"I don't recall."

"Did you tell Lieutenant Krueger that your father had terminated your employment?"

"I don't recall."

"Did you tell Lieutenant Krueger that you and your father argued?"

"I don't recall."

"Did you ever talk to your mother about who the perpetrator was that caused your father's death?"

"Yes."

"Did you immediately go to B and B Floral shop after your father was killed?"

"Immediately."

"Okay. And did you take charge at that time?"

"Yes."

Snider began to, again, gradually tighten the focus. "The day your father was shot and while he was in the hospital, do you recall Mr. Wartnick coming to the shop to help fill orders?"

"Yes."

"Okay. Did you end up inheriting fifty-one percent of the business from your father?"

"There is no business."

"Well, at the time of your father's death, there was a business."

"It never came. We never got—we never talked about it. We never got to that point. We closed the business prior to ever getting to that point."

"But you did run the business. Is that correct?"

"Yes, I did."

"Why did you close the business?"

"We weren't able to run it profitably."

"At the time of your father's death, other than obtaining an interest in the business, did you get anything else? Did you inherit anything else?"

"What did I inherit? I don't have anything other than some personal mementos."

"No cash?"

"Not that I'm aware of, except some proceeds from a lawsuit."

"From the wrongful death lawsuit against Mr. Wartnick?"

Bobby nodded.

"You have received benefits from that?"

"Some."

"How much have you received?"

"Probably under five thousand." Up to this date, Wartnick had paid almost twenty-five thousand dollars toward settlement of the judgment.

"There was some indication that the records of B and B were destroyed in a fire. Was there some fire that destroyed the records?"

"I don't know."

"You were in charge, were you not?"

"Of the shop, yeah."

"Okay. What role did your mother play?"

"She ran the office."

"Did it ever come to your attention that your mother was sexually intimate with Officer Krueger?"

Bobby stopped the chair, eyes narrowed. His response was slow. "No," he hesitated. "I don't recall that."

"Do you know why your grandfather accused you and your mother of being implicated in your father's death?"

"Do I know why?"

Snider nodded. "Yes, sir."

"I have no idea."

"There's one other question I meant to ask you about," Jerry said. "You mentioned in your testimony—in response to my questions about an insurance policy that Midwest Floral had on the life of your father. When did you first gain knowledge that there was such a policy?"

"At its inception. I mean, my father and mother talked about it when Midwest wanted to take it out."

"So, is it your testimony that at the time you were working side by side with Mr. Wartnick [the day of the shooting], that you knew Midwest Floral had a life insurance policy on the life of your father?"

The sneer returned. "Yeah."

CHAPTER 16

ONE WEEK LATER

TUESDAY, MAY 30, 1989

"It's been sixteen years and we still don't know what it's like to rest." Betty Nachtsheim, now Prokosh, sat in Snider's hot-seat, petite hands clasped daintily to the right of her chin, but her words were hurled toward her questioner with a smoker's rasp.

Betty Nachtsheim's most noticeable feature was the poufy bubble of heavily sprayed, bottle-blonde hair above eyeglasses the size of large lemons. A polka-dot, polyester bow covered the lower half of her long, stiff neck and extended halfway across each shoulder. A permanently down-turned pucker etched thin lips. Rarely did she move except a wary shifting of her gaze from Snider, in front of her, to her attorney, Ron Meshbesher, on her left or to her daughter, Terry, to her right beside the door.

Liberko noticed Betty was neither somber nor emotional about the loss of her husband until the video camera turned on, but he thought that could be due to passage of time.

Snider was unfazed by Betty's stated inability to rest. "But you want to find out who—"

"I want to find out, I need to give that to Bob because Bob had a right to life and," she glared at Wartnick over Snider's shoulder, "somebody took that life from him."

Norm steadily returned her gaze. *Yes*, he thought. *Somebody did.*

"Do you agree with Bobby's testimony that he had not talked with his dad for six to nine months?"

Betty recoiled from the question with disdain. "I don't know if I believe that. I know that Bob was going to call him the night before—"

"Was going to call him?"

"Yes, and ask him to please come back to work." *

"Did he call him?"

"No, we were really very tired and a friend of my family's was in St. John's hospital dying, so Angie and I went to my mother's and picked her up and went to St. John's and prayed for a while—this was my mother's friend—and, um, came home and Bob was asleep. He fell asleep. He hadn't called Bobby. I

---

* - Here and elsewhere, Betty's testimony directly contradicts Bobby's earlier testimony regarding whether and when he might have been called.

do, I think, I don't know because I didn't talk to Bob." Her fingers covered her mouth. Mother and daughter avoided eye contact.

"But you have no knowledge if he called him or not."

"No, but I do know he was going to."

"Did Bobby ever tell you that he had discussed sticking up his old man?"

"No, I don't think Bobby ever did. And I don't think Bobby ever would."

"Did he ever tell you he discussed it with some of his friends, including Roger Nordstrom?"

"After the fact. He said that it was, umm, at their party or some—I think they were talking that the Federal Reserve was being moved, or ways to, you know, I don't know, but—"

"Mrs. Nachtsheim—I'm sorry. I don't remember your new, married name."

"Prokosh. P-r-o-k-o-s-h."

"Mrs. Prokosh, are you basing that on Bobby's testimony last week?"

She shook her head. "I must have heard it through the years. I don't know."

"Did it ever come to your attention that Bobby had discussed with his friends getting fifty-one percent of the B and B florist business?"

No response. No movement.

"When your husband died?" Snider pressed.

Betty looked down at the finished edge of the conference table. "Yeah, I guess it did."

"How did that come to your—"

"Oh, I don't know. That was just a bunch of chatter. At that time, Bob was—I really don't know. If Bobby told—I don't think Bobby did—I remember one night Bobby called me—I don't think Bobby told me and I don't think I knew when Bobby called me and I was in with Bob and the nurse gave me her telephone and he said, 'Mother, whatever you hear, I don't—you know—don't pay any attention to it.'"

Snider repeated her statement. "'Don't pay any attention to it?'"

She nodded. "And I, I do believe that's what that was about."

"Did he *say* that was what it was about?"

"No." She jumped on the question. "He didn't tell me what it was about, but he called and I guess I thought that's what it was."

"After your husband was shot, Bobby went back into the florist shop. Is that correct?"

"We called him that morning."

"And he went in?"

"You bet he did."

"And that's the first time he had been in the shop for six to nine months?"

"I don't know if it was that long. That seems like an awfully long time to me."

"You don't necessarily—"

"I don't think—"

"—agree with what—"

"—it was that long."

"—Bobby said?"

"I just have a hard time—but maybe."

"Okay. For a long period of time he had—"

"For a period of time."

"—not been in the shop."

Betty straightened. "We were not without Bobby all that great length of time."

"And he had not talked to his father during the time he was away from the shop?"

She shrugged. "I don't know."

"He testified he did not. Do you have any reason to disbelieve him?"

She shrugged again and hesitated. "No."

Snider's gaze was serene. "Do you believe Bobby is a truthful person?"

Betty flinched backward as though Snider had struck her. "Yes, I do."

"You don't think he'd lie?"

"I don't."

Silence settled into the room as Betty awaited the next question. Snider glanced through exhibit pages. Liberko finished off several interrupted notes. Wartnick felt the rhythmic plod of his heart as it thudded within his chest. Then Betty spoke again. "That depends. I, I think he'd tell me he didn't go out drinking because I would disapprove."

"Did he tell you that he stole from his father?"

"He didn't steal from his father."

"Your testimony, Mrs. Prokosh, is that you are not aware and you have no knowledge that Bobby was stealing flowers, selling them, and pocketing the money?"

"Not when Bob was alive."

"But you're saying he did this *after* Bob was—"

"He might of. I don't know. I've heard this. People have told me that."

"Who's told you that?" Snider asked without looking up.

"I don't know. I don't know. I've heard that and I've asked him."

"You've asked Bobby?"

"Yeah, and it depends. I mean, what do you call stealing?"

"Taking, selling, pocketing the proceeds."

"Well, it was his business, too."

Now Snider did look at Betty but without expression. "It was his business at that time?"

"That's right." She looked down. "It was ours. And it was his as much as it was anyone else's as far as I was concerned."

"Okay," Snider shifted aside several pages. "Did it come to your attention that Bobby was selling drugs out of the shop?"

Betty shook her head. "I don't believe he was."

"Did it ever come to your attention, though, that he was—"

"Oh, yeah. A lot of these things have."

"And you thought for a while he was involved in the shooting, did you not?"

"I didn't know what I thought."

"Didn't you tell Officer Krueger you believed Bobby may have had something to—"

"I don't know that I said that I *believed* it. Everybody told me Bobby could have."

"You love your son, Mrs. Prokosh?"

"I love him deeply." The words resonated from deep inside her.

"And whatever he says you want to believe, is that correct?"

"No. Oh, no. I walked through all this long before today, when it was a lot more painful, and I'm convinced my son did not kill his father nor did he have anything to do with it." The scowl deepened. "But there was a period of time, thanks to people like yourself, that I had to wonder that."

"Mrs. Prokosh, you did tell Lieutenant Krueger that at one time you thought Bobby had shot your husband, did you not?"

"Of course, I probably—" Betty pressed back into the chair, her head pulled away from her interrogator, shoulders drawn toward her ears. "Maybe I did." She glanced from Snider and Wartnick, to Meshbesher, to Terry, and back to Snider with wary jerks. "I don't remember saying that."

"Okay," Snider nodded. "You got some benefits in an economic sense from your husband's death, did you not?"

"Bob had a three thousand dollar life insurance policy that paid six because he died accidentally. That buried him." Betty's glare punctuated her statement.

"You also had credit life on the mortgage taken out on your home to start the business. Is that correct?"

Wartnick sent up a silent thank you. Ten years earlier Wartnick had begged Gainsley to ask that question. Tom Evers had testified early in MPD's investigation that the morning of the shooting, before she even went to the hospital, Betty had come into the office at B and B looking for insurance papers.

"That was not a credit," Betty replied. "That was a gesture by the bank. I did not know, when Bob died, that they would pay the house back."

"Your testimony is that you were not aware of the credit life insurance—"

"No, I was not."

"—policy? You were keeping the books at B and B, is that correct?"

"Sort of." She had begun to relax. "But they went to an accountant. I kept the records, [then] they were all turned over to Brodkorp."

"And you're telling us today that you did not know there was a credit life insurance policy on the mortgage that was taken out on your house?"

Betty pushed her left palm toward Snider like a shield. "I did not know that until Bob was dead and I went back into the bank for whatever reason and it was a gesture on their part. We took a loan out for twenty-three thousand against our house and I think the bank demanded a life insurance policy on Bob, and when he, in fact died, they gave us the—they attached that to the house. I don't think they had to do that."

"So the bank had a life insurance policy—"

"That's right."

"—on the life of your husband which they collected on?"

"That's right. That's right."

"Did you ever think the bank was involved—"

"Oh, no."

"—in the death of your husband?"

"No!"

"But they got a benefit from it. They got the mortgage paid."

"But they didn't. They paid the house back up because we had financed our house."

"You got a benefit when your—"

"Well—"

"—husband died. An economic benefit. Is that correct?"

"I guess."

"In that your house was paid off." An uneasy quiet crept into the room. Snider was unmoving, eyebrows raised, blue eyes targeted on Betty.

The seconds ticked off in Wartnick's head. He was intensely aware of Snider's size, his presence in the room, his calm pursuit of the truth.

Betty exhaled abruptly. "That's right," she finally acknowledged.

"When you arrived at B and B on the morning of May 24, did you talk to any of the employees there?"

"No."

"Lieutenant Krueger was the first person you met with—"

"That's right."

"—at the hospital? Who called Bobby?"

"I think Angie did at home. I didn't call anybody. I kind of gave her orders, though. I asked her to call my sister and ask her to go to the store so there was somebody there, and maybe Sister called Bobby. I don't know."

"You don't know who called him?"

"I just felt like somebody should be at the store so Bob wouldn't be angry with us for going to him." Betty glanced down to her right. Behind the large, round spectacles genuine sorrow relaxed her muscles and revealed, for the briefest instant, that she had become gaunt and worn.

"But you just don't recall—"

She shook her head slowly. "I don't."

"—who made that call?"[19]

"But Bobby was at the store when I got there. I saw him."

"Was already at the store when you arrived?"

She nodded.

"Did you speak with him?"

"No."

"Okay. Do you remember Lieutenant Krueger telling you he wanted to leak a story that Bob had regained consciousness long enough to identify the perpetrator?"

"He never said that to me."

"He never asked you about that?"

She shook her head in an emphatic No. "He really wasn't there very much. All he did was ask me that morning if I remembered anything and gave me a card. And I just didn't know anybody that wanted Bob dead." Her blink-rate had increased. Wartnick felt her glare.

"So you never told Lieutenant Krueger that you refused to let that story be leaked?"

"No."

"And what was your relationship with Lieutenant Russ Krueger?"

Another long pause was filled with shuffling papers. Terry coughed into the silence.

"I really depended on him."

"Did you find him to be generally an honest and truthful person?"

"I don't know. I guess I wanted him to be."

"Did you find him to *not* be honest and truthful?"

"I don't know that, either."

Snider flipped to a clean page in his yellow pad. "Now there came a time when you contacted this Peter Hurkos in California?"

"That's right."

"What contact did you have with Mr. Hurkos?"

"I went out there."

"One trip to California?"

"Two."

"Two trips to California? Can you tell me the dates of when you went, please?"

"I can't remember the exact dates, but I went, I suppose, in '75 or '6 or '4. I don't know."

"You just don't have a calendar that would help refresh your memory?"

---

19. Angie Nachtsheim would later testify that she could not remember calling her brother nor could she remember who might have. In fact, she could not even say for sure that he had ever actually been called. Angie also verified they had left the house within fifteen minutes of the call from B and B, and that Bobby was already busy at the store when they arrived.

"No, I went in—" the pause was long enough that discomfort descended on the room. "Then he came here. We found the gun in the river and I took it back out to him, then he—"

"Wait a minute," Snider glanced up. "What gun was found here?"

"A part of a gun. I took that back out to—"

"How did he react to that?"

"Well, he said it was the gun—it was exactly the way he said we would find it."

"Who found it?"

"The police."

"Do you know where that gun is now?"

"I have no idea. It's part of a sawed-off shotgun, and it was chiseled or sawed-off the way Peter said it would be."[20]

"Did you believe in Peter Hurkos?"

"I was willing to, and he convinced me that I could."

"And he convinced you that what he said was truthful and accurate?"

"Most of it."

"And he told you that Norm Wartnick did not physically shoot your husband, did he not?"

"Well, he did at times, and at other times he—. My understanding of psychic perceptions is that they get mixed up. He came here and he went into Norm's place of business and Norm—"

"Were you there?"

"I drove him. It was ninety-five [degrees] outside. Peter went in. Norm ran from him—"

"Did you see him run?"

"No," Betty said, agitated. "I only have what Peter told me. And Peter kept saying, 'Death. Death. Death.' And he was ice cold when he got in the car."

"Who was ice cold?"

"Peter Hurkos."

"Who kept saying, 'Death. Death. Death'?"

"Peter did."

"He was saying—"

"Norm was the killer."

"He came back from seeing Norm, and—"

"From going into Midwest. And Norm ran to the back of the store and—"

"But you didn't see him run?"

"No," she rasped, "this is what Peter told me. You asked me and that's all I know, and—"

---

20. The shotgun was eventually determined not to be a match to the Nachtsheim murder but was connected to another, more recent event. Jerry Snider always believed the shotgun was never found, there being—like so many other aspects of this case—no evidence for it except Betty Nachtsheim's testimony.

Snider waited. She shrugged. "Okay," Snider said, "What did he say after he came out?"

Jack Mason interrupted. "Excuse me. I wonder if in fairness to the witness you could let her finish her answers just as she is letting you finish your questions."

"That's an excellent idea, Mr. Mason," Snider said. "Thank you for your suggestion."

"He," Betty tried again. "That's—. I have what Peter told me. I dropped him off there and that's what he told me. I only have what I observed in Peter Hurkos—that he was definitely ice cold and he was really not real coherent, if that makes sense."

"How much did you pay Peter Hurkos for that—"

"Twenty thousand dollars."

"You gave him twenty thousand dollars?"

She nodded slowly with a stubborn jut of her jaw. "All told."

"For how many visits with him?"

"Three."

"Where did you get the money?"

"Through our store."

"From B and B?"

"I went to the bank and bought a cashier's check. I discussed it with our banker and he understood what I was doing, and I needed to do that."

"Is that one of the reasons your business failed?"

"I don't think so. It was hard to work there. We walked over the spot where Bob laid—it never came up." The rapid blinking began again.

"Well, twenty thousand dollars was not an insignificant amount of money to be taken from that store, was it?"

"No." The blinking was even faster. "But we did well. We just didn't like it," Betty finished with bravado.

"How many days was Peter Hurkos in—"

"I don't know."

"You had three visits with him. Once in California—"

"The initial visit, and then when they found the gun I took it back out to him."

"The Minneapolis police department allowed you to take a potential murder weapon on an airplane to another state to show to a psychic?"

She shrugged. "Russ said no one would care."

"Okay," Snider inhaled deeply. "The initial visit—how long did that take?"

"A couple of days, maybe."

"Is that when Lieutenant Krueger came out?"

"Um-hum."

"And Lieutenant Krueger met with—"

"Yes, he did."

"—Peter Hurkos. Is that correct? Now, is it true, Mrs. Prokosh, that you had one or more intimate encounters with Lieutenant Krueger during the early part of the 1970s?"

Betty nodded.

"How long did this intimate sexual contact with Lieutenant Krueger last?"

"Very brief."

"What year was this?"

"Oh, probably '73."

"Several months after your husband was shot in May of 1973?"

"No."

"In the fall of 1973?"

"Probably." Betty contradicted herself.

"Did you ever meet Lieutenant Krueger in California?"

"Nothing happened in California."

"You were not intimate with Lieutenant Krueger while the two of you were in California?"

"No, only here in Minneapolis, at the Leamington Hotel."

The room's occupants were quiet as Snider referred to a list of questions based on Russ Krueger's sworn deposition taken the week before. "Isn't it true, Mrs. Prokosh, that you told Lieutenant Krueger that Bobby hated his dad?"

"Oh, I don't know. I mean, I could have said almost anything at that time; and maybe at that time, maybe I thought Bobby hated him. I don't think so."

"Would you deny, if Lieutenant Krueger testified that you told him that Bobby hated his dad, that you said that?"

Betty paused. "I don't know."

"You don't know if you would deny it?"

"Oh, I think—there were times when Bobby hated his dad. I think there still are times. It depends upon what you call hate."

"Well, my—"

"Sometimes we hate the things and people we love."

"My question to you is not whether he did or didn't hate his dad; my ques—"

"I don't think he did."

"—tion is whether or not you made that statement to Lieutenant Krueger."

"I don't think so. Right then he was mad at his dad."

"And if Lieutenant Krueger testified that you told him Bobby hated his dad, would you deny that you made that statement?"

"I guess I couldn't."

"Didn't you tell Lieutenant Krueger that you were concerned Bobby might want to take some vengeful action against his father?"

"No."

"You deny that you made—"

"I certainly do."

"—that statement? You never said anything like that to Lieutenant—"

"No."

Snider studied Betty's face, made direct eye contact. "Did you ever tell Lieutenant Krueger that Bobby was capable of killing his dad?"

"No."

"Did Lieutenant Krueger tell you that Bobby is still a suspect?"

Betty scowled. "No."

"The entire time that you visited with him?"

"Oh, I think he always said that. I think I knew that whether he said it or I just knew it."

"Did Lieutenant Krueger ever tell you Bobby *told* him he hated his dad?"

"No," she said and scowled again.

"Did Lieutenant Krueger ever tell you he saw no bereavement in Bobby after his father was shot and died?"

That one seemed to catch Betty off-guard. She hesitated then spoke slowly. "No."

"And your husband had angry relations, did he not, with his son, Bobby?"

"Oh, yeah."

"And they argued a lot, did they not?"

Betty nodded.

"In fact, they were coming to blows one time in the florist shop, weren't they?"

"I don't think so. I don't think they ever hit one another."

"Why did you call the police in Roseville to help you get the car back [from Bobby] earlier in the spring, before Bob was shot?"

"I don't know. I didn't have—. Dad—Bob went to get the car, not me."

"Was he afraid of his son?"

"No."

"Then why would he involve the police?"

"I don't know."

"He didn't tell you why?"

She emitted a raspy noise that insinuated 'No.'

"And after Bob was shot, did you ever have any conversations with Tom Evers?"

"Very few."

"What conversations did you have?"

"Very few. He showed up at the hospital with Paul and all of this garbage started, and—"

"All of what garbage started?"

"Oh, about this party and all this stuff, and I really didn't want to hear any of it."

"You didn't want to hear about the party that Bobby—"

"I didn't want to hear anything. I didn't want to hear anything."

"Did Lieutenant Krueger ever mention to you any conflicts in statements made by Debbie Feist?"

"No."

"Did he ever tell you that in one instance Debbie Feist said she left Bobby asleep on the sofa while she and some of Bobby's friends went out for pizza?"

"I don't remember a lot of that, I really don't. It's just such a lot of—"

"Did he ever tell you that in another instance Debbie testified she never left Bobby's side all night, the night—"

Betty shook her head. "I don't remember that, either."

"—of the 23rd of May? Does your daughter-in-law, Debbie Feist, have a good relationship with you?"

"We're fine. I go out there and I stay in their home and I—." She sighed and looked down again. "Yeah."

"Did it ever come to your attention that Bobby was making statements that he wished both of his parents dead?"

Another question that caught her off guard. "No."

"Did you know an individual by the name of Domagalski?"

"Oh, many, many, many, many, many years ago."

"Did you have an affair with Mr. Domagalski?"

"I wasn't married; he was a friend of mine."

"Did you have a child by him?"

"Yes, I did." That child, a girl, would have been born in the late 1940s.

"And how did Paul Nachtsheim know about that?"

"Because I told Bob."

"And Bob told his father?"

"Um-hmm."

"Where's that child today?"

"She's in St. Louis."

"Did you ever ask Bobby why the night before his father was shot he was talking about robbing his father?"

"Well, I think I'm reconciled to the fact that had Bob not been shot, these would have been just normal kids' stuff."

"'Normal kids' stuff' to talk about robbing your father?"

"Well, they've taken on a different perspective. I don't know that Bobby talked about it, either; he just said that it would've been easy. They were just talking about robbery," she said with a flip of her hand, then suddenly looked very uncomfortable. "I don't really know. To me the kids, they were kids growing up in a very difficult time and a lot of things went on in their lives that now they have to answer for—would have just been 'growing up' had their dad not died the way he did. And I think," her assertiveness had returned, "there are more victims to this than Bob Nachtsheim."

Absolutely, Wartnick thought then pushed away thoughts of what his own children had been forced to endure. Although heat rushed up his neck, the referee's stoic expression stayed firmly in place.

Snider shuffled papers. After several moments, Betty spit out, "I think there's a dark side to all human nature, even *yours*. And you're forcing us to expose ours."

"Well," Snider responded calmly, "you don't have any problem with the fact that you used a lawsuit to vindicate rights, do you, Mrs. Nachtsheim?"

"I don't think a lawsuit is to vindicate rights. I think that the system I used in a lawsuit was all that I had; it's the system that protects this country. I did not feel like I abused it, and I would be awfully angry to see it manipulated on points of law rather than on justice."

"What about facts?"

"Facts?"

"You still interested in the facts?"

"I'm interested in the truth. That's what I want. That's what we all want. But I think somebody's muddying the waters again."

"What do you mean 'muddying the waters'?"

"Ack! Somebody does that all the time. That's why Bob's murder was just lost in the shuffle, because somebody walked in with a lot of garbage and now we don't know what really happened."

"What garbage did someone—"

"Oh, the kids and all of this party stuff. They're just a lot of kids, and we got sidetracked, didn't we? And it was my hope to get it back on track. We had a week of trial," Betty opined. "We had every opportunity to bring it out. That's our system." Betty glared at Snider. "That's who you work for. And that's who I live for. That's all I've got."

"Well, you have an unsatisfied judgment against Mr. Wartnick. Is that correct?"

A glint flashed in her eyes. She dared not look at Norm. Instead, she scowled again and said, "I'd rather not have that. I'd rather see Norm Wartnick in prison."

Bull! Wartnick thought. Betty did not love Bob, but the money was huge to her. Whatever she might have said was for others to read. What she wanted was the money.

Five days before deposition of Betty Nachtsheim-Prokosh, a videotaped record had been made of Russ Krueger's version of the facts, and the two versions did not always match. Betty freely admitted Bobby was running the shop after Bob's death, but Krueger insisted several times, "Not to my knowledge. No."

Though Betty could not bring herself to fully admit her own son's habitual drug use, less-than-wholesome associations, or tendency toward violence, much less that he may have been involved in his father's death, Russ Krueger said, "Well, she was concerned because there was some bad feelings between her son and her husband. I know the old man accused him of stealing, and he was using drugs heavily, and the old man booted him out, and there was some real hard feelings about it. She was concerned Bobby'd want to take vengeance against his father."

"Did it ever come to your attention Bobby made statements that he hated his old man?"

"Oh, yeah." Krueger nodded. "I knew that. He *told* me he hated him." Moments later he added, "He wasn't a likeable person. Easy to dislike."

"Bobby?"

"Yeah. He was a first-class jerk, in my opinion. Bobby lies like some people breathe."

Another subject on which Betty and Krueger's testimonies did not agree was Roger Nordstrom. Betty categorically denied ever knowing him until after the shooting and said she had never told Krueger that Bobby and Roger Nordstrom were dealing in guns. She swore no recollection of Nordstrom or his shotgun, or herself, being present when Bob reclaimed Bobby's car. Krueger's recollection was different.

"Didn't Betty Nachtsheim tell you that Roger Nordstrom was a gun collector?"

Krueger began to nod.

"And didn't she also tell you that Bobby Nachtsheim and Roger Nordstrom were selling guns and selling drugs?"

Krueger's lips pursed as his round head continued its slow backward-and-forward progress. "Yes, she did say that. Yes." He stopped nodding and redirected his attention to a food stain on the end of his tie, pushed twice with his cheeks to lift his glasses to the bridge of his nose.

"And didn't Mrs. Nachtsheim tell you that Bobby had told her Roger Nordstrom would shoot a man for two hundred dollars?"

"Yes, she did."

"Didn't Betty Nachtsheim also tell you that a couple of weeks before Bob Nachtsheim was shot, that both Betty and Bob Nachtsheim went to Bobby's apartment to pick up a car, and that Roger Nordstrom was at Bobby's apartment?"

"Yes, she did." The nodding began again.

"And threatened Bob Nachtsheim—"

"Yes, she did," he said, still nodding.

"—to shoot him with a shotgun?"

"That's correct. That's correct."

Snider studied the face of the deponent as he asked, "Did you follow up on that lead?"

The nodding stopped, the tie was dropped back onto his belly. "Yes, I did. I couldn't find Nordstrom."

"You never sent anybody to Texas to try to locate him?"

"They wouldn't spend the money for me to go to Texas."

"Did you ever talk with Betty Nachtsheim about funding your trip to Texas to try to find Roger Nordstrom?"

"Not to my knowledge."

"Who funded your trip to California to meet with the psychic, Peter Hurkos?"

"She did."

Betty Nachtsheim had begged Lieutenant Krueger to go to California with her. Being a disbeliever in 'that hokum' and a married man, he had refused. She went with her daughter, Angie, and initially met with Hurkos, alone. Soon Hurkos was agreeing that it would be helpful to have Lieutenant Krueger bring them a map of the Twin Cities, so he called the police officer and requested he come. Betty made the arrangements.

"She paid your way out. Was that with the approval of the department?"

"They could care less. They don't have to spend any money."

"Did she pay for your expenses out there?"

"She paid for all expenses out there."

"Where did you stay when you were out there?"

"Same motel. I can't recall the name of it."

"Did you stay with Betty Nachtsheim in that motel?"

"She stayed in another room with her daughter."

"When you had your affair, was that in California?"

"Right."

"On this trip?"

"Right."

So Krueger's testimony was that their affair had taken place in California. Betty's testimony was nothing happened in California; it occurred afterward, at the Leamington Hotel in Minneapolis. Joe Friedberg commented later they were probably both right.

"Mr. Krueger, Betty Nachtsheim was a suspect in this case, was she not?"

"Oh, the wife is always a suspect any time her husband's killed."

"Well, I believe you've testified she would have benefited, at least to the extent of the insurance proceeds paying off the loans."

Krueger pursed his lips, shook his head, and scratched his ear as he said, "She was never a serious participant in this."

"Did the fact that you had an affair with her enter into your decision that she was never a serious suspect?"

"No, that wouldn't have bothered me one bit if we could've proved something against her I would have admitted the affair after she was charged. It wouldn't have bothered me. Murder is murder."

"Did Betty Nachtsheim admit to you that she had an affair with a man named Roy Benson?"

110

"I think she did. It's in the back of my mind. I think she did."

"Did you attempt to ascertain whether or not there were any jealousies involved in this murder?"

"Well, I questioned Betty extensively about, 'did she ever catch her husband with another woman or any other woman calling the house,' or vice versa, 'did he ever catch you with any other man.' There was nobody I could question to prove a jealousy."

"Well, you had plenty of witnesses tell you that—"

"Correct, but nobody could come up with any names."

"What about Roy Benson?"

"Well, that's, that was self-explanatory."

"Why was it self-explanatory?"

"Because they were in business together, and it was an incident."

"But it was an *incident* fairly close to the time Mr. Nachtsheim was shot, was it not?"

"Yeah, but we had checked it out. There was nothing to make Mr. Benson a suspect."

"There's a reference to Betty Nachtsheim having an affair with a man named Domagalski. Did you check that out?"

"I got a hold of Betty and asked her. She denied it. And I caught a hold of Domagalski by phone and he denied it."

"Did you try to determine whether or not Betty had a child by Domalgalski?"

"She had a child by somebody. I can't recall who it was. I think the child, if I can remember was adopted. She's in St. Louis, Missouri." Betty's testimony was that her first daughter's father was Domagalski.

"There are other statements [by] Betty [that] she knew of no reason for anyone to shoot her husband, and she, again, denied having any affairs. Did she continually deny that to you?"

"No, she later admitted it."

"So she wasn't telling you the truth earlier?"

"Well, I don't remember what the deal was, but she, she finally admitted she'd had one session with one person. She didn't consider that an affair."

"Did you try to ascertain why Betty was hiring an attorney to bring a divorce action against Mr. Nachtsheim?"

"I think we discussed it, but I can't recall what the discussion was. I think she told me she had filed for divorce."

"The fact she had filed more than once for divorce against her husband, who ended up being murdered, was not a significant factor for you?"

"No."

"Did it ever cross your mind that because you had this intimate relationship with Betty Nachtsheim, that it would be best for you to refer this case to some other investigator at the Minneapolis Police Department?"

"Nobody wanted it."

"But did it ever occur to you?"

"It didn't compromise the investigation."

"Did it ever occur to you that—"

"No."

"—you should have done that?"

"No."

One thing Betty Nachtsheim and Russ Krueger did agree on was Norm Wartnick's potential involvement in the shooting of Bob Nachtsheim.

"And you knew that Mr. Wartnick had been asked to take a lie detector test?"

"His attorney advised him not to talk to me or take a lie detector test."

"Well, again, we'll get to that in a moment, but I'd like to focus on my question. You knew that he did not take a test."

"I sure did."

"Was that a factor in what appears to be your judgment from this record, that Mr. Wartnick had something to do with the death of Mr. Nachtsheim?"

"No doubt about it as far as I'm concerned."

"Because he followed his attorney's advice and didn't take a lie detector test?"

"Nope, he's the only one that gained."

"Well, we're going to talk about the gaining business. I believe you've admitted to me that if Bobby inherited the shop, he had something to gain from his father's death. Is that a fair statement?"

"If that's what actually happened, he inherited the shop and the business, then he would have something to gain. Yes."

"All right. The next issue is insurance coverage. Wasn't there a credit life policy that Betty Nachtsheim had on the life of her husband?"

"Yes."

"And that resulted in her [home, business, and vehicle] mortgages being paid free and clear?"

"But I have that on mine, too."

"Well, regardless if you have it or not, it is true. That is the case?"

"Oh, sure. Sure."

"And you would agree with me, would you not, that at least from the standpoint of the Betty Nachtsheim mortgages being paid off, she had something to gain from her husband's death?"

"Oh, sure."

"So it's not true, is it, that the only person that had anything to gain by the death of Mr. Nachtsheim in a monetary sense was Mr. Wartnick?"

"Well, the way you put it there—but the one that was not a member of the family, the one who had nothing to do with the family—he was the one who gained, Wartnick."

"Well, Mr. Wartnick didn't have a personal life insurance policy on Mr. Nachtsheim's person, did he? Wasn't this Midwest that had—"

Krueger leaned forward and stabbed a finger onto the tabletop. "Well, who was Midwest? Wartnick."

"Well, who *was* Midwest? Did your investigation reveal that?"

"Sure. He was the president."

"Well, did it reveal the ownership of Midwest? How much ownership did Mr. Wartnick have of Midwest? Did your investigation reveal that?"

"I think it did at the time. I can't recall."

"Do you recall it being something like thirty percent of the business?"

"I think we did see that, yeah."

"That being the case, why did you focus on Mr. Wartnick?"

"Because he renewed that policy within twelve days of the homicide. He had absolutely no reason to renew a policy."

"Well, they told you why they renewed it, did they not?"

"Oh, well," Krueger shrugged and re-examined his tie.

"He wasn't trying to hide that fact from you, was he?"

"No." Krueger shrugged. "Because he was talking about it. He didn't hide it."

Snider thumbed through several sets of documents, extracted two, and handed them to the court reporter. "I'd like to mark as Krueger Exhibit One, please, pages four-o-nine through four-twenty-four of the trial transcript, *Nachtsheim against Wartnick and Midwest.*"

The pages were passed to Krueger, who thumbed through them while he adjusted his glasses with his cheeks.

"At the bottom of the page," Snider said, "there's a statement or a soliloquy you're giving that states, quote, It's beyond comprehension that a man can get an insurance policy on another man and thirteen days later he's shot in the head and killed, and the only man that benefited from it was that man right there, end quote, and you're pointing. Who were you pointing to?"

"Norm Wartnick."

"You're pointing to Mr. Wartnick. And you, obviously, raised your voice. Correct, Mr. Krueger?"

"I probably did." He thumped the transcript page. "[The judge] said, 'Keep your voice down.'" Then Krueger yawned. "What time is it anyway?"

"It's twenty past four. I'm almost through, Mr. Krueger. The judge admonished you to keep your voice down. He also struck that portion of the transcript. Is that correct?"

"Yep."

"Mr. Krueger, it's just simply not true, is it, that the only person that benefited from Mr. Nachtsheim's death was Mr. Wartnick."

"A hundred-thousand dollar policy it is."

"Well, it's also true Bobby Nachtsheim benefited if he obtained the business. Is that correct?"

"That would be correct."

"And it's also true Betty Nachtsheim benefited because she received insurance benefits. Is that correct?"

"Sure."

"Do you admit, Mr. Krueger, that you could be absolutely dead wrong that Mr. Wartnick was the perpetrator here?"

"Could I be dead wrong?"

Snider leaned toward the witness. "Yes."

"Sure, I could be."

CHAPTER 17

JUNE 26, 1989

Terry Nachtsheim Peters's deposition was taken. Sixteen years had dulled neither Terry's pain nor her anger at losing her father. To sit within ten feet of Norm Wartnick, the man whom she believed had pulled the trigger, was painful. She bore it with fortitude, seemed to genuinely want the truth—seemed stunned by several facts in the case when Snider presented them.

Had there been less innuendo and accusation flying through her family and more genuine search for truth on the part of her mother, Terry might have been spared those years of pain. Betty's goal to win no matter the cost had put her daughter through years of misery. And today Betty sat and watched the pain in her daughter's eyes, and knew she had the solution.

Snider asked, "Did it ever come to your attention that there was a party at your brother's apartment the night before your dad was shot?"

"Yes." Short replies were given with a quick nod of her head.

"And did it come to your attention there was a discussion at that party about robbing your father early the next morning?"

"Yes."

"Did it come to your attention that your brother drew a sketch of the florist shop for one of the party participants by the name of Nordstrom? Roger Nordstrom?"

"I think I heard at some point there was a sketch drawn. I don't think I ever knew who drew it or anything else."

"Did it ever come to your attention that Lieutenant Krueger believed, and still believes, that Roger Nordstrom is the missing link in this case?"

Her eyes widened, then narrowed. "No."

"Did you ever talk to Lieutenant Krueger about Roger Nordstrom?"

"I don't know." She shrugged. "I may have."

"Did you ever meet Tom Evers?"

"Yes." She searched her memory for a moment. "I think at one point I may have dated a guy that was a friend of his, and then may have seen him occasionally."

"Did you see him at the hospital during the days that your father was in the hospital prior to his death?"

"Yes, I did." Growing agitation sent her chair rocking back and forth.

"Do you have any reason to believe that Mr. Evers had any involvement in causing your father's death?"

"As I recall, Dad arrived—you know that was during a busy time, and Evers at that point, I believe, worked at B and B and, you know, that information had come from within."

"And you believe Mr. Evers may have provided some information on that?"

"He may have," Terry said with confidence.

Snider's steady baritone voice and his calm search for truth provided a pressure release for the tension in the room. "And what are you basing that on?"

"What I've learned in sixteen, seventeen years of trying to find out what happened to my father. It may have come from Krueger, from talking with my mom, from Mr. Meshbesher."

"So what you're saying is you're really basing it on speculation. Is that correct?"

Her laugh was cynical. "If everyone around me is speculating, then I guess I am. Yes."

"And have you undertaken any investigation, yourself, into your father's death?"

"I've gone to the police. I went to see Supreme Court Justice Scott. I went to see Lieutenant Quinn; talked to police chief Bouza; saw everybody and anybody I could."

"What did you say to Mr. Scott?"

"As I recall, I went to him for an explanation as to why there was never an indictment, or why it wasn't presented to the grand jury."

"When you talked to him, were you talking about why whatever evidence existed against Mr. Wartnick was not presented to a grand jury? Or were you talking about it just in general?"

"I'm sure that specifically I was referring to evidence against Mr. Wartnick."

"Why were you referring to Mr. Wartnick in your discussion with Mr. Scott?"

Fire ignited in her eyes. "Because I knew Norm pocketed a hundred-thousand dollars."

"Any other reason?"

Snider's steady response caused Terry's ire to wane. "I knew he pled the Fifth Amendment." Her chair bounced with each accusation. "I knew he was sitting across the street in a station wagon a week or ten days before my dad was killed. I knew there was an orchid box laying on the floor and the only reason it would have been out is for another wholesaler."[21]

"That's what your mother told you?"

She gave a quick nod. "And from having been around B and B prior to Dad's death."

Snider listed each of her accusations, individually, and requested whatever proof she had for their accuracy. Her response for each was her mother, Lieutenant Krueger, or Mr. Meshbesher. She could provide no other evidence or witness, and eventually Terry seemed to realize there was importance in that fact.

"I guess the only evidence I have is I knew my dad well enough to know that if someone were nine inches away from him, holding a gun, he wouldn't stand there unless it were someone like Mr. Wartnick who my dad would think would never pull that trigger."

"And what are you basing that on?"

"Because I know my dad was quick. My dad was not dumb, and he would not have put himself in that position. He would not have opened the door to a strange person."

"Mrs. Peters, did you get any inheritance from your father?"

"No."

"Did you get an interest in the B and B business?"

"I don't believe so. No."

"Did it ever come to your attention that your brother, Bobby, had stolen three thousand dollars from his father?"

Terry was stunned. "No."

"Do you know why he was fired from the business?"

"No, I don't."

"You obviously know your sister-in-law, Debra Feist Nachtsheim. Is that correct?"

"That's correct."

"How long have you known her?"

"I don't think I ever met Debbie until—. I don't remember when I met her. I don't think I knew her at the time of Dad's death."

"Did you know her at the time she and your brother got married?"

---

21. These are only some of the allegations Betty Nachtsheim made against Norm Wartnick which would never be corroborated by any other witnesses nor would have any evidence supplied which might indicate any truth to them. Those allegations included Norm had parked across the street from B and B to watch the store, when Norm had come to help at B and B on the day of the shooting he had 'run around like a chicken without a head,' Bob had left Midwest because Wartnick was distributing pornography, and Bob would only have gotten a flat of orchids out of the cooler that morning for another wholesaler who wanted to buy some. Betty also promoted the idea that Bob would have turned his back on Wartnick because he would have considered Norm 'too much of a coward to pull the trigger.' Betty's statement that Wartnick had run from Peter Hurkos would be attributed by others to have actually been the actions of her son, Bobby.

"I'm not sure I had even met her before that."

"Do you know Larry Strehlow?"

"That name also rings a bell. You know, there were a lot of people that come and go in your life, and the name rings a bell with me, but that's all it does."

"Did it ever come to your attention that Mr. Strehlow was at your brother's party the night before your father was murdered?"

"I don't recall."

"Are you aware that Larry Strehlow died in the cemetery where your father is buried, with a gravestone on his head?"

She nodded. "Yes. We went to the cemetery and looked at where he died versus where my father is buried."

"And they're within sight of each other, I take it?"

"That's correct."

"If you stand where Mr. Strehlow lost his life, you can see where your father—"

"That's correct." She nodded again but this time it was accompanied by the clearing of her throat and release of a deep breath. Then Terry gave unusual testimony not mentioned by any other members of the Nachtsheim family. It began toward the end of questioning by Mason's associate, Melissa Draper, who attended Mrs. Peters's deposition in Mason's stead.

"You testified," Draper said, "that you went to the cemetery at some point to see where Mr. Strehlow had died?"

"Yes."

"Was there any particular reason you did that, other than just curiosity? To see how far it was from your father's grave?"

"Well, I went to see my father. I went to see where it was and how it happened because it was strange, and then I went to the Roseville police."

"And why did you go to the Roseville police?"

"There was a male figure standing up on the hill a lot of times when any of us went to see my father; and that, in itself, was strange. I reported anything that ever happened to me that was strange because I didn't know if it was connected."

"Okay. But you don't have any idea who that male figure was?"

"No."

"And what did the Roseville police do?"

"They came to the cemetery. They, you know, talked with us at length about it. I don't know what they did with it."

Ms. Draper changed the subject.

Later, in his redirect questions, Jerry Snider raised it again. "I have a few follow-up questions, Mrs. Peters. I want to ask you about this male figure on the hill. How many times did you see him?"

"I have no idea. I mean, I didn't keep track of how often I saw him there."

"How often did you go there?"

"That varied. I may have gone once a week, I may have gone once a day, I may have gone there once a month."

"And more than a few times you saw this male figure on the hill?"

"Yes."

"What time of day would it be?"

She shrugged and gave a half-laugh, more of scorn than humor. "It would vary. You know, I would stop at the cemetery on the way home from work, go there at eight o'clock at night, seven o'clock in the morning. But not every time we went to the cemetery."

"Right, but enough that—"

"I felt watched."

"You felt watched. Was he looking at you?"

"I couldn't see his eyes. I have no idea."

"Do you have any way of knowing whether this figure was looking at your father's grave or any other particular grave?"

"Really, I had no—. But I felt like he was watching me."

"What did he look like?"

"You couldn't see him. It was too far away. I mean, you couldn't look at him and pick him out of a crowd."

"Even though it was some great distance, you can't identify any characteristics of this man at all?"

"No."

"Was he tall, short, heavy, thin?"

"I think, as I remember—in talking with my family I think we kind of decided that he had Larry Strehlow's features. I mean, he was kind of the same build as Larry Strehlow. Whether it was, in fact, Larry Strehlow, we never knew."

"So you saw this figure on the hill prior to the time that Larry Strehlow was killed?"

"Yes, but I don't recall ever seeing him after that."

Larry Strehlow's death and Terry Nachtsheim-Peters's encounters in the cemetery, like many of the threads knotted into this web of unsavory events, remains unpursued and unsolved.

CHAPTER 18

FRIDAY, JULY 14, 1989

Friedberg described friend and former law partner, Doug Thomson, as a short little guy who looked like Mr. Magoo. Today Thomson, Wartnick's former criminal defense attorney, was at Faegre for deposition. Jack Mason was also present.

"We've determined," Snider said, "there was a time in which you were consulted by Mr. Wartnick. Is that correct?"

"That's correct." Thomson's words were delivered in soft, clear tones.

"And what brought it about?"

"Mr. Wartnick was referred to me by a Minneapolis lawyer, Phillip Gainsley."

"And did Mr. Gainsley tell you the purpose of that referral?"

"I believe Mr. Wartnick was a suspect in a recent homicide and he wanted to know if I'd be interested in representing him. I said I would. I believe we met in Mr. Gainsley's office."

"And you had discussions with Mr. Wartnick and Mr. Gainsley at that time?"

The deponent shook his head. "I was introduced to Mr. Wartnick at that time. I don't recall any discussions [at that time] regarding the reason for my retention."

"Okay. Did you have subsequent meetings with Mr. Wartnick?"

"In my office, I did. Yes."

"Mr. Wartnick has waived the attorney-client privilege in this case for purposes of pursuing his legal malpractice claim against Moss and Barnett and against Phillip Gainsley, and I'd like you, Mr. Thomson," Snider glanced to the deponent, "to tell us and state on the record as best you can recall the substance of what Mr. Wartnick said to you."

"Well, he categorically denied that he had any responsibility whatsoever for the death of Mr. Nachtsheim. He consistently maintained his innocence."

"Do you have a practice when you counsel with suspects in homicides to tell them that they need to come clean with you, so to speak?"

"Well, one of the standard procedures—I, in fact, recall saying to Mr. Wartnick if he wanted the proper advice, it was necessary that I know exactly what happened. If he didn't tell me exactly what happened, I could give him the wrong advice, and he was the one going to prison, not me. That's rather standard."

"And once these comments were made to Mr. Wartnick, he continued to tell you that he had no involvement in this homicide?"

"That's correct."

"Did you believe him?"

"Yes, I did." Thomson nodded and reached for his coffee mug.

Exhibit 1 was presented—an affidavit by Phil Gainsley filed July 11, 1988.

Exhibit 2 was a copy of a letter from Phil Gainsley to Thomson dated June 30, 1988.

Exhibit 3 was a cover letter from Joseph Friedberg to Scott Herzog of Moss & Barnett with an affidavit by Doug Thomson.

They began with Exhibit 1. "All right," Snider said. "I want to direct your attention specifically to page two, beginning with paragraph two, and I'll read this portion. The second sentence, [Gainsley] states, 'I was well versed in the inferences of his Fifth Amendment rights, and made the considered judgment that he had no choice but to assert his constitutional right to silence.' And then if you'll let me skip down a sentence, Mr. Gainsley states, 'Moreover, I confirmed my advice with retained criminal counsel, Douglas W. Thomson.' My question to you, Mr. Thomson, is did you have any discussions at any time with Mr. Gainsley about Mr. Wartnick asserting his Fifth Amendment in his deposition in that civil case?"

"No. I don't believe I've had any contact with Phil Gainsley regarding the civil case whatsoever."

No one spoke as Snider flipped pages and found the next portion in question. "I'd like to ask you if you would describe for the record what your fee was for undertaking the counseling and representing of Mr. Wartnick back in 1973."

"It was a $5,000 retainer."

"Is it or is it not the case that Mr. Gainsley asked you for a portion of the $5,000 retainer that Wartnick paid to you?"

"Yes. The situation, as I recall it, was that Mr. Gainsley was more or less acting as a go-between between me and Mr. Wartnick regarding the amount of the fee. I was in one office and Mr. Wartnick was in another office, and I believe Mr. Gainsley's father may have been in a third office. I don't recall specifically what the negotiations were, but five thousand was agreed upon, then Mr. Gainsley said that they would want a one-third referral fee."

"Phil Gainsley said this to you?"

"Yes."

Questioning soon moved to if and when Mr. Thomson, as a criminal attorney, would polygraph a client. He acknowledged it was "very routine" to "make arrangements to have your client polygraphed independently, and if the client passes the polygraph test or is cleared, as they say, then you call the law enforcement agent back and say, 'Fine. Be happy to take the polygraph test.' If he's not clear or flunks the polygraph test, then you tell them, 'I've advised my client not to take a polygraph test because I don't believe in it.'"

"In your experience," Snider continued, "is that fairly routine practice of experienced criminal lawyers in the Twin Cities area?"

"Very routine."

"I want to ask you a question on another subject matter, now, Mr. Thomson. If a client is asked in a civil lawsuit to give a deposition, what factors do you consider in deciding whether or not you're going to instruct or advise your client to take the Fifth Amendment?"

"Well, there are probably several ingredients that'd go into that. Number One, has he given a preexisting statement? Number Two would be whether or not he could, indeed, incriminate himself. Probably ninety-nine times out of a hundred there would be no reason to take the Fifth Amendment, and the only concern would be that his testimony is consistent with the prior existing statement. Usually you advise your client of the consequences of *not* asserting or *of* asserting, and let him make up his mind what he wants to do."

"What advice do you give your clients with regard to the consequences of asserting or not asserting the Fifth Amendment in a civil deposition?"

"Well, in civil procedure in discovery and in request for admission, if you assert the privilege, the request is deemed admitted. In interrogatories and depositions, if you assert the privilege then an unfavorable inference can be drawn."

"Do you find it to be the practice of experienced attorneys representing an accused in civil litigation that the experienced practitioner in the Twin Cities explains to the accused the concept as you've explained it?"

"That would be my under—"

"Object to," Mason barked. "—as calling for a conclusion of the witness without foundation. Move the answer be stricken."

Snider looked up at the deponent. "You understand that Mr. Mason makes objections from time to time, and if you want the question read back at all, you can have that done, Mr. Thomson. If it distracts you."

Humor showed itself only in Doug Thomson's eyes. "Okay."

Soon it was Jack Mason's turn. Thomson shifted to face the man charged with defending Phil Gainsley. Thomson was not intimidated when speaking to Mason, and he did not let Mason's stray eye distract him.

"As you, I think, know," Mason began, "I represent Phil Gainsley and the law firm he works for. You're, I gather, a friend of Joe Friedberg's?"

"Yes, I am."

"And I gather you see Mr. Friedberg on a regular schedule, frequently socially?"

"I do. Yes."

"Have you had other matters referred to you by Phil Gainsley back in 1973?"

"Not that I recall."

"And you understood what your task was to be?"

"Well, my understanding, I was to be Mr. Wartnick's lawyer and advise him regarding the criminal investigation that was then going on."

"Do you recall the date of the last service you rendered in connection with your representation of Mr. Wartnick?"

"It would be my phone call to Gary Flakne regarding the insurance proceeds."

"And what is it you understood you would be doing for Mr. Wartnick as his attorney?"

"Well, I would be advising him of what his rights were regarding the investigation. I contacted the Hennepin County Attorney's office, advised them I was representing him and there was an ongoing investigation. You advise the prosecuting authority that you're representing the client. It has two effects: Number One, they don't make any attempt to contact the client personally; they do it all through the lawyer. Number Two, if any charge should be made, they'll usually call you and give you the courtesy to bring your client in without going into the formality of arrest. And there are other matters, reasons why you contact the county attorney—that's the purpose of my representation."

Mason said, "I've had the reporter mark as Deposition Exhibit Five a letter dated September 14, 1973, from Gainsley's firm to you. Did you receive that letter on or about that date?"

"Before you answer, Mr. Thomson," Snider said, "could I inquire of counsel where this letter came from? Is this out of the Moss and Barnett files?"

"This is out of the file that I have, Yes," Mason acknowledged.

"Well, I want to state for the record that this is not a document that's been supplied to us, even though there's a representation in the interrogatory answers that all files have been produced to us. And I'd like to simply bring that to your attention, Mr. Mason. If there are other things, other portions of the file beyond this, I'd like to have them produced to me because we're entitled to them and we've asked for them."

"Well, I assure you, Jerry, that I have only the statement that you asked for this. I've given them to you, and if there are documents that we haven't provided, of course, we're—"

"Well, you're the attorney representing this client, and I suggest to you that you collect your files. But what I've indicated on the record is true and correct."

Mason turned to Thomson. "Did you get Exhibit Five on or about the date it appears on the letter with the materials it makes reference to?"

"Well, the copy of this letter is not in my file. I have no independent recollection of the letter; however, it may be that—" Thomson scanned the page. "This letter refers to the insurance policy, and it may be that I have another file independent of the homicide investigation file."

Mason passed along another photocopy. "I've had the reporter mark as Deposition Exhibit Six a document bearing date October 12, 1973, to you from Phil Gainsley. Did you get this letter on or about the date it bears?"

"I have the same comment on this document." Snider reached for the page. "It appears, Mr. Mason, there's an entire file that we haven't seen when there's been the representation very early in this case that all of the files had been produced to us. That's clearly not the case. If this came out of Moss and Barnett's files—"

"Well, you'll have to provide me—" Mason began.

"Well, we'll do it, Mr. Mason. I think you know that request has been made, but we'll give you book and page."

"That would be helpful, and then, of course, we'll give you anything that you don't have. The problem we have—when Mr. Gainsley gave you files, he didn't number them, so it's a matter of whether he did or didn't, and his assertion to you that he did and yours that he didn't.

"Are you saying that he did give us this?"

"I think so, yes. I don't know what he gave you. I know what I have, and you're welcome to see whatever I have that's material. But like I said, Jerry, it would really be helpful to me if we can proceed with this."

"Sure."

Mason produced a document and had it marked Deposition Exhibit Seven, which Snider again stated for the record he had never seen. Mason continued, "This letter dated October 15, 1973, from Phil Gainsley to you. Did you receive this letter on or about the date it bears?"

"I don't recall, but I probably did."

"Is this a letter that's in your file?"

"No."

"Incidentally, Jerry, is there a reason you haven't provided me with Mr. Thomson's file?"

"Just because I haven't seen it, myself, which is a pretty good reason, I think."

A series of documents were produced, letters from Gainsley to Thomson, which Doug Thomson did not recall receiving and could only presume were intended to keep him informed on how Gainsley's case was proceeding. Then Mason, again, turned to Exhibit 3, the copy of the $1,666.66 check, to the photocopy of the endorser's signature. "Do you know who affixed the handwritten words on page six, 'Phillip Gainsley,' with the misspelling of attorney Gainsley's first name?"

"I have no idea."

"Did you ever learn from Mr. Wartnick whether he had taken a polygraph or been offered a polygraph test?"

"No."

"You did make an effort to learn from Mr. Wartnick everything he had said to the police and they had said to him?"

"Yes."

"And you did not learn from him in the course of that that he had been offered a lie detector test?"

"I don't recall that."

"Did you ever review the police file in this matter?"

"No."

"Did you ever interview any witnesses with respect to this matter?"

"No."

"Did you ever give Mr. Wartnick advice relative to the Fifth Amendment?"

"No."

"Did you ever learn from Mr. Gainsley that he was recommending that Mr. Wartnick take the Fifth Amendment in his deposition when it was taken in 1979?"

"I never discussed the civil matter with Mr. Gainsley."

Mason glanced up at the deponent. "When did you first become aware Mr. Wartnick had taken the Fifth Amendment in his deposition?"

"I believe after the [1986] verdict." Thomson returned Mason's gaze.

"Isn't it a fact that in 1979, Mr. Gainsley told you he was recommending that Mr. Wartnick take the Fifth Amendment in his deposition?"

"I have no recollection of that whatsoever."

"And isn't it a fact that in this conversation you expressed surprise to Mr. Gainsley that the civil action was still pending?"

"No, I wasn't aware of the civil action pending, I don't believe."

"And isn't it a fact that after expressing surprise, you told Mr. Gainsley, 'Well, that's sure the right thing to do about the criminal matter,' or words to that effect?"

"I have no recollection of that."

Mason concluded his questioning.

Snider had an additional inquiry. "You were asked a couple of questions by Mr. Mason regarding an alleged conversation Phil Gainsley had with you in February of 1979 in which you allegedly agreed with Gainsley's advice on instructing Mr. Wartnick to take the Fifth Amendment. Do you have any recollection of that conversation *ever* taking place?"

"None whatsoever."

"Would it have been sound advice for you to have agreed with Mr. Gainsley on his Fifth Amendment—"

"No."

"—and interpretation?" Snider concluded. "Nothing further. Thank you."

"Move to strike the latter answer," Mason interjected, "as an opinion of the witness without foundation."

CHAPTER 19

MONDAY, JUNE 5, 1989

Liberko telephoned B and B's former bank manager. He was directed to John Hart, an attorney. Mr. Hart said there would be no problem for Faegre to review records—with a subpoena.

Days later, Hart called Liberko. "I've been through the bank's records of transactions and located a stack of papers approximately eight inches thick, paperwork associated with Nachtsheim matters." In a June 10, 1975, letter from the bank to Betty Nachtsheim were these words: "I am still amazed at your apparent lack of concern for B and B."

TUESDAY, JUNE 20, 1989

"Mr. Friedberg? Jack Montague, here. Got your letter yesterday requestin' our firm see about locating a Mr. Roger Nordstrom. I wanted to let you know we turned him up right off the bat.

"Yes, sir, here in Austin. Looks like he's been here since at least '76.

"Yes, sir, only a preliminary; just puttin' our finger on him. We can get ya more if that's what ya want. Okay then, I'll see what I can pull together. Talk at ya soon."

LATE JUNE 1989

Liberko continued his interviews of accountants, bankers, Nachtsheim family members and friends. He spoke with Tom Whalen, owner of Twin Cities Wholesale Floral, one of the largest wholesale florists in the Midwest since the late 1960s. "It would have been stupid for Norm to buy a gross of orchids from Bob," Tom said. "Why would he? Norm could easily order them from either me or Jimmy Goldstein."

Tom explained there were two reasons it made far more sense for Norm to call him or Jimmy. First, their inventories were significantly larger than Bob's; Norm's cost would be less. Also, Tom and Jimmy's inventories would be much fresher and in better condition.

He also confirmed that one of the first things, back then, a wholesaler did in the morning was to pull his orchids out of the cooler to let them warm up.

No, he had never been contacted by Mr. Gainsley or anyone on Norm's behalf, even though he had offered.

It was Norm Wartnick's first turn in the hot seat. Snider sat near his client in a room with plain walls, a long table, and carafes of water and coffee and their necessities laid out on an otherwise bare counter.

Mason hunched over the table, assorted papers scattered around him. Once the basics were out of the way he asked, "Have you at any time, after the trial to which we made reference, talked with Mr. Gainsley about the quality of his representation of you?"

"Yes."

"Is it the case you told him numerous attorneys had called you and discussed with you the quality of his representation?"

"Yes," Wartnick nodded, "after the Appellate Court and after the Supreme Court denial."

"So, to put this in a time frame, there was a trial before Judge McCarr, then there was an appeal to the Court of Appeals, then there was a petition to the Supreme Court, sequentially. Is that correct?"

"Yes."

"You said there were some matters to which Jack, your brother, expressed the view that a first-year law student could have handled better. What was that about?"

"He was concerned about [Gainsley's] opening statement—about a lie detector test not being allowed into court."

"Anything else?"

"Oh, he had many concerns. I just don't remember. He did most of the talking."

"Did you, at that meeting, have any concerns?"

"Oh, I had a lot of concerns."

"Is your memory such that you are able to tell us today what those concerns were?"

+

WEDNESDAY, NOVEMBER 25, 1987

Norm watched from the office doorway, over his brother Jack's shoulder, as Phil Gainsley stood behind his desk. Gainsley nodded at Norm and extended his hand to Jack, "Good to see you again," then Gainsley gestured toward a tall man in a Sears and Roebuck suit. "This is Paul Neimann,* head of our litigation department. Norm, I believe you've already met Paul."

"If I have, I don't remember. How are you?"

---

* - not the actual name

"Fine, Mr. Wartnick. I want to assure you I'm here only to verify there are no unanswered questions."

"In what respect?" Jack countered.

"I understand there is potential here for an action against Mr. Gainsley."

"Please, gentlemen." Phil raised an inviting hand for peace and gestured toward an armchair. "Have a seat. Cup of coffee, Jack? Norm, some tea?"

"No," Norm answered for both brothers as they seated themselves on Moss & Barnett's brown vinyl. "I don't think we're going to be here that long."

"I see." Gainsley settled into his own chair behind the desk.

Neimann remained standing. "I understand you may have concerns regarding how Mr. Wartnick's case has proceeded."

Jack glanced at Norm. Norm nodded. Jack spoke. "An assortment of people have indicated they thought Norm's defense was less than what it should have been."

"I can understand why you would feel that way. It's perfectly natural, actually, in the circumstances. I imagine it's disconcerting to find yourself suddenly owing what must seem a surreal amount of money."

Neimann casually moved to stand beside his associate. "But I can assure you, Moss and Barnett is thoroughly satisfied with the work Mr. Gainsley has done on this case. Hopefully, over time, you'll arrive at the same realization—that your attorney did all he could within the circumstances and the law. Mr. Gainsley has, indeed, met the appropriate standard of care for your case, Mr. Wartnick."

Silence filled the room and insinuated neither Norm nor Jack had a reply. Norm's chest tightened. After a lifetime of self-confidence, overflowing with a lighthearted casualness toward life, this was a new sensation for Norm; new, at least, since the devastating verdict a year-and-a-half earlier.

The brothers' lack of verbal response made Gainsley assume he had the advantage. "If I had to do it all over again, Jack, I would make no judgments differently from those I've made during the past thirteen years."

"Oh, it's not a question of just the judgments you made," Jack responded. "It's a question of your overall competence. We've been told that the way you handled Norm's case—well, that some of the things you did even a first-year law student should have known not to—"

"Mr. Wartnick," Neimann interrupted. He smiled. "Jack, if I may. Moss and Barnett's team of partners reviews all litigation occurring within these offices. They found Mr. Gainsley had done a reputable job. We have, indeed, been reviewing his work right along. While unfortunate that your brother's case turned out the way it did, Phil Gainsley cannot be held responsible for what any jury may or may not decide."

"We think there were actions that should've been taken before we even went to court," Norm countered. "Witnesses who should've been talked to, maybe even recorded."

"Witnesses who would have thrown a much different light on the surrounding circumstances," Jack added.

Neimann stepped toward Norm. "You cannot know they would have made any difference to this jury."

Jack focused on Gainsley. "You made no attempt to call those witnesses and now Norm has lost everything. Everything."

Gainsley pursed his lips together. He seemed to be humming but Norm could not be sure.

"Gentlemen, again, I can appreciate your irritation." Neimann's smile stayed glued to his lips. "Your response is normal in your situation. I'm sure that over time you will settle down, your reactions will settle down, and you'll see—"

Norm faced Gainsley. "The jury was almost unanimous against me in what should have been a no-lose game. The Court of Appeals rubber stamped McCarr's Order and the Supreme Court gave us a one-liner but wouldn't even give us a hearing."

"Well, that's not entirely accurate, Norm," Gainsley said, "but I'm sure that makes little difference considering the size of the judgment against you."

"It seems accurate enough."

"Well, we did win the insurance claim completely."

"The insurance claim?"

"I had no reason to believe that the state legislature would revise the wrongful death statute just for this case, ten years after—"

"The insurance claim? Meshbesher was accusing me of murdering Bob Nachtsheim."

"It's easy at this juncture to second guess ourselves. Judge McCarr, himself, made a statement to me following the Supreme Court's denial of review. He said that the matters covered by this lawsuit were—and here I quote Judge McCarr: 'a hot potato.'"

"Absolutely," Neimann said. "Judges are accountable to the people."

"And therefore," Gainsley continued, "will naturally feel the pulse of public opinion. There are too many people who do not want to see Norm 'get off free' on this count."

"Wait just a—" Norm sputtered.

"The United States Supreme Court, however, is accountable to no one—"

"The United States—Are you kidding?"

"They might look at this differently since the legal issues should be resolved in Norm's favor."

"Wait a minute," Jack said. "Law's not determined by public opinion!"

"I don't mean to intimate it is," Gainsley smiled. "Judges, however, are human and, therefore, just as susceptible to public sway as you or I. And further complicating this case was the almost impossible task of showing justification for your renewal of the insurance policy, Norm, after Nachtsheim left your employ."

"We're not saying it's an easy case," Norm said, then stood. "Only that it was definitely mishandled."

Jack also rose. "We wanted to hear what you'd say." He turned to his brother. "Heard enough?"

+

Wartnick blinked away the memory and looked toward Jack Mason. "Mr. Gainsley told me and my brother we'd been a victim of the judicial system. The six jurors weren't favorable since, in this case, he felt they didn't understand the law. He was also disappointed the Appellate Court gave such a verdict, said court members were appointed to their positions by votes of the people and it wasn't a good year for them to overturn because of the repercussions that might come in the newspapers."

"And this was said by Mr. Gainsley?"

It seemed to Wartnick that Mason's crossed eyes might be focused on him. "That, and other things that were said to my brother in answer to his questions."

Mason's volley of questions continued regarding coverages and losses and retirement plans; about whether or not Wartnick had threatened or manipulated Bob into taking the physical required to initiate the policy; about when and how and where and under what conditions Wartnick had intended to transfer the policy to Bob at age sixty-five.

Snider watched how Wartnick fared under Mason's grinding. He was satisfied they had sufficiently prepared Wartnick for the defense attorney's methods.

"And whose life," Mason continued, "were you insuring for your benefit?"

"Not for my benefit."

"For Midwest's benefit."

"Bob understood the policy."

"And you understood that you needed his permission?"

"Yes."

"And is it the case that you told him you were going to transfer it to him at a time prior to the time he had given you permission?"

"I'm going to object to the form of the question," Snider interrupted. "I'm sorry. I don't understand."

Mason smirked. "All right. If these are hard questions, just let me know."

Wartnick decided to continue as though nothing had happened. "I'm sorry. I don't know."

Snider did not take Mason's remark lying down. "That one is just unclear, Jack," he said calmly.

So Mason continued as though nothing had happened. "What was the reason for telling Mr. Nachtsheim at the time that it was your intention to transfer the policy to him when he turned sixty-five?"

"I wanted Bob to know how important he was to us, and this was a package that we were willing to pay for and would be his."

"And did you foresee that unless you made some sort of promise to Mr. Nachtsheim that he might not agree to have his life insured for your benefit?"

"No."

"In August of 1972, when Mr. Nachtsheim left, what, please, took place? Did he advise you in person or by letter that he was leaving, or what?"

"Bob handed me a letter. I believe it was possibly no more than one, maybe two lines, that he was leaving the company."

"And where were you when he handed you that letter?"

"About twenty-five feet away from him, within the main store."

"Did he approach you with the letter across those twenty-five feet?"

"Yes, I believe so."

"And who was present besides you and Bob Nachtsheim?"

"The entire crew was standing around us. I really don't recall."

"Do you recall what the letter said?"

"'Effective this date,' and then there was no date, 'effective this date,' something to the effect that 'we terminate our employment,' 'I terminate my employment.'"

"Was Mrs. Nachtsheim working for Midwest Floral, too?"

"MFC next door. It was a company designed to handle the hard goods."

"What did Bob Nachtsheim say when he handed you the letter of resignation?"

"I don't remember specifically. He handed me the letter and then I said, 'Let's sit down and talk for a few minutes in my office.' He said fine. We talked about fifteen minutes."

"As nearly as you can recall, tell me what the two of you said to one another."

Snider wondered if Wartnick was churning on the inside, his face occasionally revealed a hint of irritation; but Mason saw only a calm, steady tenacity.

"I wished him good luck in his new venture and offered to give him his job back at any time—he knew he was an important entity to our business—and I told him the door was always open for him. We shook hands, and he left."

Mason launched into a long hour of questions on how the timing of Bob's resignation was related to the timing of Betty's and theirs to the timing of Bobby's. Who was first? What period of time elapsed? Where had they been standing? How had they been standing? How far apart had they been standing? "Did it strike you as a peculiar event these members of the family coming in one after the other, a minute or two apart, offering their resignations?"

"No."

"Isn't it a fact that what, in fact, happened was that Mr. Nachtsheim offered his resignation and said he would stay on for a couple of weeks, and you threw him out and fired his son and his wife?"

"No. No, absolutely not."

"What you say happened is that first Mr. Nachtsheim, then a minute or two later Bobby Nachtsheim, and a minute or two after that Mrs. Nachtsheim came in and offered you their resignations?"

"No. I say Bob handed me the resignation which was one sheet of paper. Bobby handed me a sheet of paper identical to Bob's, and Betty came in and handed me a sheet of paper identical to Bob's and Bobby's. All within three or four minutes, total."

"All right. Tell me what you say happened. When did you invite Bob into your office?"

"I'm going to object. Asked and answered." Snider looked at Wartnick. "You don't have to answer that. I instruct you not to answer."

Mason scribbled on his notepad. "Grounds of instruction?"

"Repetitive. He already answered it. You're repeating your questions, Jack."

"Was the note from Mrs. Nachtsheim identical to that of Bobby Nachtsheim?"

"Objection. Asked and answered. I instruct you not to answer. Next question."

"All right," Mason said. "I will accept that instruction. If the transcript discloses there is no answer, we shall reconvene the deposition for the purpose of getting an answer to that question."

"There's an answer to the question, so next question," Snider replied, still calm.

"The same is true of other objections," Mason said. "If the transcript, in fact, discloses there is not an answer, then we will bring Mr. Wartnick back down here."

"Next question." Snider still appeared unperturbed.

"What did Mrs. Nachtsheim do after she handed you this piece of paper?"

"I don't remember." Wartnick shrugged.

"How long after Mrs. Nachtsheim handed you her resignation did you invite—was it before you invited Bob Nachtsheim into your office?"

"Objection. Asked and answered. I instruct you not to answer. Next question."

"Can you remember what the time period was?"

"He answered that. Next question."

"I tell you what. We'll take a recess and have the reporter find the answer." So Wartnick mentally ticked off the minutes as the court reporter read page after page of previous testimony which confirmed the topic was asked and fully answered.

Mason continued as though nothing inconvenient had occurred. "All right. Having in mind that testimony, please answer this question: Is it the case that after Mr. Nachtsheim handed you his letter of resignation, you said, 'Let's sit down in my office'?"

"I don't know if it was immediately, until I had received all three of them—or two others, a total of three."

"Isn't it a fact that what, in fact, happened on this day, that Bob Nachtsheim told you that it was his intention to leave and start up a competing business and you said to him, 'You're leaving right now'?"

"No, that's not true."

"Isn't it a fact that you told Mr. Nachtsheim that he wouldn't have two weeks, that he would leave immediately?"

"No, I didn't tell him that."

"Isn't it a fact that you told Mrs. Nachtsheim that she was discharged at once based on her husband's resignation?"

"No."

Snider was pleased with the way his client withstood Mason's tactics, but Jack could still wear down Wartnick. And Mason's assault came as unrelenting extraction of picayune points.

"Another subject," Mason continued. "Did you at some point sell your business to J. W. Perry?"

"Yes."

"I'm handing you what has been marked as Deposition Exhibit Seven. Does this represent the agreement of sale as well as the exhibits and the employment agreement which were entered into in connection with that matter?"

"I don't know. I haven't got the original. If this is the original, I don't know. I haven't seen it for a long time."

Snider stepped in. "I was under the impression, and it's my belief that we have asked for all of Mr. Wartnick's files from Mr. Gainsley. This is not a file Mr. Gainsley has turned over to us, to my knowledge. I have never seen it before. Since we do have a request for all those files, it's disconcerting to see this for the first time as an exhibit in Mr. Wartnick's deposition. I'd ask you *again* to produce all of Mr. Wartnick's and Midwest Floral's files to him."

"Well," Mason replied. "I'll be glad to give you whatever I have in this respect. As I recall, the request was for Mr. Wartnick's files, and Mr. Gainsley and his law firm responded by giving Mr. Wartnick his files. You are now asking for Midwest Floral's files, and we'll respond to that by giving you Midwest Floral's files, too. These documents came from Midwest Floral's files."

Then Mason slid a document across the table toward Wartnick that he neither identified nor marked as an exhibit. Snider intercepted it.

"This is another one of those documents," Snider said, "which we've previously requested. I believe you indicated on the record, Mr. Mason, that you had supplied Mr. Wartnick with all of his personal files. I think this proves conclusively that that is not the case. I also note the next document that you're marking, which will be marked Exhibit Nine, is another document we've not seen. It seems to me that when a demand is made for files that are exclusively within the possession of your client, particularly when those files are Mr. Wartnick's files, it is unfair not to have produced them. If there are other such files, I would make the demand that you produce them right now."

Mason did not even blink. Instead, he handed a document to the court reporter, who marked the document. Mason slid the page toward Wartnick. "Showing you what has been marked as Exhibit Nine, is this a handwritten letter by you to Phil Gainsley?"

"Yes, I would say so."

"And was that sent to him in response to the letter marked Exhibit Eight?"

"I don't know if it was sent or handed to him. I have no way of knowing."

"In order that we can be clear in the reading of your handwriting, would you read Exhibit Nine aloud, please?"

Wartnick glanced at Snider, who nodded ever-so slightly. "'Phil,'" Wartnick began. "Umm, I don't know what the name is up in the upper right-hand corner. 'I got the copy from T and Y Service. I do not remember the work but the boys there are honest and if they say so then I must have. Only thing I can think of is that I was forced to use the car while one of the other trucks was down. So if I must—I must have felt that they owed this one, owed me this one. I then asked Del, the owner, if I ever had done this before or after this date or on any other unit and he said, 'No, never that he can remember.' Phil, I am confused. Are we waiting because you think I have erred or are we waiting for another case, maybe? The rest of that letter you sent me is bull.' And 'bull' is emphasized," Wartnick concluded.

Mason did not look up from the stack of papers in front of him. "Then turning to page two of Exhibit Nine, is that a copy of the record which was altered to appear to have work done on a company truck instead of a family vehicle of yours?"

"It appears so, yes."

"If we're at a convenient place here," Snider interrupted. "Mr. Mason, I again, if you have other documents that are Mr. Wartnick's documents or Midwest Floral Supply's documents, we've asked for those. We have interrogatories where we have asked for those. I'm going to demand that you produce them."

"Well, you've asked in your interrogatories, Interrogatory Number Four, I think," Mason replied, "and I think those have been provided. I told you I would verify that, and I've also tendered to you documents in addition to those. If there are files of Mr. Wartnick's or Midwest's, as I said to you then and I repeat now, you're welcome to look at any of them."

"Well, these files belong to Mr. Wartnick and we are making a demand for them on this record just as we did the other day. If you have those files in your possession, we want them now."

"Well, I'll arrange for that at any time. Sure."

"What I think is unfair," Snider continued, "is when we have a representation made by your client before you were in this case that the entire file involving Mr. Wartnick had been produced. It's disconcerting to sit here and see documents produced that haven't been given to us."

"Well, I'm sorry you feel that way. As I say, if you want to get those, the thing you should have done was to have asked for them in the first place, but now—"

"Well, we did. I think we've covered that in the interrogatories."

"If it'd make you feel better," Mason said, straight-faced, "I can recess this deposition and make the search right now, if you would prefer to do it that way."

"All right," Snider began to collect his notes. "Since these files belong to Mr. Wartnick or his previous company maybe you can just have them carted over to us, or we could send someone to pick them up."

Mason nodded. "I'll be glad to do that. I think what I'm going to have to do is number them. That's going to involve some time and cost and we can discuss that, and we don't need to do it on the record."

Snider shook his head. "I'm not interested in paying costs, particularly when those documents belong to Mr. Wartnick."

CHAPTER 20

WEDNESDAY, AUGUST 2, 1989

Steve Severson deposed former B and B employee, Alan Mentes.

"Do you recall that there came a time that Bobby was terminated from the company?"

"I thought he quit."

"When you say you thought he quit, what do you base that on?"

"Well," Mentes's hands began to tremble as suppressed emotions were evoked by memories—vivid in the horror of their reality. "I still knew Larry and Bobby pretty well, then, and I recall that's what he told me." He exhaled forcefully and groped in an empty shirt pocket. "Ya know. That he quit."

"That's what Bobby told you?"

"Yeah."

"Did it ever come to your attention that, in fact, Mr. Nachtsheim had fired him?"

"No."

"And you considered yourself to be a friend of Roger Nordstrom's back at the time that you were at B and B?"

"Yeah."

"Did it ever come to your attention that Mr. Nordstrom had a confrontation with Mr. Bob Nachtsheim regarding the repossession of a car?"

"No, I don't remember that at all."

"Do you know where Mr. Nordstrom is today?"

"Yeah. Texas."

"Do you know where in Texas?"

"I have no idea."

Severson changed topics. "Was there a time that you dated Debra Feist?"

"Right."

"Who is Debra Feist?"

"A girl I met at a party."

"When did you date Debra Feist?"

"That's rough. Early '70s, maybe."

"Was it while you were working at B and B Wholesale?"

"Yeah."

"Did there come a time when your relationship with Ms. Feist ended?"

"Right."

"When did she start dating Bobby Nachtsheim?"

"As soon as we broke up."

"Was the time that you broke up with Debra Feist before Mr. Nachtsheim was shot?"

"Yeah, I think so. Shortly before. Yeah."

"Who ran the B and B Wholesale shop after Mr. Nachtsheim was shot?"

"Bobby."

"And so, I take it, that you continued to work for Bobby, then?"

"Right."

"Do you know Norm Wartnick?"

Mentes nodded and rubbed trembling fingers across his forehead. "I did a few deliveries at Midwest, but I never really met the man until the morning Mr. Nachtsheim got shot."

"Okay."

"He, he came in to help out." Mentes cleared his throat.

"So tell me about that day when Mr. Wartnick came to help out."

"Well," Mentes shifted nervously in his seat. "Calls came in as people came and picked orders up, and he'd just help Bobby on the phones."

"Other than working with flowers and answering phones, do you know what else Mr. Wartnick did to help out?"

"No. Soon as the ambulance left and it got down to doing what we're—you know, what I did, I just got out of there. That was it. I stayed on the road as much as I could."

"Mr. Mentes, what I'd like to have you do for us now, if you would, and I understand this may be painful, is just describe for us what you observed when you came to work that day."

"Well, I followed Larry in, and I went to the bathroom first, I think." Again fingers probed the shirt pocket and again came out empty. He slumped back into the seat and closed his eyes. "Oh, God, I tried to forget this."

The testimony of Alan Mentes and Larry Kramlinger to police was that they had arrived at the shop together, about seven o'clock that gray and rainy morning. Both front and back doors were shut but not locked. Mentes had headed for the bathroom, but Kramlinger heard a gurgling sound coming from the work room and went to check it out. Sometimes the Nachtsheims' youngest son, seven-year-old John, would hide and play tricks on them early in the morning.

But the gurgling did not come from young John. Kramlinger hollered for Mentes, who saw the victim lying, face down, on the floor in a large pool of blood. Mentes went to see what was the matter and put his hand under the victim's head to raise it out of the pool of blood so Nachtsheim could breathe. That was when Mentes saw what looked like a hole on the right side of Bob's head, just behind his ear. Because of the position of Mr. Nachtsheim's body, Mentes first thought he had fallen and hit his head on the work table, then he realized there was no blood there. His boss had been shot.

Larry telephoned police. Bob Nachtsheim, though barely able to breathe, tried to speak, tried to move, even tried to get up. Mentes stayed with Nachtsheim until the ambulance arrived, stayed to hold his head up and to hold the man down because Bob was struggling so.

Once released from his grisly labor, Mentes had tried to go to the bathroom to wash the blood off his hands, but a detective had insisted he go to the front of the store and not touch anything until police had finished looking over the back of the shop.

"Did Mr. Nachtsheim have a practice with respect to inspecting flowers in the morning?"

"Yeah."

"What was that practice?" Severson's tone was calming.

"Well, after—the coolers were locked. After opening the coolers, he'd kind of look around the whole place and, you know, check and make sure—cut flowers don't last very long, so you know, he'd—I was usually never there in the morning when he got there. He always got there before everybody. But during the course of the few, very few times I did get there before him, after he unlocked the coolers, he usually looked around, you know, see what kind of shape everything was in."

"Okay. And that included the flowers?"

"Yeah."

"Did you ever observe him taking flowers out of the cooler in the morning?"

"All the time, yeah."

"And do you know why he did that?"

"He always inspected them outside the cooler because that's when he put them on the packing table, and he looked at them before they got packed to ship."

"I see, and would that include boxes of orchids?"

"Oh, sure. They're the most delicate. They don't last very long."

"Now, you indicated that you testified at the [original] trial?"

"Uh-huh."

"Who called you to testify?"

"Somebody that works for Ron Meshbesher."

"Prior to the time of the trial, were you interviewed by Mr. Gainsley?"

"I don't recall."

"Do you know who Phillip Gainsley is?"

"No."

"Okay. Do you recall ever being contacted prior to the time of the trial by anyone representing Norm Wartnick?"

Alan Mentes shook his head to indicate no.

"Do you recall the last time you spoke to Bobby Nachtsheim?"

"Halloween party five, six years ago. A long time ago."

"Did you have occasion to speak to Bobby Nachtsheim about the shooting of his father?"

"No. Never. If anybody ever brought it up, I'd drop the conversation or walk out. I just as soon not talk about it or hear about it or—" his voice trailed to silence but the hands still shook.

Severson waited to see if Mentes would finish his sentence. He did not. So Severson reached into a file and pulled out two sheets of paper, stapled together, and slid them across the table to Mentes. "I'm going to show you what's been marked as Deposition Exhibit Two and ask you to tell me whether you can identify that exhibit."

"I can't remember ever seeing it before. No." It was a report from Krueger's MPD file on the Nachtsheim murder.

"Okay," Severson said. "If you would, please, focus your attention on the first paragraph after the line on the first page. Do you see where it says, 'These two young men'?"

"Uh-huh."

"Okay. Would you read that paragraph, please."

"'These two young men stated that they're,'" Mentes stopped to clear his throat, "'that they had arrived at the shop about seven a.m. and when they entered through the rear door which was unlocked but closed they found the victim lying face down in a pool of blood just outside of the walk-in cooler door in the workroom—" Mentes inhaled deeply, then cleared his throat again. "—the workroom. They had noted that the cooler door was standing ajar. There was a large box of orchids approximately three feet by eighteen inches and six inches deep on the work table near the pool of blood[22]—'" he inhaled. "I'm pretty nervous."

"Just take your time."

Mentes nodded. "—which the young men said was [previously] lying on the floor just east of the feet of the victim, and again just outside the walk-in cooler door. They informed me that this box of orchids normally would be kept in the, in the walk-in and that the victim normally handled all the orchids himself and it was not usual that he would have entered the—'"

"It was not usual or not unusual?"

"'It was not *un*usual—sorry—not *un*usual that he would have entered the cooler in the early a.m. hours and removed said box for purposes of repacking or whatever.'"

"Thank you, Mr. Mentes. Does this paragraph refresh your recollection as to what you told the police following the shooting of Bob Nachtsheim?"

---

22. It was, elsewhere, established that before police arrived Larry Kramlinger had picked up the box of orchids lying, inverted, on the floor outside the cooler at Nachtsheim's feet and had placed them, upright, on the work table under which Nachtsheim had fallen when shot.

"Yeah."

"Okay. And did you, in fact, tell the police following the shooting that a box of orchids normally would have been kept in the walk-in and that 'the victim normally handled all of the orchids himself, and that it was not unusual that he would have entered the cooler in the early a.m. hours and removed said box for purposes of repacking or whatever'?"

"Yeah," Mentes nodded and looked away.

FRIDAY, AUGUST 11, 1989

"Hey, Steve, look at this." Joe Friedberg's son, Mike, held up a copy of a memorandum. Mike Friedberg had one year of law school left to complete. This summer he was clerking for Snider.

Severson glanced through several pages of the document, then whistled. "Would you look at that. Where'd you get this?" Severson spun the box around to read the label. "Is this the one you just picked up?"

"Right."

Severson rifled through the contents. "There's no order to any of this," he said. The pages faced rearward, frontward, right side up, upside down, skewed, and helter-skelter with no organization of any kind. "I wouldn't put it past Black Jack to have thrown the whole batch down the stairs," Severson said moments later. "Jerry, though, may not be completely satisfied."

"And why is that?" Snider strode into the room.

"You won't believe what Young Friedberg, here, has stumbled across." He extended the memo to Snider. "But Gainsley's time records still aren't here."

Snider scanned the documents. His eyebrows rose. "Yes, indeed. Mike, call your dad."

In Snider's office, Joe Friedberg glanced from the memo to Snider. "Got a hornbook[23]?"

Snider nodded. "Dan, find a copy of *McCormack's* for Joe."

"So this is Lerner's answer to Gainsley's smoking-gun memo," Joe said in disgust. "Complete ignorance." He flumped into his regular seat in front of Snider's desk and looked around at the others in the room. "While we're waiting, anyone find out from Norm about that T and Y receipt?"

---

23. "In United States law, a hornbook is a text that gives an overview of a particular area of law. Hornbooks summarize and explain the law in a specific area. They are distinct from casebooks, which are collections of cases (or parts of cases) chosen to help illustrate and stimulate discussion about legal issues." — "Treatises, hornbooks and nutshells are secondary sources that cover specific areas of the law. Unlike the casebooks used in most first year law classes, these three sources provide explanations, analyses, criticisms and overviews of legal topics in narrative form. Students can use treatises, hornbooks, and nutshells to obtain a solid overview of legal topics and to review concepts learned." (en.wikipedia.org/wiki/Hornbook_%28law%29 and library.lawschool.cornell.edu. Accessed 7-16-2011.)

Mike looked up from his notepad. When no one answered, he replied, "He and Mrs. Wartnick were down to their last vehicle and had no money because it was time to pay on the judgment. If he was going to do his job for—What was the name of the guy who took over Midwest?"

"J. W. Perry," Severson said without looking up. "But that's a company, not a guy."

"Yeah. That's it," Mike said. "Norm was picking up and delivering flowers and running all sorts of company errands, and Norm says Perry never reimbursed him."

"And in the sales agreement for Midwest, J. W. Perry promised Norm a company car, which they never delivered on," Jerry added as he continued with Liberko's memorandum.

"That's right." Mike nodded. "Anyway, the Wartnicks were way overdue on the oil change, and Norm figured Perry owed it to him."

Mike's dad shook his head. "Sounds about right." Then Joe added, almost to himself, "Wonder how long it'll be before this guy gets a break."

The *McCormack's* arrived. Joe flipped to the passage quoted by Lerner, turned it toward Snider. "She's completely off." He thumped a finger against the heading. "Pulled it from the criminal section, not the civil. Lerner had no understanding whatsoever of the consequences of tailoring her answers to what Gainsley wanted to hear. Besides that, if you're gonna rely on secondary sources, gonna find your answers in a hornbook, you're—"

"You're completely negligent," Snider and Friedberg finished together.

CHAPTER 21

THREE WEEKS LATER

WEDNESDAY, AUGUST 23, 1989

"These people are incredible," Liberko said and extended summaries of depositions to Snider. "What an amazing set of events. Norm Wartnick is very sane, and no amount of money he might have obtained would ever be worth the hellish scrutiny he and his family have endured. Nothing adds up, unless you consider that maybe this murder was motivated by hate, or revenge."

Snider passed a set of the photocopied summaries to Severson and then to Friedberg, who had followed Liberko into the office.

The investigative work, for now, was completed. Liberko had formed strong opinions during those hot days trudging through dirty streets. His understanding of the Nachtsheim family, their doings and acquaintances, were valuable to Snider as he deposed the Nachtsheims and Russ Krueger. Liberko sat with Snider through those depositions, and as he summarized the transcripts he noted not only where one deponent's testimony contradicted another but also where their words did not stand against facts.

Had Betty known Roger Nordstrom? Had she heard from Bobby that Nordstrom would kill someone for two hundred dollars? She denied it. Krueger said she had. Drugs, anger, greed, and lies; but what most astounded Liberko was Betty's muddy insistence, then retraction of her statement that Angie had called Bobby the morning of the shooting. Placed alongside Krueger's inability to locate any evidence Bobby had ever, actually been called, Liberko thought a truer picture had begun to emerge.

Now the Wartnick team collected in Snider's office.

"Any of you catch Russ Krueger on TV?" Severson asked. "Talking about unsolved murders in the Cities?"

He surveyed the room. Mike Friedberg sat at the other end of Snider's couch from Severson and doodled on the top page of his legal pad; Liberko sat quietly near the door, as usual. Joe Friedberg stood in front of Snider's desk and Snider sat behind it; each flipped through Liberko's memos, though Joe's examination was less all-encompassing.

"He talked about Wartnick?" Severson said. "The Nachtsheim murder? On *Twin Cities Live?*"

Friedberg shrugged, "He's a loose cannon," and continued to peruse Liberko's reports.

Snider moved only his eyes as he glanced up to Severson. "Interestingly he made a point to say Nachtsheim's murder was the only case he'd never solved—was still working on it."

"Think it'll do us any harm?"

Friedberg dropped his sheaf of photocopies to the coffee table and took a seat in front of Snider's desk. "Biggest concern is how it taints the jury pool. Won't know that 'til *voir dire*[24]. I'm more concerned about what we've lost in Davis's order."

Nine days earlier, on August 14, 1989, Friedberg, Snider, and Jack Mason had argued in court on whether or not plaintiff could amend their complaint to include recent discovery of Gainsley's kickback request and his perjury in sworn affidavit that it had never happened. It stuck in Joe's throat that Gainsley charged Wartnick by the hour to conduct a case he was not competent to handle.

In court, Friedberg had argued: 'What Mr. Meshbesher did to Mr. Gainsley is something one should never be able to pull on *any*body who's been admitted to the practice of law. Mr. Meshbesher testified that from the day he served [his first complaint] he kept waiting for the other shoe to drop. He felt sure he would have to notify his own malpractice [insurance] carrier. But Mr. Gainsley, from 1976 to 1985, never raised the statute of limitations."

In October of 1976 when Meshbesher filed his original unjust enrichment complaint, he had exceeded the three-year limitation set on the filing of a wrongful death complaint, but after Wartnick's Fifth Amendment deposition in 1979, Meshbesher had a wrongful death case against the defendant. He went into action to remedy his malpractice of letting the limitations run. Meshbesher wrote a friend, a state legislator, and suggested that victims of civil wrongs caused by murder deserved equal rights with victims of criminal actions, therefore the limitation of three years mandated by Minnesota's wrongful death statute should be eliminated retroactive to any and all open cases.

During the 1979 legislative session, Meshbesher's bill enjoyed easy passage through the state House but never arrived in the Senate. In 1982 it successfully traveled the Senate's road to passage but died in the House. Meshbesher honed the two previous bills into a document acceptable to both legislative bodies and concluded, "There is no good reason why a person who may be proved to be a murderer three years and one day after the killing should escape civil liability based upon a restrictive statute of limitations." Meshbesher submitted

24. "In American jurisprudence, *voir dire* is an important part of the jury selection process. During *voir dire*, prospective jurors are asked a series of questions to determine whether or not they are fit to serve on the jury. Lawyers for both sides and the trial judge may ask questions and dismiss jurors, and it is hoped that the end result of *voir dire* is an impartial jury which will sit fairly in judgment on the case" (www.wisegeek.com/what-is-voir-dire.htm. Apr 2, 2011).

the draft to "Concerned Legislators," confident his third attempt would see passage of a new Wrongful Death Statute. On June 14, 1983, Minnesota Governor Rudy Perpich signed Meshbesher's wrongful death statute into law and Meshbesher proceeded with *Nachtsheim v. Wartnick.*

Now, in 1989, Friedberg and Snider had wanted to amend their initial complaint to include issues they believed further proved Gainsley's ineptitude and greed, his negligent practice of law. "We're asking for offensive summary judgment," Friedberg had argued before Judge Davis, "on the failure to raise the statute of limitations. There wouldn't have been a judge on any bench anywhere who wouldn't have chucked out the case if it had been raised." During this 1989 court session, Gainsley, through Mason, also made another motion for summary judgment. Davis's subsequent order did not favor the Wartnick team. Now they had a defeat to discuss.

Now seated in Snider's office, Joe raised other issues involved. "And why won't Mason stipulate our protection orders? Evers, I'm sure, can take care of himself, but that Kreuser—Dennis Kreuser—he's not gonna say a word without it." He turned to Snider. "Speaking of sleaze bags, how'd it go down in Texas?"

Snider leaned back in his chair and stared hard at the notepad in the center of his desktop. "Roger Nordstrom's a scary guy. Reeked of alcohol at nine in the morning. Unshaven, like he'd been out all night. Empty," he paused and gave an small, unconscious shake of his head, "empty, bloodshot eyes—stared at me while we were setting up. His head swiveled with this blank expression as he followed me everywhere I moved. Followed me with those empty eyes." Snider reached for his coffee. "You'll notice on the video he wore dark glasses during the actual taping."

+

August 21, 1989 – Texas Law Center, Austin, Texas

Snider checked one item off his list—Nordstrom testified he had never been contacted by Gainsley or any attorney from Moss and Barnett. "Have you ever been interviewed by the Minnesota authorities or any other authorities concerning the death of Bob Nachtsheim?"

"No." Nordstrom replied in the briefest syllables. The acrid stench of him fogged the windowless room.

"Do you know Bobby Nachtsheim, or the person we'll refer to as Bobby Nachtsheim?"

"Yes."

"And tell me how you know him, please."

"Went to high school with him; roommates for a length of time."

"When did you room with Bobby Nachtsheim?"

"Maybe four months prior to his father's death."

"So four months prior to the time Bob Nachtsheim was murdered, you were rooming with Bobby?"

Nordstrom seemed to sway slightly. "I can't recall at what time I was his roommate, or if it was after the fact. But at the time he was working at—I think it was B and B Florist, trying to keep it going."

"So you were rooming with him after Bob Nachtsheim was killed?"

"I don't recall. I don't recall the date."

"You don't have a recollection that it was before or after Bob Nachtsheim was shot?"

"I think it was after he was shot that he was trying to keep it going."

"Have you had any contact with the Nachtsheim family since 1973?"

"A time or two, but, you know, Good Lord, not probably for fifteen years."

"When was that time or two?"

"Well, you know," Nordstrom was stiff, motionless. "Run into him at a bar or a party or something."

"When did you do that?"

"I don't recall. It was just one of those things from the neighborhood, you know."

"Do you have a recollection of how you got notice that Bob Nachtsheim had been murdered?"

"If I remember right, I think Bobby told me. Or told me his father had been killed, whatever."

"Where were you when he told you this?"

"I have absolutely no idea. Possibly at the house; maybe, you know, got a phone call, whatever."

"I want to ask you some questions, now, about a party that people have testified to, and I just want you to testify to the best of your recollection on these events. Did you ever attend a party where drugs and alcohol were used and Bobby Nachtsheim was present?"

"Yes."

"You have used drugs with Bobby Kaufmman?"

"Yes."

"Okay. Have you attended a party with Bobby when he made statements that if something happened to his dad he would become part owner of his father's business?"

Nordstrom paused. "Not to my recollection. As far as I knew, it was a family business."

"You never heard Bobby make a statement that if something happened to his old man he would get fifty-one percent of the business?"

"Not to my recollection. No," Nordstrom said. The only thing that moved was his mouth.

148

"Did you ever attend a party where Bobby Nachtsheim talked about how easy it would be to rob his dad early in the morning before anyone else arrived at the B and B Florist shop?"

"No."

"Your testimony is unequivocal, I take it, Mr. Nordstrom, that you have no recollection of Bobby Nachtsheim ever making statements about 'robbing his old man'?"

"Not to my recollection. No."

"Were you ever at B and B Florist shop before Bob Nachtsheim was shot?"

"Not that I recall."

"You were only at B and B after the shooting. Is that correct?"

"As far as I recall. Yes."

"Did you talk to Bobby about the murder of his father?"

"I would imagine that we talked about it. It was one of those things that—. You know, apparently they didn't know anything about it, and, you know, we—you know, of course, your friend's father is shot, you're going to talk about it."

+

Snider set his coffee mug on his desk. "He, of course, denied any and everything—being at Bobby's when Bob repossessed the car, knowing Dennis Kreuser, selling drugs. In spite of that, we've almost accumulated enough evidence to convict him of the murder, if we were moving that direction."

The room went quiet except for the agitated drumming of Joe's fingers on the arms of his chair. Friedberg was not bothered by men like Nordstrom. He had seen life's putrid depravity and knew the hopelessness of its end. What bothered Friedberg was a different type of danger, the type which appears tidy and polished on the outside.

"We got screwed by the judge's decision on Gainsley's failure to raise the statute of limitations," Friedberg barked into the quietness that had settled in Snider's office. "He should have objected back in '76 and gotten that original case thrown out."

"That's what we argued, but Davis didn't agree."

"Well, I won't understand that decision if I live to be a hundred. Meshbesher even admitted he'd let the statute run; he had to scramble to correct his own malpractice. And Mason's still trying to establish that taking the Fifth Amendment was attorney judgment, that Gainsley flapping his jaws about the polygraph [in opening statement] was just trial strategy."

"So," Liberko interrupted, "by definition, Gainsley can't be negligent if it was just a judgment call. Correct?"

Snider nodded.

"Does Mason have any idea how bad an attorney his client is?" Severson wondered aloud.

During the next half hour, Snider and Friedberg discussed options still available to them after Davis's latest order, then they distributed assignments and dismissed the team.

"Joe." Snider halted Friedberg as he stood to leave. "Regarding Robert Sheran. He let me know that several weeks ago Phil Gainsley approached him wanting to talk about a legal malpractice problem. Sheran said because of that he felt awkward about being an expert witness on Wartnick's behalf. He'd decided not to be engaged by either side."

"Well, that'll save some serious quid. I wasn't comfortable with Sheran, anyway." Friedberg tapped the side of his head. "He's not doing so well these days."

Snider agreed. "I told him as far as I was concerned he was free to undertake engagement on Gainsley's behalf should he choose to do so. Turns out, Sheran *will* be testifying on Gainsley's behalf."

"Right," Friedberg acknowledged, then added, "Have you read Sheran's supreme court decision in Parker against Parker? I looked it up the other day. He says a plaintiff can't use the Fifth Amendment to shield himself from examination, which is exactly what Gainsley had Wartnick do. Sheran's also used the 'reasonable hypothesis of innocence' theory. If he does side with Gainsley, it's a piece of cake to impeach[25] with that. When's Norm's next deposition?"

"Tomorrow, but I've instructed him not to go. Jack had agreed to turn over all the documents to us before the next deposition. They haven't done that—we still don't have time records. I sent Jack a letter this morning and reminded him of that, so we'll see what he does."

---

25. The testimony of a witness is impeached when statements they make are inconsistent with their earlier statements; impeachment challenges the credibility of a witness. (*West's Encyclopedia of American Law*. ed 2. 2008. The Gale Group, Inc.)

CHAPTER 22

THURSDAY, AUGUST 24, 1989

Jack Mason hunched over a conference table at Dorsey & Whitney. His sandy gray hair and beard looked disheveled, even after a fresh hair cut and shave. Thick glasses magnified his grey eyes, the right one a wandering star.

The time was nine forty-five. The court reporter was the only other person in the room.

"I'm going to use the speaker phone to call Jerry Snider. You record the conversation."

"Yes, sir."

The call rang through.

"Jack Mason, here. I've a court reporter and she's transcribing this telephone call. I had previously marked as Deposition Exhibit A my letter of August 16 confirming the deposition of Mr. Wartnick to be taken at nine-thirty today and as Deposition Exhibit B your letter of August 17 in which you state, quote, You are correct that we have agreed to recommence to finish the deposition of Norm Wartnick on Thursday, August 24, 1989, at nine-thirty A.M., end quote. We have been here, now, since nine-thirty, and we ask that you appear with Mr. Wartnick."

"Jack, as you know, I sent you a letter yesterday by messenger informing you that you still had not produced all the documents to us that you had agreed to produce. I want to make sure the reporter is getting my statement as well. Is that happening?"

"Yes, sir," the reporter said.

"Great," Snider continued. "And I'd told you that we would continue those depositions as soon as you got all the files and documents to us. And you know from correspondence that's been going on, we do not have all those files and documents yet, and the letter I sent to you yesterday asked that you respond to us, particularly with respect to Mr. Gainsley's time records. We don't have those. Since we don't have those time records, I think you understood that we weren't going ahead with it today.

"You might also recall that at the second deposition session, we continued that deposition until the documents could be produced to us and we would have those documents, because it turns out that interrogatory responses and statements made by Mr. Gainsley were in error. All documents were not produced to us and you knew, at least as of yesterday, that we were not going to produce Mr. Wartnick for deposition until those documents were produced. So I assume the decision for you to go ahead and get your court reporter over and make what you perceive to be a record is basically your own doing, and I think that's fine."

"Well, first," Mason began, "the time records you requested have nothing to do with the deposition and completion of Mr. Wartnick's deposition. And second, if you did request those documents—"

"Jack, just a moment. I'm going to hang up. I am not going to enter into a telephone proceeding with you. I think I made my statement. What I'd really prefer you to say is that you'll provide the documents to us, which you have not done. If you provide the documents to us, we'll go ahead with the deposition. That was the understanding weeks ago. We don't have the documents. I think you're grandstanding, and I think you're posturing, and I see no reason to continue with this."

"Can we take the depositions of your experts, or is that also something—"

"Yes" Snider said. "I'd like to take the depositions of your two experts as soon as we can."

"When can we take Mr. Flaskamp's deposition?"

"Well, are you ready to produce Bob Sheran and Judge Kane to us?"

"When can we—"

"I think I have a question pending."

"My question precedes yours," Mason snorted.

"Jack, if you want to talk about it like a gentleman, I'll be glad to do so."

"Gentlemen honor their promises," Jack retorted.

The court reporter recorded: "May the record show that the line has been disconnected by Mr. Snider."

CHAPTER 23

ONE MONTH LATER

MONDAY, SEPTEMBER 25, 1989

The clerk of the court of the Honorable Michael Davis stood and read, "Next case, *Wartnick verses Gainsley and Moss and Barnett.*"

Judge Davis nodded to counsel from the bench. "Good morning."

Jack Mason spoke first. "Your Honor, may it please the court—"

"Counsel, note your appearances for the record," the judge interrupted.

"Jack Mason. I appear for the defendants in this matter. I'm with Dorsey and Whitney."

Accompanying Mr. Mason but not noted for the record was a young African-American associate who was not involved in the case in any way, indeed had no clue even what the case was about. Friedberg and Snider would later say it was their opinion Mason brought him along simply to sit at counsel's table, the Honorable Judge Davis also being African-American.

"Joe Friedberg for Plaintiff Wartnick in this case. Appearing with me is Jerry Snider with Faegre and Benson." Friedberg and Snider then watched Mason give an argument that, to anyone other than this handful of attorneys, made absolutely no sense. Friedberg's take was that Mason just stayed true to form and expounded on something in left field.

"May it please the court," Mason said again, "our motion substantiates two motions. Plaintiffs made that motion without any justification in fact. Second, plaintiffs failed by the promise to appear for discovery. Our proposed order asks that the court require plaintiffs to honor their promise and appear for depositions; secondly, to impose sanctions on counsel for their conduct. We need the protection of this court. Plaintiffs are represented by three attorneys and a legal assistant. They've taken seventeen depositions revealing nothing, so we recognize the Court's powers are limited, but we have presented to the Court clear evidence of a situation which requires that the Court protect us from this kind of thing. We substantiated from evidence and the law, and ask the Court to issue an order in the form prayed for." Mason sat down.

Friedberg stood. "Your Honor, may I approach the bench?" At Judge Davis's nod, Friedberg took the seven strides required to hand the Court a document. "Your Honor, there's really four things on this morning. One is the motion for sanctions because the defendant claims our request for protective order back in March was ill-founded.

"I've just presented the Court an affidavit of Dennis Kreuser that says he told our investigator he was concerned for his life and the safety of his children. In addition to that, we had the same type of evidence from Mr. Evers—he kept guns all over his house waiting for a confrontation from Mr. Roger Nordstrom and made the statement on pages twelve and thirteen that, quote, big fellows don't stop bullets, end quote.

"We brought a motion for protective order. It was denied. We gave the information and the names to Mr. Mason a long, long time ago. Prior to giving the names, we offered to him the names if he maintained the sanctity of this [request] and not tell other people about it. He turned that down. The depositions and affidavits support the fact that witnesses have been afraid for a number of years and they didn't want to come out. [Since then] they have and it's over with. Our motion for protective order was brought in good faith, no question about it.

"As far as his motion to finish Mr. Wartnick's deposition, Mr. Wartnick has appeared three times in Mr. Mason's office. Each time he's deposed, Mr. Mason comes out of the box with documents we haven't seen.

"We also said, 'Mr. Mason, give us the time records of Mr. Gainsley because Mr. Wartnick keeps getting asked about meetings with Mr. Gainsley.' We haven't seen the time records, so we can't go over them. Either Mr. Mason should say, 'Mr. Gainsley never kept time records'—which is highly unlikely since he billed on an hourly basis and Mr. Wartnick paid him over one-hundred thirteen thousand dollars—or Mr. Gainsley destroyed the time records. That wouldn't be nice but it might be true. So, either give us the time records so we can adequately prepare Mr. Wartnick for his fourth deposition or tell us they're not around. That's real simple.

"Now, we have some important motions before this Court. Mr. Mason's attempting to color us in a bad light. That's nonsense and isn't the way to practice law. He knows he won't deliver the time records or tell us why they're not here."

Mason stood again. "May I reply briefly, Your Honor?"

"You may."

"They submit for today's hearing, again in violation of the Rule, the affidavit of Dennis Kreuser hoping that the Court will accept as true what Mr. Kreuser says in this self-serving affidavit, rather than what Mr. Kreuser said on cross-examination in his deposition. There's no justification offered by way of evidence, documents, affidavit, deposition testimony, or Mr. Liberko's notes as to Mr. Evers. They made a motion as to him, too.

"So we simply are here seeking the protection of this court," Mason continued. "If it's a smear on the Faegre and Benson firm to call attention to the fact they're sending three attorneys and a legal assistant every time they appear in court or depositions, think what it means to the defendant to have the kind of things said about the defendant by Mr. Snider and Mr. Friedberg that are wholly without any justification and done for the purpose of obtaining their fee and thirty percent left goes to Ron Meshbesher."

Friedberg leaned back in his chair at counsel's table and chuckled. "If Mr. Mason can tell us how we can enhance our fees by having fifty lawyers in here on a contingent fee case, I'd like him to write it out for me so I can understand it."

CHAPTER 24

ONE MONTH LATER

MID-OCTOBER 1989

Norm paced his den as if it were the sideline of a basketball court during the last moments of a hard-fought game. "Davis recused! I can't believe it. On the eighty-eighth day of his ninety day window. Recused! Why now? Why'd he wait so late?"

"What was going on behind the scenes?" Butch wondered aloud.

That stopped Norm in mid-step. "Now *that's* a question—when you'd want to be a bug on the wall." The quick strides began again. "Witnesses were lined up, experts ready, exhibits made it a slam dunk. Phil's probably ecstatic."

Babe and Connie watched from the couch, each lost in her own misgivings.

"You know," Norm continued, "I just learned the Gainsley family's been pals with one of the other district judges for decades. Schiefelbein. Bob Schiefelbein." He stopped to glare at the wall. "I wonder if there's a connection."

"Stop." Babe stood. "No more. It only grinds dirt into the wound to start making insinuations you can't prove."

Norm spun toward her. "Don't you know what this means?"

"Just because I don't want to talk about it, you think I don't know what's going on? Of course I know what this means. It means we've got to start all over, all the way from scratch. It means this is never going to end!"

THURSDAY, OCTOBER 19, 1989

"Judge Meyers* got to Davis," Friedberg growled. "I know he did."

"And Davis did the right thing," Snider replied. "He's a fair-minded man; has integrity."

Friedberg's gaze stayed fixed on his steak and baked potato. The two men were seated at the dining room table in Snider's home. Snider's wife had suggested the location—it was quieter, more secure than the attorneys' offices or a noisy restaurant. And the two attorneys had much to discuss.

Word of Judge Michael Davis's recusal at the eleventh hour had sputtered through the courthouse grapevine. There was rumored involvement by Judge Meyers—whose chambers were near Davis's and who was a personal friend of Phil Gainsley's father. Had Meyers pushed Davis to decide in Gainsley's

* - not the actual name

favor? Made circumstances difficult for the judge? Affected his objectivity? Few people knew. Judge Davis will not discuss it, but in dealing with the situation he took the high road and removed himself from a difficult situation.

"It's unconscionable," Friedberg sawed against another chunk of steak—rare, the way he liked it, "that a man who's been through what Wartnick has should have to start over. I can't believe how much Severson said the poor guy forked over at his last garnishment hearing." He thrust the bite into his mouth and ground at it. "And he's got another garnishment hearing in less than a month. I don't see how he's making it. How long's it going to take for another judge to be seated?"

Friedberg and Snider discussed attributes and advantages of various members of the local judiciary. The name Robert Schiefelbein arose. "You know," Friedberg said, "back in the day, he and Gainsley's old man went to lunch together every week—had offices next to each other or down the hall, something like that. What are the odds Schiefelbein'll come up in rotation?"

"There are fair judges, Joe, and it's our job to push for one who's fair and impartial."

TWO MONTHS LATER

MID-DECEMBER 1989

Connie Clayman set down her cup in shock and stared across the coffee shop table at Babe. "Seventy-six-*hundred* dollars?! The guy who did your audit is either greedy or insane. Where does he think you're coming up with that kind of money?"

"No use wondering about it. We'll have to figure out something. Let's go, you still need gifts for your girls. I don't want to get too warm in here; makes it harder to go back outside."

The friends emerged from the warmth of the coffee shop into a twenty mile-per-hour arctic blast of snow. Ropes of evergreen boughs festooned with giant, red bows and strings of twinkling lights lined France Avenue; they shivered and swung and glowed outside each shop—necessities at a latitude where the sun was gone by four-thirty on winter afternoons.

Connie pulled her knit scarf up and cap down until only a slit was open to peep through then followed Babe's flapping coattail through the rush of harried shoppers. Without warning, Babe stopped. Connie followed her line of sight to a pine-green pant suit in a shop window. One glance at Babe's face revealed the depth of her longing for something new to wear, something pretty, just this once, for the scores of family gatherings and community events mandatory during this holiday time of year. It had been years since Connie's frugal friend had worn something new.

Connie prodded Babe with an elbow and nodded toward the shop door. "Have a holly, jolly Christmas" jingled as they opened the outer door of the airlock. Connie pulled her scarf below her chin, scrubbed the fuzz off her lips, and said, "You've got to at least try it on. It's been forever!"

"It'll only make it worse."

"Nonsense. It might be just the pick-me-up you need. Go on."

Before she could talk herself out of it, Babe yanked open the inner door.

"Merry Christmas," a sales clerk greeted them. "How can I help you?"

"The green pant suit in the window. I'd like to try it on."

The clerk sized her up. "I'll meet you in Dressing Room G."

Connie gave her the look that told Babe her friend was trying too hard to cheer her up.

Babe deposited her coat in a chair. "It's just a pant suit. Sit down." Several minutes later Babe stepped from the dressing room wearing the two pieces and crossed to the three-way mirror. The color was perfect with her complexion, the fit was exquisite, one of those rare times it felt as though a garment had been made just for her.

She caught her friend's expression in the glass. Connie thought the same.

The swell of fierce desire crashed against a solid wall of realism. Babe spun toward Room G. "I'm fooling myself to even toy with this."

MONDAY, DECEMBER 25, 1989 ~ CHRISTMAS DAY

Tom Evers's home smelled like smoked turkey, pumpkin pie, and beer, but a few bottles of beer were left. They had been set aside to be consumed during a rare Christmas Day edition of Monday Night Football. Evers fully expected the Vikings to trounce the Bengals.

Gifts had been opened and teenagers were fighting over the year's hot item, Nintendo's Game Boy. Evers decided to spend the afternoon finishing up long overdue inside chores.

At four-fifteen the phone rang. Evers took the finishing nails from between his lips and hollered, "Which of you knuckleheads is going to get that?" No response. He shook his head, set down the hammer, and picked up the receiver. "Evers."

The longer he listened, the more still Evers became. John Nachtsheim's voice screamed from the other end of the line: "I don't care—even if you have twenty-one guns stashed around the place, it won't be enough."

"Kid." Evers stood as unmoving as a stone fortress. "If you want to start something, you'd better carry a big one, 'cause you even seriously *think* about trying to hurt my family and you'll be laying alongside your father, but this time I'll be the one to put you there."

Dan assembled support materials for a motion they would file on Friday—Plaintiff's Third Amended Motion to Reconsider Plaintiff's Motion to Amend the Complaint. His office telephone rang. "This is Dan."

It was Tom Evers. Liberko listened, scribbled notes, then nodded. "I suggest you do so. I'll let Jerry know."

Moments later Liberko had Snider on the line. "Tom Evers just called." Liberko relayed the facts Evers had given him regarding John Nachtsheim's threats on Christmas Day, then said, "He asked whether or not I thought he should file a statement with the police. I suggested he do so. That's right. Yes, sir, I'll type that up. And actually that's why he called—said if anything happens, he wants that conversation on record."

In his own office, Snider hung up the telephone and looked through the day's mail. Correspondence included a letter from the newly-assigned case judge. *So,* Snider mused, *after nine weeks and 12 more recusals, it comes down to Judge Robert Schiefelbein.*

Pre-trial conference was set for February 22, 1990.

TWO DAYS LATER

FRIDAY, DECEMBER 29, 1989

Liberko's office phone rang. It was Tom Evers. John Nachtsheim had called again and this time his threats sounded serious.

Evers had been awakened at three o'clock that morning by an anonymous phone call Evers believed was related to John's call on Christmas Day. Evers also said his younger brother, had received the same type phone call around the same time that morning—Young Evers and John Nachtsheim had gone through school together. Evers also reported that the emergency brake cable on his brother's car had been cut and his sister-in-law had received a string of harassing, insulting phone calls.

Dan called Snider and then, at Snider's instruction, placed a call to Inspector Otto of the Minneapolis Police Department.

Within days the official request came through. Faegre was to send the MPD copies of all depositions and any other pertinent materials related to the case. Inspector Otto wanted to pull together some of the missing pieces regarding the murder of Bob Nachtsheim.

CHAPTER 25

THURSDAY, FEBRUARY 22, 1990

The courtroom of the Honorable Robert Schiefelbein, Judge of District Court, was small as modern district courtrooms go. Light walls, straight-backed chairs, one long table near the front at which representatives for both plaintiff and defendant were seated.

"Both of you have motions," Judge Schiefelbein opened the session. "Before I accepted the file, I read some of the material, so I think I can appreciate some of the flavor of the litigation, and you can assume that." He focused hard on Snider, then Friedberg. "Now, why don't we divide up the time, and I don't know who is the original moving party, but whoever that was can have five minutes of rebuttal."

"Both sides are moving, Your Honor," Friedberg said. "I think it's our motion to amend the complaint, and I believe our motion for summary judgment. Mr. Mason has motion for sanctions against us. Then there's what I generically refer to as the discovery hassles. Can't remember who moved for what there."

"All right. Fine." The silver head stayed bent over whatever the judge was reading.

"Your Honor, for the record, I'm Joe Friedberg. I represent the plaintiff, Norm Wartnick. Co-counsel is Mr. Snider and Mr. Severson from Faegre and Benson." No one looked up.

Friedberg started with Nachtsheim's death in 1973 and began a brief summary of the details of the original, *Nachtsheim v. Wartnick* case. He detailed how Meshbesher had gerrymandered his original 1976 complaint against Wartnick and had filed a veiled wrongful death complaint in his claim for unjust enrichment with the addition of a request for a million dollars in punitive damages.

An unjust enrichment complaint cannot have a request for punitive damages, though it may request *pecuniary* damages. *Pecuniary* means money; a pecuniary loss in this instance describes the financial loss a family suffers from the death of a family member. By asking for *punitive* damages, however, Meshbesher showed he was thinking about much more than just the alleged unjust enrichment. He was looking forward to a wrongful death complaint, which he could not do in 1976 because it would have pointed out the fact he had passed the time limit allowed to file that complaint.

Judge Schiefelbein interrupted Friedberg's explanation of the timeline to state he did not believe Friedberg's claim that Meshbesher's original, 1976 complaint was a veiled wrongful death action. Friedberg's assertion, Schiefelbein said, could not be substantiated.

"Your Honor, our position is that it was either a wrongful death action or it was nothing. The death was in May of 1973. Meshbesher was retained in October of '74. The statute of limitations for wrongful death expired in May 1976, and it wasn't until October of that year that Meshbesher brought his complaint.

"Now," Friedberg continued, "Meshbesher, in his deposition, said, 'That's an embarrassment to me.' He blew it. He had his own malpractice. He was not concerned to a great degree about that, Your Honor, because he didn't have any evidence that Mr. Wartnick was involved in this homicide. He was concerned about his own professional reputation—being sued for malpractice—and what he did here was gerrymandered a cause of action and entitled it unjust enrichment to get around the wrongful death statute."

"Well," Judge Schiefelbein responded, "the prayer for relief wasn't for pecuniary loss to the heirs was it?"

"No, it wasn't, Your Honor. He brought it for one-hundred thousand dollars because he didn't want what he was doing to be transparent."

"Well, the nature of the claim was the insurance policy. Correct?"

"Yes, and no. There was also a claim for a million dollars in punitive damages which, obviously, you can't tack on to [that type] claim, Your Honor."

"Well, but isn't the nature of the action contemplated an action for the injury caused by the wrongful act rather than the proceeds of an insurance policy which exist and are recoverable where there's injury caused?"[26]

"No. Not in this situation. There would be no claim were it not for the death of Mr. Nachtsheim."

---

26. This passage is confusing. During our discussions, Snider speculated, "this passage is confusing because the judge was confused. He was trying to make an argument that the insurance claim was really about the injury (death of Nachtsheim) suffered by the Nachtsheim family and not about the insurance policy. Meshbesher's complaint really made no sense because he'd let the statute of limitations run on a wrongful death action and his way of correcting that was to plead unjust enrichment for which punitive damages are not permitted; yet Ron asked for punitive damages in his unjust enrichment complaint, when under the law he was not entitled to do so.

"What Schiefelbein was trying to do with his obtuse questions is anybody's guess. One possibility is that Schiefelbein was trying to make a case that the [1976] unjust enrichment complaint against Wartnick was really a tort claim—which would probably then enable Schiefelbein to [not allow] Wartnick's malpractice claim because it was not filed within six years from the unjust enrichment action."

"Sure there would," the judge retorted. "When his death occurred, whether it was caused by injury or not, that would trigger the payment by the insurer. Correct?"

"Oh, that is certainly correct."

"Okay."

Snider could feel the judge's glow of satisfaction.

But Friedberg was not finished. "And there would be no action like this [claim of unjust enrichment]. The only thing Mr. Gainsley was right about in this case is that there was an insurable interest. There's no question about the fact that there was an insurable interest. The Supreme Court said so. But there's no such claim as unjust enrichment in this state. It's a complete nonentity. So, in this situation, the injury that takes place is what triggers the possibility of a claim."

Schiefelbein did not respond to the contradiction, so Friedberg picked up where he had left off with the timeline and eventually arrived at 1979. "An amended complaint is served in March, and the Court should look at that because in that amended complaint Mr. Meshbesher is no longer ambiguous. He accuses Mr. Wartnick of causing or procuring the death of Nachtsheim. This is clearly a wrongful death allegation. He's accusing him of murder."

Schiefelbein studied his notes rather than look at Friedberg. "What's the gist of Meshbesher's claim? That Wartnick cannot accept the proceeds of the insurance policy because he procured the death which triggered the insurance?"

Friedberg nodded. "And Meshbesher asked for punitive damages because he now squarely accused him of killing."

"Okay," the judge glanced at Friedberg. "Still no claim of pecuniary loss to next of kin?"

"I don't think so. At this point, Gainsley—who *has* Prudential's Answer which raised the issue of limitations—files his amended complaint but he does *not* raise the statute of limitations. And he does not raise the other stanza of the wrongful death statute."

"And the underlying premise of that point," Schiefelbein interrupted again, "is that it's a wrongful death statute. If it's a wrongful death action, that statute is what? Two or three years?"

"Three years," Friedberg said.

"Okay. I think it used to be two. But, in any event, the underlying premise of that argument is, if it's a wrongful death action rather than an action arising out of a contract, then the applicable statute has expired."

"That's correct, Your Honor."

"As Mr. Mason points out rather ironically, since in the [original, 1976 unjust enrichment] case Wartnick prevailed. Correct?"

"Oh, yes. He had to. And that's not a surprise. Mr. Gainsley was right about that point. There is no such cause of action. Mr. Meshbesher then goes to the legislature and gets the statute changed, because he's got a case. The wrongful death statute was *not* activated by Mr. Gainsley. The statute of limitations *was not raised* by Mr. Gainsley."

"Is that what you're asking damages on?"

"There's going to be a big issue of credibility in this case. Mr. Gainsley is going to say, despite this memorandum showing he does *not* know the ramifications of the Fifth Amendment, that he explained the ramifications of the Fifth to Mr. Wartnick. Mr. Wartnick is going to say, 'I never heard of the Fifth Amendment until he told me five minutes before the deposition, handed me a card, and told me to read it.' That's the credibility issue."

"Yes," Judge Schiefelbein acknowledged. "It's my understanding that that would appear to be not only a factual dispute but a viable claim of negligence on the part of counsel."

"There isn't much question," Friedberg continued. "After Mr. Gainsley was advised by his law clerk on the problem that he, himself, had created on the Fifth Amendment, Mr. Gainsley wrote to Mr. Meshbesher and said, I'll tell you what. I'll give you a deposition on Wartnick on the condition you don't use the first one. Meshbesher, obviously, said forget it. Gainsley never told Wartnick about that letter because he was concealing the negligent advice he'd given him.

"Now, in relation to sanctions for the protective order," Friedberg produced an enlarged copy of new pages from the Minneapolis Police files. "This is a recent police report made by Detective Otto."

"I read that," Schiefelbein said.

"We're talking about murder," Friedberg said. "If we'd had our protective order, none of these threats would have taken place. That request for a protective order was brought in good faith. People involved in this case have died since the murder."

"I must admit," the judge said, "it resurrected old memories—when I [appeared] before *your* close personal friend, Judge Lord. It was a civil matter arising out of an arson and I sought to protect the name of an informant who was a member of an arson gang. Judge Lord ordered the disclosure, and that night when the informant left the plant, the arsonists and his colleagues were at the plant gate. My witness disappeared."

"We weren't trying to keep a secret for a nefarious purpose," Friedberg said. "We were quite willing to disclose it to Mr. Mason. We just didn't want the people who *found* out about it to *find* out about it! It was brought in good faith."

The judge nodded. "I'll be interested to hear Mr. Mason's comments because I, admittedly, knew about Mr. Evers's association and that was no secret. The claim is that they weren't aware that he was now talking. Is that the situation?"

"That's correct," Friedberg nodded. "He *and* Mr. Kreuser. Both of them. I'm glad the police are involved in this case. Thank you, Your Honor," Friedberg concluded and sat down.

Schiefelbein turned to Mason.

"To me," Mason said, "the Court has already articulated—and I'm just going to jump to that so we can get that behind us. The Court has already articulated what's wrong with plaintiff's theory and has read our materials. The one thing that we didn't focus on is how it can be explained that Prudential, which did believe the Statute of Limitations, would give a seventy-five thousand dollar settlement [to the Nachtsheim family] if this was a knockout punch."

"How did the Fifth Amendment play at that trial, Mr. Mason?" the judge asked.

"It was a role in that discussion and I—that's an interesting point, Judge. An essential argument here is that, '*but for* the alleged Fifth Amendment advice and the failure to discover witnesses.' Ironically, since the day of that trial, Mr. Wartnick has submitted to deposition and they've taken extensive discovery. No exculpatory evidence has been found. But in his deposition, Mr. Wartnick admitted that the victim had quit [his employment at Midwest] and admitted that the night before the murder he, Mr. Wartnick, had played racquetball with the insurance agent who sold him the life insurance policy on Mr. Nachtsheim. He admitted in his deposition that within hours of the murder he called Mr. Gainsley to see what he should do about it. So we have substantiation from Mr. Wartnick's own lips that shows had he not taken the Fifth Amendment he would have been worse off."

Judge Schiefelbein eventually closed the hearing. "We will *not* be trying the issue regarding the so-called failure to 'assert a Statute of Limitations defense' in what this Court views as *not* [being] a wrongful death action. I want to move this case along, so let's get the show on the road."

CHAPTER 26

Monday, April 16, 1990

'73 Murder of Florist Haunts Widow, Accused Killer
by Staff Writer, *Star Tribune*

This is the story of two people crying out for justice. Both are haunted by ghosts of long ago, unable to count the sleepless nights they have spent since May 24, 1973, when Minneapolis florist Robert Nachtsheim was struck by the shotgun blast that was to kill him four days later.

The case was never solved. No one was ever arrested. But these two people—one, the accused, and the other, his accuser—have kept it alive for 17 years, suspended in a limbo of byzantine lawsuits and circumstantial evidence that seem to pose no answers, only more questions.

Liberko, Severson, and Mike Friedberg were in a small, windowless conference room. Mike organized documents in the Wartnick case. Severson had spent the last hour in his office on continued analysis of the Peter Hurkos tape transcripts; he had stepped in with a question for Liberko but stayed to hear Liberko read aloud from the *Star Trib* article.

"'Wartnick,'" Liberko continued, "'might also have been hurt by several legal tactics, one of which was pleading the Fifth Amendment—continued on page—'" Newsprint crackled as Liberko thumbed the top corners. "—eleven, thirteen, fifteen—here it is. —'one of which was pleading the Fifth Amendment, thereby declining to answer questions during questioning by [Betty] Prokosh's attorney,' and on, and on." Liberko scanned the article. "I was wanting to read you one of Norm's quotations. Here it is. 'It's like going to the batter's box with two strikes against you,' said Wartnick. 'You're going to swing at the next pitch.' Prokosh wants the strikeout.'"

"I'm sure she does," Severson quipped.

"It actually mentions," Liberko continued, "there's no evidence except, well—quote, he had just taken a large box of orchids out of the store cooler when he was shot. That's about it. End quote."

"What's the big deal about the orchids, anyway?" Mike interjected. "So he's in a flower shop. What's that got to do with why he was murdered?"

Dan looked at Mike over the top of the paper. "Or if Wartnick did it?"

"Exactly, because—"

"Because," Severson said, "the widow made some big deal about, 'it had to be another wholesale flower guy or her old man wouldn't have been getting them out.'"

"So," Mike's cocked eyebrow revealed understanding, "if it's his regular routine—"

"That shoots her statement out of the water. Exactly."

"What's she got against Mr. Wartnick?"

Mike's question hung in the air, unanswered.

"Hey," Liberko's voice again came from behind the newspaper. "It actually mentions the party at Bobby's apartment. 'Bobby said robbing the store was never discussed. Instead, he said, the conversation centered on how easy it would be to take his father's billfold—' Ha! They actually mention the bathroom door."

"Let's see that. Does it talk about the insurance?"

"Oh, sure. Right there. And look at this precious picture of Betty gazing wistfully at a tiny photo of Bob."

"They should see the video of her deposition. Not so soft and sad then."

"Mentions some of the threats received. Huh, Betty says she got one, too; says some guy with a gun actually broke into her house. Now, this is more like it. Listen to this. Prokosh says Wartnick, quote, was the only one who had something to gain, unquote—from the death of course—and she 'deeply resents that suspicion has been leveled at her and her son.' Yeah, I bet she does."

"Let's see that. Look there, a mention of the reopened police investigation." The article continued:

> In the meantime, at least two lives are stuck on a treadmill of uncertainty.
>
> Wartnick, 49, will likely spend the rest of his life making payments toward the civil judgment. He can have no checking or savings accounts and his credit is ruined. One-quarter of his salary is deducted from his biweekly paycheck. But what's much worse, said Wartnick, is that he's marked as a murderer to his friends, his acquaintances, many of whom wonder how it is that a killer is allowed to roam free. "I've lost a lot of friends," Wartnick said. "I don't sleep."
>
> Betty Prokosh hasn't slept much either. Lately, she's tossed and turned trying to figure out ways to convince someone,

anyone, that what she believes to be true is right. She said the case has made her feel like she's coming apart.

Ironically, Prokosh would benefit financially from Wartnick winning his malpractice case. That's because Wartnick would have to apply a good deal of any money he wins in the lawsuit to paying off his judgment to Prokosh.

But Prokosh said that money doesn't interest her. "I don't want that money," she said. "This whole thing isn't about money and never was. I'm glad because every time Norm sees his paycheck, he knows Bob was alive."

Dan closed and folded the paper. Severson noticed that Liberko seemed intently focused on his own, speeding thoughts; his eyes shifted left to right, back and forth as though he was speed reading the pages of a book. "Where'd you go?" Severson chuckled.

"Huh?" The query brought Liberko's thoughts back into the room. "Oh, just trying to wrap my brain around what it must be like to be Wartnick when these articles come out."

"He says the attention doesn't bother him." Severson popped the tab on another Diet Pepsi.

"Right. And Pope John Paul's not Catholic." Liberko stood and crossed to the coffee decanter. "At least this article didn't quote that stupid remark from out of nowhere that Phil Gainsley's bimbo made in that article several months ago."

"Bimbo?" Mike glanced at Liberko over the pile of documents.

"Former receptionist," Liberko said as he poured. "She swears whenever Wartnick came into the office he always greeted her with 'Hello, Killer.'" Liberko took a sip and burned his lip. "Blessed mother of—Since when has the coffee in that thing been hot?!"

Severson chuckled. "Since they brought it in while you were behind the paper."

"Could of warned me."

"What fun is that?"

"Aaaaand?" Mike said, still behind the pile of files.

"And what?" Liberko set the offending mug on the table.

"'Hello, *Killer*'? There's got to be more to that story."

"No, that's it. No one else in the office ever heard him say it or anything like it."

The receptionist's claim was never substantiated. Her willingness to make a false statement on Gainsley's behalf, however, revealed the legal community's deep desire to vindicate Phil Gainsley, even as it denied justice to an innocent Norm Wartnick.

Phil Gainsley's time records were eventually made available at Dorsey & Whitney. Dan Liberko picked them up. Friedberg and Snider examined them and noticed the date of an important, alleged meeting the week prior to Wartnick's Fifth Amendment deposition was significantly out of chronological order. Friedberg chuckled, "The ink's still wet."

The time records directly contradicted Gainsley's testimony of if and when he had discussed with Wartnick the use of the Fifth Amendment in a civil deposition. Or, to be plain, nowhere in the time log was there found any time when Gainsley might have prepared Wartnick for his February 1979 deposition nor, indeed, any indication he ever discussed with Wartnick the consequences for taking the Fifth Amendment in his civil deposition. It appeared Gainsley's time logs confirmed Wartnick's version of the story.

As significant as the time logs were, however, their appearance could not alleviate the growing concern that the real threat was no longer Gainsley so much as it was Judge Schiefelbein and the power of the judicial system.

Common thinking within the legal community is that attorneys can exceed their bounds because they want to win their case but that what a judge says is absolute truth. "There is nothing you can do [when faced with bias and prejudice in the courtroom] because of the power the judge has in our system," Jerry Snider has said. "There's a presumption that whatever a judge says is correct. All you can do is try to make your record for the appeal."

ONE WEEK LATER

APRIL 24, 1990

Judge Schiefelbein handed down his Order on Plaintiff's Motions. Their motions to amend, for summary judgment, for sanctions, attorney's fees, to set a trial date, and to compel discovery were all denied.

170

CHAPTER 27

MAY 17, 1990

Friedberg and Snider filed their Second Amended Complaint. Added was another of "defendants committed acts and omissions": Gainsley failed to "mitigate the damage done at the deposition by offering Wartnick unconditionally for a second deposition on those matters as to which he pled the Fifth Amendment privilege."

Friedberg's original complaint, filed back in January of 1988, had merely named Wartnick versus Gainsley and Moss and Barnett as the parties involved, had established the required attorney-client relationship, and had stated simply, "That Defendants were negligent in their representation of Plaintiff," and "That Plaintiff has been damaged by Defendants' negligence, which negligence proximately caused Plaintiff's damages." Friedberg had fully intended to give Gainsley plenty of opportunity to explain himself. Friedberg would back out of the case if Gainsley had done the job right.

By late February of 1989, though, sufficient evidence had been collected showing Gainsley had been negligent and, since Gainsley continually insisted he had done nothing wrong, Friedberg and Snider amended their complaint to include specifics. They claimed Gainsley failed to assert that the three-year statute of limitations had passed when Meshbesher filed the 1976 original complaint; Gainsley had instructed Wartnick to assert the Fifth Amendment during the 1979 deposition while Gainsley, himself, did not understand the results of doing so. Other specifics within the complaint included Gainsley's failure to allow Wartnick to make his own informed decision on whether or not to assert the Fifth Amendment; failure to argue that there was insufficient evidence against Wartnick in the first place; introducing inadmissible and highly prejudicial evidence into the trial during his opening statement by referring to Wartnick's refusal to take a polygraph test; and his failure to conduct even minimally adequate investigation into the Nachtsheim murder, including the failure to obtain the complete police report, failure to interview and depose key witnesses and suspects, and failure to present any alternative theories as to who killed Bob Nachtsheim.

In that February 1989 amended complaint, Wartnick's legal team also mentioned the severe emotional distress, pain, and suffering Wartnick and his family had endured with Wartnick being publicly branded a murderer.

+

Babe lowered the Buick's visor against a shaft of sunlight that pierced through a gap in the thunderclouds overhead. She wished the sun would make up its mind. She also wished the rush-hour drivers packed along Highway 100 would make up their minds. Unless someone took off her bumper first, there were only two more errands to do and she could go home. She parked in front of the cleaners and hurried inside. Two lines of customers waited, arms draped with dirty clothes.

"You here to pick up?" A spunky teenage girl with a face full of freckles and a mouth full of braces called from behind the counter. "What's the name?"

"Wartnick," Babe called back, then groaned. How could she have made that mistake again?

Silence descended heavier than the thunderstorm. Every adult in the store turned to stare.

She lifted her chin and forced lightness into her tone. "Babe Wartnick."

"How many to pick up?" Freckles smacked her gum and seemed oblivious to the riveted judgments of the grown-ups around her.

"Three." Babe stepped between the two lines and up to the counter. She prayed she had enough cash in her wallet to make this a quick exchange.

+

Friedberg and Snider were confident that both Phil Gainsley and Moss and Barnett's representation of Wartnick bespoke a fiduciary duty to the man. Friedberg and Snider felt they had proven that duty had been breached and that such breach of duty was the immediate cause of the damages inflicted upon Wartnick and his family.

In Jack Mason's response to Friedberg and Snider's Amended Complaint, he argued that Meshbesher's 1976 complaint was for "unjust enrichment," therefore the wrongful death statute of limitations could not apply. "Furthermore, if Plaintiff *had* a legitimate basis" to bring up the statute, it was too late—they had passed the six year limitation on legal malpractice claims.

Mason also asserted that Wartnick could no longer advance the opinion that Gainsley should have made efforts both to obtain the full police file and to develop alternate theories—those issues, he said, had already been addressed within Judge Davis's partially granting Gainsley summary judgment the previous October. And, Mason argued in his Response, Judge Davis had stated that determining if evidence was sufficient was a judgment every attorney had to make so was not subject to challenge.

Now, two-and-a-half years after Friedberg filed the original complaint, he and Snider filed their own Motion for Summary Judgment. They hoped the Court would find Gainsley "liable to plaintiff, as a matter of law, for all damages caused by his negligence." With their May 1990 Second Amended Complaint, they hoped Defendants would be compelled to provide complete discovery.

"Look at this. Look at this." Butch Clayman slapped the *Star Tribune* onto the kitchen table. "The shotgun's lost. It says right here, 'and the weapon found in the river back in 1974 is missing.' They don't know where it is." He slapped the article again with the back of his hand. "And Otto says the case is unworkable. Well, whodda thunk."

Norm set four Diet Cokes on the table. "Can't imagine why the guy's surprised the county attorney's file's gone missing." He shrugged. "It's on par with the rest of MPD's stellar performance in this case."

Connie came around the peninsula that separated the main kitchen from the eating area and added her bowl of lime Jell-o salad to the collection of dishes on the table. "Butch, where's that quote from Betty you read to me in the car? Let me see that. Wartnick says…. Otto says…. Here it is. Betty says she's 'tossing and turning to get someone, anyone to believe that what she believes is true.'"

"Not going to happen." Norm closed the utensil drawer. "'Cause it's not true. And even if I win this thing, she's going to get almost all the money."

The oven door banged. Salt and pepper shakers perched atop the raised back slid off and shattered onto the stove top. Norm and the Claymans turned to see a red-faced Babe grab the Dustbuster and grind ferociously at the confusion of black and white as she wiped away tears.

Connie nodded to Norm, "You going to spread out those forks or you want me to do it?"

"I got it."

Butch snapped the paper closed. "I'm tired of the grieving widow act. If Betty cared for Bob, she'd want the real truth no matter what it was."

Norm nodded. "Joe's been talking to me about possible legal action against her."

Connie's gaze was still on Babe. "How'd the recent garnishment deposition go?"

Babe set the hot dish on the table then stood there and stared at it. "Over and over, the same questions, same insinuations, same pushing, pushing, pushing—like they're trying to prove there's so much more for them to uncover. But there isn't!" She lifted her gaze to meet Connie's. "There isn't any more. There isn't *anything* anymore."

CHAPTER 28

Bruce Rubenstein, professor of history at the University of Michigan–Flint, published a detailed article in *The Minnesota Journal of Law and Politics.* He wrote,

> Early in the investigation, Krueger and Betty Nachtsheim began socializing together, often at downtown Minneapolis' Blue Ox cocktail lounge. Krueger was part-time bouncer, a side job that was considered proper then but is now against department rules.
>
> Terry Nachtsheim, Betty's daughter, sometimes accompanied her mother to the Blue Ox. She remembers Krueger's behavior there as frightening. "I remember him getting into a drunken argument with some people and waving a loaded pistol around," she says, "and I was thinking 'this guy's a cop; he could shoot somebody and get away with it.' He scared me."
>
> The fact that Krueger was working when he was at the Blue Ox came as a complete surprise to Miss Nachtsheim. "I always thought he just hung out there and drank," she says. "That was how it looked."

Rubenstein would eventually include this saga as a chapter in his compilation, *Greed, Rage, and Love Gone Wrong: Murder in Minnesota* (University of Minnesota Press. 2004).

MAY 25, 1990

Judge Schiefelbein ordered a mandatory settlement conference. "Continuance shall not be granted. Failure to comply will subject the parties to appropriate sanctions, to include the assessment of costs against the delinquent party, dismissal, or other relief as the Court may deem appropriate."

Schiefelbein would continue to push hard for settlement.

Friedberg and Snider spent the summer of 1990 attending depositions of their expert witnesses and deposing defendant's experts. While Snider's depositions of defendant's experts were brief and to the point, Mason's deposition of plaintiff's experts were lengthy, tedious processes—often extended for additional days.

Plaintiff's expert witness Marcy Wallace, a trial lawyer with over twenty years of courtroom experience, stated that she gleaned valuable information from the Peter Hurkos audio tapes: namely, Bobby Nachtsheim was shown not credible; Dennis Kreuser was also not above suspicion; Lieutenant Krueger's statements were inconsistent and, since Betty had gone over Krueger's head and accused him of being a potential suspect, he feared the ruining of his career. At the time of the interviews with Hurkos, Betty Nachtsheim could no longer live with the belief that one of her own children had committed the murder.

Wallace also stated that attorney Gainsley had exposed Wartnick to very substantial risks of punitive damages and, if he had truly been concerned about polygraph issues being raised by Mr. Meshbesher, Gainsley should have made use of motions *in limine*.[27]

Her strongest words were spoken against Gainsley's advice on the taking of the Fifth Amendment. "Mr. Wartnick would necessarily have to sacrifice the civil case if he were going to plead the Fifth Amendment. Yet Gainsley did not advise his client to sacrifice the case nor proceed as if it *were* a sacrificed civil case. Instead he proceeded as if it would be a potentially acceptable strategy."

John C. McNulty, a lawyer with thirty years of trial experience, stated, "it was erroneous and not a good idea for Wartnick to plead the Fifth Amendment in 1979. … I don't see that the client needed to have a choice, to tell you the truth. Mr. Wartnick—there is no evidence that he committed the crime. He has always denied it. And as a civil lawyer, not a criminal lawyer, I believe that people who take the Fifth should not take it if they are not guilty unless they're trying to hide some other crime that'd come out in the process. Certainly to advise somebody to take the Fifth who has not committed the crime I think would be wrong advice. My conclusion is it is malpractice. It fails to meet the standards of the community."

McNulty also concluded that "no real investigation was made of Bobby or any attempt made to get Bobby back as a witness or in some way get his testimony, to in some way back up that particular bit of information as part of an overall program where you try to shift the blame for the murder to some person other than the defendant."

Michael Berens, with the law firm of Kelly and Burns, had been a law clerk to U. S. Supreme Court Justice Harry Blackman and had accrued over twenty-five years of courtroom experience. Mr. Berens testified that Gainsley failed to exercise reasonable care regarding Wartnick's informed consent and "there are, frankly, no significant factors" which could be presented to argue

27. *In limine* (lim-in-nay) n. Latin for 'at the threshold,' a motion made at the start of a trial requesting that the judge rule certain evidence may not be introduced in trial. (http://dictionary.law.com. Accessed 4/25/2011.)

for assertion of Wartnick's Fifth Amendment rights. Mr. Berens's opinion was that Phil Gainsley did not accurately know nor did he communicate the legal ramifications in taking the Fifth and therefore "did not exercise reasonable care. ... Gainsley ought to have utilized the familiar tools that lawyers utilize [including motions *in limine*] to keep highly prejudicial information away from the jury. Having not done that is a failure to exercise reasonable care. ... I view it as crucial for him to have proposed an alternate cause for the death and let it come out in a reasonably persuasive fashion."

William D. Flaskamp, known as "Flash" and consistently recognized as one of the state's best trial lawyers, was incredulous that attorney Gainsley would have discussed Wartnick's case in front of the insurance agent, Zola Friedman. Flaskamp referenced Gainsley's statements that his preparation of Wartnick was done on the Saturday morning prior to the 1979 deposition—the date indicated by the "wet ink" record in the time log—a meeting at which the insurance agent, Gainsley said, was also present. "Well, one," Flaskamp said, "amazement that he'd discuss the sensitive nature of this with a total stranger. That was amazing to me. Attorney-client privilege just would have evaporated with that."

Flaskamp also stated, "I don't know of any 'pro' in the Fifth Amendment. If a man hasn't indicated he's guilty of the crime, I can't see anything that would be anything but disastrous by asserting the Fifth Amendment." Regarding mention of the polygraph in Gainsley's opening statement, Mr. Flaskamp had strong words. "That was gross negligence ... a gross error. I can't fathom anybody saying 'my client did not take a lie detector test,' ever. Ever."

Earl Paul Gray, former Hennepin County Public Defender, Assistant U.S. Attorney, and Assistant Federal Prosecutor, said, regarding Gainsley's instruction for Wartnick to take the Fifth Amendment, "Well, I would say that would be negligence on his part—on Gainsley's part—not to allow Mr. Wartnick to make an informed decision as to whether to assert the Fifth Amendment. ... It's nonfeasance in not sitting down with your client and letting the client decide. It's his *right* to testify or not testify."

During Mason's deposition of Gray, the deponent said, "From what I read, the only reason Mr. Gainsley gave was that he was afraid of Mr. Meshbesher and he thought his client's demeanor and personality would be a problem, and that just doesn't cut mustard with me. I don't think that's a justifiable reason, number one, and number two, I don't think Mr. Wartnick made it; I think Mr. Gainsley made it and I think he made a mistake, and I think he compounded that by not sometime after that scheduling a deposition without any *quid pro quo.*

"I don't think," Gray continued, "a lawyer with knowledge of the law and the facts in this area would have done what Mr. Gainsley did. I just can't believe that a competent lawyer trying a case as important as this would have done that."

"In the course of your practice," Mason then asked, "from time to time you receive telephone calls from persons who believe themselves to be suspected of a crime. Is that true?"

"Yes."

"When a lawyer of competence in a *criminal* area receives such a phone call and the client questions whether he ought to, or she ought to talk to the police, what should be your general advice or a lawyer's general advice on that subject?"

"Well," said Gray, "the first thing I would do is ask them to come in and talk to me on a one-on-one basis and establish a lawyer-client relationship; find out what the facts are as the person sees them. After that, make a decision whether or not he or she should talk to the police."

"And what would be the factors for and against talking to the police?"

"Well, basically—unless I've been provided copies of the police reports—I very seldom allow my clients to talk to the police. The factors against it would be anything that's said that could be held against the person. You don't know if you have all the facts."

"So the risk you're guarding against," Mason asked, "is that a client would unwittingly give to the police a fact which could assist in the conviction of the client even though it's a seemingly innocuous fact?"

"Yes."

"So one of Mr. Gainsley's initial responsibilities as Wartnick's attorney was to assist Wartnick in avoiding indictment and avoiding conviction for murder?"

"Yes."

"And that assignment really continued right up to the time Mr. Gainsley stopped representing Wartnick?"

"It stopped at one point in time because he had referred his client to a criminal lawyer named Douglas Thomson."

"Getting back to the scenario you described earlier ... where the client decides not to testify, you would put on the record that you've told them they have the option to testify and you've advised them and they've made the election. Correct?"

"Yes. In a trial, yes. Outside the hearing of the jury, of course."

"And you'd do the same thing if a client elected not to testify and put on the record—"

"No," Gray cut off the repetitious question and reasserted, "If he chose *not* to testify, I'd do it. If he chose *to* testify, then I wouldn't [because] he's taking the stand."

"You wouldn't record, out of the hearing the jury, the fact that you told the client he had an option not to?"

"No, I wouldn't do it then. Just if he's asserted the Fifth. If he decided *not* to testify, because you have to put it on the record that it's *his* decision. *It is his decision.*"

Mr. Gray had thoughts on another aspect of the case, as well. "In [Gainsley's] final argument—and the whole trial of his case—he didn't come up with any theory of defense.

"The guy was murdered. No question about that. And your client has a hell of a motive, and you have a preponderance of evidence, you'd better find the other alternatives or you're going to lose and lose big."

"What?" Mason asked.

"I've experienced that. In this case there *were* alternative theories. I thought one of them—well, maybe I'm getting off the track, but—"

"Well, go ahead."

"Krueger having sex with the widow. I would've had some fun with that."

"In what way? How would that lead to suggesting an alternate suspect?"

"Don't know as much as an alternate suspect so much as she's the Plaintiff, isn't she? If she was loose right after the death, she probably was loose before. Who knows if she had a boyfriend? Who knows if she didn't have a gun? Who knows? Even if they would have said, 'Well, she didn't do it,' I think in my mind it would have diminished the damages, you know, because maybe she did do it. At least she wasn't going to have that much of a loss because she was in bed with some other dude shortly after.' And this was a cop that was supposed to be investigating the case, which is just not done. I mean, that's like it came out of a mystery novel or something."

"Or," Mason said, "on the other hand, the jury might conclude, 'This murder had such a horrible impact on her it even led her to this kind of behavior,' and increase the damages?"

"Sure, I agree with you they may have done that. But it just seemed to me that woman might've had some loose morals before her husband died and, you know, jurors read books and they like to think that the spouse did it or hired somebody to do it."

"And the problem with suggesting robbery as a motive," Mason continued this previous line of questioning, "is that the victim had a big wallet sticking out of his pocket. Right?"

"Well, you *could* use robbery, too. Clearly you could use robbery. The guy blew his head off, went for his wallet, heard something, panicked, and ran— or maybe he stole something else, or maybe somebody came on the scene. Robbery isn't ruled out because the billfold's there."

Mason changed the subject. "As far as interviewing witnesses, there would be no reason to do that if you've already got the interviews from the police, would there?"

"Oh, yes. Especially in a civil case. What happens if one of these witnesses take the Fifth Amendment—like Bobby Nachtsheim or somebody? That'd just blow [Betty] Nachtsheim's case out the water, I think. And you don't know what this kid will do, because—just exactly what happened in this case—Gainsley was cross-examining, I think it was Krueger, and tried to get in these hearsay statements, and he was blown out of the water. He had to call the person. That's the one thing nice about civil cases: you've got all that discovery."

"Did you form a conclusion as to whether Gainsley would have learned something by interviewing these witnesses that they didn't say in the police report?"

"I guess I couldn't form that conclusion because I don't know what the witnesses would have said, but I know one thing: if you have your investigator talk to them—I would venture the guess that if that'd been done these guys wouldn't have talked to him because they didn't have to; then I would have laid a subpoena on them or taken their deposition and said, 'Isn't it true in 1986 Mr. Jones went to talk to you and you wouldn't talk to him? Who told you not to? Do you have something to hide?' – Play the same darn game Meshbesher was playing."

"If you had taken the deposition of Bobby, you'd have put into admissible evidence his denial of the murder and his establishment of an alibi, wouldn't you?"

"Yes, but as I read those police reports, he was gone for a period of time, partying that night and doing drugs. I think you'd take his deposition. He didn't have a plausible explanation."

"You don't need Bobby present to suggest to the jury that he did it. Right? I mean, it isn't Perry Mason where if you have him there he'll say, 'Oh, you got me.'"

"Yes, you want to put him on the stand," Earl Gray said, "and explain what he was doing that morning, even if he denies it. That's what you want to put in front of this jury: 'Look at what this kid was doing.' Yeah, you do have to have Bobby there. I wouldn't expect him to admit it. I'd want him to deny it."

"Or you'd want him to be *not* present at all," Mason said. "That would also have implication, wouldn't it?"

"I don't know how you could get into that information if you don't have him there. I mean, that's what happened to Gainsley. He tried to get it in through Krueger and he got blocked."

"It's clear," Mason said, "at least from reading Meshbesher's final argument, that he drew the conclusion that Gainsley was pointing the finger at Bobby?"

"Yes. Yes, in fact, I thought—"

"And then [Meshbesher]," Mason interrupted, "made the argument, 'How dare he make such a suggestion? We all have arguments with our kids, but they don't murder us for it.'"

"Right. And he also said there was no evidence of anything to tie Bobby into this; it was just Gainsley's assertion—which [Meshbesher] was right on, too, because there wasn't any evidence. Gainsley didn't have the evidence. I know what the police reports say, and I know if you did your proper investigation you'd be able to get into evidence and make a reasonably good argument that there is more than one suspect in this case, because the strongest motive in the world—'And we all know, ladies and gentlemen of the jury, that almost all murders such as this happen within the home by family members.'"

THREE MONTHS LATER

AUGUST 3, 1990

Jack Mason filed a motion with Judge Schiefelbein to grant Defendant summary judgment as "particularly appropriate here because plaintiff's claims are based upon disputes as to the exercise of judgment. Malpractice may not be premised on judgmental decisions."

AUGUST 21, 1990

Betty Nachtsheim-Prokosh filed to stipulate that she would receive both "notice of the receipt of any monies paid," and "a judicial lien on the proceeds of the verdict, judgment, or settlement." It was so stipulated.

LATE AUGUST 1990

Minneapolis Police Department Inspector Otto informed Dan Liberko there was insufficient evidence to move any further on the Nachtsheim murder case.

Not only was the shotgun no longer in the possession of Minneapolis's law enforcement but the Hennepin County Attorney's office had no file and no record of where the file might be. It was assumed within the County Attorney's office that they had 'accidentally destroyed' every trace of the file on this open murder investigation, ostensibly as the department progressed into the computer age. The bulk of the MPD file was also missing, and Krueger testified he no longer knew where his copy was. "I've moved around quite a bit, lately," he told Snider. "Must've lost it during one of the moves." Friedberg and Snider were both unmoved by his plight and forced to proceed without what could have been vital information.

People who may otherwise be responsible employees can find themselves at a point where it seems more profitable to be induced to speak or act against better character, caught in compromising situations, or ignore a colleague's callousness or cowardice rather than lose their job or deal with other unpleasant working conditions. Did that occur in this case? People driven by an agenda are manipulative, influential, and easily sniff out sheep to do their bidding. Does that explain this tangled bungling of the evidence? If so, who were the manipulators? What were their goals? Too many of those involved are gone, their stories locked away by death, as unretrievable as the County Attorney's file on Bob Nachtsheim's murder.

CHAPTER 29

FOUR MONTHS LATER

DECEMBER 20, 1990

Snider's office telephone rang. It was Schiefelbein's secretary: "I could mail Judge Schiefelbein's Order to you, or you can come pick it up." Snider decided sooner was better. At the courthouse, he received the packet of papers and, as one page flipped to the next, Snider became more and more flabbergasted.

Unable to settle the case, Judge Schiefelbein ordered Plaintiff's Second Amended Complaint dismissed with prejudice.[28] Schiefelbein also ordered Gainsley's Motion for Summary Judgment "granted in its entirety." Judge Schiefelbein had declared Norm Wartnick's case dead in the water.

Snider wondered how could they lose on every single count on a summary judgment motion.

It was a long walk back to the office. When he arrived, Snider called Friedberg. "I picked up Schiefelbein's Order. The fix is in."

Friedberg was silent.

"This is beyond a mere decision," Snider continued. "You just can't lose a case this way if you're given a fair hearing."

Friedberg's disappointment was palpable, and yet—was Schiefelbein's Order so bad it was almost good? Friedberg and Snider had both lost cases, but not this way, not losing on every single point they had tried to make, on every single thing the judge could rule against them on.

Snider braced himself for the onset of 'See, I told you it was a no-good case' from certain Faegre partners and began making notes regarding Schiefelbein's overwhelming ruling.

---

28. *Dismissal with prejudice* means the case is dismissed and the plaintiff can never again pursue legal action on the same claims. Dismissal with prejudice is a final judgment. A court has inherent power to dismiss an action with prejudice if there is a failure to offer admissible evidence that shows disputed issues of material fact. (Jerry Snider)

Friday, January 11, 1991

The Wartnicks had to come up with $5,110.56 toward the judgment against Wartnick. Their family's holidays had been smaller and quieter than even the recent past, but they were together. Babe had become skilled at adapting to each new circumstance, so few acquaintances realized the depth of the growing darkness that hung over them.

SEVEN MONTHS LATER
Monday, July 15, 1991

Friedberg slammed the arm of the chair. "What are the odds it'll even *get* a fair hearing?" He rose, checked his watch, sat back down, and swore. The Wartnick team had decided to appeal.

Snider shifted forward to sit straighter, flipped open the file on his desk, and uncapped his pen. "We'll win if it gets a fair review—"

"You really believe that?" Friedberg said with the pitch of his voice toward the top of its range. "*You*'ve argued in Appellate Court."

Snider rested the pen on the table. "We both know it's illusory to believe the Appellate Court always gives cases the consideration they deserve, but—no, let me finish—but this is a good case, and Norm Wartnick—"

"Wartnick deserves it. Who are you talking to here?" Silence thudded into the room. Moments passed, then Friedberg tried again. "So, what are we gonna say that's any different than what we've already said?"

"Joe, let me tell you something that happened back in January." Snider leaned a forearm on the table's edge. "Not too long after Schiefelbein's order came down, I met again with the litigation committee. They supported our efforts, but after the meeting Faegre partner Bob Oliver pulled me aside and said, 'You've got to get rid of that no-good case. You and I both know you're only wasting more time with it if you appeal.'

"I said, 'It's a good case. He deserved fair and speedy justice,' but Oliver was adamant. 'It's an embarrassment to our firm that you're going after my friend, Phil Gainsley!'

"Later—hold on, there's more. That was in January. Last week, I was walking and chatting with Bob and we passed Gainsley. I said, 'Morning, Phil.' He nodded, acknowledged me—and Bob Oliver had no idea who we'd just passed. Didn't know Gainsley from Adam, but he knows Judge Meyers's whole family."

"It's got to be force exerted by Meyers," Friedberg said.

"To let anyone exert that type pressure is to forfeit our right to seek justice. We fight this—within the law, but we show justice is possible."

"At least Davis left us a case to try," Friedberg grumbled. "Schiefelbein's summary judgment opinion was terrible. It's astounding how judges are given such deferential treatment in this system. They can do no wrong unless you can *prove* they have."

"Odland voluntarily disqualified himself," Snider reminded him. "Acknowledged his bias—said he couldn't hear the case because he was in the county attorney's office with Krueger back in the '70s and thought Wartnick was guilty. That's two of the three presiding judges, Davis and Odlund, who've done the right thing."

"Well," Friedberg still looked ready to burst, then gradually he exhaled. "Okay." Now he inhaled deeply and tipped his chair backward. "Let's get started polishing your argument and hope for the best. Steve finish going through those Hurkos tapes?"

"Here are a few choice morsels." Snider pulled Severson's report from a file and passed it to Friedberg, who read a number of important, private admissions that Betty Nachtsheim had made during her visits with the psychic back in May of 1974:

- o Dennis Kreuser hated her guts. Bobby told her Kreuser would kill them both.
- o Bobby admitted he'd told someone Bob Nachtsheim always had a lot of money in his wallet.

A bulb lit in Friedberg's mind. "A lot of money in his wallet. Didn't Bobby say in his deposition he'd told someone his dad always carried something like five or six hundred dollars?"

"That was Betty or Krueger, I believe."

"But the police report said his wallet was protruding from his pocket and he only had $300 on him when they inventoried his belongings."

"Okay."

"There's $200 missing—the price Betty alleged Nordstrom said he'd kill a man for."

Snider's eyebrows rose. He settled back in his chair and rubbed his jaw through his beard for several seconds then said, "Impossible to prove. I wouldn't even mention it." He leaned forward again and picked up his pen. "But it gets better. Keep reading."

- o A representative of the local crime organization came into B and B when it first opened. Bob had kicked them out.
- o Betty asked Russ Krueger if he had killed her husband; she heard he had done things like that and thought he might have done it or knew who did.
- o The crime boss threatened Betty over her accusations against Russ Krueger.
- o Krueger had told her that it would hurt her more if the police actually solved the murder.
- o Krueger told her Bobby killed her husband.

o   Betty said she could not live her life thinking her kids had killed their dad.

"What a family." Friedberg leaned back and took a deep breath. "Too bad you can't bring up any of this in Appellate Court on Thursday."

FIVE WEEKS LATER

Wartnick managed, with Babe's help, to pull together the new garnishment demand: $9,937.62. He also wrote a letter to Snider:

"I want you to know that Babe, my children and myself really appreciate what you and your law firm have done for us over the last 3 years. There are times I thank God for folks like you. … Until I met you and your firm I had lost faith in what most people call law.

"It is truly amazing that it has been 3 years. It seems like yesterday when we took Phil's deposition. At that time it looked like an easy case to get to the jury. Not necessarily easy to win but at least get a chance to be heard. Little did anyone of us know what we were up against. You took depositions of some of the weirdest and in some cases most dangerous people I have ever seen or met.

"I can't tell you how many times I have tried to defend the court system to my friends when they've asked. … I've had to make a lot of changes in my life over the last 20 years. … Jerry, I'm scared. I don't have much going for me now. I know we are still hanging on the appellate court ruling but to tell you the truth what scares me is what is next. I'm going to be 51, soon 60. I work 12 to 15 hours a day now. I know I can't keep that up. …

"I fear for the time when you say, 'Norm, we've done what we can.' I've dreamed of the day I would be free of this curse, the day I could work only eight hours then go home and cut the grass. Does it appear to you that some people are meant to be winners and others to be losers?

"I love life. I have tried to stay calm during the storm. I'm not sure I can make it. But for the grace of God go I. Not a bad saying.

"Your friend always, Norm."

CHAPTER 30

SIX WEEKS LATER

WEDNESDAY, OCTOBER 2, 1991

Appellate Judge Roland Amundson[29] rubber stamped Schiefelbein's district court order that granted Gainsley summary judgment.

At Faegre, partner Bob Oliver mocked, "That's really too bad, Jerry. I guess you think you've got to keep going." Snider nodded politely and kept walking.

"We clean our house from the inside, Jerry," Oliver's words reverberated down the quiet corridor. "Your career may do better when you decide to keep that in mind."

Ten days later, Snider was inducted as a Fellow in the American College of Trial Lawyers[30] at its annual meeting in Boston.

SATURDAY, OCTOBER 26, 1991

Friedberg, Snider, and Wartnick sat around a late dinner at Senser's Sports Bar and Grill. The Minnesota Twins were in the World Series and the Twins were down two games to three. Every pair of eyes in the place was fastened onto a television screen for Game Six—all pairs but three.

Wartnick pushed a bit of sirloin around his plate. "I don't see what the problem is. They either accept it or they don't."

"Requesting a Supreme Court review should never be taken lightly," Snider said. "It's never trivial—in this case especially."

"Why this case? You mean because I'm going after a lawyer?"

Friedberg propped his elbow on the table and bore down on Wartnick. "You have any idea what the buzz is at the courthouse?" He took a side glance at Snider. "Or at Faegre?"

---

29. In 2002, Roland Amundson was found guilty and sentenced to two years in prison for embezzlement of over three-hundred-thousand dollars from a trust fund set aside for the care of a severely mentally disabled woman. Then-Hennepin County Attorney, Amy Klobuchar, made a name for herself in the Amundson case when she went after a sitting judge. (http://news.minnesota.publicradio.org/features/200202/26_stawickie_coajudge/ and http://www.nytimes.com/2006/01/13/national/13inmate.html. 5/12/2011.)

30. Less than one percent of all attorneys in any state are inducted into the College. Jerry Snider achieved this fairly early in his career. Joe Friedberg was also inducted into the College.

"Faegre?" Wartnick turned to Snider. "Like what? I thought you said they were behind you."

"Most are. Some, though, tell me I should get rid of the case."

"Who—what—"

"I tell them it's a good case—because it is, Norm. If we can find a fair and level playing field, the facts will stand on their own."

A groan rippled among the bar's patrons as the Braves' shortstop, Belliard, slid safe into second base.

Snider leaned toward Wartnick. "But just because we petition for review doesn't mean they'll accept it."

"They only review about one in eight cases," Friedberg shrugged, "and those are almost always criminal. To get a review of a civil case is, well—"

"—almost nil," Snider finished.

The crowd groaned loudly as two runs crossed the plate for Atlanta.

Friedberg, Snider, and Wartnick withdrew, each man into his own thoughts, so absorbed not one of them realized the Twins were back up to bat.

"But it's worth a shot, at least!" Wartnick said into the tension of the fifth inning. "It's not your lives that have been racked up by this thing. If we lose this, I've got, got—"

Friedberg watched the throbbing in Wartnick's jaw and glanced at Snider.

The crowd erupted as Dan Gladden crossed the plate on Kirby Puckett's fly ball to center field. The Twins were up by one.

Wartnick chewed his last bite, turned toward the game, and willed himself to relax. Friedberg and Snider would not make a decision tonight no matter how hard he pushed.

The Braves tied it in the top of the eighth inning. It stayed tied through the top of eleven. Now Kirby Puckett was back at the plate and took ball one.

"Hey, guys." Wartnick turned back to Friedberg and Snider.

Puckett watched strike one cross the plate.

"Come on," Wartnick said. "If the Twins can win the Series, surely we can petition the supreme court."

Puckett took ball two. Friedberg responded with a lopsided grin.

Snider said nothing, simply turned toward the television screen in time to see the Braves' pitcher hang a changeup toward the plate. Puckett's muscles rippled as he launched the pitch into the left-center-field seats. The restaurant crowd erupted. Snider glanced back at Friedberg as Jack Buck's voice hollered into history, "And we'll see you tomorrow night!"

Friedberg shook his head and swallowed the last of his beer. "Think the Twinkies have a Game Seven left in them?"

188

Wartnick petitioned the Minnesota Supreme Court for review of *Wartnick v. Gainsley and Moss & Barnett.*

CHAPTER 31

SIX MONTHS LATER

TUESDAY, MAY 5, 1992

Jerry Snider presented oral argument before the Minnesota Supreme Court in the case of *Wartnick v. Gainsley and Moss & Barnett.*

FIVE MONTHS LATER

FRIDAY, OCTOBER 2, 1992

The State of Minnesota in Supreme Court filed their decision which included: "the presentation of conflicting expert testimony regarding whether an attorney's actions met the appropriate standard of care raises questions of material fact, making summary judgment inappropriate." The Opinion was written by Justice Sandra S. Gardebring.

Schiefelbein erred in granting a summary judgment. Now it was going back to him for trial.

TWO MONTHS LATER

MONDAY, DECEMBER 7, 1992

Jerry Snider appeared before Faegre's in-house Litigation Policy Committee. Legal minds debated grounds to request Judge Robert Schiefelbein recuse himself from the case at hand: "But will Schiefelbein believe he's actually done anything for which he *should* recuse himself?"

"He's been close friends with the defendant for years. Any judge is obliged to recuse if there's any appearance—"

"There's no law against friendship," Bob Oliver jumped in. "You'd have to go out state to find someone not on first-name basis with half the attorneys in the county."

"It's the *appearance* of impartiality that matters. In this case there seems to be definite prejudice and appearance of, an abundance of—"

"Schiefelbein's never going to admit that."

"Not with his chronic case of black-robe-itis. This is a waste of time and resources."

"Then we have to give him an out."

"I agree. Some way to recuse and still save face."

"Well, Schiefelbein's original order giving Gainsley summary judgment just shouts partiality."

"Why did Davis recuse?"

"No one knows. He won't talk about it."

"God, he would have been a good one to have presiding."

"Isn't it *U.S. v. Hollister* that states it's fundamental to our judicial system to avoid even the appearance of impropriety?"

"I think, rather, that it states that avoiding the appearance of impropriety *is as important* to developing public confidence in the judiciary as avoiding the impropriety itself."

"Well, that'd be a start."

"You'll never prove it," Bob Oliver leaned back in his chair.

"Gentlemen," Snider said, "if I might draw your attention to the district court's ruling against us on the same issues which the Supreme Court said *are* involved in this case." He flipped through several pages of a stapled sheaf. "Here. Schiefelbein states, 'There are no genuine issues of material fact as to whether Gainsley was negligent or whether his conduct caused plaintiff's damages.'"

"And the high court obviously disagreed."

"Yes," Snider said. "They held there were definite questions of material fact which could not be decided without a full trial."

"Issues they said were central to this case?"

"Like what?" Oliver demanded.

Snider answered calmly. "Plaintiff's claim that the defendant failed to mitigate the damages from his repeated assertion of the Fifth Amendment in his initial deposition."

"That's a big one."

"Exactly. Judge Schiefelbein obviously rejected all expert testimony and reached his own conclusions about standards of care."

"I think you have cause, Jerry. If the Court already thinks plaintiff's claims have no merit then a request for recusal is in order."

"Jerry, do the research, write the brief, and get back to us," concluded managing partner Jim Halls.

"I want to read everything before any motion's filed." Bob Oliver threw his pen to the table top and crossed his arms in front of his chest.

"Good. Anyone else want to read it before it's filed?"

"Absolutely."

"I think that goes without saying."

Agreement was reached and the memorandum was drafted, then reviewed and approved by the committee. Snider filed his motion on Wednesday, December 16, 1992.

THURSDAY, FEBRUARY 25, 1993

Judge Schiefelbein's order was short and simple: "Based upon all the files, records, and proceedings herein, it is hereby ordered that Plaintiff's Motion for Disqualification is denied."

CHAPTER 32

TWO WEEKS LATER

MARCH 10, 1993

Jack Mason sent Friedberg and Snider his Defendants' Second Supplemental Response to Plaintiff's Interrogatory No. 3, Set 1.

> The Honorable Stanley Kane, identified in a previous interrogatory as an expert witness for defendants, is now deceased. His deposition testimony may be used at trial.
>
> In general, defendants anticipate that their experts will testify that Mr. Gainsley's representation of Norm Wartnick met the applicable standards of care, that the alleged incidents of malpractice upon which plaintiff relies were not negligent, were legitimate exercises of an attorney's judgment, and were not a substantial factor in the outcome of the *Nachtsheim v. Wartnick* litigation.

APRIL 23, 1993

Norm Wartnick, the referee, knows that wasted ticks of the clock lose games. The year 1993 marked the seventeenth year Wartnick had borne the pressure of Betty's extreme attempts to garner all benefits from Bob Nachtsheim's death. Even if Wartnick ultimately won his case against Gainsley, he could never regain that lost time. In those years of calling games, though, Wartnick had learned that to dwell on the lost time was to entertain discouragement, and discouragement led to ultimate loss. Norm refused to entertain that type of defeat.

The Wartnicks paid $10,411.98 toward Betty's judgment against him.

MAY 20, 1993

Friedberg and Snider sent to Mason their Plaintiff's Supplemental Response to Defendants' Interrogatory No. 25:

> In addition to the previously identified expert witnesses, Wartnick intends to call F. Lee Bailey as an additional expert. Mr. Bailey is expected to testify as follows: that Mr. Gainsley accepted a case which was well beyond his level of competence,

failed to bring in qualified help from an experienced trial lawyer, and badly botched his client's case as a result....

Mr. Bailey is expected to testify on the issue of proximate cause that application of the 'but for...' test yields a very clear answer, declared by [attorney] Meshbesher on the day of the [1979] deposition: '[but for] your advice, I didn't have a case.'

FOUR MONTHS LATER

EARLY SEPTEMBER 1993

Snider introduced Wartnick to the newest member of his team. "Norm, this is Chuck Webber. Dan's become a law clerk with another firm in town and Severson's a partner now, here at Faegre, and needs to give more attention to his practice. I invited Chuck to come and give us a hand."

Wartnick wondered if Webber was up to the challenge. Tall, dark-haired, and lithe, Webber seemed more polished, television news anchor than hard-nosed attorney.

"Chuck's already researched both judicial bias and damages awarded in malpractice cases," Snider said.

"That's right, Mr. Wartnick," Webber extended his hand. "I'm looking forward to helping you any way I can."

The kid had a firm grip. Wartnick watched Webber nod at Snider and exit the office.

"When we get through here, Norm," Snider said, "I'll introduce you to Walter Duffy. As you know, Judge Schiefelbein is always keen to settle. Joe and I've been wondering the best way to go about it—we seem to have developed some animosity between us and Mason. Too much punching, so to speak." Snider smiled and turned toward his chair behind the desk. "Actually, it was Chuck's idea to bring in Duffy—and you might be interested to know Duffy's acquired the nickname 'Pioneer' since he has a tendency to be an early settler." He chuckled at Wartnick's wary expression and retrieved a notepad from his desktop.

Wartnick seated himself at the front side of Snider's desk.

"According to Lee Bailey," Snider flipped several pages and found the spot he wanted, "it was negligence on Mr. Gainsley's part to not reopen the deposition so you could answer all of Meshbesher's questions. Gainsley was under obligation to undo the mistake—to admit it—perhaps even become a witness to testify that the mistake was his and not his client's—yours."

"So he should have let me answer like I wanted to."

"You, actually, Bailey says, had no right to even claim the Fifth. He believes that the self-protection of the Fifth Amendment is a right and a privilege and, being an innocent person with nothing to hide, you weren't in a place to have that right available. No guilt, no Fifth."

Wartnick absorbed the information with an air of relief.

"And mentioning the lie detector in his opening statement, he says, is a mainstay of our case. Without those two mistakes, Bailey says, the case would never have reached a jury."

"He studied the case that well?" Wartnick finally spoke. "Will he testify?"

"He knows the legal issues, Norm, and he said he'd be glad to testify on your behalf—*if* we go to trial."

Wartnick straightened. "What do you mean, '*if*?'"

"The push is strong from Judge Schiefelbein to settle this, and we're running out of viable options."

"What—"

"Judge Schiefelbein's refusal to recuse leaves us very few alternatives. We either fight for the best settlement we can get or we proceed with a trial which is likely to be very contentious—to get very ugly. That's not what I want," Snider leaned toward Wartnick. "But I promise you there will never come a time when I say, 'Sorry. We did the best we could.' If I have to, Norm, I'll leave the firm and try the case on my own."

"But—"

"I stepped up to go to bat for you, Norm. Fortunately there are enough people here at Faegre who think we're doing the right thing—one of the advantages of a big firm—and," Snider smiled, "our God tells us that what He thinks is good, what He requires is for us to do justice, to love kindness, and to walk humbly with Him. So," he leaned back in his chair, "have we mentioned anything to you about ALAS?"

Wartnick blinked as he tried to absorb all he had just heard.

"No? They're officed in New York—an insurance company—that is, they provide liability coverage for big, member law firms like Moss and Barnett. If you win your case against Mr. Gainsley, the money for the settlement would not come from Gainsley but from ALAS because they carry Moss and Barnett's malpractice insurance."

Wartnick shrugged.

"I mention this because ALAS has asked me to come to New York—both Jack Mason and me. They're going to push to settle this thing, Norm, so," Snider uncapped his pen, "let's talk about realistic amounts we could settle for."

ONE WEEK LATER

WEDNESDAY, SEPTEMBER 15, 1993 – NEW YORK CITY

"Hello. Joe? Joe, are you there?" A burst of static. Snider yanked the receiver away from his ear. "Seems our connection's not very good." Friedberg agreed.

"Just got out of the meeting with Mason and the ALAS representative," Snider said. "Name's Mendrzycki. No, like 'mends,' as in 'He mends a garment.'

An unfortunate analogy. Right. Right, but he had no interest in settling. No, totally closed his eyes to the evidence. Of *course* we showed negligence—and causation. The meeting itself? About ten minutes. We were totally rebuffed. I don't even know why they called us to come out here." Snider listened. "Interesting observation. What *does* he know that we don't?"

"Don't ask me," Norm held Babe's jacket for her to slip into it. "Butch just said, 'We're taking you two out tonight.' You ready to put this on?"

"Why would he do that? No, I'm already too warm. Did he say if he would try to make it to the trial on Monday?"

"No one needs to be there Monday. It's only the first day. Jerry says they'll hash out rules and stuff, then they'll pick a jury and yada yada. Things'll probably get going on Tuesday—"

"Don't you 'yada yada' me, Wartnick! Nothing about this thing's been routine *or* easy!"

CHAPTER 33

Attorneys gathered within chambers before Judge Schiefelbein. "Counsel, please indicate your appearances for the record," the judge requested without looking up from the files open on his desk.

"John M. Mason with the firm of Dorsey and Whitney, with Ed Magarian who is also with Dorsey and Whitney."

"I'm Jerry Snider with Faegre and Benson, representing Norm Wartnick."

"And I'm Joseph Friedberg with the mega-firm of Joseph S. Friedberg, Chartered, representing Mr. Wartnick."

"Walter J. Duffy, Jr., Faegre and Benson, with Mr. Snider and Mr. Friedberg."

Then the Court acknowledged Mr. Friedberg to speak.

"Your Honor, first there are two issues we believe should be revisited. The first one indeed should be first, because I'm going to ask the Court to reconsider our motion for recusal. In order to do that, I need to reminisce a bit." For several moments Friedberg recounted Judge Davis being the first judge to preside over the case, then said, "after sitting on some important motions for somewhere around ninety days he—to everybody's surprise, I believe—recused himself without giving a reason, as is his right. I've never understood why he did it. I did ask him one day if I had anything to do with it, if I'd done anything wrong, and his answer was no. Outside of that, I have no further insight into it.

"The case was assigned here," with a nod Friedberg indicated Judge Schiefelbein, "and his Honor, to use the vernacular, threw the case out in relation to all causes of action. In addition to that, his Honor threw this case out on Mr. Mason's motion to dismiss for statute of limitations grounds, which was never considered by the Court of Appeals. And it has always been my belief, and I believe shared by Mr. Snider, that in addition to dismissing our case—which is never a good feeling—the Court did make more than a few gratuitous comments which gave us insight into what appears to be the Court's feelings that this is just a case of 'hindsight is 20/20' and we're picking on a lawyer.

"I believe that the findings of fact made by this Court were really without foundation. The Court of Appeals did *not* look behind this Court's finding of fact and it affirmed this Court. The Supreme Court *did*, however, look behind the findings of fact and determined that on three or four grounds, at least, we're entitled to submit this case to the jury.

"When it was remanded to this Court, we brought a motion to recuse based, really, on the fact the Court had taken a rather harsh position in the first place. Some things have happened over the past months. On several occasions, Judge Meyers—who used to have chambers next to Judge Davis—has gratuitously made comments to members of the Faegre firm about 'You're the firm prosecuting my friend, Phil Gainsley.' On numerous occasions, when seeing me, he's gratuitously raised the issue of, you know, why am I picking on his friend, Phil Gainsley.

"Yesterday morning, I ran into Judge Meyers, who I happen to consider a friend and I think he considers me one, and he again indicated more than a simple awareness of this by stating, 'You're starting that case with my friend tomorrow morning in front of Judge Schiefelbein.'

"I believe that a member of this Bench is extremely close friends with Phil Gainsley, that he is extremely interested in this case and, at the very least, that relationship creates an appearance of impropriety for our client. We're uneasy about it when added to the fact that you've thrown us out of here before. I just have to candidly say that worries me, and I'm again moving for you to recuse yourself."

The session lasted almost two hours. As they were leaving, two things occurred. Jerry Snider requested the conversation regarding Judge Meyers be kept strictly confidential. Judge Schiefelbein seemed to appreciate the request and all present stipulated to confidentiality. Then the judge requested a private meeting with Faegre attorney Walter Duffy to discuss settlement issues.

With the elevator doors firmly closed on Friedberg and Snider and their descent begun, Snider spoke in hushed tones. "'No person for whom he has greater respect,'" he quoted Judge Schiefelbein's statement about Judge Meyers. "'Probably the most ethical and honest person Schiefelbein's met? I wonder if he's seen the desk drawer full of files on this case that Meyers's keeping."

Friedberg cast a quick glance at Snider, his eyelids narrowed.

Snider gave a quick nod. "He showed them to me. Quite proud of how informed he's stayed."

The elevator doors slid open. "It seems more and more that this case is not about justice for merely one man," Snider said, "but now for the whole rule of law. If we let the Schiefelbeins and Meyers of this world get away with this, there will be no justice at all."

"Mr. Meshbesher represents the heirs and next of kin of Mr. Nachtsheim," Judge Schiefelbein began proceedings from behind the bench, "specifically, Ms. Nachtsheim-Peters, and has asked leave of the Court to make a motion with respect to the order of the Court regarding sequestration of the witnesses. Mr. Meshbesher?"

Sequestration of witnesses excludes them from the courtroom and protects against one witness influencing the testimony of another.

"Yes. Thank you, Your Honor." Meshbesher rose from a seat in the gallery. "It's my understanding that yesterday the Court ruled that Terry Nachtsheim Peters be excluded from participating as a spectator in this trial since she has been subpoenaed by plaintiff's counsel.

"She came here from Florida, Your Honor, with the express purpose of monitoring this trial for a number of reasons. First and foremost, she's been under therapy for a number of years as a result of the trauma of her father's death. Her therapist is very strong in recommending that sitting through this trial is an important adjunct to the therapy she's been participating in for a number of years."

Meshbesher explained that Terry's years as both a legal assistant and an active member of homicide victims' groups should indicate she would do nothing to prejudice the plaintiff by her presence in court. "She would be pleased to accept a court order that allows her to sit here with the understanding she cannot convey any remarks or thoughts to the defense in this case."

The judge nodded. "Mr. Friedberg?"

Friedberg rose partially from his chair. "We'll agree."

The Nachtsheims again had their eyes and ears on the inside. ALAS representative Mendrzycki was also present throughout the trial.

Tuesday, noon recess

Snider had set aside a small, windowless conference room at Faegre that was christened by Wartnick's team as "the war room." A large white board dominated the wall space beside the door. Bare walls surrounded an obliquely-shaped conference table. Telephone, message pad, and paper clip dispenser were corralled upon a small work table in the corner of the room.

When court was not in session, Wartnick, Webber, Friedberg, and Snider strode the four long blocks through the office-tower canyon between the courthouse and Faegre's offices in Norwest Center. Rather than remove his badge from his wallet, Snider's routine often gave people who witnessed it a chuckle—a unique way to buzz the men past Faegre's security. He backed up to the electronic entry pad and bent his knees until the i.d. in his back pocket triggered the scanner.

Once settled in the war room they shared coffee or lunch as they conferred, planned, and prepared for the next session. Lunch was usually sandwiches from a shop on the street—tuna for Snider, turkey for Wartnick and Webber, and whatever sounded good to Friedberg.

Today they discussed Schiefelbein's rulings against them during the morning session. Phrases like "emasculating a major portion of the case," "despite clear Minnesota case law," "despite how the Supreme Court ruled," and "regardless of what the evidence was going to be" were said in varying degrees of irritation and determination. But they all agreed that what was most damaging was Judge Schiefelbein's declaration that both Wartnick's successful polygraph exam and Phil Gainsley's February 1979 "Dear Jane" memo were not admissible. They must now leave the jury with the impression that Wartnick was afraid of flunking a lie detector test and that he, himself, had made his own decision to take the Fifth Amendment.

CHAPTER 34

"It's my intention, now, to have the clerk go down and get a jury panel," Judge Schiefelbein began.

"Your Honor," Friedberg stood. "I've got a certified copy of the judgment. The only matter of damages outstanding is that it's been our belief that inherent in this is our claim that lawyer's fees paid to Mr. Gainsley should be added on to this judgment. If the Court wants to see the judgment—"

"No, I don't have any quarrel with that if it's properly certified."

"But so it's clear," Friedberg continued, "we're not asking for *our* fees, we're asking for the return of the fees paid to Mr. Gainsley. That's based on our claim that his representation was negligent. It totals one-hundred twenty to one-hundred thirty thousand dollars, Your Honor."

Judge Schiefelbein looked toward defendant's end of council's table. "Mr. Mason?"

"He's simply apprising us of his point of view. There's nothing for me to respond to."

"The reason I raise it, Your Honor," Friedberg spoke up again, "is because I'm going to make an opening statement soon and—"

"Sure, sure." Judge Schiefelbein interrupted. "Thank you. I appreciate that. Rachel," he turned to the court employee, "why don't you go down and get a jury panel."

For the briefest moment, Friedberg looked like a landed fish, then he sat down and leaned toward Snider. Attorneys shuffled papers and whispered to each other and sometimes to their clients; the court reporter rearranged objects on her desk, security repeatedly straightened his belt, air ducts rattled, and in the distance the elevator bell chimed. Then, just as boredom had comfortably settled the anxious occupants of the room, a side door opened.

Today's entrance was made by a wary group of fidgeters set to endure their civic duty for the shortest time-span possible. This pool of potential jurors was mostly women—a fact, Friedberg later remarked, that was in their favor due to Mason's brusque manner and sharp, abusive tactics.

The activity which followed their entrance soon settled to an occasional rustle. Attorneys for both sides were prepared to begin proceedings.

Without a word, Judge Schiefelbein stood and strode from the bench.

All eyes watched the door slam as he disappeared, then each person in the room turned to the person seated beside them with expressions of puzzled concern. Another waiting time began. Long moments passed, then Judge Schiefelbein's law clerk stepped into the courtroom. She announced that Jerry Snider had a telephone call and should take it, if he would, please, in the court reporter's office.

"This is Jerry Snider. Duffy? What are you—? Schiefelbein called *you*?! On the lie detector claim—is he kidding? That directly contradicts the Supreme Court decision. There's more to come? He actually *said* that? I know Schiefelbein doesn't joke about this, but—. Yes, but we both know he just wants to fix the case against Wartnick. In fairness we cannot allow that to happen." Snider paused to listen. "But that won't even cover half the judgment. Well, that's generous to think of Babe," he bristled, "since she's been writing personal checks from her family's trust fund."

Snider felt the gazes of the room full of people as he crossed back to Friedberg seated at council's table. "We need to talk."

Moments later, Friedberg leaned against the bathroom counter and glared. "Norm, don't you dare settle. There's always a way around a roadblock."

"That amount includes two-hundred-thousand for Babe," Snider said.

"To cover all those checks she wrote." Wartnick wanted verification.

Snider nodded.

"Then all this is for nothing." Wartnick slowly shook his head. "The investigation, depositions, subpoenas, witnesses, your trips to Texas, to Florida, everything. All for nothing."

An hour later Wartnick was again seated in the row of chairs in front of the rail which separated the gallery from the front of the courtroom. He watched Snider and Mason enter through the main doors. Snider took his seat beside Friedberg at counsel's table. At the other end of the table, Mason and Gainsley put their heads together and held a brief but intense conversation.

"All rise."

Judge Schiefelbein's black robe flowed behind him as he returned to the bench.

"Be seated."

Mason remained standing. "Your Honor, in spite of the Court's rulings in our favor, both parties are in agreement. A settlement has been reached for $1.2 million."

"Good. I'll give you tomorrow for the parties to work out the specifics and we'll reassemble in my chambers Friday morning to finalize." The gavel banged. "Court adjourned."

Friedberg strode from the courtroom without a word.

Friedberg, Snider, Mason, and Meshbesher assembled off-the-record in Schiefelbein's chambers. "Well, gentlemen," the judge began. "Are we ready to finalize this settlement?"

"Oh, there's not going to be any settlement." Mason spat out the words as though they were rancid meat. "Not when we've had such a serious breach of confidentiality."[31] He had everyone's full attention. Mason nodded toward Friedberg, then stated that the previous evening Friedberg and Meshbesher had dined together and during the course of their conversation it had been revealed to Meshbesher that the judge had earmarked a portion of the settlement for Babe.

Negotiations crumbled. Meshbesher requested a meeting with the judge. Schiefelbein agreed to meet with Meshbesher and the Nachtsheim family in his chambers after the lunch break.

The attorneys filed out of Schiefelbein's chambers and headed for the elevator, all of them except Joe Friedberg.

"Judge," Friedberg stopped in the doorway and turned back toward Schiefelbein. "Purely for informational purposes, just wanted to let you know that if this case doesn't settle, we'll again raise the motion for recusal."

Schiefelbein looked up.

"I intend to honor the stipulated confidentiality of the Meyers matter," Friedberg said, "but the recusal motion will be coming again if the case proceeds to trial. Enjoy your lunch."

That evening, Snider gathered his documents from counsel's table, dropped them in his brief case, and snapped the locks into place. He was tired. No, weary. Weary and frustrated and, and still determined Norm Wartnick was going to get a fair deal. The walk toward the elevator was quiet, but as he reached the lobby outside chambers' secure hallway, the judge, himself, appeared from within. "Evening, Judge."

"Jerry. Been quite the week."

Snider nodded. "Got an interesting weekend planned?"

"Should be nice, especially if this sunshine continues. You?"

"Oh, paperwork and raking leaves."

The elevator doors slid open and Snider gestured for the judge to precede him through the opening. Brief moments later they both sauntered into the lobby.

"Enjoy the weekend, Your Honor. Hopefully we'll have this thing settled when we see you on Tuesday."

Judge Schiefelbein nodded. "See you then."

---

31. No confidentiality agreement was connected with either this case or its settlement (Snider).

"Say something," Butch begged from the privacy of the Wartnicks' patio. "Where's Mr. Positive—the guy who always sees silver linings?"

Norm slowly shook his head and flipped a hamburger patty to another part of the grill. He gazed at the bands of color that hovered above the darkening horizon. "I can't do it."

Meat sizzled as another patty was flipped. "And I'll never be able to provide for my family—never get to sit up there and tell my side—never say, once and for all, I had nothing to do with Bob's death. I'll never get to hear those words bounce off the courtroom walls and into the ears of some decent folks who'll actually listen and do something about this constant dripping, this constant reminder that I'm never going to be able to support my family; never going to ref a game without people booing me the whole game; never going to work at a decent job without the constant nagging at me, scraping at me for another five thousand or nine thousand or fifteen thousand or whatever amount they say we owe this time."

Norm saw Babe's face hover briefly in the kitchen window. Her ears and eyes were red—sure signs she was crying.

"They're going to chip away pieces of me for the rest of my life."

CHAPTER 35

LATE MONDAY AFTERNOON, SEPTEMBER 27, 1993

Snider propped himself on the corner of his desk and listened for the muted ding of the elevator. The Wartnick team had gathered.

Friedberg moved his chair to a back corner of Snider's office and leaned it against the wall. From there he glanced first at Webber, then at Duffy. They, too, silently awaited Wartnick's arrival; their expressions reflected the gray, glowering clouds which hung at eye level outside the expanse of glass.

Wartnick entered.

Snider stood. "Have a seat, Norm." He indicated a chair at the round table in front of the window.

"Mr. Wartnick," Duffy shook hands with Wartnick and finally spoke. "I've spent the day with Mason putting together a package. It doesn't look good for our side."

Wartnick pulled out the chair. "Okay, let me have it."

"Nine sixty-eight. Final offer."

"Thousand?!" Wartnick sat down hard.

Friedberg leaned toward Wartnick. "If you settle, I'll never talk to you again."

"But how—how's that supposed to even scratch the surface when Betty has a three million dollar motive to see me hang?"

THE NEXT MORNING

TUESDAY, SEPTEMBER 28, 1993 – TRIAL DAY FIVE

Friedberg and Snider met early at the courthouse to finalize paperwork. That concluded, they took the back stairway up one floor and began their trek down the secured chambers' corridor on their way to the courtroom's back entrance. Toward the other end of the hallway, Judge Schiefelbein and Jack Mason engaged in animated, agitated conversation. The two men glanced up at Friedberg and Snider's approach. Schiefelbein abruptly turned and disappeared into chambers. Mason redirected his ire toward opposing counsel.

"Guess you two think you're real smart," Mason snarled, "but this isn't over."

They watched Mason turn and exit through the security doors into the elevator lobby.

"Got a clue what that was all about?" Friedberg asked.

Snider did not restrain a grin. "Not even one. Can't say I necessarily *want* to know. Can't be too bad, though, if Jack's that hot under the collar."

Friedberg and Snider met Wartnick and Webber in the wide, public passage that ran the length of the Courts Tower. A windowed wall invited viewing of Hennepin County Government Center's atrium and the lobby seventeen floors below. "Joe!" Meshbesher strode toward them. He extended pages toward Friedberg, then Snider. "Before you go in."

The three attorneys continued through the doorway. Wartnick followed. Webber entered last. Friedberg and Snider already had their heads together; one whispered while the other nodded.

"All rise."

Once ensconced, Judge Schiefelbein spoke. "Who wants to address the Court?"

"May I, Your Honor?" Meshbesher stood in the aisle, briefcase on the seat beside him.

"Yes, Mr. Meshbesher."

"I have a motion to intervene." He gazed steadily toward the bench. "It may be premature unless parties indicate they're going ahead with the settlement. If a settlement has been reached, then my motion to intervene, I believe, is timely and I think the Court ought to hear me."

Schiefelbein's stare took in both ends of counsel's table. His eyes narrowed as his glance reached plaintiff's end. "Who would like to speak on behalf of the defendants with respect to the request?"

Snider interrupted. "Your Honor, I received this motion ten or fifteen minutes ago. My basic position is we don't oppose Mr. Meshbesher's motion to intervene. Happy to have him."

Mason riffled through the pages with quick flips. "If the court please, no proposed order was submitted. We've no objection if it's for the purpose of having a role and being heard on the issue of disbursement of settlement funds—if a settlement is accomplished," he added with a snarl.

"A proposed order is on the way to the court," Meshbesher affirmed, "and I'd be happy to work out the terms of the order with the parties, Your Honor."

"How much time do you need to advise me whether the case is settled or not?"

"I believe, Your Honor," Mason answered, "in the next hour-and-a-half we'd be in a position to advise the court in that respect."

"Fine," the judge concluded. "We'll stand in recess until 11:30."

Wartnick followed his attorneys back into the hallway and found a pay phone. "Babe, we're recessed. Yeah, to give everybody time to finish working out the details. No, I don't know!" he said, then sighed. A sudden movement from Snider caught his attention. "Wait a minute. Something's going on. I'll call you back."

Wartnick hurried over to Friedberg. "What's going on?"

Friedberg extended papers to him. "Read this."

The papers were affidavits by Ron Meshbesher and Betty and Terry Nachtsheim regarding their Friday afternoon meeting with Judge Schiefelbein. Wartnick read slowly and, as he did, he winced and shifted his stance to straighten his back. His neck flamed. He glanced again at Friedberg. "Am I reading this right? Ron says that Judge Schiefelbein actually said I'm guilty?"

Friedberg nodded. Fire had returned to those brown eyes. "Told that to the Nachtsheim ladies last Friday afternoon. Jerry's calling Duffy now." Friedberg leveled Wartnick with a steady gaze. "You realize Gainsley's not the biggest bad guy here. Judges are given great deferential treatment in our system. They can do no wrong unless you can prove they've done wrong, but," Friedberg waved his rolled-up copy of Meshbesher's affidavit toward Schiefelbein's courtroom, "we got him this time. He prejudged the case. No appeals court in the country will let a judge get away with that."

Mason stood behind counsel's table. "May it please the court, we've made diligent efforts to settle this case. We've been unable to do so. We ask that the matter proceed to trial with a selection of a jury as soon as possible, this morning or this afternoon."

Friedberg stood. "Your Honor, although I hadn't been as intensely involved in the negotiations as Mr. Duffy and Mr. Snider have, I believe that statement is correct. Every indication I have is that there've been diligent efforts to settle this case. I believe the case is, with one exception, ripe for trial—."

"Sit down, Mr. Friedberg," Judge Schiefelbein ordered. "Folks," he pointed toward the Nachtsheim family and a news reporter—"you're not parties to the lawsuit." Schiefelbein's volume increased with every phrase. "I'm going to ask you to leave my courtroom. I've got something to say to the lawyers and it's just between the lawyers and myself. Meshbesher can remain."

As the spectators filed out, Schiefelbein turned to the clerk and demanded, "Lock the door."

"Last Friday morning, Mr. Friedberg *and* Mr. Snider," the judge was reading from a yellow legal pad, "when everyone else including Mr. Duffy had left, made another *ex parte* communication to me. They said they intended to renew their motion for me to recuse myself.

"The record will reflect the number of motions to recuse and the bases claimed. Mr. Mason has claimed it was made to intimidate this court. I ignored that claim. . . .

"I did not consider their motion for recusal improper because I respected the lawyers and the firms and would not entertain any ulterior motive. Since that time, counsel have renewed the motion repeatedly, including a motion which included Judge Meyers, impliedly claiming he influenced me. That is not true and is not, repeat *not*, the reason I recuse myself."

Friedberg leaned back in his seat and exhaled. Mason leaned forward and planted his elbows on the table. Snider's shoulders relaxed, but not completely.

"The cumulative effect of the renewed motions," Schiefelbein continued, "and notice that it will continue has forced this court into an adversarial posture with counsel.

"This court cannot remain immune to attacks on my integrity—I will *not* permit Mr. Friedberg or Mr. Snider to appear in *my* courtroom again! I will recuse myself from *all* cases involving Faegre, if that's the firm's wish, although I have no problem with the firm if Mr. Snider is *not involved*."

Judge Schiefelbein collected himself. "I apologize for any inconvenience or delay to Mr. Mason or his clients."

CHAPTER 36

"*His* courtroom?" Judge Bruce Hartigan shook his head and stared at Snider. "It's not his courtroom, it's the *people's* courtroom."

Snider could not wipe the smile from his face. "Well, that's what he said. And I can't tell you how relieved I am—how relieved *we* are. If Schiefelbein had continued the back-room antics, it would have gotten ugly. The unfairness would have permeated the entire decision. No doubt about it. I would have been forced to make a record of this very contentious trial."

SEVEN MONTHS LATER

EARLY APRIL 1994

"A few more things to pass along," Snider said to Wartnick as his legal team assembled in Snider's office. "We've received official notice that Phil Gainsley has left Moss and Barnett to form a new partnership."

"When he's not being a big shot back East," Webber said.

Wartnick turned a quizzical expression toward Webber.

"You didn't know? He's got some cushy spot with the Met or the Boston Pops—some big, fancy gig back on the East Coast. He's a 'Stump the Expert' quiz panelist. It's an intermission thing. I've heard tell he's pretty good."

"Keeps him from mangling people's lives," Wartnick muttered and began to pick at the seam of his trousers.

Silence followed Wartnick's remark. Snider's gentle baritone eased the tension. "As you know, Chief Judge Burke has assigned young Judge John Stanoch to this case—"

"Wasn't he Governor Perpich's campaign manager?" Webber asked.

Wartnick was more curious about how many judges had recused themselves this time.

Friedberg shifted in his chair, reached for his coffee, and addressed both questions. "Eight more recusals. And Stanoch was appointed to the bench during Perpich's last week. Mason's okay with him because he's a Democrat."

"We're okay with him because he seems unbiased," Snider quickly added. "Doesn't seem impressed by fancy suits."

"Or black robes?" Wartnick asked.

"To be determined. We'll hope not."

Wartnick wasn't satisfied. "What happens if Stanoch turns out to be another Schiefelbein?"

"We go to trial and make a record. All you can do is try to make your record for appeal."

"What's a record? Record of what?"

"Norm, a judge is to be a fair, neutral referee—"

"You bet!"

"—calling balls, strikes, and outs. But when that doesn't happen, you stand up and say aloud in court, so the court reporter records it that, 'Your Honor, I'd like to make a record of this.' And he can say, 'Record of what?' 'Your conduct, Your Honor,' and you lay out your thoughts and reasons for—'You're refusing to listen to my objections,' or 'You didn't allow me sufficient time to respond,' or whatever he's doing."

"What in the blazes good does that do besides make him even hotter?"

"Nothing," Friedberg said "if he's determined to throw the case."

"What you get, then," Snider said, "is a record of it for an appeal."

Wartnick was still not satisfied. "He's going to stop you. Tell you to sit down."

Snider nodded. "Every time a judge tries to stop me, I say, 'You're depriving me of making my record, Your Honor.' Then even that's on record."

"Recusals are rarely done," Friedberg added. "But when they need to happen, you have to step up and do it."

"The more obstinate the judge becomes, the more forceful I become," Snider leaned back. "Let me tell you—in a small, country town I had an actual case where the judge and the other attorney were good friends. The other attorney said, 'Your Honor, here's what I think you should do,' and the judge did it, without even giving me a chance to speak. So I stood up and said, 'Your Honor, I'm going to ask you to step aside in this case. You didn't hear from me, didn't give me a chance to respond, and have created prejudice in this case, and I'm going to have to ask you to recuse yourself.'

"That judge was a gentle, soft-spoken man and it really kind of shocked him, I think. He thought about it for a while, then did come back in and recused. Had buyer's remorse afterward—was angry about it, but he knew it was the right thing to do. If that's the only tool in our arsenal, Norm, then that's what we have to do. But I don't think it's going to come to that. I really don't.

"Any more questions along those lines?" Snider scanned the faces in the room.

"No? Then I need to let you all know that Mason has named his polygraph expert. A Mr. Yeschke."

"Yeschke?" Friedberg straightened. "*Charles* Yeschke? So the bow-tied bigot is defense's polygraph expert?"

Snider raised an eyebrow.

Webber laughed. "I smell history."

Apparently very pleased with the announcement, Friedberg settled back in his chair. "Talk about Schiefelbein's beehive of prejudices—Mason's handed us the polygraph issue. You remember Yeschke," he turned to Snider. "Testing a suspect, turned off the equipment, muttered 'Hot-blooded Cuban!' or something along those lines. He was censured for it."

Snider began to nod.

"He'll be a piece of cake to discredit," Friedberg continued. "Can't wait to get the guy under cross. And it'd be good if the jury was multiracial. What a bigot. You know, he perjured himself once, too. Shoot, that's the best news we've had since Schiefelbein spit out the bit."

"Discredit, yes. Antics, no." Snider replied. "We'll be gentlemen whenever we're in the courtroom, especially with Jack Mason."

"Not a problem." The grin stayed stuck to Friedberg's face. He glanced at Webber, nodded to Wartnick. "So you know, we could've foregone all this polygraph stuff, but we wanted the issue in because Norm passed it. It's worth it to open ourselves up so the jury hears Norm passed that poly. And not once, but twice."

"Mason's associate," Webber said, "Ed Magarian, has deposed our polygraph expert. But Magarian reserved the right to reconvene regarding some documents we don't have. I didn't commit one way or the other."

"How'd it go?" Snider asked.

"Mr. Shaw holds his own very well; gives concise, understandable explanations of the test, itself, and of the procedure. I think he'll do well at trial."

Wartnick shrugged. Friedberg and Snider's buoyancy was good enough for him. "Guys, I hate to run," he leveraged himself out of his chair, "but I've got a game to ref. Anything you need from me?"

Wartnick went around the room shaking hands. "Thank you, again. I really appreciate what you guys are doing for me." With a last nod he was gone.

"Before we drag this meeting out further than needed," Snider watched Wartnick disappear down the corridor, "let's discuss proposed jury instructions and the matters still pending before the court. First is clarification on damages due to emotional distress."

"That's gonna be a tough one. That man," Friedberg pointed toward the doorway, "he's a hard worker, was a happy guy. It destroyed his life. Listen to some of his long-time friends—the few who stuck around. They tell me he used to be Mr. Laid-Back, a great one for laughs."

"He hardly ever even smiles," Webber said.

"Exactly. So," Friedberg turned to Snider, "how do we convince the judge that emotional distress damages are not only warranted, they're essential?"

THURSDAY, APRIL 28, 1994

"What?" Wartnick's jaw dropped. "No! No, he can't do that!"

"He can and he did."

Webber updated Wartnick on progress with the case every few days via telephone, and if Webber did not call Wartnick then Wartnick called Webber. Today's meeting, though, was face-to-face at Faegre.

"Stanoch ruled we can't use the 'Dear Jane' memo at *all*?"

"Nope. Nor mention the conversation when Gainsley gave you the note card, *nor* the conversation Meshbesher had with Gainsley after the deposition. But we *can* still, well here," Webber handed Wartnick a copy of Stanoch's ruling and pointed to a paragraph where the judge had quoted from the Supreme Court's decision. "Read this paragraph."

> Plaintiff will be allowed to establish in this case that he took a deposition in 1979, that he asserted his fifth amendment right not to testify at that deposition, that he asserted his fifth amendment right based on the advice of his attorney Gainsley, and that the assertion of the fifth amendment based upon the advice of his attorney Gainsley caused damage to his defense in the civil case. Additional inquiry relating to the alleged negligence of Gainsley's original advice will not be allowed.

"But notice," Webber said. "Stanoch denied the other defense motions."

"You mean there was anything left?"

"Oh, sure. Relax, Norm. Joe and Jerry are disappointed, but not worried." He flipped sheets and thumped part-way down the page. "At least we get to refer to the police file. See here: Mason wanted to use Bobby and Betty's polygraph info but can't. But we *can* use the rest of the police report. That's a big point because we can show what Gainsley should have known—well, if he'd actually had the report like he said he did."

"So, what about these other things?" Wartnick flipped pages. "'Defendant's motion denied, motion denied,' What's all that about?"

"Let's see it. Stanoch said—okay—'Defendant's motion that this Court rule as a matter of law that an unconditional offer to make plaintiff available for a second depo—yada-ya—not have made the first depo inadmissible is Denied.' In other words, Mason's wanting to just say, 'the law says offering the second deposition wouldn't have helped. Meshbesher would still have been able to use the first deposition.' Stanoch says, 'No, the law doesn't say that. It must be argued at trial.'"

"What do our experts say?"

"They each have slightly different takes on it. Mostly that it was for a jury to decide, which is why Gainsley was negligent. He didn't give the jury anything to work with, didn't bring it up or offer it so the jury had something *to* decide."

"This says, 'Plaintiff does not seek a recovery of his attorney's fees.' You know Joe and Jerry should get paid." Wartnick glanced up. "It can't come from me. I've got nothing left."

"Right, but it's not a separate issue for the jury to decide. Joe, Jerry, and Ron will figure all that out based on what the jury awards—probably all based on what Betty's willing to settle the judgment for. It really comes down to Betty and her judgment against you."

FIVE MONTHS LATER

THURSDAY, SEPTEMBER 29, 1994—TRIAL DAY THREE

Judge John Stanoch spoke from the bench in open court, but no jury had been seated. "We're here this morning because we have at least two issues I want to address for purposes of the record, both of which we had some discussion about yesterday in chambers."

And so commenced the third day of trial. Snider and Mason jockeyed back and forth, and Judge Stanoch repeatedly requested Mr. Mason clarify. Wartnick felt it was hours later when Judge Stanoch said, "I'm prepared to rule now on the polygraph issue. Mr. Snider, why don't you make your motion and we'll see what Mr. Mason has to say."

The polygraph issue was a difficult one with which to deal. What was basic fairness in the interest of justice? Both sides had an opinion, and young Stanoch was forced to wade through the swamp. He eventually came to a decision.

"I believe that the interest of justice dictates that I allow plaintiffs to add this claim back into their complaint and make it available for trial. However, I'm not going to allow plaintiffs to pick and choose what they want. I think that would be, as Mr. Mason indicates, allowing the parties to choose their outcomes in a way that I can't support. If it's going to be in the case, let's put it in the case and let's give both sides a way to address the issue."

Score one for the plaintiff.

"With regard to the fee issue, let me just state that I have informed the parties that while I have denied defense requests to inquire as to the fee arrangements Mr. Wartnick has with his attorneys, I've also indicated to plaintiff's counsel that—and I want to simply memorialize this for the record—that if, during the course of this trial, plaintiffs contrast their investigation and preparation with Mr. Gainsley's investigation in the underlying case in such a manner that it becomes a main point or focus of this case, I'm going to consider a defense request to inquire about the fee arrangement plaintiff has with his attorneys.

"So, I'm not changing my rulings on that, but I want plaintiffs on notice: one of the things that came up in your brief is that 'We want to take the jury by the hand and lead them through what a proper investigation would have looked like' and, to the extent that's a focus of your arguments, I think the defense is going to be allowed to inquire about your fee arrangements."

"Judge," Friedberg stood, "there's no reason for us to be cute. We said exactly what we intend to do. We're going to show what we found."

"I guess I'm saying, don't be surprised if Mr. Mason makes a motion for me to reconsider the portion of my ruling that restricts inquiry regarding the fee."

Friedberg grinned. "Oh, we'll not be surprised."

"All right," Judge Stanoch said. "The other issue I want to address this morning and place on record is the claim that Gainsley failed to present alternative theories of who caused the death of Bob Nachtsheim. My view is that this is not part of this case and I'm not going to allow plaintiffs to argue that to the jury."

Snider rose. "Let me just put one thing on the record, if I could, Your Honor. As a matter of fact, the trial transcript, which I think the court will see as we proceed through this trial, reflects that Gainsley never had a theory in place as to who committed this offense. He never offered any evidence on that point. We can obviously live with the court's ruling, but I don't want the court to believe that the underlying trial in this case presented any alternative viable theory. There was none."

"Yes," the court acknowledged. "And my concern is obviously this: as we go through this investigation issue, to the extent that what you're driving at is, 'If they had done all this investigation they would have been able to present this list of A through Z suspects, and that was the negligent act'—" Judge Stanoch looked directly at Snider, "that's not coming into this trial."

CHAPTER 37

This was it. In moments they would begin what had been eight, well really twenty-one years in the making. Twenty-one years since Bob Nachtsheim had died that gray morning in May.

The side door squawked open. The jury filed into the loft set aside to separate them from the gallery. It had been eight years since Wartnick had seen a jury sworn in. This time it was easier to watch.

Judge Stanoch addressed the jury. "Good morning, members of the jury. I'm going to give you an idea of what we're going to do this morning. I'm going to give you some preliminary instructions that will guide you as you hear the testimony in this case.

"You are the sole judges of whether a witness is to be believed and of the weight to be given to the testimony. In determining believability and weight you should take into consideration, One, the witness's interest or lack of interest in the outcome of the case; Two, their relationship to the parties; Three, their ability and opportunity to know, remember, and relate the facts. Four, their manner and appearance; Five, their...."

An image sprang to Wartnick's mind: Russ Krueger lounging in the witness box during the first trial, picking his fingernails and wrinkling his cheeks to push up his glasses. Then that mental image was replaced by one of Phil Gainsley sitting at counsel's table while Wartnick was on the witness stand being drawn and quartered by Meshbesher. Wartnick's advocate had gazed beyond the ceiling with his hands clasped behind his head—that was how he sat for much of the original trial.

Wartnick glanced at Friedberg. He intently studied each jury member, one by one. Snider alternately studied the jurors, studied Stanoch, and made notes. At defendant's end of the table, Gainsley gazed at nothing and drummed his fingers on the arms of his chair, like he was off in the Bahamas or maybe Boston.

"Mr. Friedberg, at this time is plaintiff prepared to proceed with opening statement?"

Friedberg stood. "We are, Your Honor."

Norm wondered why Stanoch had decided not to allow any emotional damages, then he shrugged. Hey, Friedberg and Snider had gotten him this far. Now it was time for fireworks—and to hope for the best.

"You may proceed."

"If it please the court," Friedberg nodded to Judge Stanoch, glanced toward Snider, then nodded to Mason, "counsel, members of the jury." Friedberg moved leisurely around the end of counsel's table and ambled forward until he stood, empty-handed, before the jury.

"This is an attorney malpractice case, an attorney negligence case." Two, three steps then stop, look another juror in the eye. "That doesn't mean we're making a broad sweeping denunciation of the ability and character of Phillip Gainsley or the law firm of Moss and Barnett. It simply means we're alleging that in this case he handled for my client, Norm Wartnick, he made an error, and the error raises itself to the dignity of what we call malpractice."

Wartnick felt the jury's gaze. All six of them. Women again, well all women this time. Friedberg said it was a good thing. And it was a good mixture of backgrounds and ages. One was indigenous, probably Ojibwa, native to this region of Minnesota; three others had Latina, African-American, or a mixture in their pasts. It looked like an intelligent group, Wartnick thought. Friedberg had done his job well.

Friedberg strolled toward counsel's table and stood in front of Snider. "Were I to kill somebody, murder Mr. Snider, and it be a defenseless act, then the state of Minnesota—assuming I did it here—could and probably should indict me for first degree murder. That's a prosecution, a criminal case. They'd prosecute me and, if they convict me, they'd send me to prison for life.

"Now, completely aside from that—whether the state convicts me or I'm acquitted—the widow and children of Mr. Snider may sue me civilly for what's called wrongful death. That's a civil case brought by the survivors of Mr. Snider who sue me for what I've taken from them. And the only thing the law can give them is money, and that's what a jury would be asked to do.

"Now, let me get to the story—"

An hour-and-a-half later, Webber grinned and popped the pull tab on an ice-cold 7-Up. Court was recessed so the attorneys could hash out Mason's latest objection. "We interrupt this Opening Statement to request a mistrial. Did you notice Betty Nachtsheim?" Webber's grin broadened. "While Joe was saying 'she did this' and 'she did that'? No? I thought she was going to explode all over the courtroom."

"'…and tapes were made where she said she believed Bobby murdered her husband.'" Wartnick paced from wall to wall in the little conference room provided by the court and tried to stretch out his back. "Yeah, I'm sure she loved that."

"Or 'She's slept with the chief investigator. Wouldn't that compromising of the investigation have been interesting for a jury…?' You want something to drink? Mason already knows he's sunk. He's got to tug for every inch he can get. Coffee? Oh, forgot—you're like me—not a coffee drinker, either. Want some water or something? No? Joe's bringing Gainsley's Fifth Amendment advice into opening was calculated, Norm. He thought it was important enough to risk it." Webber took a long chug from the soda can. "Relax. They won't be in chambers long."

"Members of the jury," Judge Stanoch spoke from the bench, "I apologize for the delay. A couple of things before we resume. First of all, I'm ordering you to disregard Mr. Friedberg's last statement. I'm going to order it stricken from the record and you're not to consider that statement in any way.

"Further, as I told you earlier, you'll hear testimony in this trial that the Nachtsheim's family attorney, Ron Meshbesher, took Mr. Wartnick's deposition in 1979. That deposition was taken in connection with the Nachtsheim family's claim that Mr. Wartnick had been unjustly enriched in the amount of one-hundred-thousand dollars.

"In the 1979 deposition, Mr. Gainsley instructed Mr. Wartnick to assert his Fifth Amendment rights in response to Mr. Meshbesher's questions about the murder. Testimony about that instruction to Mr. Wartnick will be offered in this trial only to provide some context to plaintiff's claim that Mr. Gainsley failed to mitigate the damage done by instructing Mr. Wartnick to invoke the Fifth Amendment at his 1979 deposition. Therefore, you cannot base your decision in this case in any way on Mr. Gainsley's advice to assert the Fifth Amendment.

"Mr. Friedberg, you may resume your opening statement."

Another hour and a dozen talking-points later, Friedberg summed up. "Ladies, there was a trial, and the evidence will show that the trial that took place for that good, honest jury wasn't anything like what should have taken place because of the negligence, the failure, and the laziness of Mr. Wartnick's lawyer. The jury never knew about the party, never knew about the plot. That evidence was never before them."

"Objection, Your Honor," Mason interrupted. "That's not part of the argument in this case. We'd ask the jury be instructed to disregard that."

"Mr. Friedberg, if you want to move along, please."

Friedberg nodded. "Ladies of the jury, I want you to evaluate the testimony that is given. I want you to take a look at the witnesses that are called. I want you to determine what Mr. Gainsley knew, what he should have known, what he did, what he didn't do.

"And then we want you to make a decision that it's, more likely than not, the reason that Norm Wartnick has got this unremovable, permanent judgment against him is because of the negligence of his lawyer.

"Then, when the case is over, I'm *not* going to ask you for any money for damages to his feelings, or any money for damages to his reputation—nothing like that. We're going to ask you to remove this judgment, to give him the amount of money to pay the judgment off because that's all he can do. And if the judgment is removed, he can go to work, keep his pay, take care of his family. That's all we want you to do is get that judgment off his back. That's why this case was brought. Thank you."

The jury got a five minute break, then it was Mason's turn.

"My mother used to tell me," Mason began, "that when you're right about the facts, you raise the facts and you pound the facts. When you're right about the law, you raise the law and pound the law. And when you're not right about the facts and you're not right about the law, you raise your voice and pound the table."

Mason waited for the laughter but instead cleared his throat amidst the booming silence and started again.

"There are things that just aren't open to doubt, and we'll show you some of those facts." Unlike Friedberg's fluid hand motions, Mason's were short, jerky, rushed. "And the facts are these: That in May 1973, early in the morning, Bob Nachtsheim was shot. Mr. Wartnick has *not* been charged *criminally* with that. A criminal case takes evidence beyond a reasonable doubt.

"But in 1986, a civil jury, people just like you, heard evidence after a five-day trial, and on the basis of that trial they concluded that Mr. Wartnick had murdered or caused the murder of Mr. Nachtsheim. The jury heard the evidence and we're not here to have another trial. This isn't a whodunit. We're here because Mr. Wartnick claims 'It wasn't me. Nothing I did. It was my attorney's fault.'

"But he's more specific than that, and I want to call your attention to what it is he claims his attorney did wrong."

Mason erected a large, white board at the front of the courtroom near the bailiff. For the next half-hour he revisited the complaints against his client listed upon that white board along with a chronology of events which favored his client and which his experts would support. He even had those experts in the courtroom, had each one stand as he introduced them.

"There are thousands of trials that happen every week," Mason said, "and in every trial there's somebody who wins and somebody who loses. That's going to happen in this trial. The party that loses doesn't necessarily lose because their attorney did something. The party that loses, loses perhaps because that's what the facts show. ...

"If O. J. Simpson is convicted, will that mean that his attorneys are incompetent? Or that they were negligent? Or if O. J. Simpson is acquitted, the facts will show that doesn't necessarily indicate the state was incompetent or negligent.

"The prevailing attorney in this case was Ron Meshbesher. Ron Meshbesher has won a lot of cases. Lawyers who lose to Ron Meshbesher don't necessarily commit malpractice."

CHAPTER 38

Ron Meshbesher maintained his air of dignity within the confined space of the witness box. Polished reading glasses were perched mid-way down his nose as he perused the document Snider had handed him.

"And the summons bears the date of October 13, 1976. Is that correct?" Snider said.

"That's correct."

"Would you tell the jury what a summons is, please."

"A summons is a notice to a defendant who is being sued. It indicates to the defendant they are being served a complaint and they have twenty days to file a formal answer to the complaint. If they don't file an answer, the plaintiff—the party bringing the lawsuit—has the right to get a default judgment."

"And what is a complaint? Would you just define that in layman's terms, please?"

"A complaint is merely a written statement of the facts that the plaintiff believes entitles them to money, in most cases, or [to] some kind of relief from the court. It's basically a list of the facts and the accusations against the defendants."

"Now," Snider said. "You had indicated that the fall of 1974 is when you were retained by Mrs. Nachtsheim. Yet you filed a complaint some two years later—on or about October 13, 1976."

"Correct." Meshbesher nodded.

"Why did it take you two years to file a summons and complaint?"

"I originally told Betty Nachtsheim that, from what I knew and from what she told me, we only had a motive for Mr. Wartnick. I was uncomfortable accusing him of the death of her husband without any more evidence. Betty stayed on my back, so to speak, periodically asking me to take steps. I said, 'Betty, there's nothing new' [until] finally I came up with this theory of unjust enrichment. And," Meshbesher continued, "I thought it should be against public policy for insurance companies to issue policies to people who had no interest in or connection to the insured. It was an invitation for some kind of mischief."

Snider stood before the witness, Exhibit Seven in hand. "Did you have any law checked on this unjust enrichment theory at the time you caused the summons and complaint to issue?"

"Well, I did some research and I recall it was against public policy in a number of states. In Minnesota it appeared not to be, so I knew that if I pursued this we would have to make new law by taking appeals to the Minnesota Supreme Court."

"Your Honor," Snider turned to the bench, "I offer Exhibit 7 at this point."

The judge received the paper. "Mr. Mason."

"We object. It's only part of the record. There's another summons and complaint that was issued a short time after that, and that should come in at the same time."

"Well," Snider said, "it's going to come in, Your Honor. I can only offer one at a time."

"I'll conditionally receive this one until the subsequent exhibit is offered. At that time we'll see if we can clear it all up."

The jurors could still reference the chronology on Mason's white board.

Snider returned to Ron Meshbesher. "Did you, in this complaint, accuse Mr. Wartnick of committing the murder of Bob Nachtsheim?"

"No. I did not."

"What was the reason for that?"

"I just felt in good conscience I couldn't make that allegation—accuse somebody of murder without having more facts."

"In October of 1976, when you filed this action, did you then take some further action to try to conduct discovery in your case?"

"Not for a while." Meshbesher pulled a note card from his suit jacket's inside pocket and smiled at the jury. "I've got a little list of chronology here to pique my memory because it's been so long ago. I know that on February 16, 1979, I took Mr. Wartnick's deposition in my office."

"So that was some three years after you filed the complaint. Is that correct?"

"About two-and-a-half years."

"Okay. Can you tell us why it took you so long to take the deposition?"

"There were a number of factors. One, I was hoping more evidence would develop in the police investigation, or something would come forward I could sink my teeth into and proceed with more confidence in the case. ... Also, I have a vague recollection that Mr. Gainsley and I had some understanding that I wouldn't require an immediate answer until we had done some discovery— had an exchange of information; that's what I mean by discovery."

"And, as you've testified, in February of 1979 you did that discovery. Correct?"

Meshbesher nodded. "We did the deposition of Mr. Wartnick, which is one part of the discovery process."

"Did Mr. Wartnick answer your questions?"

"Well, he answered them in a fashion."

"Please explain what you mean." Snider ambled back toward counsel's table.

"He gave his name, address, and where he worked, I believe, and his family situation. And then, when I asked any questions pertaining to the murder, he took the Fifth Amendment."

"What do you mean 'He took the Fifth Amendment'?"

"He refused to answer on the grounds of the Fifth Amendment, which means, to a lawyer, that the answers would tend to incriminate him."

The jury was quiet as their glances shifted to look at Wartnick.

"And did he do that more than once in that deposition?" Snider continued.

"He did it to every question I asked concerning anything that had to do with the murder of Mr. Nachtsheim."

Friedberg glanced over his shoulder at his client. Deep emotion had reddened his neck and flamed his ears. Friedberg gave Wartnick a quick, reassuring nod.

"Did you take any action following that deposition, with regard to your pleadings against Mr. Wartnick?"

"Yes, I did."

"Your Honor, may I approach the witness again?"

"You may."

"Let me show you Exhibit 23, please. Would you identify that for the record."

"Exhibit 23 is, again, a summons with an amended complaint."

"And what changes did you make in your amended complaint?"

"For the first time I accused Mr. Wartnick of either causing or procuring the murder."

Several women of the jury scribbled in their notepads.

"What had happened since October 13, 1976, that caused you to make this amendment?"

"Mr. Wartnick's taking of the Fifth Amendment at the deposition."

Few people in the courtroom noticed the minute hand circle the clock face as Snider questioned Meshbesher on the chronology of the Minnesota legislature's passage of his bill to eliminate the statute of limitations on situations amounting to murder; on the differences between his first complaint against Wartnick for unjust enrichment and the second complaint for wrongful death—"Without the taking of the Fifth Amendment I really had no basis to proceed with his wrongful death complaint"; on Gainsley's Motions for Summary Judgment which were denied in all respects "because the Fifth Amendment itself was enough to allow a jury to find in favor of the plaintiff, to find that Mr. Wartnick had something to do with the death of Mr. Nachtsheim."

Snider had Meshbesher read aloud, then comment on Gainsley's conditional offer for a second deposition. "I didn't respond in writing. ... I told him that without the Fifth Amendment I have no case. ... I was afraid if I took Mr. Wartnick's deposition and he answered all the questions, a judge might rule that I couldn't use the previous deposition."

"If Mr. Gainsley," Snider said, hands clasped respectfully in front of him, "had offered on an unconditional basis, would you have taken that deposition, Mr. Meshbesher?"

"I don't think I'd have a choice. If he's presenting him to me, if I'd have said 'No, I'm not going to take it,' he may have brought a motion that required me to take it or else waive my right to use the Fifth Amendment."

Snider turned slightly toward the jury. "It's hypothetical, I take it, because there *was* never an unconditional offer for another deposition. Is that correct?"

"No, there wasn't."

"And at the time of the trial, did you have occasion to use the 1979 deposition transcript of Mr. Wartnick?"

"Yes."

"And would you tell the court and jury how you used it."

"I had Mr. Wartnick as a witness, and I had him read the answers to the questions I had put to him at the deposition. In other words, we had a script. If I might explain."

"Please do." Snider again turned casually toward counsel's table.

"Ordinarily, when a witness testifies [during a trial] from a deposition, somebody other than the witness will read the deposition. I was prepared to have a lawyer from my office do that, and Mr. Gainsley objected to it and said, 'Why don't you have Mr. Wartnick go on the witness stand? He can answer his own questions.' So I—"

Snider spun toward the witness. "Wait a minute. *Who* suggested that?"

"Mr. Gainsley did."

"Ooh-kay."

"And with that suggestion—I certainly accepted it—Mr. Wartnick took the witness stand and I asked him verbatim from the transcript the same questions I'd asked him at the deposition, and he had to read his answers exactly as they were in the deposition transcript. He took the Fifth Amendment."

"He refused to answer?"

Meshbesher nodded. "He refused to answer."

Snider allowed a moment of silence—time for the reality of that situation to sink into the imaginations of its hearers as he bent over counsel's table to retrieve pages from that day's stack of intended exhibits.

Most of the afternoon session consisted of refinements to Meshbesher's opinion of various memoranda, case briefs, etc. as they pertained to the underlying trial. Then, almost to the end of the afternoon, after a short break, Snider turned the questioning toward another document found in Mr. Meshbesher's files.

"Mr. Meshbesher, would you just identify what Exhibit One Hundred Thirty-E is, please."

"One-thirty-E represents a copy of the police report in connection with the investigation of the death of Bob Nachtsheim and comprises forty-five pages."

"And where did you get these documents?"

"I got them from the Minneapolis Police Department and Mr. Krueger."

"And when did you get them?"

"I can't remember the date. I had them before the deposition of Mr. Wartnick."

Exhibit 130-E was received into evidence.

"Now I assume, Mr. Meshbesher, that after you got this report you obviously read through it. Is that correct?"

"Yes, I did."

"Were there any individuals listed in the report that you followed up on in terms of a deposition or an investigation?"

"By telephone, I know, I talked to some witnesses, but we didn't take any depositions of any of these witnesses listed in the police report."

Snider nodded. "Mr. Friedberg, in his opening statement this morning, listed a number of people who attended a party the night before the murder. Were you familiar with that?"

"I was," Meshbesher confirmed, "from the police report."

"Did you undertake any effort to investigate the party after you read it in the police report?"

"No, I did not."

"Would you tell us why you did not?"

"Because the information hurt my case considerably. I wanted to stay away from it."

"Okay." Snider walked to the large white board. "And Mr. Friedberg, during his opening statement, wrote here on this board a number of people that attended the party. Bobby Nachtsheim, Roger Nordstrom, Dennis Kreuser, and a woman by the name of Debra Feist. Correct?"

"Yes."

"Did you take any depositions of these people?"

"No."

"Did you send an investigator to interview any of these people?"

"No."

"And would you tell us why you didn't?"

"Because the police report indicated they had a conversation at that party about robbing Mr. Nachtsheim. That was devastating to my case. I wanted to stay as clear away from them as I could."

"Why did you want to stay as clear away from them as you could?"

"Because our case focused on Mr. Wartnick as the killer. If I got involved with these people, or took their deposition, they would detract from my accusation against Mr. Wartnick. They would give the jury an alternative suspect."

"Did you have an expectation that Mr. Gainsley, the attorney for Mr. Wartnick, might interview and depose these people?"

"I certainly thought he would." Meshbesher nodded and removed his reading glasses.

"Why is that, sir?"

"Because it helps his case. For Mr. Gainsley to show to the jury there were other possible suspects [who] would detract from the evidence against his client. The jury never heard about these other possible suspects because he never called them as witnesses."

Snider ambled toward the jury box. "So if you're trying to prove someone did *not* commit a murder, do you consider it important to show that somebody else *did* commit a murder?"

"If I had admissible evidence to that effect, I absolutely would use it."

"Did you have any fear that the individuals listed here in connection with the party might show up at the trial?"

"Absolutely I did."

"*Did* any of these people show up as witnesses at the trial?"

"No."

"If you were representing Mr. Wartnick and somebody else was representing Mrs. Nachtsheim, would you have interviewed these witnesses?"

"Objection," Mason said. "Asking for an opinion of a lay witness."

Snider turned calmly toward the bench. "He's not a lay witness, Your Honor."

"The witness is not identified as an expert," Mason argued. "I object to that. He's called as a lay member of the profession so it's not something he can testify to."

The judge nodded. "Mr. Snider, I think I'm going to sustain the objection."

Snider nodded and again faced the witness. "Mr. Meshbesher, you gave us your credentials earlier in your testimony. Do you hold any office or positions within any of those organizations you identified?"

"I can save some time." Mason spoke up again. "I don't doubt that Mr. Meshbesher is one of the best trial lawyers in the state of Minnesota, maybe the nation."

Meshbesher chuckled. "I want a copy of that."

Laughter fluttered through the jury and across the gallery of spectators.

Mason did not look amused. "We don't need to lay a foundation that this guy is a pretty darn good trial lawyer, if I could phrase it that way."

"Could we get Mr. Mason under oath to say that, Your Honor?" Friedberg spoke from his seat behind counsel's table.

Snider turned to Judge Stanoch. "Is that sufficient foundation, Your Honor, for me to ask him the question that I wanted to ask him regarding his expertise as a lawyer and what investigation he would have done?"

"Why don't you step up here so we can discuss this. Okay?"

Mason shuffled to the bench and the three men began an animated conversation.

Wartnick turned in his chair to see who was in the gallery and caught sight of Terry Nachtsheim. Her clenched jaw and stern, hostile expression was one of few such expressions in a courtroom full of smiles.

"Mr. Snider," the judge said as he brought attention back to the front of the room.

"Thank you, Your Honor. Mr. Meshbesher, if you were representing someone in a wrongful death case where the death was caused by murder—if you'll accept that as my hypothesis—and you had knowledge and information that there were other suspects out in the community, would you interview and depose those suspects?"

"I would do both."

"And tell me why."

"Because I had a duty to my client to investigate every bit of evidence that would have helped my client's case. If I could establish that someone else committed the murder, it'd relieve my client of any liability."

"In your opinion, as a professional endorsed by Mr. Mason as he's done on this record," the twinkle in Snider's blue eyes was seen only by Meshbesher, "would it be negligence, in the hypothetical that I just gave you, for an attorney *not* to investigate and depose those potential suspects?"

"Yes. I believe it would be."

"Mr. Meshbesher, was there any knowledge that came to your attention that would cause you to investigate whether or not Roger Nordstrom and Bobby Nachtsheim peddled drugs and guns?"

"There was an indication in the police report that the police got that information from some witness. I saw no reason for me to investigate it because it hurt my client's case."

"In what way?"

"It would point to possible suspects. We had a lawsuit against Norm Wartnick and for us to establish those facts would damage the case that I had against him. That was his lawyer's job, not mine."

CHAPTER 39

Wartnick grimaced as he watched Friedberg and Snider shoot sandwich trash into the round can on their way out of the war room. Snider's shot went wide left. Friedberg's took a lucky bounce off the wall. "Don't give up your day job," Wartnick called as they disappeared through the doorway.

Webber scooped up the wad on the floor and successfully deposited it. "He scores!"

"You realize my wife's best friend's going on the stand right now and I'm not there to encourage her."

"Distract her, you mean." Webber laughed.

Webber reminded Wartnick they, as the plaintiff, were first to present their evidence, and Mason, as the defense, could cross-examine their witnesses and call their evidence into question, as much as the judge allowed—those were the current proceedings. Once they were finished—had rested—it was Mason's turn to present his witnesses and evidence, and Friedberg and Snider would cross-examine and call into question what they could.

"Your turn to testify," Webber said, "—to tell that jury what you want them to know—is first thing tomorrow morning. Both Joe and Jerry want you ready, so, one more time—here's the list we're to cover. Item One. They say, 'Remember, Norm, just relax. You're in good hands.'"

"Just skip to the part where you tell me where I'm supposed to look when very-cross-eyed 'Black Jack' is standing in front of me asking me very serious questions."

Wednesday, October 5, 1994 – trial day seven

Wartnick stood before the bailiff and again, eight years later, raised his right hand and swore to tell the truth, the whole truth, and nothing but the truth, so help him God.

Friedberg stood behind counsel's table and smiled at him as Wartnick adjusted himself into the tight quarters of the witness box. The court reporter was to his left on the other side of a three-foot-high oak divider and not even an arm's length away. Judge Stanoch's bench rose on the other side of the court reporter, elevated several feet higher than Wartnick's head. "How old a man are you, Mr. Wartnick?"

"Fifty-three."

"And how old were you back in 1973? The hard questions come later," Friedberg smiled again.

"Well, that's a tough question. How age flies. Born in 1941; that'd make me—In '73?"

"Why don't you just subtract twenty-one."

"All right. Thirty-one. Thirty-one years old."

Joe nodded. "Okay. Would you please tell the jury whether or not you have ever killed or participated in any way in the killing of any human being."

Wartnick looked at the jury panel mere feet away to his right. Their gazes nailed him. "The answer to that is No."

"Did you have anything to do with the death of Bob Nachtsheim?"

"No."

"And how long have you been living under the shadow of that accusation brought against you by the Nachtsheims?"

"Twenty-one years." The crushing grip on Wartnick's soul loosened ever-so slightly.

The courtroom began to refill after the mid-afternoon break. Friedberg had spent most of today on questions that detailed facts surrounding the events of that cold morning twenty-one years before. Now Friedberg was reloaded and ready to finish strong.

Wartnick, in the witness box, used his referee focus to avoid watching Phil Gainsley plod into the room. Connie had commented before dinner the previous Saturday, "I just read a quote from Ezra Pound. 'Affable, suave, moderate men, all of them perfectly and smugly convinced of their respectability.'[32] Doesn't that just scream *Phil Gainsley* to you guys?!"

"Mr. Wartnick," Friedberg's voice burst into Wartnick's thoughts. Wartnick blinked and refocused.

"Mr. Wartnick, did you ever speak to Mr. Gainsley about how he planned to defend you?"

"No."

"Did you ever have a conference with him about whether he was going to investigate the case?"

"No."

"Did you have any expectations of what he was going to do?"

"My expectations would be that he was going to do the job he was hired to do and that was to defend me."

"All right," Friedberg nodded. "Now, was there any question in your mind that you were being accused of bringing about the death of Mr. Nachtsheim?"

"Not after the amended complaint."

"And at that point did Mr. Gainsley ever call you in and say this is how I'm going to investigate the case? This is what I'm going to do?"

32. Ezra Pound. "Polite Essays" in *New Directions*. 1937. 116.

"No."

"Did you have any expectations of how a lawyer would defend you in relation to being accused of a murder?"

"Well, I had expectations somebody would go out and talk to somebody. My wife and I talked on that, too. There was nothing getting done, nobody was being subpoenaed, nobody was being asked questions. It was almost as if we were going no place."

"Did Mr. Gainsley ever sit down with you and go over the police reports?"

"Never."

"Did he ever discuss with you any other suspects?"

"We had a brief discussion about Bobby, at one point when it came closer to trial and that was about the only suspect."

"Did you ask him what he was doing?"

"I challenged him many times, you know. Where were we going? What was going on? I called a lot over the years. I tried to keep informed, but I guess, you know, what he told me I believed."

"What did he tell you?"

"He told me that things were progressing nicely."

"Okay. Did you ask him for any detail on that?"

"Well, he had some problems with the first case which was unjust enrichment. He didn't understand that. And he kept saying, 'Norm, that just doesn't make any sense to me.'

"As far as other issues were concerned," Wartnick continued, "I asked him, he'd come up with some real good answers and I guess, you know, being as I am only—well, just a layman—I thought they were the correct answers, so—." He let his words trail off, uncertain what to say.

"Were you ever told anything about a party where a plan was developed to rob Bob Nachtsheim?"

"Never."

"Did you ever hear about it during the trial you sat through?"

"No."

"Was any other person who could possibly have killed Bob Nachtsheim ever brought up to you by Mr. Gainsley?"

"Other than Bobby? No."

"Ever bring it up in the trial or in discussions with you?"

"No."

"Did you continue to receive bills?"

"Yes."

"Did you ever get any bills for investigation?"

"No."

"Did Mr. Gainsley ever advise you that a statute had been amended to change the nature of your lawsuit?"

"Yes."

"What did he tell you about that?"

"Well, he told me that when the wrongful death act had been filed against me, that Mr. Meshbesher had gone out and got the law changed so there was no longer a limitation on murder in a wrongful death act, and it was made retroactive back to my case, back to 1973."

"Okay. Did he tell you, discuss with you at all, in the years from 1982, 1983, forward, why he'd instructed you to take the Fifth Amendment?"

"No."

"There were some interrogatories put in this case where you take the Fifth Amendment again. What happened there?"

"Well, I received them in the mail. I've got to tell you, my mailman—I got a lot of mail. Mr. Gainsley sent me material. It had notes: 'sign here.' I signed and sent it back. I just, I guess when it said that 'You refuse to answer on the grounds,' or whatever is specifically in the Fifth, I just assumed it was a continuation of what was going on the first time I took the Fifth, that I was still under Phils protection saying I should, you know, his instructions that that's my answer."

"Did you receive copies of a lot of correspondence that Mr. Gainsley sent in this case?"

"Yes."

"I want to show you Plaintiff's Exhibit No. Fifty-One, which is in evidence, and it's a letter sent by Mr. Gainsley to Mr. Meshbesher, February 26, 1985. Was there a copy sent to you of that letter?"

Wartnick glanced at the page he took from Friedberg. "No."

"Why don't you read that out loud to the jury."

"Dated February 26, 1985." Wartnick complied as Friedberg turned and ambled toward counsel's table, head bowed, listening. "'Dear Ron: I am thinking of having my client waive his Fifth Amendment rights and, if you wish, allowing him to submit himself for a deposition. I would do so, however, only with the written understanding that a trier of fact would not be advised that he once took the Fifth Amendment. If you wish to pursue this further, please advise.'"

"Mr. Gainsley was saying he was thinking of having," Friedberg turned toward Wartnick, "you waive your Fifth Amendment rights and allow Mr. Meshbesher to take your deposition *if* he would agree to forget about the first one where you were instructed to take the Fifth. Did he ever discuss that with you?"

"No."

"Did he ever discuss offering you to Mr. Meshbesher for any kind of unconditional deposition?"

"No."

"Did he ever discuss with you the ramifications of taking the Fifth Amendment in a civil case?"

"No."

"When you arrived the first day at trial, had Mr. Gainsley made you aware of the ramifications of taking the Fifth Amendment in a civil case?"

"No."

"Had he told you it was the taking of the Fifth Amendment, which he'd instructed you to do, that allowed the case to go to a jury at all?"

"No."

"Had he explained to you any Fifth Amendment law?"

"No."

Friedberg shrugged. "Had you ever told him anything incriminating?"

"Objection," Mason growled. "How does the witness know?"

Friedberg addressed Judge Stanoch. "Be the best one to know, Your Honor."

"All right. Overrule the objection."

Wartnick had watched Mason during that interchange and forgot what Friedberg had asked. "Could I have the question one more time, please?"

"Had you ever yet told Mr. Gainsley anything incriminating?"

"No."

"As you sit here today, do you have any understanding of why that man gave you that card and told you, signaled you to read it?"

"No."

"Did he ever ask you to attend a deposition of any of these people at the party?"

"No."

"Did he ever tell you there was a person in this world named Roger Nordstrom?"

"No."

Friedberg took a few steps toward Wartnick. "Now, you've said this before, but you heard the evidence going in front of that jury. If you were a juror, would you have found against yourself?"

"Yes."

"Why?"

"There wasn't anything that pointed to anybody else but me."

"And who were you counting on to point some other way but you?"

"Mr. Gainsley."

"What did he tell you about whether a jury could understand a case like this?"

"Well, as the case progressed—and it only took a week—he said a jury doesn't have the intelligence to understand a case of this magnitude, so he expected to lose at this level."

"He actually told you he expected to lose?"

"Well, Mr. Gainsley told me that the jury, not being capable of making this decision, would have to—the only ones that could really make a decision of this type would be the Appellate Court. And we filed the proper papers to go to the Appellate Court, I'll tell you the truth, with the understanding that it would be overturned."

"Did you pay him additional funds to appeal the case?"

"We were in arrears on payment. I got a call from his office saying if I didn't bring the account up to relatively current he wouldn't take it to the Appellate Court. Somebody came out to the house, brought my wife a box of candy, and we gave him a sizeable check."

"After the trial, did you write Mr. Gainsley a letter?"

"Yes, I did."

Friedberg turned to counsel's table, lifted the sheaf of papers off the top of his stack, and crossed toward Wartnick. "Showing you what's marked as Plaintiff's Exhibit Ninety-Three—"

Wartnick took the papers and made sure his referee's face was in place.

"—I ask you if you could identify this letter. Did you write it?"

"Yes, I did."

"And did you send that to Mr. Gainsley?"

"Yes, I did."

"And was that letter a reflection of your feelings, both emotional and intellectual, at the time you wrote it?"

"Yes, it absolutely was."

"All right. And is this the best record of how you felt back then?"

Wartnick paused and, though he looked at the letter, he saw again the darkened basement and the green glow of the computer monitor. "It was a time I sat down at the computer and wrote what my heart believed to be wrong and right." He pulled himself back up to look at Friedberg. "Yes, it was the best. Yes."

Friedberg turned to Judge Stanoch. "Could I have permission to have this read to the jury, Your Honor? It's offered."

"Mr. Mason."

"The issue is whether this should come into evidence?"

The judge nodded. "That's the first issue. Right."

"No objection to that."

"All right. It's admitted."

Wartnick's gaze returned to the lines on the page in front of him. They blurred.

He heard Friedberg's voice. "Ask that it be read, Your Honor."

"We object to that. It's four pages long and it's not fair to the jury."

"All right. I'll overrule the objection and allow it to be read."

Wartnick noticed that the courtroom was quiet. He looked up. Friedberg nodded to him.

"It's marked 'very personal.'" Norm read. "'Dear Phil: This letter is being put together on a computer so you will have to forgive the spelling and all the errors in paragraphs. I was never really good at that. … I did receive your letter today with the results of all the work my wife and you and her attorney had been doing over the last few months. … I always felt that I should never meddle in law since I did not know a thing about it. I left that to you experts. …

"'You have always treated me fairly, beginning with the old days. Now it is the new days. I have lost a case which many thought I could never lose; a case where I thought the idea was to try and prove that others, other than myself, had a motive to see Bob dead. I know now we never did much towards that goal. …

"'You say that the results of the trial were hard to deny. Well I do deny them. I feel now that I did not push you hard enough towards our goal, that of showing other motives, and because of this I've been forced to destroy my entire life's work.

"'Some say it was the judge, so do I sue him for not being fair? You know I cannot. Some say it was the way my attorney presented the case. I don't want to believe that. I have worked for years, like you, to make a life for my family and I see it going down the drain.

"'This letter is very hard to write as I feel that I'm dumping on you, but who else should I blame? Police officers and attorneys, friends of mine have asked me over and over again: Why? Why, after thirteen years can this happen? A case that was buried as long as this now comes to life and kills me. I have to answer to my children and my friends and of course members of my—my family and my wife's family. Why? Why did I let this happen?

"'I guess I was caught like this was just a fairy tale, was not real. But now I see my life is gone, wasted because of some judge and facts that weren't allowed into court. …

"'Now for money. I said you should also know how much this case has cost me over the years. I have spent during the last—during the time it was with your firm I spent over $20,000 trying to, as you told me, not make waves. Take the Fifth, lay low and quiet, do not make noise. And when you left your firm and went with the firm of Moss and Barnett I was to drop—I was to drop my case. That was hard to take, that was hard to take.'"

"Norm," Friedberg glanced up from his copy. "Read it exactly."

"I'm sorry."

"Start with 'do not make noise.'"

"Okay. '—do not make noise. And when you left your firm and went with the firm of Moss and Barnett and I was told that if I did not keep my account current you would have to drop my case. That was hard to take. I had trusted you and your firm to do a job for me and my family and now I'm not sure I trusted the right person.

"'I know I spent over forty thousand dollars with your firm over the last year or so. I'm not, and never have been, a wealthy man. Is this not the end of the well? I've been working with a rope and getting deeper. The rope is falling

237

away from me, from my grasp. I do not know if I will ever be able to see the light again. …

"'My family has been great and I knew they would be, but I have college children and who is to come through? Not me. I don't have the money. It is gone. …

"'Thank God my wife hired her own attorney. Now I have two attorneys to pay, but at least he informed what our rights were. He told us what to do.

"'You and I talked over what our next move was, sell and dispose of money legally, within the law, so that in the end, other than paying your fee and other attorney's fees, that I would have nothing left for her to get. Now after I talked with you on the phone a bit ago, you acted surprised that I did, in fact, pay Dayton's and Visa and other bills. You knew what I was doing and you told me it was okay.

"'I pay you more and more and now the well is getting deeper. I'm at my wits end. I lost a case I should never have lost. Now it is over and the next twenty years are going to be a bitch with everything going to her, my family doing without. Appeal? How? How? I do not have the funds to do so.

"'You already told me that an appeal would be a waste of your time and mine, so I guess it's over. She has won, and we have lost. I, my entire life, and to you just another case. What can be done?'" Wartnick choked and blinked hard. "I do not know. Does this firm of Moss and Barnett feel that all the blood from the Wartnick family is gone?'" He sniffed, then cleared his throat, "'Or do they feel that what has happened now should be a lesson to others to have lots of money before entering into a law case that took over fourteen years to crop up and let's move on to bigger and bigger fish.'" Wartnick hiccoughed. "'I wish my dad was alive—'"

Wartnick choked on the swelling in his throat and could no longer stem the tears; they fell despite all the control he could muster. "Excuse me."

Silence hovered throughout the room. A juror sniffed. Someone in the gallery coughed, then someone else. Wartnick did not want to know who.

"I told the jury I would have them out by four-thirty." Judge Stanoch's voice gently pushed back the silence. "I don't know how much is left."

Wartnick stayed glued to the page in his lap. "Just a short bit, Your Honor."

Friedberg nodded. "Probably ten minutes."

"Do we have members of the jury that have buses they have to catch? Okay. Why don't we take a break here for the day. If you can be back at nine-fifteen tomorrow morning. Rather than nine o'clock, nine-fifteen. All right. Have a pleasant evening. Remember, do not talk to anyone about the case. Do not allow anyone to talk to you about the case."

CHAPTER 40

The city lights of Minneapolis sparkled in the clear autumn night like diamonds, rubies, and amber. Looking north from atop Foshay Tower, the city's buildings stepped downward until they disappeared completely, swallowed up in the darkness of the Mississippi River valley.

At the base of that tower, Friedberg and Snider sat on two sides of a table covered with white linen. Outside the window, passers-by did double-takes at the face they saw every night on television news, for next to them, in a position to almost face the window, sat F. Lee Bailey. He ordered Scotch and a steak, rare, set right in the middle of a bare plate—no frills, no garnishes, just barely grilled meat.

Bailey had stopped overnight in Minneapolis on his way from Florida to California to assist in the O. J. Simpson criminal trial. The timing for his stop-over in the Twin Cities had been fortuitous—with the leniency of the Court and Mason's begrudging acquiescence.

Friedberg and Snider had picked up Bailey at the airport and brought him to dinner at Café Un, Deux, Trois to prepare for his day on the witness stand. He needed little preparation and was well versed in all the legal aspects involved in the case.

THURSDAY, OCTOBER 6, 1994 — TRIAL DAY EIGHT

Wartnick repositioned himself in the witness chair. The pain in his low back twitched worse than usual. Friedberg stood directly in front of him and pointed toward a line on the last page of Wartnick's personal letter to Gainsley. "Would you briefly finish reading this. You can start from there."

Wartnick nodded. "Why have I not said anything earlier? I am not very good in person and not good on the phone. I hate to hurt any person, even when they hurt me, but now who really cares? I've been crushed. I'm a broken man working for Betty and Moss and Barnett. ..."

The letter concluded: "'So here we are at the end of our rope, or *the* rope anyway. In fact, I'm just plain worn out. I do not sleep and I'm on heavy medication to help me relax.

"'Phil, this has taken me a long time to write so please read it. I do not hate, and I do not hold grudges but I just feel that I now and will for the rest of my life be going nowhere. ... I thought I would never say uncle, but maybe it's time. Uncle. Uncle. I have no more to give.

"'Do whatever you must and I'll try to keep you current in money, but how do I do that with Betty and family and you and my wife's attorney, only so many hours in the day and so many days in the week. I'll work until you are paid and I promise you that. I have never cheated anyone out of a buck and never Bob, that I promise you. You will get your money.

"'Good luck and God speed. Norm Wartnick.'"

He slid the letter onto the wooden shelf in front of him and listened for Friedberg.

"Mr. Wartnick, are you working now?"

"No." He looked up to where he knew Friedberg must be standing.

"How are you supporting your family?"

"I'm an umpire. I do sports and I work in the evening."

"Okay. Up until recently did you have a job?"

"Yes."

"How long did you work there?"

"Seven years."

"What happened?"

"My position with the company was no longer there. It was just simply eliminated."

"Okay. Did you work last night?"

"Yes."

"What did you do?"

"I umpired volleyball games."

"What type of umpiring do you do? You do that year round?"

"I do volleyball. I do basketball. I do slow pitch and fast pitch for high schools and for Park and Rec, so it's an all-year-around job, yes."

"Let me ask you about your family. How long have you been married?"

"Thirty-three years."

"To how many wives?"

"One."

"It's your only marriage?"

"Yes."

"Were you married to her when Mr. Nachtsheim was killed?"

"Yes."

"Have you remained married through all of this travail?"

"Yes."

"Does your wife work?"

"Yes."

"What does she do?"

"She's a special needs teacher, and she's the lead teacher that goes in in the morning, starts about seven, quarter to seven; takes the children that have to have a place to go while the parents go to work. She also handles problem children who have difficulty with reading and other school problems where they have to have special treatment so there's more of a one-to-one relationship with the teacher versus a classroom of twenty-five or thirty children."

"How long has she done that?"

"Well, she graduated from the University of Minnesota as a teacher. She taught for several years and then we decided to have a family. And then she went back to work part-time as the children grew older. Now that the money has become an issue, she's gone to full-time."

"How old were your children at the time Mr. Nachtsheim was killed? Approximately."

"Well, my eldest daughter right now is twenty-eight and Bob has been gone for twenty-one years, so she'd be approximately seven years old; seven or eight. My second child would have been, is two years younger so would have been either five or six, and my next child is two years younger than that, which would have made him three to four."

"Okay. And did they graduate from school?" Friedberg had begun his slow amble around the front of the room.

"Yes. All three of my children went through—My daughters, both my daughters graduated valedictorian; my son with high honors. Both my daughters went on to the University of Minnesota. One is in accounting, and the other became an aerospace engineer. She was an intern for Louis Nassau down in Houston and now works for the Louis Nassau Center in Cleveland. She's married. My son graduated from the University of Minnesota as a computer programmer and a computer analyst."

"How did you manage to get them all through school?"

"Financially?"

"Yeah."

"It wasn't because of me." Wartnick hated that pinch in his chest. "My wife's father was a prominent doctor in Minneapolis and he put away money for all his grandchildren's education. That's the money they used."

"All right." Friedberg nodded. "Have they been supportive, your whole family, of you during this entire time?"

"Yes."

"On the morning that Mr. Nachtsheim was killed, did you see your children?"

"Yes."

"Did you tell Mr. Gainsley you had seen your children that morning?"

"Yes."

"Did he ever interview them?"

"No."

"Did you observe, in the course of your representation by Phillip Gainsley, any attempt to investigate and find out who had done this?"

"No."

"Why didn't you complain to him about it?"

"I did."

"Did you accept—" Friedberg hesitated. "What kind of answers did you receive?"

"Well, Mr. Gainsley was my attorney. When Mr. Gainsley told me that he was doing what he felt his job responsibility was, that he was doing it well—. He worked for a good law firm. Harry Gainsley was his father. I always felt Phil was, you know, going to be at least as good as his father, hopefully. Always felt very comfortable that Phil was doing the best he could do."

Soon it was Mason's turn to cross-examine. Mason stood beside his white board and pointed. "Okay. On May 24, 1973, Mr. Nachtsheim was fatally shot shortly after he arrived at work."

"That's correct," Wartnick nodded.

"And the evidence suggested that the killer was somebody Mr. Nachtsheim knew."

"Object to that as argumentative." Friedberg leaned back in his chair with his thumbs in his pants' pockets. "Beyond his ability to deduce, Your Honor."

"Overruled. The witness may answer."

"I'm sorry," Wartnick shook his head. "Could you repeat the question, Mr. Mason?"

"Right. The evidence suggested that the killer was someone Mr. Nachtsheim knew," Mason repeated.

"I wasn't aware of all the evidence, so I guess, in all fairness, I couldn't answer that."

"Okay. Now here we are twenty years later and you've been paying a certain amount of attention to the evidence in this case?"

"Yes."

"And having heard that evidence, you'd agree, wouldn't you, that the evidence suggests that the killer was somebody Mr. Nachtsheim knew?"

"I'm not sure I'd interpret that all the evidence I've heard shows that."

"He apparently had let the killer in before opening for business?"

"I don't remember anybody saying 'Let him in.' I don't know that for a fact."

"There was no evidence of a robbery or a struggle?"

"That's correct."

"The killer shot Mr. Nachtsheim in the head at close range from a visible position."

"I guess that's correct."

"And after hearing all the evidence, the jury decided that you did murder or caused the murder of Bob Nachtsheim."

"Yes."

"And you contend that you never did anything to lose your case."

"Object to the form of that question," Friedberg said without moving.

"Overruled. The witness may answer."

"Would you please rephrase," Wartnick said.

"You contend that you never did anything to lose that case," Mason repeated.

"Myself, personally? No, I did not do anything personally. No."

"You contend that Mr. Gainsley was negligent."

"Yes."

"You contend that Mr. Gainsley, in fact, did three specific things that were negligence. Right?"

"Yes."

"One of those things that you claim," Mason tapped the white board, "is that Mr. Gainsley was negligent by injecting inadmissible and highly prejudicial evidence into the trial by referring in opening statement to the fact 'Wartnick had refused to take a polygraph test when asked to do so by the police detective investigating the Nachtsheim murder.' That's one of your charges, right?"

"Yes."

"And your second charge is that he was negligent in, quote, failing to conduct even minimal adequate investigation into the Nachtsheim murder by failing to interview and depose key witnesses and suspects in the murder. Right?"

"Yes."

Mason paused and faced Wartnick. "And who are the key witnesses and suspects?"

"Not until later on did I know, but at that time he didn't interview anybody."

"Right. The question now is, who are the key witnesses and suspects?"

"At that time I thought Bobby was a key suspect."

"Okay. Anyone else? I'm asking you for the names of the key witnesses and suspects."

"You're asking me a hypothetical based upon one moment in time. After I was able to learn more about the case I learned there were a lot more people that needed to be questioned."

"Well, I'm not really asking you that," Mason looked somewhat miffed, "so I'm going to be a little more specific so it'll be easier for you."

"All right."

He took a step forward and shook his index finger toward the witness box. "You're sitting in that chair now in 1994. As you sit in that chair today, tell me and the jury the names of people you consider key witnesses and suspects in the murder."

"At that time, I did not know."

"No, no, no. *Today.*"

"Oh, today."

"Yes, sir."

"Today, with the knowledge I have, I would—"

"Key witnesses and suspects, please."

"I was surprised that he didn't investigate the party that took place the night before."

"No, no, please," Mason moaned. "I'm asking for a name, a name of a person, and that person, if you name that person, should be a person who is a key witness and suspect as you understand it today."

"Dennis Kreuser."

"Dennis Kreuser," Mason repeated.

"Roger Nordstrom."

"Uh-huh."

"Alan Mentes."

"Uh-huh."

"Bobby Nachtsheim."

"All right."

"Larry Strehlow."

"Okay."

"Debbie Feist," Wartnick concluded. "There were others. Right now, you know, those are the people I'm thinking of."

"And I believe we were interrupted here," Mason returned to the board. "The first and second claims we've covered. And the third claim of negligence says that Gainsley was negligent in failing to mitigate the damage done at the deposition by offering Wartnick unconditionally for a second deposition on those matters as to which he pled the Fifth Amendment privilege. That's your third claim?"

"Yes, sir."

"And the deposition we're talking about is that first deposition where you did plead the Fifth Amendment?"

"Yes."

"Then another of your claims is that this negligence of Gainsley caused the jury verdict. Right?"

"Yes."

"And another of your claims is that, but for this, the jury verdict would have been different."

"Yes."

"And that's your case against Mr. Gainsley. Right?"

"Your Honor," Friedberg leaned forward, a sheaf of papers in hand. "Could we have this marked for identification so the record will indicate that it's there?"

"Mr. Mason?"

"Sure. Can we do that at a break rather than take up time here?"

"Sure." Friedberg smiled and leaned back again.

"I'm sorry, Mr. Mason. Could you repeat the last question you asked me?"

"Sure."

Madam Reporter read back, "And that's your case against Mr. Gainsley. Right?"

"The answer to that one was Yes."

"You've used the Gainsley firm on a number of matters?"

"Yes."

"Over the years you met with Mr. Harry Gainsley, his dad?"

"Yes."

"And met with Phil?"

"I'm not sure how many times I met with Mr. Gainsley, senior, myself. It was Mr. Gainsley and my dad and Mr. Stoller that met. I knew Mr. Gainsley, senior, please understand that, and then eventually I knew Phil Gainsley. Yes."

"And you never had any complaints over the years up through 1973?"

"No."

"You asked the Gainsley firm for help to collect the insurance when you weren't able to do it on your own."

"That's correct."

"But that was still in 1973, wasn't it?"

"I don't know. It could be if you say it is. I have nothing in front of me to show that it is."

"In 1982 you came to him when you sold your business to J. W. Perry?"

"Yes."

"October of '84 you came to him when you were sued for wrongful death?"

"Yes."

"And when you went to see Mr. Gainsley in 1984, he had represented you for eleven years since the murder. Right?"

"Yes."

"You wouldn't have gone to him in 1984 if you didn't think he was doing a good job up until then, would you?"

"Yes, that's correct."

"You *would* have gone to him if you thought he was doing a bad job?"

"No. I would have gone to him because I thought he was doing a good job."

"You would complain a lot?"

"I complained about, you know, not being able to get a hold of him, not getting information in the mail that pertained to my case."

"And you concluded he had done an excellent job with thorough preparation."

"From the knowledge I had at the time, yes."

"Now, you testified yesterday that you told Mr. Gainsley it was standard procedure for florists to take flowers out of the cooler in the morning. Right?"

"Yes."

"You didn't tell him that at the trial but you told him prior. Right?"

"I might have told him at both places."

"Well, what you testified to yesterday was that you told him prior to trial but not at trial."

"I said—I'll say right now that I did tell him beforehand, before the trial. It was standard procedure, yes."

"And you testified yesterday that you didn't tell him at the trial. Right?"

"Objection. Mischaracterization. He never said that."

"Sustained."

"Oh, really?" Mason feigned mock surprise. "What's your testimony on that subject, sir?"

"I thought I told him—you know, it's been a long time. Maybe it could be that I told him prior to trial and not at trial itself."

"Well, it hasn't been a long time from today to yesterday. Isn't that what you said yesterday? That you didn't tell him *at* trial because you had already told him *prior* to trial?"

"If that's what I said, that's what I said."

"Isn't that your memory of it, sir?"

"If that's what I said, that's what I said."

"In any event, isn't that the fact?"

"Yes, if that's what I said."

"All right. And the reason you told Mr. Gainsley prior to trial was that he'd shown you the police report where Mrs. Nachtsheim had said what she did about the flowers. Isn't that a fact?"

"I never saw the police report."

"That's not the question, sir." Mason jerked forward a step. "The question to you is, isn't it a fact that the reason you told Mr. Gainsley about the flowers and what you claimed the practice was *prior* to trial was that you had seen the police report and discussed it with Mr. Gainsley. True or false?"

"I said I did not see—" Wartnick glanced at Snider, inhaled, and said, "That's false."

"All right. What was the reason? How did it come to your attention that you should say something about flowers to Mr. Gainsley?"

"Because the case was known as The Orchid Murder, and I wanted to explain to him why the orchids were out of the cooler."

"Everybody else knew it but you? It had become known as The Orchid Murder case and you didn't know about that?"

"Know about what, Mr. Mason?"

"Well, isn't it a fact that you and Mr. Gainsley had discussed this so-called orchid situation prior to trial?"

"Yes."

"And it's because there was something in the [police] file about that. Isn't that a fact?"

"I don't know. I didn't see the file."

"And this—" Mason stepped to defendant's end of counsel's table and shuffled papers. "Do you have Plaintiff's Exhibit Ninety-Three? This letter that you were reading?"

Wartnick glanced down to the shelf in front of him. "Yes, sir."

"That letter was written on August 5 of 1986?"

He found the date. "Yes, sir."

"Why didn't you write to Mr. Gainsley a letter like this in April or May of 1986? After the trial?"

"I thought long and hard about responding to Mr. Gainsley's actions in the courtroom. As expressed in the letter, I don't do well on the phone and I don't do well in public, so after giving a great deal of thought, I had to get it off my chest. I just couldn't sleep at night. I couldn't live with this anymore. I had to tell Mr. Gainsley my feelings, so I wrote the letter."

"The verdict was in April some time? And May, June, July, and now it's August fifth. Why did you write on August fifth of 1986?"

"Again, as stated, that was the time, after I'd pondered and decided whether or not there was something that I had to do."

"Well, the fact is, you wrote the letter because you learned that Mrs. Nachtsheim's attorneys were starting to actually try to collect on the judgment."

Wartnick nodded. "That could also be true."

"Well, that *is* what is true. Isn't it?"

"I don't have the specific dates when they started to collect money."

"The fact is, you'd gotten a letter from Mr. Gainsley telling you that Mrs. Nachtsheim's lawyers were seeking to get judgment entered."

"Do you have a date or something for me? I'll be glad to read it."

"August 4, 1986."

"That may have prompted me to write this letter," Wartnick nodded, "after pondering about it. If that's the date I received the letter, it was time to take some action."

"And they believed that you had been transferring funds to avoid the effect of the judgment."

"I don't have that in front of me."

"I'll give it to you," Mason grabbed pages off counsel's table and walked them to the witness. "I hand to you Defendant's Exhibit One-Fifty-Three, which is a letter to you dated August 4, 1986, from Gainsley to Mr. and Mrs. Norm Wartnick. Would you review that letter and confirm that's a letter that you got on or about August 4 or 5, 1986."

"I have no reason to doubt this."

Defendant's Exhibit 153 was presented and received. Then Mason read the letter aloud which closed with, "The court will no doubt enter the judgment, but I will ask the court to stay the entry until such time as it hears our motion for a new trial, or for other relief preparatory to an appeal."

"Yes," Wartnick nodded.

"And on the attached affidavit they recite, in paragraph three, 'That Nachtsheim has voluntarily stayed the entry of that judgment while the possibility of reaching a settlement between the parties has been explored.' Is that true?"

"Yes."

"And they say, 'That from April 25, 1986 to the present, Wartnick has engaged in the following transactions,' and they list 'a' through 'h,' some examples of you transferring assets. Right?"

"Yes."

"And they conclude—without taking the time, the jury will have this to review—they conclude, 'That in light of the above-mentioned transactions, Nachtsheim wishes to have the judgment entered immediately.' Right?"

Wartnick flipped through several of the pages. "Yes."

"And your letter, this August 5, 1986 letter, was written—the third sentence reads: 'I did receive your letter today with the results of all the work my wife and you and her attorney have been doing the last few months.' *That's* what this August 5 letter is all about, isn't it?"

Wartnick glanced up from the pages and nodded. "That's what prompted me to write the letter. Yes."

"And you still wanted Mr. Gainsley to be your attorney?" Mason proclaimed victoriously.

"Up through the point of the appellate court and, ultimately, the supreme court, yes."

"And he wrote you after he got this letter of yours and he said you should feel free to hire someone else. Right?"

"I don't have that in front of me."

"I'll give it to you," Mason said. Defendant's Exhibit 152 was identified, offered, and received into evidence. Mason spent time on Phil Gainsley's letter to Wartnick, parsing it into relevant bits such as, "I'm not trying to create work for myself" and "if you have lost confidence in my efforts, as suggested by your letter to me, I would be pleased to turn the file over to another attorney of your selection." Also, "I have lived with this case for thirteen years and feel comfortable taking on the appellate process." Mason concluded, "That's what he said to you, wasn't it?"

"That's what he wrote."

"And you chose to go forward?"

"Yes."

"Now, it isn't true, is it, what you said yesterday, that Mr. Gainsley said that the jury would be too stupid to understand your case?"

"That's exactly what he said."

"Isn't it that he told you they'd be too *smart* to understand your case?"

"No."

"Turn, if you would, please, to Defendant's Exhibit One-Fifty-Two, Mr. Gainsley's August 28, 1986 letter."

"I've got it." It was still in Wartnick's hand.

"Now find the paragraph that begins, 'Norm, I know of your frustrations in this matter.'"

"Yes, I've got it."

"Let me read along with you. 'Norm, I know of your frustrations in this matter, and I sense that you're beginning to be frustrated with me and my services as well. I can only tell you that I'm doing everything I can for you, and, what little comfort it is, I must remind you that I told you when you first called me about this case that it would have to be won at the appellate level.' That's true, isn't it?"

"Yes."

"And then this next sentence: 'I have always tried to explain to you that a jury would not understand why you renewed the life insurance policy on Mr. Nachtsheim when he was no longer in your employ.' That's what he said, isn't it?"

"Yes."

"I'm going to hand you Defendant's Exhibit Twelve. This is a proof of death claim that you filed on June 28 of 1973. Isn't that a fact?"

"It's my handwriting, so I'll say yes. My signature, I should say."

"Well, is that the only thing that makes you know that on June 28 of 1973 you filed a proof of death?"

"I believe I asked Mr. Zola Friedman what was needed to receive the funds for Midwest Floral Supply. He said a proof of death needed to be filed, so he went ahead and filled it out and I proceeded to sign it."

"And you don't remember talking to anybody at the Gainsley firm before you signed that. Right?"

"No. I don't remember speaking, anyway, with Mr. Gainsley."

"The first time you talked with anyone at Mr. Gainsley's office, they told you not to talk with anyone until you had a meeting. Right?"

"They simply told me not to talk with anyone. There was no mention of a meeting."

"And that was always their advice—Don't talk to anybody about anything."

"That's correct."

"And after you did meet with them and you told them the facts, they said to you, 'This doesn't look good.' Right?"

"I don't remember that."

"And you knew in your own mind it didn't look good."

"I always felt that the insurance policy that was payable to Midwest Floral was always a problem after the shooting of Mr. Nachtsheim. Yes."

"And you called the Gainsley firm after Mr. Krueger had come to see you."

"Yes."

Mason then plodded through Lieutenant Krueger's report of his 'let's just talk off the record'–conversation with Wartnick, including, "'I asked him if it was true that Midwest held a life insurance policy on the victim. He stated that they did and that it was his idea.' Is that true?"

"No. That's not entirely true."

"Well, is that what you told Mr. Krueger?"

"No."

"'Wartnick stated,'" Mason again read, "'that the policy was made out because Bob Nachtsheim was a key personnel and there was a key personnel insurance policy.' Is that true?"

"That's true."

"'I then asked Norm Wartnick when he made the last payment. He stated he thought it was somewhere around the first of April.' Is that true what you told him?"

"Again, Mr. Krueger wrote what he did not take notes on. I thought I'd made it sometime the latter part of April or May, but if he wrote April first, that's what he wrote. I don't think that's what I told him."

"Well, Mr. Krueger wrote that you, quote, stated that he thought it was somewhere around the first part of April, closed quote, that you made the payment on the insurance policy. Is that what you said to Mr. Krueger?"

"No."

"Asked and answered, Your Honor," Friedberg spoke at the same time Wartnick answered.

"The answer can stand."

"That wasn't true, was it?" Mason growled.

"I believe I answered that if Mr. Krueger put a date in there and the date is incorrect, then the date would be wrong. But I did state that the policy had been paid at a given point."

"Well, again with this, is there any reason Mr. Krueger would write down, 'He stated that he thought it was somewhere around the first part of April,' if that's not what you said to him?"

"I can't speak for Mr. Krueger."

"But you'd figure that unless you stated it, he wouldn't write it?"

"No. I said I can't speak for Mr. Krueger."

"In any event, we now know that it isn't a fact that you paid that premium some time the first part of April. We know it was on May 11th, don't we?"

"That's correct."

"'I asked him how much money did he make in a premium payment,'" Mason again quoted from Krueger's report. "'He said he thought it was $1,050.' Was that true?"

"The number sounds very close. Yes."

"Did you tell him, 'Well, look, I didn't make the payment. It was a corporation decision and Mr. Stoller, this was a joint deal'?"

250

"It would have been paid by the corporation and decided upon by the Stollers and myself," Wartnick nodded. "It wouldn't have been anything that I would have made the decision on myself."

"But that's not what you told Mr. Krueger."

"Mr. Krueger, again, did not take notes. Mr. Krueger simply wrote down what he wanted to write down."

CHAPTER 41

The courtroom was packed. Clerks and courthouse employees who could wrangle time away from their desk and every attorney whose presence was not mandatory in another courtroom had wedged into any spaces big enough to hold them. Standing room was even fully occupied. Those who watched the O. J. Simpson trial on television every night now had the celebrity attorney seated in their midst.

"Members of the jury," Judge Stanoch brought the rustling crowd to silence. "At this time we're going to interrupt Mr. Mason's cross-examination of Mr. Wartnick and we're going to allow the plaintiffs to call their next witness. When we're through with Mr. Bailey's testimony, we'll resume with Mr. Mason's cross-examination and complete Mr. Wartnick's testimony. Mr. Snider, you may call your next witness."

"Thank you very much, Your Honor. I thank counsel for permitting us to take Mr. Bailey at this time." Snider nodded to Jack. "Would you take the stand, please, Mr. Bailey."

Bailey was duly sworn in. He was shorter and more squarely built than most people realized, but Bailey's vim and self-confidence surprised no one.

"For the record, would you state your full name, spelling your last name," the court clerk requested.

"Francis Lee Bailey, Jr. B-a-i-l-e-y."

"Mr. Snider."

Snider seemed very relaxed, at least a lot more relaxed than Wartnick felt.

"Thank you very much, Your Honor." Snider was pure business as he started on the basics, his deep Southern drawl filled the courtroom with a genteel voice of authority.

"I was a young Marine Corps fighter pilot," Bailey said. "It was required in the squadron to have a ground duty. I was assigned as Second Assistant Legal Officer and assured I wouldn't have much work to do because I hadn't finished college at that point.

"One day the First Assistant killed himself on takeoff in a jet that blew up. The Legal Officer resigned and left the squadron and I became the Legal Officer, and very shortly I was sent in to try military cases called courts-martial."

Snider stood discreetly between the jury box and the public gallery. "And please tell the jury what kind of cases you tried at that time."

"All courts-martials are criminal cases. There's no civil jurisdiction. It's all about wrongdoing and the possibility of punishment. At the time, shortage of lawyers in the services compelled them to recruit or ask for volunteers whose name began with A, B, or C to take on these assignments.

"And we were functioning in the military courts under a brand new system, only two years old with untrained personnel who became trained in the business of trial law. We also had to attend civil courts when a Marine was in trouble, and monitor the proceedings and report back to the commanding officer as to what was being done."

"Approximately how many cases did you try before the military tribunal?"

"Probably forty or fifty. I prosecuted some, then reviewed many. I went up the ladder one step and became a Group Legal Officer. A Group usually consisted of five or six fighter squadrons or about 2,500 men."

"And then, if I heard you correctly, it was after this experience trying cases for the military that you went to law school?"

"Well, I had two years at Harvard. I went back for one semester and applied for a waiver to get into law school without graduating so the G. I. Bill would cover me through law school. That was granted and I started law school about nine months after I was discharged."

"And after you got your law degree what did you do?"

"I started immediately trying cases two months out of law school. The first jury case was a capital."

"What is a capital case?" Snider nodded toward the jury box. "For the jury."

"Where the death penalty is being actively sought by the prosecution in a state which permits that penalty."

"Were you associated with some firm at that time or simply practicing alone?"

"No. There was a case in progress being defended by a 72-year-old lawyer who thought it would benefit his client if he demanded certain polygraph evidence. He did. It went against him. He had a heart seizure and they started looking around for someone who knew about the polygraph to cross-examine the witness and then, to their sadness, the only one they could find was a 27-year-old lawyer across the river in Boston. I took over the case at that point. The lawyer did not recover, so I finished it."

"Well, you were a 27-year-old lawyer with polygraph experience?"

"Yes."

"And what experience did you have with the polygraph?"

"In 1954, in addition to being the Legal Officer for Marine Fighter Squadron 334, I was assigned as the investigations officer. Because of that, I had to work closely with the provost marshal's office and G-2, the intelligence section of the Marine Corps. They had both a civilian and a military polygraph examiner. They relied very heavily on the polygraph to weed out those people who were accused but who were not guilty. It's very important in the military not to put innocent men to trial. The men in the barracks would know it and they'd lose confidence in the system, so this was a concerted effort that I learned to rely on very heavily and to learn something about the manner in which it operates."

"Did you take any special instruction in the polygraph or how did you master it?"

"I studied books, I sat in on polygraph tests, observed them, talked with the examiners as to why they put questions in a certain way, what responses on charts could mean, who could be tested, who could not with confidence, and that sort of thing. Then, when I got out in 1956, while I was in school and in law school, I formed an investigative company serving trial lawyers only, and in criminal cases would frequently encourage the lawyer who hired me to submit his client to a polygraph test if he said he was innocent of the charge."

"So, you're a 27-year-old lawyer handling a capital case two months out of law school."

Lee Bailey nodded. "Two months by the bar."

"Are you admitted to practice in states other than Massachusetts?"

"The only other state where I'm fully admitted is Florida. I'm admitted in all of the federal appellate courts, including the Supreme Court, and in many of the federal district courts."

"Have you had occasions to try cases outside of Massachusetts and Florida?"

"I have tried or supervised cases in every state but Montana."

"Does that include the state of Minnesota?"

"It does indeed."

"And have you tried a case to a verdict in Minnesota?"

"I did."

"Have you had occasion during that period of time to take some of your cases up to the United States Supreme Court?"

"Two."

"And what are those cases, please?"

"One was *Sheppard against Maxwell*, which is today the standard for pretrial publicity. And the other was taken in by the U. S. Supreme Court and then dismissed as improvidently taken in, which is a rare bird, but is the same as if we never had it. This was after we had argued it. We went back to the Federal District Court and got the relief sought."

"What was the nature of the Sheppard case, Mr. Bailey?"

"There were many flaws in Sheppard's conviction of a constitutional dimension, but the one that was the lead flaw, if you read the opinion, appears to be the fault of the press for misconduct prior to and during the trial. Closely read, it really bottomed on the fact that the trial judge failed to control with the means at hand and to protect the defendant, such as locking up the jury and those kinds of things."

"Let me ask you about other activities that you've engaged in since the early 1960s. Have you done anything besides practice law?"

"I've done a fair amount of teaching at several of the polygraph schools at the Judicial College in Reno, Nevada. I'm the only lifetime member of the American Polygraph Association who is not an examiner and, indeed, taught a course at their annual convention in August."

"Mr. Bailey, what courses have you taught?"

"I have lectured at a great many of the law schools in the country. I've lectured for a lot of law enforcement, federal prosecutors. For police, generally, the favorite topic is how to be a good witness. For lawyers, generally, the favorite topic has been the art of cross-examination, but it's not limited to that. I've lectured on all phases of trial. In the polygraph schools, the one in Chicago, in New York, and now in San Diego, the Baxter School, I generally lecture about what is called the legal aspects of polygraph testing, which is a fairly broad perspective."

"Mr. Bailey," Snider strolled to counsel's table. "Let me just ask you to focus on your polygraph work. Have you used polygraphs in your practice over the years?"

"Very extensively." He nodded again.

"And would you please describe for the jury in what way you've used polygraphs."

"Many defense lawyers don't want to know if the client is guilty because if the client is guilty and tells you so, you cannot put him on the witness stand, ethically—at least according to my ethics. But to defend a guilty person as if he's innocent stands a good chance of making mistakes and getting him convicted. Conversely, if you think a person's guilty and he's not—which is what happened to Dr. Sheppard in his first trial—and you defend him as if he *were* guilty, you may well get a conviction which is not deserved and about which you can do nothing."

"Mr. Bailey, do you have an understanding of how the polygraph works?"

"Yes."

"And would you please describe that for the jury."

"In its simplest terms—"

"Objection," Mason called out. "This isn't a matter that the witness was tendered as an expert on."

"It is, Your Honor."

"Overrule the objection, allow him to answer. Note the objection for the record."

Bailey smiled at the ladies of the jury. "In its simplest terms, years ago there was discovered a psychological phenomenon called the fight-flight-holding syndrome. When a human being is threatened—a healthy, percipient human being—there are really three choices. One is to attack to protect yourself, one is to run if you think you can outrun the dangerous person, and the other is to go into a holding syndrome hoping you won't be noticed, that he or she will look at someone else as a target.

"The phenomenon of the threat causes the autonomic nervous system to respond. The sympathetic branch will cause your blood pressure to elevate, your breathing pattern to change—you're looking for more oxygen, and causes a difference in the conductivity of the skin, which is what the polygraph measures.

"All a polygraph can ever tell you is that this subject believes—not is correct, now, but believes—all of what he or she says or, conversely, that the subject does *not* believe all of what he or she says. It's a very good instrument for winnowing out innocent people in an investigation. It's *not* a good instrument for identifying guilty people. It simply means they can't be eliminated at this stage."

"Mr. Bailey, does it matter who is giving the polygraph test?"

"It matters enormously."

"Please explain to the jury why."

"When I began to use the polygraph and to teach, there were splinter groups all over the United States who spent more time attacking one another than they did defending their own profession. Finally they got together—realized they were going to have to have some standards and not just be a group of superstars who didn't cooperate with one another—and created the American Polygraph Association. They adopted a constitution, ethical standards, and developed guidelines that will accompany the examiner who is a member of the A.P.A.

"The superstar examiners you can identify only after working with them and watching them call some very tough tests. There's a top shelf that I'd let test me if I were accused of a crime I didn't commit. Probably about eight or ten in the country."

"Are there some that you would not let treat you?"

"There are many."

"Why is that?"

"The slightest indication of a willingness to bend in favor of the party that's using you in order to be the recipient of more business is the death knell. The polygraph examiner has to be the most honest person in the country."

"Mr. Bailey, let me turn to the topic that brings you here today," Snider began a stroll toward the white board on the other side of the courtroom. "You were retained to present some opinion testimony in connection with the *Wartnick against Gainsley and Moss and Barnett* case. Is that correct?"

"Yes."

"And in connect with that representation you've had an occasion to review some materials. Is that right?"

"Yes."

"Mr. Bailey, have you reviewed the file in the wrongful-death case?"

"To a degree."

Snider immediately checked his hesitation and moved quickly to the next question[33] without ever breaking stride. "And have you reached certain conclusions regarding whether or not Mr. Gainsley and his law firm, Moss and Barnett, committed negligence in the representation of Mr. Wartnick?"

"Yes."

"And have you reached certain conclusions regarding whether or not Mr. Gainsley and Moss and Barnett's negligence proximately caused Mr. Wartnick's losses in the underlying trial in this case?"

"Yes."

"I object to that," Mason barked, "as going beyond the scope of the proffer of this witness."

"Overruled. Objection noted."

Snider stopped beside the white board. "Your Honor, perhaps I could use Mr. Mason's board, if the court permits me. And I'm going to place in front of you, Mr. Bailey, the second amended complaint."

"Yes."

"And the second amended complaint," Snider gestured toward the appropriate line, "says that Mr. Gainsley and Moss and Barnett 'injecting inadmissible and highly prejudicial evidence into the trial by referring in opening statement to the fact that Wartnick had refused to take a polygraph test when asked to do so by the police department investigating the Nachtsheim murder.' Were you asked to render an opinion with respect to this first claim?"

"Yes."

"And do you have an opinion on it?"

"I do."

"What is your opinion, sir, as to whether or not in making that statement Mr. Gainsley and his law firm, Moss and Barnett, committed negligence?"

"In my opinion that was a negligent act on the part of counsel."

"And would you please explain to the jury why that's the case."

"Yes. Absent special circumstances, evidence of lie detector tests is wholly inadmissible in Minnesota, both in civil and criminal cases. The polygraph is

33. "When a witness, (especially an expert) says, 'To a degree,' any good opponent's question is going to be, "To *what* degree?' 'To a degree' is a red flag for a good trial lawyer—the witness is basically telling you he hasn't done a thorough review. In this case, Bailey had focused on the Fifth Amendment issues but spent little time reviewing the file in the underlying case. Mason may have been concerned about [questioning Bailey] because he didn't know what the answer would be—it's an older trial lawyer 'rule' that you don't ask a question you don't know the answer to: a 'rule' good trial lawyers also know when to violate—but it's pretty clear in context that the answer would have been good for [Mason]. 'To a degree' necessarily meant 'not entirely,' so Mason could have pushed on that." – Chuck Webber. Personal email to the author. 5/16/11.

nonetheless widely used by police, as it was in this case, to attempt to eliminate suspects and focus on other suspects."

Bailey leaned forward in his chair, elbows upon the chair's arms, his fingers interlaced in front of his suit vest. "The jury was informed in this opening statement something that they *never* could have learned had not Mr. Wartnick's own lawyer brought it to their attention. Number one, that when asked to take a polygraph test he agreed, which is good. And that on the advice of his lawyer he changed his mind and refused, which is bad. The inference is that his lawyer knew he couldn't pass it and wouldn't permit him to take it."

"Let me move to another topic," Snider said. "And, if I could use the complaint board again that Mr. Mason has used in this case. The second item is 'failing to conduct even minimal adequate investigation into the Nachtsheim murder by failing to interview and depose key witnesses and suspects in the murder.' Do you see that claim, sir?"

"Yes."

"Now, as a lawyer of many years experience and having tried numerous cases, what is your practice with respect to retaining an investigator?"

"Always, in every case where there's a factual dispute."

"And please tell the jury why you do that."

"Well, number one, because Edward Bennett Williams[34] told me to—the day after I took the bar. He was leader of the criminal bar, indisputably, then and until his death a few years ago.

"Two, because I'd been an investigators officer and knew that cases were won with facts, not with rhetoric. Or, as a great lawyer put it, if your investigator is good enough most any lawyer will do.

"Number three, because a trial is like an iceberg. What you see in the courtroom is the one-seventh that's above the surface. The investigation that you don't see is what the *Titanic* hit below the surface. It's absolutely essential to litigation to have a handle on the facts in your case and in your opponent's case, and to prove all the negatives that you can. In other words, to prove that something did not happen. There is no substitute for investigation. Taking depositions is part of that process, but a small part in my opinion."

"Why is taking the depositions a part of that process?"

"Because it is the discovery of and the limitation of what witnesses can say at trial. When they are sworn in a deposition, if they deviate at trial, absent some intervening circumstance, it's pretty effective cross-examination to show a change of testimony and a witness's credibility is thus badly damaged."

"Mr. Bailey, in your professional opinion, is the failure to interview and depose key suspects in a case negligence in itself?"

"Yes."

"And would you please explain why."

---

34. A Washington D.C. SuperLawyer. For additional, see http://www.nndb.com/people/981/000161498/. (5/16/2011)

"Well, because in order to come to court and be prepared to marshal evidence, one has to gather information. If a judge decides the information that's been gathered will be received by the jury, it's then evidence in that case. Obviously, you can't offer information you don't have. You simply have to go out and beat the bushes for information; interview people, interview neighbors, take pictures, do all kinds of things to assist the jury in recreating a moment in time when something happened, to make judgments as to who was there and what they did. That's what trials are all about. You cannot function without good investigation."

"Mr. Bailey, when you discuss marshalling evidence, would you describe for the jury what you mean by that."

"Yes. It's what's going on right now." He faced the jurors directly. "The parties have gotten information about the controversy that you're here to decide and are presenting the information to the judge. He's deciding what parts of it are legal evidence that you can hear, and that's called marshalling or presenting."

"Are you talking about evidence that can be admitted for the jury's consideration?" Snider asked, still standing casually beside the white board.

"Well, until you get it to the judge, you don't know if it can be admitted. You may suspect what he'll do based on the rules of law, but judges rule individually in many instances because many rulings are predicated on something else that happened in the trial that's not found in the books."

"Mr. Bailey, if in a given case an attorney states that he's going to rely on police reports at trial for evidence of others' involvement in a homicide, do you have an opinion on whether or not that constitutes negligence?"

"I do."

"Objection," Mason barked. "That's irrelevant unless a foundation is laid as to the police report in this case and the witness has testified he hasn't looked at it."

"It's a general question, Your Honor," Snider said.

"I'll overrule the objection."

"And what is your opinion, Mr. Bailey?"

"One cannot rely on bringing to a jury's attention the fact that others were suspected of a crime by virtue of the fact that a police report says so."

"Why is that, sir?"

"Generally speaking, police reports are hearsay and can't be cross-examined. Most judges will rule them out. In some jurisdictions, they're viewed as official records and they may come in, but that's rare."

"Please describe for the jury what hearsay is."

"Hearsay is, generally, a statement made out of court, not under oath, and not subject to cross-examination and confrontation."

"Mr. Bailey, I have one other question on our failure to investigate and failure to interview and depose claim, and it's this: If the attorney representing

Mr. Wartnick in the underlying trial states it was his responsibility to obstruct the plaintiff [Betty Nachtsheim] from showing that Mr. Wartnick had committed the homicide and that it was not his responsibility, nor did he have to show who committed the homicide, do you have an opinion on whether or not such an attitude constitutes negligence?"

"I do."

"And please tell me what the opinion is, Mr. Bailey."

"I believe that taking that position is negligent."

"And please tell the jury why."

"Yes." Again Bailey turned to face them. As he spoke, he looked each juror in the eye, one after another. "The ethical demand upon a lawyer is to advance every piece of evidence, every legal ruling, every benefit that a client can get. He's an advocate. The failure to attempt to prove with live evidence that someone other than the client committed the crime is giving up an important defense, because any jury that had some doubt about the guilt of the client— even though this is a civil case—might well return a verdict in favor of that client.

"If, not having heard that evidence, they say, 'Well, there doesn't appear to be anyone else accused of doing it,' or who might have done it or had a motive to do it, opportunity to do it, then that weighs against the client because something has been left out. So, in my view, there's absolute duty to seek out and present evidence of the likelihood that others may have committed the crime with which your client is charged."

"Mr. Bailey, let me move to the last point. This is again from Mr. Wartnick's second amended complaint. 'Failing to mitigate the damage done at the deposition by offering Wartnick unconditionally for a second deposition on those matters as to which he pled the Fifth Amendment privilege.' That's one of Mr. Wartnick's claims. Is that your understanding?"

"Yes."

"Mr. Bailey, do you have an opinion as to whether or not the failure to offer Mr. Wartnick unconditionally for a second deposition was negligence by Mr. Gainsley and his law firm, Moss and Barnett?"

"I do."

"And please tell the jury what your opinion is."

"My opinion is that the failure to make an unconditional offer, with no restrictions, to permit the deposition to be reopened and retaken on those questions where the Fifth Amendment was taken was negligence."

Soon it was Mason's turn. He stood, arms crossed, in front of the witness.

"Do you know a psychic by the name of Peter Hurkos?"

"I've heard of him."

"And who are the key witnesses and suspects in this case?"

"Well, as I read through some of Russ Krueger's reports, it appears that suspicion was cast at one time or another on Bobby Nachtsheim, and a man, a convict named Dennis Kreuser."

"You're being paid some amount, I assume, for being here?"

"Yes."

"How much are you getting paid?"

"$250 an hour."

Mason blanched and stammered, "Is, is that *all?*"

"That's all."

"Is that your standard rate?"

"In civil cases it tends to be. In a criminal case it'll be a far different story."

Mason turned back toward counsel's table. "Do you know a lawyer by the name of Ron Meshbesher?"

"I do."

"Friend of yours?"

"In 1966, right after the Supreme Court upheld the reversal of the Sheppard conviction, Ron Meshbesher was in line to be chairman of the criminal law section of the American Trial Lawyers Association and, by some agreement, we were made co-chairmen and I became friendly with him at that time." Then the witness chuckled. "He's three months younger than I am, so I kind of keep an eye on him."

"You've been friends ever since?"

"We have off and on. I haven't seen him for quite some time, to be frank."

"Ron Meshbesher is a pretty good lawyer?"

"He's one of the best in the United States."

"Tried lots of cases?"

"My understanding is that he has, but I'm relying more on watching him work than on the statistics of his trial practice."

"But even Ron Meshbesher doesn't win all his cases, does he?"

"Any lawyer who says he wins all his cases isn't much of a lawyer."

"And do you consider yourself a pretty good trial attorney?"

"Fair to middling."

"Even you've had clients found guilty, even though you thought they weren't?"

"Yes."

"And in those cases you might look back and see some things you'd done that you might do differently, but that's not malpractice in your judgment. Right?"

"There's no case in which a trial lawyer can't look back with the wisdom of a Monday morning quarterback and see something that could have been done differently. I can, however, think of *no* case where an innocent man has lost because anything significant was left out."

"Now, the allegation here that I want to talk to you about," Mason changed course, "is this allegation that it was negligence for Gainsley to fail to mitigate the damage done at the deposition by offering Wartnick unconditionally for a second deposition. Now, you've reviewed Plaintiff's Exhibit Fifty-One, the so-called conditional offer that Mr. Gainsley sent?"

"Yes."

"And that was a letter in which he said, 'look, you can take a second deposition but the condition is that the first deposition won't be heard by the jury.' Right?"

"Right."

"And what you think he should have done was make an unconditional offer which would say you can take a second deposition but say nothing about the first deposition. Right?"

"Well, it should have been a two-staged process. The first was to make an offer—"

"The first stage," Mason said brusquely, "would be that he should've offered unconditionally for a second deposition?"

Bailey nodded. "Step one."

"Step one. Step two is what?"

"After the [second] deposition had been completed, to ask Mr. Meshbesher to strike that part of the first deposition that related to the Fifth and, if he refused, to ask the court to do it."

"Okay. So he should have made this unconditional offer because that increased the odds the first deposition wouldn't be heard by a jury?"

"That would have been the end result."

Mason seemed pleased. "So what you're really saying is he should have had that condition in mind and simply not put it in writing?"

"That is partly correct. Would you like me to elaborate?"

"Now," Mason ignored the offer, "you said that there would be a second step, namely after the deposition. Right?"

"Yes." Bailey nodded.

"How would sending an unconditional offer for a deposition make a deposition happen?"

"It might not make a deposition happen. That, too, might have been refused."

"Okay. And if the second deposition was taken—now we're into another 'maybe, maybe not'—suppose the deposition was taken and he answered all the questions unconditionally—"

"Um-humm."

"—you don't know whether a judge would rule the first deposition out or not, do you?"

"We never know how a judge will rule. The duty is to *ask* him to rule."

CHAPTER 42

Mason's cross-examination of Wartnick proceeded in much the same way it had begun that morning. "So you didn't take a polygraph test until you started this lawsuit. Right?"

"Correct," Wartnick said.

"And that was in—you took one twice since this lawsuit has gotten started?"

"Yes."

"First one is '86 or '88?"

"Yes. Someplace in that area, yes."

"And the last one is more recently?"

"Yes."

Mason stood directly in front of Wartnick with his arms crossed. "And Mr. Shaw threw away the tracings that related to your first test so nobody can check those. Right?"

"I don't know that."

"Object to the fact he threw them away so nobody could check them," Friedberg said. "That's a misstatement. That's an argument."

"Mr. Friedberg, please," Judge Stanoch began.

Friedberg stood. "May we approach the bench, please, Your Honor?"

Moments later the Court stated, "I'll strike the statement and tell the jury to disregard the comment of counsel. Mr. Mason, if you would please rephrase the question. I'm sustaining Mr. Friedberg's objection."

"Mr. Shaw threw away the tracings on that test. Right?"

"I have no knowledge of that." Wartnick's stomach gurgled and his lower back twitched.

"And if they're thrown away, nobody can check them. Right?"

"I have no knowledge of that."

"But you know that they've been thrown away?"

"I know they're gone."

"And you know that they can't be checked."

Wartnick leaned back and forced his neck muscles to relax. "Well, if they're gone, obviously, they can't be checked."

"And is that why you took the test again?"

"Yes."

The late-afternoon session was the same. "It's a fact," Mason, crossed arms and eyes, planted himself in front of counsel's table and said, "Bob was a great salesperson. Right?"

"Yes."

"He had charisma, could sell what he wanted to, and things people didn't even want."

"Yes."

"He was responsible for thirty to forty percent of your customers."

"Yes."

"And so you bought insurance to protect you if he died and you lost the business."

"Lost *his* business."

"Right," Mason acknowledged.

"The business that he was bringing in." Wartnick wanted that clear. "Yes."

"You didn't buy insurance, though, to protect you in case he became disabled. Right?"

"I'm not sure if that policy had any disability insurance. I'm not sure if Mr. Friedman even brought it up, to tell you the truth. So, the answer is No."

"So the life insurance policy only protected you in the event of Mr. Nachtsheim's *death*. You couldn't collect on it unless he died."

"I'm not sure. It may have contained disability, but if that's all it contained, the answer is Yes."

"Well, that's what you told the first jury. Page 894, line 19, Question: 'So this life insurance policy—'"

"Whoa, whoa, whoa, whoa." Wartnick grabbed for the trial transcript on the table placed just outside and to the right of the witness box.

"Eight-ninety-four," Mason barked.

"I'll get it." Wartnick fumbled for the page. "Okay."

"Line nineteen."

"Thank you."

"Ready? 'So this life insurance policy only protected you in the event of Mr. Nachtsheim's death. Now you couldn't collect on it unless he died?' Answer: 'That's correct.'"

"To the best of my knowledge, that is correct."

"No, no," Mason cried and stabbed at the volume in his hand. "It says here, 'Now you couldn't collect on it unless he died?' That was the question. You gave this answer: 'That's correct.'"

"The answer would be Yes."

"No, no. I'm not asking you about would be or anything else. You said in 1986 to that other jury, 'That's correct.'"

"Yes."

"And that's true, isn't it?"

"Without rereading the policy, the answer is Yes."

"And if he died after he left you, you could not only collect the insurance but you'd have one less competitor."

"That's true."

"And by May of '73 he had left and taken thirty, forty percent of your customers."

"Yes."

"He hurt your business badly."

"Yes."

"Having insurance on Bob Nachtsheim's life wouldn't protect you now."

"Not as you are speaking about it, but as to why I took it out it might."

"Your own business was in terrible financial condition?"

"No. My business was in trouble because receivables were in trouble."

"Well, your own business was in terrible financial condition. True?"

"Cash flow was bad. Yes."

"All right. You couldn't afford to lose the business?"

What? "I couldn't afford to lose the business?"

"You couldn't—you, Midwest Floral, you couldn't afford to lose the business?"

"If I lost the business, I lost the business."

"Well, you couldn't afford to?"

"Why?"

"In 1973 you took an amount that was $2,600 of money for that business and you applied it to buy a life insurance policy on the life of Mr. Nachtsheim."

"Yes."

"Is that something, by the way, that you had to talk about to your board of directors? About whether you could take company money and use it for that purpose?"

"Yes."

"And you did that?"

"Yes."

"And then you named the company as the beneficiary?"

"That was the way the board of directors wanted it done. Yes."

"Did you talk to anybody when you did that on May 11, 1973? Well, instead of making the company the beneficiary, let's make Mrs. Nachtsheim the beneficiary?"

"Midwest Floral was paying the premium. Midwest Floral was the beneficiary. That's the way it was set up."

Mason continued nit-picking, line by line, statement by statement, emotion by emotion, through previous depositions and the transcript of the previous trial—a battlefield of twisted words from Mason and objections from Friedberg.

"Then look at Defendant's Exhibit Thirty-One," Mason said. "A letter to you referring to what you've said. And it says, 'You have consistently told us, without hesitation that you were not involved in any way with Mr. Nachtsheim's death, nor are you aware of anyone who was.' Is that true?"

"That's correct."

"And that's the answer you gave at the early part of the deposition that we took, at page two hundred forty-two of your deposition. Isn't it a fact, later in your deposition you changed that answer?"

"I'd have to look at both of them. I'm sorry."

"All right. We'll turn to page two hundred forty-two."

Wartnick examined one and then another of the several volumes of his deposition that Mason had taken. "And that's in the—"

"Volume two," Judge Stanoch offered.

Wartnick retrieved the plastic-spined bundle. "This is the one I think I've got here. All right. Volume two. Which line?"

"Look at page two forty-two, line seven. Question: 'Is it true, the next sentence of the letter, "You have consistently told us, without hesitation, that you're not involved in any way with Mr. Nachtsheim's death, nor are you aware of anyone who was?" Answer: 'That is true.' You said that in your deposition when it was taken on August 2, 1989. Correct?"

"Apparently you must have been reading out of something, so that particular is correct. Yes."

"That sentence is correct? 'You have consistently told us ... that you are not involved in any way with Mr. Nachtsheim's death?'"

Wartnick glanced from the page up to Mason. "That's correct. I've always said that, and I always will. And I'm getting a little bit fed up with you telling me that I am. I'm a little fed up with the whole world telling me that I am.

"For twenty-one years I've lived with you and other people in this world that tell me that I've committed a crime that I had absolutely nothing to do with. I didn't *kill* anybody. I didn't *have* anybody killed. And I just can't seem to get that into anybody's thick skull that I'm just a little person in the world trying to make something of himself and can't do it."

CHAPTER 43

The four friends sat around the Wartnicks' kitchen table. Babe nibbled her way through a rib of celery. "Oh, come on, Butch. Out with it. You're the only one not sweating bullets about being in that box. Tell me what's going on in there."

"With Whalen," her husband intruded. Norm's long-time friend, Tom Whalen of Twin Cities Floral, had been called to the witness stand the previous week to testify about the orchids. "How'd Tom do? Did somebody finally listen to common sense?"

"Norm, you were up there for three days," Connie protested. "Didn't you see people nodding when you spoke?" She bit off the tip of a carrot. "That was a great line, by the way, that 'I've lived for twenty-one years with you people telling me I did it.'"

"Wasn't precogitated, I can tell you that much. But what did Tom say about the orchids?"

"Norm said what?!" Babe straightened. "Did you really say that, Honey?"

"He did." Butch nodded slowly. "And you should have seen Friedberg. Thought he was going to make his lip bleed he was biting it so hard."

"And you finally got to add that part," Connie continued, "about when you first saw those police reports. Joe let you get that in there really nice after all the harping Mason was doing."

"What did you say, Norm?" Babe started on another rib of celery.

"Joe asked me when was the first time I'd known about the police reports. I told him it was after he started working the case, and that's the truth. He had to subpoena the files. But what about Tom?" He turned back to Butch. "Cough it up."

Connie's burst of laughter spewed carrot pieces across the table. "Norm!" She almost choked. "Mason's eyes! Warn Babe about his eyes!" She sprang out of her chair and raced for a rag.

Norm shook his head. "Not 'til I hear about Tom."

"Okay, pouty." Connie swiped the top of the table. "I'm warning you, Babe, don't try to look him in the face. He's unbelievably cross-eyed."

"Great. I'm already nervous enough! Where do you look?!"

"Never figured it out." Norm pushed his chair away from the table. "I tried looking at his forehead, at his chin, an ear. I kept looking at whatever papers he put in front of me most of the time, but Joe told me not to do that so much—said it made me look like I was trying to hide behind them. I just did the best I could," he stood up. "Anyone want another Diet Coke?"

Butch raised his index finger.

"You don't get one 'til you tell me about Whalen testifying. Connie? Babe?"

"No, I'll wait. Supper will be ready in a minute."

"Wait just a doggone," Butch protested. "You'd make me die of thirst—"

"—unless you tell me what I want to know. You got it, buddy."

Connie straightened and sniffed. "Babe? Do you smell that?"

"My hot dish!" Babe leapt from her chair toward the oven. "Norm Wartnick, did you turn off my timer?" The casserole emerged with blackened corners. "Dry as the Mojave. Well, you'll just have to like it that way."

"Connie just adds extra cheese on top." Her smack on Butch's arm reverberated around the room. He grinned as he rubbed his bicep. "Tastes the same to me."

Norm squinted at Babe. "Butch doesn't get any 'til he talks."

"Pshaw. He's been talking all night. And he may be the only one who'll eat this, thanks to you."

"Okay, okay," Butch grinned. "It's not that big a deal. Whalen stuttered a little at first—he was obviously nervous—but he pulled it off. Now can I eat?"

"What about the orchids? What did he exactly say?"

"That it's standard procedure to get them out of the cooler first thing. Come on, you know if it hadn't gone well I would have told you by now. Give me that plate. Didn't Joe or Jerry fill you in?"

"They didn't have time. They're getting ready to put Phil on the stand next week."

Connie's fork stopped halfway to her mouth. "Huh. That'll be interesting."

TUESDAY, OCTOBER 11, 1994 – TRIAL DAY ELEVEN

Snider stood behind counsel's table and verified all documents were arranged as he wanted, then he looked toward the bench and said, "Plaintiff calls Phillip Gainsley for cross-examination."

"Schumbling." Friedberg's mutter carried only to Snider's ears. Snider glanced at his co-counsel and followed the direction of his gaze. Together they watched the defendant schlep toward the witness stand and be sworn in, head lolled to the left, with that peculiar air he wore which seemed to scream out that he had nothing to lose. His suit looked like an expensive one rescued from the closet floor.

"Mr. Snider, your witness."

"Thank you, Your Honor. Mr. Gainsley, how long have you been a lawyer?"

"Just short of thirty years."

"When you joined the firm of Moss and Barnett, you indicated to Mr. Wartnick, did you not, that you had the resources of the Moss and Barnett law firm behind you to proceed with his case?"

"I don't remember any such conversation to that effect."

"Do you *deny* you had those conversations with Mr. Wartnick?"

"I don't recall having had such conversations with him."

"You and Norm Wartnick grew up together, didn't you?"

"Yes."

"And as a matter of fact, in the underlying trial of *Nachtsheim against Wartnick*, you told the jury that you were a good friend of Mr. Wartnick's, did you not?"

"I believe so."

"And that was a true statement when you made it? Is that right?"

"I think I made that more for strategy than for accuracy."

"Oh. You didn't mean it?"

"I think I made that more for strategy than I did for accuracy."

"When you told the jury you were a good friend of Mr. Wartnick and—you're now testifying that was more for strategy than accuracy. What did you mean? What *do* you mean?"

"Oh, I think it would be something that would identify me with my client so that the words I uttered would be words that my client, if my client were to speak, would say."

"Mr. Gainsley, at the time you tried that lawsuit, were you or were you not a good friend of Mr. Wartnick?"

"Objection. Repetitious."

"He's denied it, Your Honor."

"Well," Mason snarled, "that's my point."

"Let's state legal objection," Judge Stanoch warned Mason. "If I need argument, I'll ask for it from both attorneys. Thank you." He nodded to the witness. "You may answer the question."

"I'm sorry. I don't know what 'good friend' means in that context. I certainly knew him, and I knew him well. We never socialized. I've known him since childhood but never well. Didn't go to the same school. Our wives don't know each other. That's the best I can do to answer that question."

Snider stood halfway between the bench and counsel's table and regarded the witness with an expression of disbelief. "So when you told the jury that you were a 'good friend' of Mr. Wartnick, you didn't even understand what the term meant?"

"Objection. Argumentative," Mason said.

"Sustained."

Snider turned back toward plaintiff's end of counsel's table. "Was there ever a time when you asked him if he had anything to do with the Nachtsheim murder?"

"Yes."

"When was that?"

"I think it was the second time he and I spoke on the subject, when he came into my office. The first time was on the telephone, the second time is when he came in, and we asked him at that time whether he had anything to do with the murder."

"And Mr. Wartnick denied having anything to do with Nachtsheim's death. Isn't that correct?"

"That's correct."

"And you believed what Mr. Wartnick was telling you, did you not? You were never given any reason not to believe what he was telling you. Isn't that right?"

"I wanted to believe him. He was my client. There were some suspicious facts but I believed what he told me."

"Well, you're putting a little qualification on it, aren't you, Mr. Gainsley? Do you recall when your deposition was taken on April 6, 1988, in Mr. Friedberg's office?"

"Yes."

"And on page fifty-six," he flipped until he found the spot he wanted, "I direct your attention to line eighteen—you stated: 'I believed Norm. I had never any reason not to believe what he told me.'"

Gainsley nodded. "That's a part of my answer."

Snider placed a finger on the page and glanced at the witness. "Is there some other part of the answer you want to talk about?"

"I'm just telling you that's a part of my answer."

"Was this a correct part of your answer?"

"Objection," Mason called out. "In fairness to the witness, we should read the entire answer, please. What page, please?"

Snider looked to the bench. "Does the court want to permit Mr. Mason to conduct—"

"No, no. Could we have this witness answer the question. All right?"

Gainsley said nothing.

"My question to you is," Snider took a step toward the witness, "on page fifty-six, Mr. Gainsley, when you answered: 'I believed Norm. I had never any reason not to believe what he told me,' did you mean those words when you testified to that in your deposition?"

"Yes!" Mason barked. "And our objection is that under the rules when a witness is asked a question from his deposition, in fairness we get the entire context of what the witness said and not simply the isolated question."

"Let's have this witness answer this question, Mr. Mason. At that point if you want to raise that issue, we'll deal with it then. Let's get an answer to this question."

"Thank you, Your Honor." Snider turned from the bench to the witness.

Gainsley glanced at Mason, then down to the document before him. "That's not even my complete sentence."

"My question to you, once again, Mr. Gainsley, is when you said—and I'll pick up here, it says: 'If you were to push my back against the wall, I believed Norm. I had never any reason not to believe what he told me.' That's the answer you gave in your deposition. Isn't that correct?"

"Yes."

"Thanks." Snider concluded.

"May we now have the entire—" Mason began. "We started in mid-sentence. May we have now the entire answer to the question given. In fairness to the process here, may we—"

"Could the attorneys come up to the bench, please."

There was none of the coughing and movement that normally filled these bench-session silences. Wartnick noticed again how tall Snider was, even next to Mason. Wartnick admired Snider for his gracious attitude. It was a great balancer for his tenacity and intelligence.

Mason returned to his seat.

Snider stood before the witness and smiled. "Mr. Gainsley, to put all of this in context, I believe we have to go back to page fifty-four, beginning on line ten, and this question is asked, is it not? 'And so still in 1976, when the lawsuit was commenced, you still had in mind that he had denied any complicity in the death of—' And 'he' is Mr. Wartnick. Agreed?"

"I think so."

"'—he had denied any complicity in the death of Mr. Nachtsheim in the original conversation with your father. Correct?' And your answer is, 'That's correct.' Is that right?"

"That's correct."

"Then the question is asked: 'Did you believe him?' And Mr. Herzog—who was your counsel at the time. Is that right?"

"That's correct."

"And Mr. Herzog says, 'Objected to as irrelevant. Answer if you want to.' Is that right?"

"That's correct."

"And then you state: 'I don't want to.' Is that the answer you gave?"

"That's correct."

"Then Mr. Friedberg asked, 'Can you tell us why you don't want to?'"

"Excuse me," Mason dropped a heavy hand to the table top. "Objection to the colloquy by counsel."

"Judge, I thought we wanted to read it in the context."

"I did," Mason said, "but the witness's testimony, not—"

"Please." Judge Stanoch said.

"—your oral arguments—"

"Please." Judge Stanoch said louder.

"—and the lawyer's testimony."

"Mr. Mason. If you want to argue, come up to the bench."

"So the question on line fifteen," Snider resumed immediately, "page fifty-four is: 'Do you believe him?' Is that correct?"

"That's the question."

"And it was correct, wasn't it, that you did believe Norm?"

"What I testified to, thereto, was correct."

"Now the early case that was filed was known as an unjust enrichment case. Is that correct?"

"Yes."

Snider returned the deposition pages to a stack on the table. "And the issue was whether or not the corporation was a proper beneficiary. Is that right?"

Gainsley sighed and his head lolled to the left. "The question in that lawsuit was whether the corporation would have to cough up the hundred thousand dollars it got resulting from Mr. Nachtsheim's death."

"In the testimony that we read I believe you said it presented, literally, an unbelievable state of affairs, or something to that effect?"

"Yes."

"If that's the case, can you tell me why you didn't just tell Norm to write a check for one hundred thousand dollars to Mr. Meshbesher for the Nachtsheim family?"

"Well," Gainsley shifted in his seat and tugged his suit coat closed. "The corporation was the proper beneficiary of the insurance policy."

"And, at least in the early stages, that was the only lawsuit. Is that correct?"

Gainsley nodded, lips pursed. "That was the only lawsuit."

"And that was, in your words, just a hundred-thousand dollar lawsuit. Is that right?"

"Yes."

"Merely for the insurance proceeds?"

"Yes."

"Can you explain to the jury how Midwest Floral could in any way be responsible for returning those insurance proceeds to the Nachtsheim family?"

"Well, that's why Mr. Wartnick came to me. It was my job to convince the court there was no reason the corporation should give up the proceeds."

"Mr. Gainsley, let me put in front of you Plaintiff's Exhibit Seven and, if you could identify for the record whether or not Exhibit Seven is a copy of the initial complaint that was filed in this case by the Nachtsheim family against Mr. Wartnick."

He glanced over the page with no movement of his head. "I believe so."

"And this is the lawsuit that was merely for the hundred thousand dollars. Right? The insurance proceeds?"

"That's correct."

"If that's the case, Mr. Gainsley, can you explain why, on page four of the complaint," Snider flipped the pages, "there is a claim for one million dollars in punitive damages attached?"

"Can I explain that?"

"Yes, sir." Snider's penetrating gaze was locked onto Gainsley.

"No, I can't explain that."

"It is *not* the case, is it, that this was merely a complaint for one hundred thousand dollars? This was a complaint for one hundred thousand *plus* a million dollars in punitive damages. My question to you, sir, is did you give Mr. Wartnick any advice on the punitive damages aspects of this case?"

"Yes."

"What advice did you give him?"

"Not to talk to anyone under any circumstances about this matter."

"Is that because of the punitive damages aspects?"

"It's because of the entire lawsuit."

"Do you recall any discussion with Mr. Wartnick about that million dollar punitive damage claim?"

"No."

"Did you just ignore it, Mr. Gainsley? The fact that there was a million dollar punitive damage claim against Mr. Wartnick?"

"No."

"What action did you take on it?"

"I did investigation. I took depositions. I interviewed people, did requests for production of documents, did interrogatories, did research—kinds of things lawyers do when their clients get served with summonses and complaints."

"What investigation did you do, Mr. Gainsley, with respect to the unjust enrichment case?"

Gainsley examined the ceiling tiles. "I got hold of the police report. I interviewed Russ Krueger at least once, I think twice, at least twice, maybe three times. I interviewed people whose names came up in the police report. I interviewed Wartnick a *lot*. I interviewed Zola Friedman. I interviewed the Stollers." He sighed. "I had many conversations with counsel for Prudential. They had far greater resources than Norm did and I relied upon a lot of their investigation."

"May I approach the witness, Your Honor?"

"You may."

"Let me place in front of you Plaintiff's Exhibit Forty-Two, if I could, Mr. Gainsley, and this is a letter that Mr. Johnson, representing Prudential, wrote to you. Is that correct?"

Gainsley glanced over the page and nodded. "Yes."

"And what he's doing is enclosing a copy of the police file to you. Is that right?"

"A copy of the police file. Right."

"Now," Snider stood in front of the court reporter. "Is it the case that, even though this lawsuit started in 1976, you didn't get a copy of the police report or the police file until August of 1982?"

"No."

"You got it earlier?"

"Yes." Gainsley pursed his lips.

"When did you get it?"

"I got portions of the police file as early as 1973. I got more in 1976. I got some as late as 1985. I got the police file as the police file was being accumulated."

"Oh, you got it as it was being accumulated?"

"I mean, I didn't get things in 1982 that weren't created until 1985."

"Your Honor, I offer Exhibit Forty-Two." The letter from Roger Johnson was received.

"There's a reference at the bottom of the first page that says: 'I think it might be worthwhile for us to subpoena the police department file at some point so that we can get a legible copy of the whole file.' Do you see that?"

"Yes."

"Is it the case that the file that Mr. Johnson sent to you was not legible?"

"Some parts of it were; some parts of it weren't."

"And you ultimately did subpoena the police file at the time of the trial, did you not?"

"For trial purposes I did. Yes." Gainsley nodded.

"And is it your testimony you had the entire file prior to that?"

"There were, I think, maybe two minor areas of the file that I didn't have by the time trial came. Everything else I had."

"And you got it from Prudential?"

"I got it from the police. I got it from Prudential. I got it from even Meshbesher as late as 1985. It was the last place I got it. Mostly from the police."

"Who gave it to you from the police, Mr. Gainsley?"

"Actually, I think Jane Lerner got it from the police, but I think—I'm not sure who from the police, but I got it from the police."

"What did you do with that file as you were getting it, as you testified? Did you take any action on it?" Snider leaned against counsel's table.

"Yes. One of the things that struck me," Gainsley was slightly more animated, "was an interview Lieutenant Krueger said he had with [insurance salesman] Zola Friedman. Somehow it came to my attention Zola Friedman denied ever meeting with Mr. Krueger, and I wanted to interview Friedman and go over with him what Krueger almost verbatim said was a conversation, almost a precise description of the meeting they had. That was one of the things I did with the police report. I talked a lot with Prudential about the grandfather—the Paul Nachtsheim statement, and discussed with them how we should treat that statement."

"*Now* you testify that you talked about the Paul Nachtsheim state—"

"Yes."

"Isn't it the case that you *never* got the Paul Nachtsheim statement?"

"I know I testified I didn't, but it occurs to me I did have it. I discussed it, in any event."

"Well, you do agree with me that in your deposition you testified that you were not aware of the Paul Nachtsheim statement?"

"No. I did not say that at all."

Snider retrieved the deposition transcript from the stack on counsel's table. "May I approach the witness, Your Honor?"

"You may."

"Showing you your deposition, Mr. Gainsley. Again, that was taken by Mr. Friedberg in April of 1988. Was this question asked and is this the answer that you gave?"

"Page, please," Mason said.

"Page ninety-six, beginning on line twenty-two. 'Did you receive a narrative statement taken by Attorney Johnson from Paul Nachtsheim, the deceased's father?' And the answer that you gave is, 'I don't think so.' Is that correct?"

"You were asking me there if I *received* it, and I said I don't think so. That's correct."

"Oh, are you trying to draw a distinction between knowing about it and receiving it, Mr. Gainsley?"

"That's correct."

"And you said you knew about it from Mr. Johnson, is that right?"

"Yes."

"And you knew in this statement from Paul Nachtsheim that Mr. Johnson had taken on behalf of Prudential, that, among other things, Paul Nachtsheim was accusing his grandson, Bobby, of committing murder against Bob Nachtsheim. Is that correct?"

"I knew that from conversations I, myself, had with Paul Nachtsheim."

"And you knew about this report and you never asked to get a copy of it?"

"That's not true."

"You *did* ask to get a copy of it?"

"I don't know whether I asked or not, but I did get a copy."

"So when you testified that you don't think you received a narrative taken by Attorney Johnson from Paul Nachtsheim, you said, 'I don't think so,' you now have a recollection that you ultimately did get it?"

"Yes, that's correct."

"So you have a different recollection today. Is that correct?"

"Yes, that's correct."

Snider returned to counsel's table and retrieved two large, bound documents. "Now, this is the entire trial transcript in the underlying case, Mr. Gainsley. I'd like to take a minute and have you take a look at, if you would, please, page seven hundred ninety-two in Volume Two. Do you have that?"

Gainsley took his time to fumble through the stack of bound documents. "Yes."

"If we look at the index," Snider flipped to the front, "we see that [your] witnesses in this trial were Roger Walker, Norm Wartnick, Tom Evers, and Babe Wartnick. Correct?"

"I think that's correct."

"Members of the jury," Judge Stanoch interrupted, "at this time I'm going to let you go for the day. Be back at nine-fifteen tomorrow morning. Don't talk to anybody about the case; don't let anyone talk to you. Nine-fifteen tomorrow morning."

WEDNESDAY, OCTOBER 12, 1994 – TRIAL DAY 12

"Why did you call Roger Walker?" Snider resumed cross-examination of Gainsley, whose suit was even more wrinkled than the day before.

"I called Roger Walker, who is the head of the economics department at Hamline University, to show the value of [Nachtsheim's] earnings in his business as a way to counter the amount of damages that Mrs. Nachtsheim was trying to prove."

"In effect, Dr. Walker was a damages expert. Is that correct?"

"Yes."

"And you wanted him to show that if Mr. Nachtsheim had lived up to his expected date of retirement he'd have made less money than the plaintiffs were claiming through their expert. Isn't that correct?"

"That's essentially correct."

"And Dr. Walker had absolutely nothing to do with identifying any alternative suspects in this case. Is that correct?"

"That's correct."

"Now, yesterday you testified that periodically you received portions of the police report. Do you recall that testimony?"

"Yes."

"May I approach the witness, Your Honor?"

"You may."

"Let me put in front of you Plaintiff's Exhibit Seventy-Three. Would you identify Seventy-Three for the record."

Gainsley barely glanced at the page. "It's a photocopy of a subpoena that I caused the court to issue to the Minneapolis Police Department for purposes of this trial."

"And the date of the subpoena is April 17, 1986. Is that correct?"

"That's correct."

"Now previously, yesterday, we offered and it's been received into evidence, Plaintiff's Exhibit Forty-Two. And let me, just to refresh your recollection, put Exhibit Forty-Two in front of you. And Forty-Two is a copy of Mr. Johnson, representing Prudential Insurance Company, transmitting a copy of the police file to you. Is that correct?"

Gainsley nodded. "He enclosed a copy of the police file Paul Nachtsheim had given him."

"And if you read further down, Mr. Johnson tells you: 'I think it might be worthwhile for us to subpoena the police department file at some point so that we can get a legible copy of the whole file.' Did I read that correctly?"

"Yes."

"And it's true, is it not, Mr. Gainsley, that the first time you got the police file—contrary to what you testified to yesterday in front of this jury—was in August of 1982?"

"No."

"And it's also true, isn't it, Mr. Gainsley, that the file you got in 1982 was not legible?"

"No."

Snider spun toward counsel's table. "Do you recall filing an affidavit with the court in this very case back in July of 1988?"

"Yes."

"What I'd like to do is put in front of you a copy of that affidavit." He laid the pages on the shelf in front of the witness. "Actually July 11, 1988. Is that correct?"

Snider waited. "Exhibit One-Thirty-Four-B?" He prompted. Again he paused for an answer.

None came. Phil Gainsley flipped back and forth through the few pages, his lips pursed.

"Is that an affidavit that you filed with the court? It has your signature on it."

"Well, there's markings on it and crossing out."

"I'm only going to ask you to focus on the first page, Mr. Gainsley. That is an affidavit that you signed. Is that correct?"

"This is an affidavit that I signed, but it didn't have the markings, the deletions, the crossing out."

"I'm not offering the affidavit in evidence. I do want to read, if you would, in the first paragraph of your affidavit, the sentence that begins five lines from the bottom of the page."

Gainsley located the point and nodded.

"And you state in your affidavit, do you not, as follows: 'The state of the record is that I received the police reports *twice*: *once* during pretrial discovery from Prudential Life Insurance Company and the second time *at trial* by subpoena of the Minneapolis Police Department.' Is that a sentence that you put in your affidavit back in July of 1988?"

"Yes."

"And isn't it the case, Mr. Gainsley, that Exhibit Forty-Two, which reflects illegible copies of the police department file being sent to you from Prudential, is the first time you got the police file?"

"No."

"You deny that?"

"Yes."

"And isn't it further true that the only time you got a legible copy of the police file is when you issued your subpoena on April 17, 1986, for trial?"

"No."

"And is it the case, Mr. Gainsley, that the reason you didn't investigate this case, and the reason you didn't take depositions is that in 1982, when you first got the file, it was illegible. And by the time you got to trial and you issued a subpoena and you got the police records, it's too late to conduct an investigation. Isn't that correct?"

"Objection. The question is multiple and argumentative."

"Overruled."

Gainsley's eyes focused back and forth between Mason and Snider. "You—you'll—," he stuttered, "you'll have to break it down. You have to break that question down because I can't answer it in the form that you gave it to me."

"You can't answer the question, Mr. Gainsley?"

"No, because it assumes things that are not true."

"So you can't answer the question?"

"Not the way you phrased it."

"When you issued the subpoena, did you get files from the Police Department, sir?"

"When I issued—"

Snider paused, waited. "On the eve of trial."

"For the trial? The trial subpoena?"

"Yes, sir," Snider said.

"I got what the police department said was the file. Yes."

"Mr. Gainsley, let me show you Plaintiff's Exhibit Six, which is a file copy of a letter that you sent to Prudential Insurance Company of America on December 16, 1973." He waited for Gainsley to look at the page. "Is that correct?"

"Yes."

"Your Honor, we offer Plaintiff's Exhibit Six."

"No objection." Mason did not even look up.

"It's received."

"Now, Mr. Gainsley, back on December 9 you tell Mr. Wartnick that, quote, As of this time and for a considerable period of time in the future, the

280

police department and the county attorney have no intention of abandoning their investigation, end quote. Do you recall that?"

"Yes."

"But less than ten days later you're writing a letter to Prudential Insurance Company, Plaintiff's Exhibit Six, which states, quote, Your file in this matter is being returned to you and I wish to confirm our telephone conversation in which you advise that upon receiving the file my client can expect remittance of the hundred thousand dollars together with interest, end quote.

"Your letter goes on to state, that the draft should be made payable to Midwest Floral Supply *and* the Gainsley law firm, and should be forwarded to your office. That's the letter you sent, is it not?"

"Yes."

"Mr. Gainsley, did you ever get a signed fee agreement for a percentage of those insurance proceeds that your firm received?"

"I don't believe so."

"But you *did* ask Mr. Wartnick for *twenty-five percent* of those insurance proceeds that were payable to Midwest. Is that correct?"

Gainsley cleared his throat and studied the ledge in front of him. "Yes."

Snider let the answer hang in the air.

"Now," he turned back to counsel's table. "I want to focus for a moment, Mr. Gainsley, on the failure to investigate the case, if I could. And you testified yesterday that Mrs. Nachtsheim's was the only deposition that you took during the litigation but that you interviewed Russ Krueger and, I believe, Zola Friedman. I want to make sure—give you a chance to answer. Did you do anything else in terms of an investigation other than interview Russ Krueger and interview Zola Friedman, and take Mrs. Nachtsheim's deposition?"

"Yes."

"What else did you do, sir?"

"Went over to the Ramsey County District Court to take a look at Mrs. Nachtsheim's two divorce actions. I worked with Roger Johnson, the attorney for Prudential, a *lot*. Interviewed people at Prudential who he would make available. Interviewed—got the Prudential investigation file on the matter. Did my discovery, formal discovery. Probably that's all I can think of now."

"You never devoted any of your attention through any of these discovery devices to get to the bottom of the party that Bobby Nachtsheim and Roger Nordstrom and Debbie Feist and Dennis Kreuser had the night before the murder. Is that correct?"

"No. That's not correct."

"Please expound for us, if you would."

"Well, I talked to Russ Krueger about it. I read the reports about them, made some decisions about them."

"You never interviewed or took any depositions of the participants in the party. Correct?"

"I *had* interviews of the participants. I did not take depositions."

"Well, the interviews you had were from the police department file, isn't that correct?"

"That's correct."

"You never *did* any interviews yourself—your office never did any interviews of any of those people, did it? And your office never took any depositions of any of those people. Is that correct?"

Snider waited.

"That's correct."

"In your earlier deposition, starting on line eleven: 'I knew that as long as he remained silent, he could not be misconstrued or make any *faux pas*, and I just concluded, based upon my conversations with him, my knowledge of the law, the depositions that either I took or participated in, that hiring an investigator would not have served any useful purpose.' What did you mean, that there was really nothing further for you to investigate as long as you kept your options open to permit Mr. Wartnick to testify at trial?"

"I gave that answer in response to the question why didn't I hire an investigator. I didn't hire an investigator because I had someone in my office do investigation for us. I had the police department who could do investigation far beyond anything I could do or have available to me."

"Who in your office served as your investigator, Mr. Gainsley?"

"Jane Lerner."

"If Jane Lerner did those investigations, those investigations would be reflected on her time records. Isn't that correct?"

"I believe so."

Persistence to acquire Gainsley's time cards again paid off. Wartnick's team could and would prove Jane Lerner had done no investigation into any matters concerning the murder of Bob Nachtsheim.

"You aren't testifying that Jane Lerner did any investigation of Bobby Nachtsheim, Roger Nordstrom, or the drug and alcohol party, are you, Mr. Gainsley?"

He was slow to answer. "No."

"She was investigating things like Mrs. Nachtsheim's filings for divorce and that kind of thing. Isn't that correct?"

"She did legal research; she did factual research."

"Okay. And the factual research either concerned the domestic relations matters of Mrs. Nachtsheim or it involved the issue of the insurance proceeds. Is that a fair statement?"

The witness focused on his fingernails. "The issue as to why a company like Midwest Floral could have a policy on someone who no longer worked for it."

"Mr. Gainsley," Snider persisted, "at no point in time did either you or Ms. Lerner *ever* conduct any factual investigation for any suspects alternative to Mr. Wartnick involved in this murder. Is that the case?"

282

"Yes."

"In your deposition, directing your attention to page seventy-two, line one. Mr. Friedberg asked you this question, quote, What attempt, if any, in twelve years did you make to find out who had in fact been responsible for the death of Mr. Nachtsheim? Close quote. And the answer you gave was: 'My responsibility was to obstruct Mrs. Nachtsheim from showing that Norm had done it. It was not my responsibility, nor did I have to show who did do it.' That's the answer you gave. Is that correct?"

"Yes."

"That was your strategy in representing Mr. Wartnick in this case where he was accused of causing the wrongful death of Bob Nachtsheim. You were going to try to obstruct Mrs. Nachtsheim from showing Norm had done it, *but* you were *not* going to show who did do it. Is that correct?"

"That's correct."

"Now, Mr. Meshbesher took Mr. Krueger's deposition. Do you recall that?"

"Yes."

"And shortly before that deposition was taken by Mr. Meshbesher, you discovered that Betty Nachtsheim and Lieutenant Krueger had an intimate affair. Is that correct?"

"Yes."

"And your response to that information was simply to take no action on it. Isn't that correct?"

"That's not correct."

"Isn't it the case," Snider pressed, "that you did not attempt to do any independent investigation of the affair between Betty Nachtsheim and Lieutenant Krueger?"

"No, I did not do an independent investigation of their affair."

"Mr. Gainsley, did you at some point in time have a suspicion or belief or even an inkling that the perpetrator of this crime may have been Bobby Nachtsheim?"

"No."

Snider's eyebrows rose in full view of the jury. "You never had a belief that Bobby Nachtsheim may have been involved in the homicide? Is that your testimony?"

"No, it's not. That's not my testimony."

"So you *did* have a belief that Bobby Nachtsheim may have been involved in the homicide?"

"That's not correct either."

Snider bore down on the witness with an incredulous stare. "Maybe I'm missing something, Mr. Gainsley. Would you explain your answer."

"Sure. Early on when Wartnick came to see me, when the 1976 lawsuit was brought, he told me what he characterized as an acrimonious relationship between Bobby and his father. And we talked in my office a lot about that, and what I was trying to weigh was do I come into court and show that a boy killed his dad? —which would be one of the options available to me.

"I told Norm that I could find some support in the police report for that because there was some evidence in the police report or some statements made by one of the nine police officers who compiled the report that Bobby didn't get along with his father.

"So I decided, rather than having a shotgun approach as to who might have killed him, I said if you can testify that there was animosity between the two of them, then maybe what we ought to do is focus on one. Let's not go into court and say the whole world killed him, everyone killed him but you. Let's go into court and point to one person. Whether I believed it or not wasn't relevant to anything. It's the strategy that we decided to use."

"I take it, Mr. Gainsley, it was your strategy and judgment that you were going to try to, at least in some way, point the finger at Bobby. Is that correct?"

"Yes."

"The fact of the matter is you never did it. Isn't that correct?"

"No." Gainsley proclaimed with a jut of his jaw.

"You think you did point to Bobby as the perpetrator of this crime in your defense of Mr. Wartnick?"

"Yes."

"How could you make a judgment or a strategy call without even knowing what Bobby had to say on the subject, Mr. Gainsley?"

"I was satisfied with the interviews that he gave to the various police."

"It was only one police investigative unit and that's the Minneapolis Police Department. Correct?"

"That's correct."

"And you were satisfied with that?"

"Yes."

"Would you agree, Mr. Gainsley, that if you want to put witnesses on the stand to testify, it's helpful for you to know not only what they're going to say but how they're going to testify? Their demeanor, the manner in which they testify, for example?"

"Yes."

"And how can you make a judgment call on that if you never bothered to take the deposition of someone like Bobby Nachtsheim?"

"I didn't want to call Bobby. I did not want Bobby Nachtsheim in that trial."

"Well, you weren't in a position to make that decision because you'd never taken his deposition or interviewed him. Isn't that correct, Mr. Gainsley?"

"I *was* in the position to make that decision."

"Without having taken his deposition or even interviewing him?"

"Yes."

"Do you think it would have been relevant and admissible evidence for that first jury to have heard that Bobby Nachtsheim was discussing what percentage of the business he was going to get upon his father's death?"

"That would not have been in evidence."

"I'm asking you," Snider insisted, "if that's not something you would have wanted to know at the time of the trial of the underlying case?"

"I *did* know it at the trial of the underlying case."

"You didn't get it into evidence, did you?"

"I don't know whether I did or not."

"And isn't it the case that no one asked any questions about the incident involving the repossession of an automobile some two weeks prior to Mr. Nachtsheim's murder when there were threats made against Mr. Nachtsheim by Nordstrom and by Bobby?"

"I don't recall."

"Why did you say you can't rely on what Mr. Krueger says?"

The fast switch in topics caused Gainsley to hesitate. "W-when I met with Krueger it was almost a cat-and-mouse game. I just had to be careful as to whether he was leading me on or was he telling me something that was factual. I did not take at face value certain things he told me because I knew he was trying to get information from me."

Snider moved a step toward the witness. "So you thought he was not telling you information that was factual?"

"I think that's right. I think some of the things he told me were not factual."

"Well, if that's the case, Mr. Gainsley, you've testified in front of this jury that you relied on the police report which was prepared primarily by Officer Krueger. How could you rely on Officer Krueger's report if he's telling you things you don't believe and aren't trustworthy?"

"How could I do that?"

"Yes, sir," Snider's penetrating gaze was fixed on the witness. "How can you say that you could rely on Mr. Krueger's reports based on what you've testified here about Mr. Krueger?"

"Because they weren't Mr. Krueger's reports. They were all of the police department's reports. They were Quinn's reports, there was Negethon, there was all sorts of police officers who did the interviewing and who did the narratives. I didn't rely just upon him."

"Well, you knew that Mr. Krueger was in charge of that investigation, did you not?"

"He was for a while. There was someone before him and someone after him."

"Yeah, there was someone for two days before him. Isn't that correct?"

"That's correct."

"And then he kept the case, basically, until he [retired from the force] several years later. Isn't that correct?"

"That's correct."

Snider turned suddenly toward the bench. "Your Honor, may I have Exhibit One-Thirty-E, please." The police report was retrieved. "And may I approach the witness?"

"You may."

"Mr. Gainsley, I don't want to belabor the point, but as you look through this you see Krueger's name scattered throughout this, do you not?"

"Yes."

"And it's Officer Krueger who is writing these reports. Correct?"

"Some of them."

Snider flipped page after page of the police file to highlight the number of reports completed by Krueger, each acknowledged by the witness. "And if we continue after those dates, we see Lieutenant Krueger's name scattered throughout, and he's writing a narrative of what he's investigated. Is that correct?"

"Yes."

"And you didn't believe Lieutenant Krueger?"

"Not on everything."

"Did you investigate any of the people that were suggested as potential suspects in the police report, other than Zola Friedman and the people at Prudential Insurance?"

"You mean the party people?"

"Yes," Snider gave a quick nod.

"No." Gainsley acknowledged.

"The people who testified about the altercation over the car, the police reports that talk about Bobby saying he was walking unless he gets fifty-one percent of the business. Did you ever follow up and have any investigation of those items?"

"No."

"And it's the case, is it not, that early on in this proceeding Mr. Wartnick told you he'd seen his children the morning of the shooting?"

"That's correct."

"But you never took their depositions or interviewed them. Isn't that right?"

"That's correct."

"Mr. Gainsley, how can you make a judgment on what the kids would or would not do for you if you don't even sit down and talk with them?"

"I know what my client told me."

"I'm sorry?"

"I know what my client told me."

"Isn't it the case that unless you take the time to talk with those children, you're not in a position to make the very kind of judgment call you're now testifying you made?"

"No."

"What do you mean, 'No'?"

"That's not the case."

"Why is it not the case, if you don't know what they're going to say?"

"I *knew* what they were going to say. My client told me what they were going to say."

Gainsley's answer hung in the air. The jury panel recorded more notes. Snider stepped slowly toward the white board.

"Let me move to another topic of investigation, if I can, Mr. Gainsley, and it's the issue of the flat of orchids on the floor. You agree with me, don't you, that in the underlying trial against Mr. Wartnick the orchids became a significant issue in the trial?"

"It became an issue," Gainsley hedged.

"Well, it became a significant issue, did it not?" Snider pressed.

"It became an issue."

Friedberg shook his head at Gainsley's insistence, sighed, leaned back in his chair, and prepared to enjoy another opportunity to admire the ease with which Snider could ebb and flow with a witness's statements, take advantage of a witness's words to pull out the truth or pin down an attitude, and still keep his cool.

"May I approach the witness, Your Honor?"

"You may."

"Mr. Gainsley, this is your March 15, 1990, deposition transcript at page forty-four. Isn't it the case you were asked the following question: 'Did it become a significant factor in your trial on behalf of Midwest Floral and Mr. Wartnick that there was no explanation for the orchids being out of the cooler?' And the answer you gave is: 'The orchids became a significant issue.' That's the testimony you gave. Is that right?"

"That's correct."

"And it's the truth, is it not, that in the underlying trial the orchids became a significant issue?"

"I think that's right."

Snider nodded, turned, and strolled back to the white board. "Did you *ever* learn that it was a practice and routine of Mr. Nachtsheim each morning to take his orchids out of the cooler?"

"No," the witness shook his head decisively.

"You never learned that?"

"That's correct," Gainsley insisted.

"Mr. Gainsley, Plaintiff's Exhibit One-Thirty-E, the police report, the full paragraph in the middle of page nine reflects a conversation between Mr. Krueger and Mr. Mentes, and it says, 'They informed me that this box of orchids normally would have been kept in the walk-in and that the victim normally handled all of the orchids himself and it was not unusual that he would have entered the cooler in the early a.m. hours and removed said box for purposes of repacking or whatever.' Mr. Mentes's statement never came to your attention, did it, Mr. Gainsley?"

"Yes."

"About taking orchids out first thing in the morning?"

"What he said here came to my attention."

"Isn't it the case, Mr. Gainsley, that at the time of trial you didn't have a legible copy of this police report so you would know that's what Mentes was going to say?"

"No, that's not the case."

"Are you telling this jury that before Mr. Wartnick's trial you had knowledge that Mr. Mentes made a statement to the police that the victim handled orchids, himself, and it was not unusual for him to enter the cooler in the early a.m. hours and remove the orchids for purposes of repacking? You had knowledge of that?"

"I had knowledge of that."

"And you had knowledge before the trial started?"

"Yes."

"How do you reconcile the testimony that you just gave about knowledge of Mr. Nachtsheim's practice with regard to orchids, with the testimony you gave on page forty-five that you do *not* remember whether you learned that it was a practice and routine of Mr. Nachtsheim each morning to take his orchids out of the cooler?"

"You're asking two different questions. Those aren't the same thing."

"Do you remember it now, Mr. Gainsley?"

"Do I remember *what* now?"

"That it was a practice and routine of Mr. Nachtsheim to take the orchids out of the cooler?"

"After he put on his smock in the morning," Gainsley said as he hurriedly scanned the page, "that would be one of the things that he might do. He was shot before he even put his smock on. I think Wartnick told me that you put on your smock because whenever you go in the cooler you get wet."

"Mr. Gainsley, you just gave testimony about a so-called discussion with Mr. Wartnick about Mr. Nachtsheim putting on his smock. The question I asked you in your deposition is: 'Did you learn that it was a practice and routine of Nachtsheim each morning to take his orchids out of the cooler?' And your answer was, 'I can't remember now whether I had learned that.' I take it, at the time of your deposition in March of 1990, that's just not something you could remember. Is that correct? Is that what your answer meant when you testified as you did?"

"What I said in my deposition was true."

"You couldn't remember?"

"What I said in my deposition was true."

"Mr. Gainsley, I want to understand your testimony, and when I asked you if you learned about a practice and routine of Mr. Nachtsheim taking orchids out of the cooler, your answer at your deposition in 1990 was that you can't remember whether you had learned that."

"That's correct."

"All right. My second question for you is, do you remember *today* whether or not you learned that somewhere in this process?"

"No."

"You never learned it?"

"No."

"And you never investigated, you never conducted an investigation to determine whether it was a routine practice to take orchids out of the cooler each morning. Is that correct?"

"That's not correct."

Snider again turned to face the bench. "Your Honor, may I have Plaintiff's Exhibit Sixty-Two, please." The exhibit was retrieved. Snider extended it to the witness, "I'd like to place in front of you, Mr. Gainsley, and this is a brief that you prepared in the underlying litigation. Is that correct?"

"Yes."

"Why don't you tell the court and the jury what kind of brief this is."

"There was a notice of motion and motion. This was where I asked the court in December of 1985 to grant Mr. Wartnick and his company summary judgment."

"And please describe what a summary judgment is, Mr. Gainsley."

Gainsley squirmed further down into his chair. "It's what the name implies."

Snider waited. The jury began to squirm.

"It's where the court would order judgment summarily—" Gainsley finally answered, "—without the necessity of trial, based upon what the court has before it at the time."

"In other words, in a summary judgment it's the judge that decides the case, decides if there's insufficient genuine issues of material fact for the case to go to a jury. Is that correct?"

"That's correct."

"And your purpose in filing this motion for summary judgment, I assume, is to not let the case ever get to a jury?"

"That's correct."

"If you'd look at page two of your memorandum there's a discussion about Mrs. Nachtsheim's futile attempt to lay her husband's death at the feet of Mr. Wartnick or Midwest. Do you see that?"

"Yes."

"And you argue, further down the page, that, quote, Mrs. Nachtsheim has utterly failed to produce a shred of evidence, notwithstanding the twelve years that have elapsed since Mr. Nachtsheim's death, close quote. Is that correct?"

"That's what I argued."

"And you believed that when you argued it, didn't you?"

"I don't know what my belief is. This is what my client retains me to do is to make these arguments on his behalf."

"Well, Mr. Gainsley, you're not telling this jury you'd make arguments that are not true?"

"I make arguments to advance my client's causes."

Snider looked incredulously at the witness. "Mr. Gainsley, you don't put false information in your briefs that you file with the court, do you?"

"False information?"

"Yes, sir."

"No."

"So if you put something in a brief that you file with the court, you expect the court to rely on it, I assume. Is that correct?"

"That's correct."

"And when you prepared *this* brief, you meant to be fair and accurate with respect to the facts, with respect to your argument about the facts. Is that correct?"

"Objection," Mason called out. "Misleading and irrelevant."

"Overruled. The witness may answer."

Gainsley straightened a bit in the seat. "It was not my function to be fair. It was my function to state my client's cause as I could state it."

"Did you believe, at the time you wrote these words, that, quote, Mrs. Nachtsheim has utterly failed to produce a shred of evidence against Mr. Wartnick, close quote. Did you believe there was evidence against Mr. Wartnick?"

"I thought there was sufficient evidence that a court was going to deny my motion. And I also thought that Mr. Meshbesher wasn't simply going to take this and agree to it; that he would respond to it and fight me off on it."

"You thought you were going to lose this and you filed it anyway?"

"No. What I said was that Meshbesher was not simply going to roll over and play dead. He would show the judge facts he thought supported a claim that the matter should go to a jury."

"There's an assertion on page seventeen of the brief," Snider continued, "if you'd turn to that, please—discussing Wartnick's refusal to undergo a polygraph examination and repeatedly asserting the Fifth Amendment to all questions relating to Mr. Nachtsheim's death. And it says: 'In Mrs. Nachtsheim's answers to interrogatories, she claims as a fact supporting her allegation, Mr. Wartnick's refusal to undergo a polygraph examination and repeatedly asserting the Fifth Amendment to all questions relating to Mr. Nachtsheim's death. Mr. Wartnick's refusal on both fronts was on the sound advice of counsel.' Is that what you wrote in your brief?"

"Yes."

"And was that factual?"

"Yes."

"And then you go on to say that 'Polygraph examinations are not accepted in this state and any reference to such tests are inadmissible in trial.' Correct?"

"That's what I said."

"And did you have an understanding that was the law at the time you represented Mr. Wartnick?"

"Well, I knew that polygraph tests are not admissible in court."

Snider again returned to counsel's table and resorted documents.

"I want to ask you, if you would, please, to turn to a portion of the trial transcript. I believe there's a Volume I in front of you. Let me ask you, Mr. Gainsley, to turn to page two-seventy-one through two-seventy-three of the transcript. You were cross-examining Officer Quinn on these pages. Correct?"

"Yes."

"And you asked this question, 'Did your investigation reveal any problems between the owner, Mr. Nachtsheim, and his employees?' Do you see that question?" Snider turned toward the witness.

"Yes."

"And Mr. Meshbesher is entering an objection—sort of like Mr. Mason has done here from time to time—and he says, 'Wait a minute. No foundation laid. Hearsay, Your Honor.' Did that take place on that page of the transcript, Mr. Gainsley?"

"Yes."

"All right. And let me call your attention, if I could please, to the next part of this; a statement that Mr. Meshbesher makes out of the presence of the jury. And could you confirm for our jury that part of the statement that Mr. Meshbesher made is: 'He's got to call those people—' in other words, the witnesses interviewed by William Quinn—'call those people in to prove it, not from this guy.' In other words, not from Mr. Quinn, the police officer."

"We'll stipulate the record says what it says in the middle there," Mason said.

"Thank you," Snider acknowledged Mason. "And then you make a statement—and the dots in this copy indicate this is not your complete statement but it's the portion of the statement that I wish to bring to the attention of the jury—and it states: 'I'm offering that to show…might be hearsay…that the thinking of the police department at the time did not focus exclusively upon Mr. Wartnick, but that there were other people who were considered as a part of the investigation, at least at this early stage.' Is that an argument that you made at the trial at this point in time?"

"We'll stipulate that, too," Mason offered.

"Okay. And then we get to the last sentence and you've got Judge McCarr—who is the Court. Correct, Mr. Gainsley?"

"That's correct."

"And the Court says: 'I'll sustain the objection. I think it's over broad and calls for hearsay in this present form.' Now what's going on here, isn't it, Mr. Gainsley, is that you're trying to present information contained in the police reports to show there were other suspects in this case. Isn't that correct?"

"That's correct."

"And the way you intended to do that was by questioning Officer Quinn as to what's in the police reports. Is that correct?"

Gainsley nodded, lips pursed. "This was cross-examination of Officer Quinn."

"Yes, sir. Cross-examination of Officer Quinn, but that cross-examination from the police report was hearsay. Isn't that right?"

"The judge sustained the objection." Gainsley affirmed Snider's statement.

"And that being the case, Mr. Gainsley, is it or is it not the case you knew that report reflected conversations police officers had with third parties, so you can't admit that evidence for the truth of what those parties state."

"That's correct."

"Okay. And do you agree with me that the only way to get evidence in, you've got to call the people that said it or else it's hearsay. It's not going to come into evidence. Correct?"

"That's generally correct."

"So, if you want to get evidence in as to what was said at this particular party, there's a number of things you can do, one of which is call Dennis Kreuser as a witness or take his deposition prior to the time you call him as a witness and ask him what he said. Is that correct?"

"Yes."

Snider took a small step toward the defendant. "Mr. Gainsley, did you try to offer the police reports at the underlying trial?"

Gainsley began to strum his fingers on the wooden shelf in front of him, then changed his mind, sat back, and cross his arms in front of his chest. "I think what I tried to do here was to offer Quinn's portion of the report."

"So, part of the police report?"

"Yes."

Another small step was taken toward the man in the witness box. "And you wanted to do that because you thought there was something in those reports that would be helpful to your defense of Mr. Wartnick and Midwest Floral. Is that correct?"

"Yes." The witness nodded, ineffectively straightened his tie, and sent a fleeting glance toward the judge.

"But you couldn't get the documents in because the court said they were hearsay. Is that correct?"

Gainsley glanced at the ceiling tiles and barely breathed. "The court sustained Meshbesher's objection."

Gainsley's belated attempts to introduce facts mentioned within the police reports, his only real defense of Wartnick, had been easily repulsed.

292

CHAPTER 44

Judge Stanoch and attorneys from both sides gathered without the jury to discuss a number of issues, the predominant one being Mason's motion to strike portions of the testimony of F. Lee Bailey.

The lengthy meeting ended with Judge Stanoch's pronouncement, "What I'm prepared to do at this time is to indicate that I believe the scope of the Fifth Amendment advice, the original Fifth Amendment advice that Mr. Bailey testified to, was too broad, and I'm not inclined to let that occur with regard to any future witnesses. [It] goes beyond the scope of my ruling. I'll indicate that now as guidance to the attorneys as you prepare for the additional experts.

"I'll deal separately with the issue of what we do with Mr. Bailey's testimony in that regard and talk to the attorneys further about that. The remainder of the issues I'll take under advisement. I'm going to have my clerk pull for me the two Supreme Court cases mentioned by Mr. Friedberg so I can research them and I'll give you some guidance.

"Now I'd like to bring the jury in so we can get going. Mr. Gainsley, I'm sure, wants to get up here and get this over with, and I'm sure the jury wants to get going, too. Why don't we get back in a trial posture. We'll go up until about twelve-fifteen."

WEDNESDAY, OCTOBER 12 THRU MONDAY, OCTOBER 17, 1994—TRIAL DAYS 12 THROUGH 15

Mason's direct and re-direct and Snider's recross-examinations of Gainsley continued through the end of the week, punch and counter-punch, including how many times during the original trial the jury heard Wartnick had not taken a polygraph. Gainsley said 'only in opening statement'; Snider proved otherwise—twice more, at least.

Falsification of the time records came into play regarding whether or not Gainsley had adequately prepared Wartnick for his 1979 deposition or, indeed, had even discussed with Wartnick the implications of taking the Fifth Amendment in a civil deposition.

"Now you testified," Snider said, "that you had previously agreed that Mr. Wartnick was going to take the Fifth Amendment. Is that correct?

"That's correct." Gainsley said.

"And you instructed him to take the Fifth Amendment. Isn't that correct?"

"That's correct."

"Okay," Snider also nodded. "Now *when* had you previously agreed that Mr. Wartnick was going to take the Fifth Amendment?"

"We had talked about it on numerous occasions and it just evolved, after numerous discussions, that that's what he ought to do."

"Who had talked about it, Mr. Gainsley?"

Gainsley straightened in the witness chair. "My partner and Mr. Wartnick; my father and Mr. Wartnick; Ms. Lerner and Mr. Wartnick; Mr. Wartnick and I. All of us." This statement would prove very important in the impeachment of Gainsley.

Snider nodded, turned, and retrieved a sheet of paper from atop a stack on counsel's table. He walked it to the witness. "Mr. Gainsley, I've put in front of you Defendant's Exhibit Forty-Two, which [you placed] into evidence through the testimony of Mr. Wartnick. Is that a document that you're familiar with?"

Gainsley barely glanced at it. "Yes."

"And is it your testimony here today that this is a letter that you sent to Mr. Wartnick?"

Gainsley nodded.

Wartnick had earlier testified he never saw the letter until the final collection of Gainsley's documents late in this case.

"And this letter purports to set up a meeting between Mr. Wartnick, Zola Friedman, and yourself on Saturday morning, February 10, at nine o'clock. Is that correct?

"Yes."

"As you sit here today, do you have an independent recollection of a meeting on February 10, 1979?"

"I believe so." Gainsley seemed quite confident.

"Can you tell us why," Snider began a short stroll to the far corner of the jury box, "in your first deposition that was taken back in 1988, that you did *not* have such a recollection?"

"No."

"Did it become important to you, Mr. Gainsley," Snider faced the witness, "that you have a day that you could point to that reflects that you met with Mr. Wartnick prior to the time his deposition was taken?"

Gainsley cleared his throat. "I'm sorry. I don't understand you."

"Well, did it become important to your defense of this case—the case that Mr. Wartnick has against you for legal malpractice—that you establish a date and a time when you met with Mr. Wartnick prior to the deposition?"

"No."

"All right, sir." Again Snider moved to counsel's table and retrieved the Gainsley law firm's time record. "Now would you please look at Exhibit One-

Twenty-Three-B and tell us if there is any time entry on your records that reflect such a meeting."

Gainsley pulled the photocopy of the time records from a stack in front of him and flipped back and forth through the pages. "Yes," he glanced up, confident. "February 10, 1979."

The "wet ink" entry.

Snider walked Gainsley through entry after entry on the time log, and nowhere were any entries found that could even be remotely misunderstood to have been meetings in which Mr. Wartnick might have been present when the Fifth Amendment had been discussed. Not with [Gainsley's] partner, not with Gainsley Sr., not even with Jane Lerner. In fact, Lerner would testify to having met with Wartnick only twice: once at Midwest Floral and once at the law firm. Both meetings were in 1976 during the early collection of factual evidence regarding the insurance claim. No indication was found that she ever met with Wartnick regarding the Fifth Amendment issue.

They arrived, in the walk-through, at the entry Gainsley claimed was his meeting with Wartnick to prepare him to take the Fifth Amendment at his deposition the following week. "February 10, 1979," Snider said. "Almost a month out of whack?"

Gainsley, again, fumbled back and forth between the sheets. "It appears that way."

"And it says, 'Conference with Norm Wartnick and Zola Friedman,' and you spent one hour doing that. Is that correct?"

"That's that Saturday morning. I think so. Yes."

"So this is the Saturday morning meeting. This ended up in your time list almost a month after the meeting is alleged to have taken place. Isn't that correct?"

"That's correct."

"Now, Mr. Gainsley," Snider took the few steps back to the end of the jury box. "Isn't it true that you falsified this entry so you could support a meeting with Mr. Wartnick?"

"No, that's not true."

"Okay," Snider nodded. "And isn't it true that the entry that you've reflected as February 10, 1979—which you posted after March 19, 1979—was typed on a different typewriter than the typewriter for the other entries on the ledger sheet in February and on into March?"

The pages flipped again. "Looks as if it's typed on a different typewriter," Gainsley agreed.

"Your Honor," Snider turned to Judge Stanoch. "I'd like the record to reflect that the item I'd like the jury to review is the February 10, 1979, entry, which is the third entry from the top of the daily time ledger sheet on the third page of the exhibit."

"So noted."

"Now, Mr. Gainsley, are you having this jury believe that you met with Zola Friedman and with Norm Wartnick for one hour on February 10 in your offices?"

"That's correct."

"And are you having this jury believe that in that meeting you discussed Mr. Wartnick's Fifth Amendment rights?"

"No, that's not correct."

Snider's square shoulders straightened. "You did *not* discuss his Fifth Amendment rights in that meeting?"

"Only to tell him that's the decision—was what we were going to do."

"Did you have some discussions about what Mr. Wartnick was going to testify to in that Saturday meeting?"

Gainsley shifted in the witness chair. "I don't think so."

"Then why did you meet with him?"

"I was very concerned about Krueger, of a meeting he had with Zola Friedman at the police department; a meeting that Zola Friedman denied ever taking place. And here is a lieutenant of the Minneapolis Police Department saying 'Zola Friedman came to see me, he was sweating, he was ringing his hands, he was agonizing.'" Gainsley picked up steam. "He said, 'Good God, I'd be in that position, too.'—he actually put words of Zola Friedman's in quotations. I just had to get Zola Friedman in there to see why there was such a discrepancy in testimony. Wartnick was my client, and I wanted him there with me, too."

"Are you telling this jury, Mr. Gainsley, that you never prepared Norm Wartnick for the deposition?"

"No. I'm not telling them that at all."

"You said you told him *at that meeting* that he would be taking the Fifth Amendment and then, I believe you said, you didn't have any discussions about what he would testify to thereafter, but you focused your attention on Zola Friedman. Is that correct?"

Gainsley flipped pages again. "You mean at this meeting?"

"Yes, sir."

"Oh, at *this* meeting. I don't recall talking about Wartnick's testimony. I recall really talking—I mean, I know that Wartnick said, 'Well, what am I going to say?' when we established that he was going to assert his Fifth Amendment rights."

Snider took a step toward Phil Gainsley. The resonance of his deep voice filled the room. "You mean when you *told* him he was going to take his Fifth Amendment rights?"

Gainsley nodded. "When I told him we were going to take his Fifth Amendment rights, that's right. And he said, 'What do I say?' and I said, 'I'll prepare a card.' But the primary focus of this meeting was this absolutely one-hundred percent contradiction over a meeting that Krueger said existed and a meeting that Mr. Friedman absolutely denied."

Snider had succeeded in getting Phil Gainsley's disingenuous duplicity on record.

The exchange between Snider and Gainsley that was most remembered by Wartnick's team, however, was when Snider asked, "Mr. Gainsley, why in the world would you have put Mr. Wartnick on the stand to take the Fifth Amendment in person?"

"Because I thought it would be a good way to introduce Mr. Wartnick to the jury."

Gainsley's response stunned Snider. "Excuse me, Mr. Gainsley?!" Both bushy eyebrows rose. "Are you saying the best way for those jurors to meet Norm Wartnick was for him to sit there and answer the question 'Did you have anything to do with the murder of Mr. Nachtsheim?' by saying, 'I refuse to answer that question on the grounds it might incriminate me'?!"

Gainsley nodded. "I thought so. Yes."

CHAPTER 45

Gainsley's time on the witness stand was followed by Plaintiff's expert witnesses Marcy Wallace, Earl Gray, and Michael Berens. Each testified according to their earlier findings:

"exposed Wartnick to very substantial risks of punitive damages" —

"My conclusion is it is malpractice. It fails to meet the standards of the community" —

"did not exercise reasonable care" — "was gross negligence … a gross error."

At the end of Friday, October 14, 1994, the fourteenth day of trial, Plaintiff rested.

Snider was pleased. He and Friedberg had presented their case as fully and accurately as possible and, more importantly, both men believed the jury had closely followed their presentation—something Mason had not yet been able to achieve. On Monday Mason would begin his defense.

Monday, October 17, 1994—Trial Day 15

"This is the matter of *Wartnick against Gainsley and Moss and Barnett*," Stanoch began. "The record should reflect we're in chambers on Monday morning, outside the presence of the jury.

"I've indicated to the attorneys this morning that I intend to strike a part of the Bailey testimony that relates to the appropriateness of Mr. Gainsley instructing Mr. Wartnick to take the Fifth Amendment. I've asked for input from the attorneys in terms of language that should be given in connection with the order to strike.

"Also, Mr. Mason has indicated he'd like to bring a motion for a directed verdict."

A directed verdict is a judge's ruling that ends the trial. A judge may grant defense's motion for directed verdict only if the plaintiff has failed to offer any admissible, relevant evidence to prove their case against the defendant. When that happens, the judge is saying that, as a matter of law, no reasonable jury could decide in the plaintiff's favor.

"Mr. Mason," the Court concluded, "you may proceed."

Mason nodded. "If the court please, the defendants move the court to grant a directed verdict on the grounds that the facts and the law the plaintiff has presented show no right to relief." Mason argued that since polygraph evidence is not admissible in Minnesota, Gainsley's reference to a polygraph in his opening statement was not malpractice because he did not refer to any admissible evidence. Mason said that Judge McCarr read an instruction to the jury at the previous trial explaining that what lawyers say in opening argument is not evidence, so the jury would never have considered the polygraph information as evidence. And when Meshbesher tried to introduce evidence of the polygraph on the grounds that Gainsley 'opened the door' to that evidence, McCarr wouldn't let him do it.

Mason's was a silly, technical argument, as if an attorney said during his opening statement, "By the way, I know a lot of people say my client is a pedophile and an axe murderer, but you should pay that no mind." What other people say about someone is hearsay and not admissible, so, by Mason's argument, it would be no problem for an attorney to make that statement because the jury would be told it was not evidence: there would be no evidence people said the client was a axe-murdering pedophile, so what's the problem?

The problem is *why would you say that in your opening statement?*

It can be a good trial strategy to tell the jury adverse facts in your case so you can spin them your way, but that is good strategy *only if* the jury is actually going to hear the adverse facts. If those facts are inadmissible as evidence, if the jury is never otherwise going to hear them, why mention them?

It was the same with Gainsley's statement that Wartnick refused to take a polygraph test. Gainsley made Wartnick sound as though he was trying to hide his guilt, and the jury would never have heard it if Gainsley had not told them.[35]

Another of Mason's arguments for directed verdict included, "On the issue of his alleged failure to conduct a minimally adequate investigation," only one of plaintiff's experts gave "evidence that was supposedly overlooked by the defendant which would have been helpful to Mr. Wartnick. ...

"There isn't evidence of *but for* causation as to any of these," Mason concluded. "The plaintiff has wholly failed in its proof and the court should grant judgment to the defendant as a matter of law."

Judge Stanoch glanced toward plaintiff's team for their response. Friedberg glanced at Snider. Snider turned with a twinkle in his eyes to Chuck Webber. Webber's eyes widened as he realized he was to offer their response. Judge Stanoch nodded. "Mr. Webber."

"The standard for a directed verdict," Webber said, "is that all of the evidence the non-moving party has put in must be presumed to be true, accurate, credible, right on the mark; and only if the evidence put in is not sufficient to justify the case going to the jury should a directed verdict be granted.

"The case that we've cited on the very first page of this memorandum says that the right to a directed verdict is to be sparingly and cautiously exercised,

---

35. Preceding explanation given by Chuck Webber—who still, nearly twenty years later, becomes animated when he discusses the issues of this case.

for obvious reasons. It's a very rare case that the plaintiff will not get in evidence enough to let the claim go to the jury."

"Let me just," Judge Stanoch interrupted, "and I don't mean to cut you off here, but let's just assume, for the purposes of this morning's discussion, that what I intend to do is take this under advisement, read your memo, before I rule. We've got the jury waiting, so if there's something that's beyond what's in your memo that you want to argue, go ahead and do so."

"Yeah, that's fine," Webber acknowledged. "What I do need to talk about is the issue on how we worded the polygraph claim in our complaint. And if I remember correctly, the way it's been stated is that Mr. Gainsley committed malpractice by negligently injecting inadmissible evidence into the trial, the wrongful death trial, in the form of reference to the polygraph. The court had some concerns about that and that's what pages three through thirteen of the memorandum are about because the court wanted cases and we gave them to the court. And there are more than what we gave.

"Mr. Mason has raised a point that what an attorney says in opening statement is not evidence as a matter of law. I suppose the argument is that if it's not evidence you can't base any sort of a malpractice claim on it. That presumes that what attorneys say in an opening statement is not to be considered at all by a jury, and that's clearly not the rule; otherwise we wouldn't have opening statements. We stand up there and make opening statements so the jury can think about them.

"The hypothetical used last week with Mr. Berens is still right on. If an attorney stands up and says to a jury: 'My client committed a heinous murder of the most gory and shallow and cowardly kind, and we have no dispute about that but, having said that, please don't pay any attention to it because I'm going to prove my client didn't commit this dastardly deed.' The jury may not be able to consider that as evidence, but there's nobody with a straight face who can say that's not a stupid thing to tell the jury.

"We've been at this for almost seven years now and not once in seven years, and not once in twelve days of trial in front of the jury have they ever complained that they're confused or bewildered or somehow in doubt about what our claim was. To stand up after twelve days of trial and say, 'Whoops, you used the wrong word in your complaint so you're knocked out of court,' is silly. To claim they're bewildered about what this claim is all about after seven years is unseemly for people who are as talented as defendants' counsel is. It's unseemly to stand up and claim bewilderment at what's going on in this case."

Laughter began to ripple through the room.

Judge Stanoch said, "Getting kind of thick."

Even Mason quipped, "This isn't the congressional record," which was followed by open laughter. "I get carried away sometimes, too, Chuck."

Webber grinned. "I feel rather strongly."

"So anyhow," the judge said, "you're opposed to the motion for directed verdict."

The gentlemen's laughter continued. The motion for directed verdict was denied.

"Good morning, members of the jury," Judge Stanoch gathered his robes and seated himself at the bench. "We'll proceed this morning with defendants' case. I'll give you more than an hour for lunch today to give you time to get out and walk around a little bit."

"In the rain?" a jury member said.

"In the rain, yeah." Stanoch's glance raked the jury as he grinned. "Who said that?"

A general lightness settled over the courtroom, brief reprieve from the heaviness of the issues before them.

"Mr. Mason, is the defense prepared to proceed?"

"We are, Your Honor."

"You may call your first witness."

Gainsley's former secretary, Kay Chismar, was shown official copies of Gainsley's time records, acknowledged her recognition of them as such, and explained the typical process by which they were assembled. "Well, we weren't probably real accurate. We posted as we had time to do the posting to get it on the pages, and maybe all of it wasn't in order."

Then it was Snider's turn. He stood behind counsel's table and said, "Ms. Chismar, you're a friend of Phil Gainsley, aren't you?"

"Yes."

"You worked for him for a long time?"

"Yes."

"I assume you liked him. Is that correct?"

"Yes."

"And you remained a friend with him right up to the present time. Is that correct?"

"Yes."

Snider began his move to the front of the room. "Ms. Chismar, you understand that no one is accusing you of committing fraud, don't you? Or of falsifying the time record?"

"I hope not."

"What kind of typewriter did you have, ma'am?"

"IBM Selectric."

"Okay. Now, do you agree that the typewriting on the February 10th entry is entirely different from the entry, for example, from March 19, 1979, which is right above it?"

"Right. Yeah. Uh-huh."

"Do you know what kind of [typewriter] the March 19, 1979, type is?"

"I'm sure it was an IBM."

"Was an IBM. But not the Selectric used on February 10, 1979, in your view?"

"No, this is my machine."

"There's a difference in type."

"Uh-huh."

"All right. I notice on all of the other time sheets there may be a few dates out of whack but nothing like an entire month. Would you agree with that?"

"I would agree that there's nothing else on here that's so out of whack."

"And it's at least possible, is it not, Ms. Chismar, that [someone] could have typed this entry six years after that?"

"No."

"Why do you say, No?"

"Six years after '79?"

"Uh-huh." Snider confirmed.

"No."

"Why do you say that?"

"Because it wouldn't have happened."

"But what's the basis of your testimony? Why do you say that?"

"Why this couldn't have been done?"

"Yes." Snider said.

"I don't have an answer."

CHAPTER 46

Former Minnesota Supreme Court Chief Justice Robert Sheran was colorless. Even his pin-striped power suit and narrow silk tie were pallid shades of gray. From the public seats it was difficult to tell where the collar of his starched shirt ended. His aura of judicial authority, however, failed to raise a speaking volume which was nearly inaudible and too often came only after long pauses. The court reporter strained to hear, even though she was within arm's reach.

"And what have you undertaken," Mason asked after the prerequisites and credentials had been established, "in connection with your responsibilities as an expert in this matter?"

"Well," Sheran cleared his throat, "I reviewed a considerable quantity of written materials: the transcript of the early trial in its entirety, numerous depositions, memoranda, the police report that was put together by the Minneapolis Police Department, and then in addition to that I refreshed my recollection with respect to what I considered to be the relevant rules of law."

Mason strode to his white board. "One of the allegations in this lawsuit has to do with the opening statement given by Mr. Gainsley." He pointed to the allegation. "Have you formed an opinion as to whether what Mr. Gainsley said in his opening statement constituted negligence?"

"Yes."

"Would you state that opinion, please."

"In my opinion it did *not* constitute negligence."

"Would you briefly summarize the reasons upon which you have formulated the opinion that Mr. Gainsley's conduct was *not* negligence. Please tell that to the jury."

"In my view, it was an absolute *imperative* for defense to present Mr. Wartnick as a person who was open, candid, direct; a person who, in face of evidence that was extremely harmful to him, would be believed by the jury.

"My experience," Sheran continued, "as a trial lawyer and as a judge tells me it's important to bring to the attention of the jury the things that you think may come to their attention somewhere during the course of the trial and might prove, if they were not forewarned, to be harmful to you. I see this statement by Mr. Gainsley as an effort to do just that."

"Let me turn to the second complaint," Mason said, "the allegation Mr. Gainsley failed to conduct a minimally adequate investigation into the

Nachtsheim murder. Have you formed an opinion as to whether Mr. Gainsley's conduct and that of the defendants was negligent?"

"Yes, I have."

"And what is that opinion?"

Sheran's air of authority was impressive. "My opinion is that it was not negligence."

"Would you summarize for the jury the grounds of your conclusion that Mr. Gainsley's investigation was *not* negligent."

"This was a case where investigation was conducted by the Minneapolis Police Department beginning a very short time after the event which resulted in Mr. Nachtsheim's death. My conviction is that this was a remarkably thorough investigation. In my judgment, it's within what would be reasonably expected of lawyers to rely on that investigation rather than to have his client incur the considerable costs involved to duplicate that investigation."

"The second issue related to that allegation," Mr. Mason spoke from beside the white board, "is whether the jury verdict was caused by any conduct of Mr. Gainsley relative to the investigation. Do you have an opinion on that subject?"

"Yes."

"What is that opinion?"

"My opinion is that it was *not* caused by any failure on his part to investigate."

"Would you summarize the grounds for that opinion, please."

"Mr. Gainsley confronted a web of circumstantial evidence tending to indicate his client was involved in this tragic event and a situation where the investigating officer, Lieutenant Krueger—an individual with thirty years experience investigating cases of this kind, an officer with experience investigating three hundred homicide cases, a person who had the opportunity to interview the critical witnesses and observe their reactions and demeanor firsthand—had come to the conclusion that Norm Wartnick was the perpetrator of this offense.

"And Mr. Gainsley," Sheran continued, "would necessarily have known that when Mr. Krueger took the witness stand to testify that, either by body language or explicit expression, he would convey to that jury it was his conviction Mr. Wartnick had caused Mr. Nachtsheim's death. So that, in my mind, became for this case an extremely difficult problem to contend with."

"We have the fact," with a quivering hand, Sheran sipped water from a glass on the shelf in front of him, then continued, "that when Mr. Wartnick was asked to explain why that was done he gave an explanation which, at least in my judgment, would seem to most people pretty unreasonable. Namely, that a disaffected employee would be coming back. That explanation seems to me to be one that most jurors would find difficult to accept.

"Then, in addition to the problem that Mr. Gainsley had arising out of these events was the circumstance that the termination of employment by Mr. Nachtsheim some eight months before had been, if not hostile, at least unpleasant. Just by the nature of things, that would tend to create the impression of a feeling of hostility."

Justice Sheran also noted that at the time of the murder, Midwest Floral was "in somewhat desperate financial circumstances."

"Unless Mr. Gainsley," Sheran began his conclusion, "as attorney for Mr. Wartnick, could identify a suspect against whom an equally strong case could be positioned, he's headed for serious trouble. Unless the outside possibility, which does occur, that Mr. Wartnick's appearance, candor, openness, frankness would be such that the jury would say, in effect, 'Well this picture looks very bad but we're satisfied, just from our assessment of you as a person, that you didn't do it.' That would be the only other possibility."

Mason stood by the white board with arms crossed over his shirt pockets. He quickly uncrossed them and stepped forward. "If Mr. Gainsley had brought to the attention of that jury that, in fact, the policy would not have totally lapsed upon failure to pay premiums, would that have been heavily in the defense of the case on Mr. Wartnick's behalf?"

"No. I think most jurors would see that as quibbling."

On each subsequent aspect of plaintiff's complaint—the need to identify a suspect, the *but for* Gainsley's lack of investigation, the failure to mitigate the damage done by the 1979 deposition and the issues raised within each, Justice Sheran's opinion remained "that was well within the judgmental ambient that applies in a situation of this kind," and "was well within the area of permissible judgment of attorneys practicing in this area," and "his conduct in that respect was not causative of the verdict."

"Finally, then," Mason concluded, "what is your opinion as to whether Mr. Gainsley committed malpractice in this matter?"

"My opinion is that he did *not*."

CHAPTER 47

Judge Stanoch nodded from the bench. "Mr. Friedberg, cross-examination."

Friedberg stood. "Thank you, Your Honor." He moved to the end of counsel's table and saw Snider's warning glance. Justice Sheran's quiet, aloof occupancy of the witness box was an austere contrast to Friedberg's swarthy vigor. *He's a former chief justice*, Snider had warned. *You've got to treat him with respect. He's eldery.*

The confident, almost arrogant bearing of the former chief justice confirmed attitude was not something from which he had retired.

Be very careful or you'll alienate the jury, Snider had said. Friedberg smirked his reassurance for only Snider to see and faced retired Minnesota Supreme Court Chief Justice Sheran.

"Mr. Sheran, are you aware of testimony in this trial that if what went on in that flower shop that morning was an attempt to rob Mr. Nachtsheim, if there had been a brief scuffle or resistance, that what the robber would have done was flee immediately? Are you aware of that?"

"Only to the extent that I heard your opening statement."

"But my opening statement, as whoever has discussed, isn't evidence. Correct?"

"That is correct." The stately, gray head nodded.

"I'm talking about testimony given by Lieutenant Krueger—the man who had investigated three hundred homicides, by your own testimony—and the fact that he testified that if this was an aborted robbery and the shotgun went off in a scuffle or through resistance, that the first thing the robber would have done was flee. Are you aware of that?"

"I'm not aware that Lieutenant Krueger so testified in this proceeding."

"Want to take my word for it?"

"Yes."

"Now, if that be so, then the body would have been where we know it was and the wallet with the money would still have been in the pocket. Correct?"

"If you accept that scenario as you've outlined it."

"All right. Now," Friedberg began to amble across the front of the courtroom. "Now, it's also true, in your entire analysis of this case and your reading of the trial transcript, that you came to the conclusion that there was no direct evidence that Mr. Wartnick was involved in this?"

"That is true."

"Not a shred of direct evidence. Correct?"

"Well, no direct evidence. I assume that includes not a shred."

Friedberg paused and chuckled. "That's my problem for trying to make a good answer better." Jurors smiled. He resumed his amble. "Now, it's classic understanding in a totally circumstantial-evidence case that the way to defend it is to show the jury what's called 'a reasonable hypothesis of innocence.' Correct?"

"Would you repeat those last few words again? A reasonable what?"

Friedberg paused in front of the witness. "A reasonable hypothesis of innocence."

"Yes."

"In fact, you yourself have *written* those words from time to time, have you not, and considered that a legal concept?"

"They sound sort of familiar."

"All right," Friedberg nodded. "And when it's a question of the identity of the killer, a reasonable hypothesis of innocence is the same thing as showing another possible killer or suspect. Correct?"

"I would say that the latter is included in the former."

"I think I said *or*, but that's true. You try to show that there's somebody else that might have done it. Right?"

"Correct."

"Somebody else that had, if we use the legal term, 'motive as opposed to reason.' Correct?"

Sheran's gray head nodded as though to convey the weighty import of the rule of law. "Those are the sign posts that you're looking for."

"And it's clear, is it not, in the law, that motive alone is insufficient to make a finding that someone has committed a homicide. Correct?"

"I believe that to be true."

"And to bring it to the jury's understanding rather than speaking in academic terms, if motive alone was sufficient to convict somebody, they probably would have arrested Lyndon Johnson when John Kennedy was shot. Correct?"

Justice Sheran did not move other than to further straighten his shoulders.

"You understand the point I'm making?" Friedberg said.

"Well, I understand the point. I don't think it has much to do with the problem we're discussing."

Friedberg glanced to Snider and received a warning lift of an eyebrow.

"There's no question," Friedberg began to meander back toward the white board, "but that there was a motive on behalf of Mr. Wartnick. Correct?"

"Correct."

"And the motive arises out of the insurance policy, and the motive is pure and simple: Money. Correct?"

"Principally so. Not exclusively so, but principally so."

"Motive plus, what you've said, some rougher feelings?"

310

"I think that would describe it."

"Now, were you aware that Mr. Wartnick has testified here that he did not dislike or hate Bob Nachtsheim?"

"I didn't know he testified to that here, but I know he has so testified on other occasions."

"You're aware of the fact that the only evidence concerning those ill feelings that Mr. Wartnick supposedly had about Mr. Nachtsheim came from *Mrs.* Nachtsheim?"

"I don't think that's accurate."

"Who else testified that Mr. Wartnick didn't like Mr. Nachtsheim?"

"I was thinking more of the circumstance. Mr. Nachtsheim had been employed in that flower shop since 1959, was their key person so far as the production of business is concerned, decides eight months before the killing he's going to leave and open a competitive business down the street. My experience tells me that when those things happen, hard feelings are generated, apart from what any testimony on the subject might be."

Friedberg stood his ground. "I believe I asked you who else testified."

"No, the question, as I understood it, was why did I feel there were hard feelings. The circumstances of the situation tell me, based on my experience, there were troubled feelings."

"Troubled feelings are not sufficient in this case. I asked you—and I'm sure what I asked—was there testimony from anyone other than Mrs. Nachtsheim that things got heated at all when the termination took place?"

"I don't recall any at the moment."

"All right." Friedberg again strolled toward the white board. "Let's discuss these issues one at a time, if you will. We've gone over this statement a lot. I assume you've refreshed your recollection as to what was said in the opening statement about the polygraph. Correct?"

Sheran squinted to read. "This is a statement Mr. Gainsley made at the time of trial. Right?"

"Yes." He faced the witness.

"Ya," Sheran's grayed head nodded slowly. "I'm sure that's it."

"Now there's been testimony here that might reasonably be interpreted to mean Wartnick had said something to Gainsley that made him think it was unwise to take that polygraph test. Do you agree with that?"

"I'm not aware of such testimony—"

"Well—"

"—in this current trial, but I'm aware of that argument. If that's what—"

"All right." Friedberg nodded. "In fact, isn't one interpretation which a jury could reasonably conclude be that Wartnick wanted to take one but 'I, Gainsley, having spoken to Wartnick, my client, have advised him not to,' and a jury could reasonably interpret that to mean that 'I really think he'd flunk the thing'?"

"That's conceivable," Sheran allowed.

"Well, isn't it also what they'd most *likely* think?"

"I don't think so. I don't think so."

"You think the jury might draw another conclusion?"

"I would if I were on the jury."

"Okay," Friedberg nodded. "And in point of fact you raise an issue." Friedberg's arms hung loosely, hands in pants pockets, his suit jacket pushed back out of the way. "When witnesses like yourself, expert witnesses, give their opinion based on their experience about how jurors might think or react to certain pieces of evidence, they're really just trying to put themselves in the jurors' minds, trying to figure out what an American citizen might think about certain types of evidence. Correct?"

"Partially correct but not completely. The judgment you're making is based, in my case, on over fifty years of experience in dealing with problems of this kind. So it's not simply a case of dropping in out of the blue and figuring out how I would deal with this problem. I think I can accurately state that I've had as much opportunity to observe the process of criminal law in the state of Minnesota as almost anyone and, in part, my judgment is based on that experience."

"How long has it been since you—well, you've tried at least one criminal case that I know of in the last ten years. Have you tried more?"

"No. Just one."

"Outside of that one, how many criminal cases have you watched?"

"You're referring now to being personally present in the courtroom while the case is being tried?"

"Yes." Friedberg recommenced his amble across the front of the courtroom.

"I don't recall any. But I've reviewed transcripts of at least a thousand of them in that period of time."

"All right. Now haven't there been literally hundreds of studies done indicating that juries tend to make decisions based on things we don't anticipate?"

"I don't know of studies, but it's consistent with my experience."

"So we really, you know, we do the best we can to lay out the evidence in front of the jury, but we really don't know what makes up their mind, do we?"

"We never know for certain. That's true."

"So each side tries to put in front of a jury as much good evidence as they can get in. Correct?"

Sheran nodded. "Yes."

"And the other side tries to keep *out* as much evidence as they can legally do, that they consider hurts their cause. Right?"

"Yes."

"And in the last analysis we count on six or twelve Americans to make a common-sense decision. Correct?"

"Yes."

Friedberg stopped in front of the jury box. "It's a bit presumptuous of all of us to think we know what goes on in jurors' minds, isn't it?"

"If you're suggesting that we're trying to say for a certainty what goes on in a juror's mind, then, yes, it would be presumptuous. But if what you're undertaking to do is make a judgment as to what jurors are likely to think, then I don't think it's presumptuous."

"All right." Friedberg resumed his slow, steady tread. "Now Mr. Meshbesher testified in this trial that there is no way in the world he would even *consider* putting in front of that jury that Mr. Wartnick had refused a polygraph test. Do you agree that's probably true?"

"Do I agree that Mr. Meshbesher said that?"

"No. We know he said it. You can take my word for it."

"Okay. I'll take your word for that."

"Do you know any lawyer, any good lawyer in this day and age, that would try to get evidence to a jury that somebody had not taken a polygraph test, or had refused to take one?"

"I can't respond to that question in terms of what Mr. Meshbesher would do or not do, but I can tell you to a certainty that lawyers frequently try to get into evidence facts and circumstances which, were they to reflect on it, [they] would realize were not admissible. Happens every day."

Friedberg spun toward the witness. "Mr. Sheran, do you know any competent lawyer in this state who would *ever* try to get in front of that jury that Mr. Wartnick had refused to take a lie detector test?"

"I-I can't identify any such person," Sheran faltered. "But my experience tells me it would not be an unlikely eventuality."

"Well, it wouldn't be admissible legally. Correct?"

"The results of the polygraph test would not be admissible. The question of whether or not a polygraph test was rejected might or might not be admissible."

"You think a lawyer," Friedberg stepped toward the witness, "could say to Mr. Wartnick, on the stand, 'Isn't it true, sir, that you refused to take a lie detector test?' without having the trial judge go absolutely berserk?"

Sheran straightened. "Do I think that's possible?"

"Yeah."

"Yes, I do think that's possible."

"A competent trial judge?"

"I don't want to make a judgment as to competency, but my experience tells me that's entirely possible."

"Do you accept Mr. Meshbesher's word that *he* would *not* have been such a lawyer?"

"I didn't—I don't recall his having said that. You tell me he did; I take your word for it."

Friedberg still squarely faced the witness. "Now you *do* concede a possible interpretation of this is that Mr. Gainsley had some information indicating to him that Mr. Wartnick might flunk and that's why he told him not to do it?"

"That's conceivable, but I don't think, in the real world, I would see it that way."

Friedberg turned toward counsel's table, inhaled, and glanced to Snider, who gave him a brief warning glance. Both now knew it would soon be possible for Sheran to impeach himself without any theatrics from Friedberg.

"Let's try this Fifth Amendment issue," Friedberg said as he stood, hands in pockets, and read the writing on the white board. "First of all, is it good or bad for a jury to hear that an individual took the Fifth Amendment?"

"It's not good. Whether it's bad or not depends on the circumstances."

"Well, clearly," Friedberg turned to face Justice Sheran, "in this case it would have been a lot better for Mr. Wartnick had the jury not heard that he took the Fifth Amendment. Correct?"

"Yes."

"There's no question but that it was damaging. Correct?"

"You separate that from everything else that occurs in the trial, no doubt about it, damaging."

"Now, honestly, Mr. Sheran, when the jury heard, 'Did you kill Bob Nachtsheim?' and then heard Mr. Wartnick say, 'I refuse to answer on the grounds it might incriminate me'—and no explanation could be given, nobody told the jury at that point it was based on the instruction of Mr. Gainsley—that was very harmful, was it not?"

"It was harmful."

"You don't want to say very?"

"The reason I don't is because you take a little piece out of the entire trial and phrase it in such a way that the whole outcome of the trial turned on that—that creates an impression which is inaccurate. I don't want to be a party to that."

"I see," Friedberg nodded; he was beginning to pick up steam. "Well, it's a lawyer's duty to do everything in the world he can do to avoid a jury being told his client has taken the Fifth Amendment, isn't it?"

"I'm not sure what you mean by 'everything he can do,' but I agree with you that taking the Fifth Amendment—having that called to the attention of the jury—is, in and of itself, a negative; so the lawyer's responsibility, within the limitations of ethics, is to prevent that from occurring. Yes."

Friedberg stepped toward the witness. "As a matter of fact, in one of *your own cases* you did everything conceivable to avoid your client having to take the Fifth Amendment, much less keep it out of evidence. Correct?"

"That is true. That's been—My experience with that is one of the reasons I feel I have as much background as anybody on this particular issue, this particular dilemma."

"And in that case, if there'd ever been a jury trial on the issue, it would've severely hurt your client if he had to take the Fifth, wouldn't it?"

"Any time that a client is required to take the Fifth in a civil case it is damaging. The degree of the damage depends on how it fits in with the overall picture of evidence as presented. To say it becomes determinative of the case—and your question implies that it would be—is grossly inaccurate, in my judgment."

"And in point of fact, one of the most important things in this case was for Mr. Gainsley to show that Norm was an open and candid person. Correct?"

"Yes."

"In fact, you testified on direct examination it was *imperative* to show that Norm was an open and candid person. Correct?"

"Yes."

"And the only way—with the Fifth Amendment stuck in the case—for anyone to show that this man was an open and candid person would've been to take the witness stand and say, 'He never wanted to do that; I made him do it.'"

"I don't agree with that at all."

"Would have been one way, wouldn't it?"

"I think it would have been a gross mistake."

"Because you think it would have been depressing and traumatic for Mr. Wartnick to have to get a new lawyer because, say two years before the trial he learns Gainsley was going to testify and take him out of the hole he, the attorney, had dug for his client?"

"Yes, I definitely think so."

"Despite the fact Doug Thomson was retained and was ready, willing, and able to try the case?"

"I'm not too sure he was ready, willing, and able to try the case."

Friedberg's cross-examination continued throughout the morning and resumed after lunch. "The Fifth Amendment in a criminal case is an absolute privilege. Correct?"

"Yes," Justice Sheran agreed. "No person can be compelled to incriminate himself in a criminal case."

"And, in fact," Friedberg added, "no defendant can be compelled to give testimony in a criminal case. Correct?"

"Yes."

"And that's true whether or not that testimony would incriminate him. Correct?"

"Yes," the gray head nodded.

"But in a *civil* case," Friedberg pressed, "that privilege is qualified by the fact that the Fifth Amendment may *only* be invoked when open testimony in a civil case would *enhance the threat* of criminal prosecution. Correct?"

"I think that's right."

"Now, let me go back to the investigation we were speaking of. It's true, is it not, based on your reading of the trial transcript in its entirety, that the original jury had no awareness of the fact that this so-called party took place the night before Mr. Nachtsheim was murdered?"

"I'm not sure of the answer to that question."

"Well, that's something we've got to be sure of. Can you recall any place in that trial—and the transcript is in evidence—can you recall any place in that transcript where the jury could have become aware of or did become aware that this party, meeting, get-together, whatever you want to call it, had taken place the night before the murder?"

"I can't recall the testimony, and the reason that I'm having difficulty is that there's considerable discussion of that in the depositions, and whether I'm thinking of things I've read in the depositions as having been said at trial, that's what I'm uncertain about."

"All right, let's try to handle it a shorthand way, then. Would you assume that no mention ever got to that jury about this party, get-together, or what have you?"

"You're asking me to assume that?"

"Yes."

"Yes, I'll assume it."

"And it's true that you have no recollection to the contrary but you're not sure. Right?"

"That is correct."

"All right. Now, do you remember the name of at least the five most-present people at that get-together? And I'll give them to you if that's easier."

"I think I do."

"What are they?"

"Bobby Nachtsheim, Debra Nachtsheim, Larry Kreuser—," he paused. "Struber? Did I say that name correctly? Struler?"

"Strehlow."

"Yes, and Mentes."

"Now, I want to turn our attention to Larry Strehlow, Roger Nordstrom, Deb—"

"Did I say Roger Nordstrom? He was there, too."

"Roger Nordstrom, Debbie Feist—later to become Nachtsheim, Bobby Nachtsheim, Larry Strehlow, and Dennis Kreuser. All right?"

"Okay."

"Did you read the depositions of those people?"

"Yes."

"Did you read Dennis Kreuser's deposition?"

"Yes."

"It's true, is it not, that when he was deposed he took the Fifth Amendment?"

"Just a moment," Mason growled. "We move to strike. That's not evidence in this case and the reason it isn't evidence is that he came here and spoke willingly to the jury."

"Counsel," the judge warned. "Approach, please."

Some jurors looked quite happy to stretch a little. Two of them scribbled hurriedly in their notebooks. Justice Sheran's quivering hand pulled a handkerchief from his inside jacket pocket and meticulously patted his forehead.

Mason's voice rose, "an illustration of what lawyers have to fear in preparing," then lowered again.

Wartnick leaned toward Webber. "What happens if Sheran doesn't—"

"First of all," the court addressed the courtroom, then looked at Friedberg, "before you go ahead, Mr. Friedberg, I'm going to instruct the jury to disregard Mr. Friedberg's last question. Mr. Friedberg."

"Mr. Sheran, did you not testify at the outset that you had reviewed a great number of materials and that your opinion was based not only on your training and experience but your review of those materials?"

"That is true."

"And in your answer, didn't you say that you had reviewed the depositions of probably not everybody in the case but a good number of those depositions?"

"Almost everybody, I'm sure."

"All right. And one of those that you reviewed was Dennis Kreuser."

"Yes."

Friedberg turned toward the bench. "At this point, Your Honor, I need direction—"

One of the jurors giggled.

Friedberg glanced at the jurors and grinned. "Not that I'm timid."

Open laughter rippled through the jury box and public gallery.

"Counsel want to come up for a minute, please."

Snider used the time to scan his notes and check off the points they had predetermined needed to be elicited from Sheran. Friedberg had made good progress.

Mason traipsed back to his seat at counsel's table.

Friedberg returned to stand in front of the witness. "It's true, is it not, Mr. Sheran, that in the deposition which you reviewed of Dennis Kreuser, he repeatedly took the Fifth Amendment when asked about the party?"

"Objection," Mason barked. "On the grounds stated at the bench."

"Objection noted." The judge did not look up. "We'll give you a—"

"—and upon the further ground," Mason interrupted again, "that there's no evidence of that in this case."

"Objection noted."

Sheran had watched the two and, when they were finished, he said, "The word 'repeatedly,' I don't know quite what that means in this context; but I take it as a given that he took the Fifth."

"All right. Now lawyers have a certain concept about the Fifth Amendment, that it's an inalienable right when taken in a criminal investigation and it doesn't necessarily mean you're hiding something. Correct?"

"That's true."

"People who *aren't* lawyers generally believe that when someone takes the Fifth Amendment they've got something to hide. Right?"

"That used to be the case. I think it's less so currently with Miranda warnings and the general understanding that the purpose of the amendment is to protect citizens from intrusions on their rights and overbearing investigative practices. But notwithstanding that, everything else being equal, it's better that you don't have it."

Friedberg paused. "It's true, is it not, that both in the police reports and in his deposition, Mr. Kreuser testified that Bobby Nachtsheim and Roger Nordstrom discussed a plan for robbing Mr. Nachtsheim. Correct?"

"Except for the use of the word robbery. And I don't mean to be technical, but what they discussed I would say was not a robbery but a burglary."

"I think you may be confusing something," Friedberg said. "Try this. Bobby Nachtsheim and Debra Feist have testified and stated that they did, indeed, discuss a plan for removing money from Mr. Nachtsheim, but it would be from his pants while he was asleep. Correct?"

"Yes. And that's a burglary, not a robbery."

"It certainly is. Dennis Kreuser discussed something else entirely, didn't he?"

"Dennis Kreuser was using the term robbery. Yes."

"And, in fact, was talking about robbery in the term of a stickup. Correct?"

"I didn't get that sense."

"You didn't get the sense from Dennis Kreuser that he was discussing Roger Nordstrom and Bobby Nachtsheim planning the robbery of Bob Nachtsheim at the florist shop?"

"Objection," Mason barked. "Irrelevant. Rule 403. Not a fact in this case, and it's prejudicial."

"I'm going to sustain this objection."

"Are you aware of what Mr. Kreuser testified to in this case? In front of this jury?"

"What he testified to was that during the course of that evening they had a conversation of how easy it would be to take money from his father's trousers, which he always hung in the same place in the bathroom before he went to bed." The former Supreme Court justice held his grey head back and his chin thrust forward. "I might add that I'm quite confident of that."

"You are?"

"The question was put to him as to what he had said, and he said this is what I said, and what he said was just as I related it, according to my recollection."

"Your recollection is that Dennis Kreuser agreed with Bobby and Debbie that the plan was to steal the wallet from his pants hanging from the bathroom door while he slept?"

"No," the witness's shoulders sagged. "I guess the point I'm making is that Bobby Nachtsheim, in his deposition, admitted the conversation and stated that what it had to do with was a plan of removing a billfold from his father's trousers while he slept. I'd term that a burglary rather than a robbery."

"No argument about that," Friedberg proclaimed.

"And it may well be that Kreuser," Sheran continued, "during the course of his deposition, was referring to *this* as being a robbery—and you've indicated that he was contemplating that it would occur in the flower shop."

"Yes." Friedberg leaned confidently against counsel's table.

"I'm pretty well satisfied from, particularly from reading Nachtsheim's deposition, that what they were talking about was this business of extracting that billfold from the father's trousers while he slept. And I may, given the hostility between Kreuser and Bobby Nachtsheim, I have may discounted what Kreuser had to say in that regard because of the, the circumstances under which it was said."

"Now you discount what Kreuser says because he had every reason to dislike Bobby because Bobby sent him to prison. Right?"

"Well," Sheran nodded, "I think he had very good reason to do Bobby Nachtsheim in, having been in effect set up by Bobby for prison on a drug bust."

Friedberg began his slow, circuitous amble again. "And you're aware of the fact that Kreuser testified *here* that the conversation about stealing from Mr. Nachtsheim made him feel uncomfortable; he and Strehlow left before the party was over. Correct?"

"Could be."

"Now let me ask you something. Do you necessarily believe that Mr. Kreuser would be telling the truth when he said that made him feel uncomfortable and he left?"

"I think Mr. Kreuser was so compromised by the fact he had been set up by [Young] Nachtsheim I wouldn't rely on his testimony in any respect. I'd have reservations about anything he had to say that had to do with Bobby Nachtsheim, that's for sure."

"And in addition to that," Friedberg took another step toward the witness, "there's nothing in his background that would indicate he'd be telling the truth when he said the discussion of the commission of a crime made him uncomfortable and he left. You wouldn't believe that for a minute, would you?"

"It would be hard for me, given his background, to see him that sensitive to a conversation about a burglary. Yes, it would."

"Or a robbery?" Another step. "Correct?"

"Or for that matter."

"Or a murder, or—"

"Well, I wouldn't—"

"—mayhem or anything else. Right?"

"Well, I think that's inappropriate to suggest that, and I wouldn't."

"If you listen to his testimony, he left 'because I felt uncomfortable. I don't want to be involved.' Right? If you credit him?"

"If you credit him, right."

"Okay. And since he's not deserving of much credit in your opinion—"

"That's true. I want to emphasize that. I think the testimony of Dennis Kreuser sitting up there in jail, anxious to get out, anxious to lay it onto Bobby Nachtsheim if he can, was not credible testimony and I haven't really given much credence to it."

"In fact," Friedberg pressed, "if he stayed during the course of the discussions about stealing from Mr. Nachtsheim and if he had participated in the discussion and a plan to steal from Mr. Nachtsheim, then that would be a crime, wouldn't it?"

"Yes, it would."

"And he would have every reason to take the Fifth Amendment when asked about it. Correct?"

"He would have *a* reason to take the Fifth Amendment, but he would have reasons to take the Fifth Amendment if he *hadn't* stayed around; so that's the problem that I'm having with your question."

Friedberg paused. "He would have reasons to take the Fifth Amendment if he hadn't stayed around? Not in a layman's view, would he?"

"Well, that's hard to answer, except if I could just make this point. The purpose of the Fifth Amendment is not just to protect the rights of citizens that are guilty; it's even more so to protect the rights of citizens who are *not* guilty and who can be maneuvered into positions by the investigating authorities where they *look* like they're guilty. That's the problem with your question."

Friedberg turned to lean across counsel's table and whispered to Snider, "Do I still have to treat him with respect?"

"Yes, you do."

"Right." Friedberg straightened and faced Sheran again. "Now, given the indication that there was such a party, given the indication that there was at least a *plan* to burglarize Mr. Nachtsheim, and given what Kreuser says about it and what Bobby and Debbie say about it and the disagreement between their statements," Friedberg focused in on the witness, "do you think all of that was not worthy of investigation?"

Sheran paused for a long heartbeat, then said slowly, "The only way I can respond to that is to say this: that if Mr. Gainsley is going to put in a defense in that case which is going to be effective, he's got to do more than dump in gossip and comments from people sitting in jail anxious to get out. He's got to put together a case that would indicate there is some other suspect at least as likely to have been the person who did it as his client. My testimony is that it just wasn't there, and it isn't there now."

"So you think that based on this he had a right to rely on the police reports. Correct?"

Sheran's response was filled with Supreme Court Justice authority. "I believe that."

"Okay. Well, if there hadn't been any police reports, then in that case he probably would have had to investigate. Correct?"

"If there had been no investigation, it surely would be called for. Yes."

"How about if he didn't have the police reports?"

"Then what?" Sheran scowled.

"Then would he have to investigate?"

"I would think so."

Friedberg retrieved photocopied pages from counsel's table and walked them over to the witness. "This is Plaintiff's Exhibit One Hundred Thirty-Four-B, Phil Gainsley's affidavit, and doesn't this say right here: 'The state of the record is that I received the police report twice, once during pretrial discovery from Prudential Life Insurance Company and the second time at trial by subpoena of the Minneapolis Police Department.' That's what it says, correct?"

"That's how it reads. Correct."

"So he just got it twice. Right?"

"That's how it reads."

"And that's under oath from him. Right?"

"Of course."

"Now, would you read Plaintiff's Exhibit Forty-Two. What's the date on that letter?"

"August 25, 1982."

"Read it out loud to the jury, if you would, sir."

Sheran cleared his throat, then began. "This is a letter to Phillip Gainsley. 'Dear Phil: Pursuant to your request, I am enclosing herewith a copy of the police file given to me by Paul Nachtsheim. As you can see, as I indicated to you by phone, much of the file is illegible because of the light copies which I received. Since Krueger has never provided us with a copy of his file, as I believe he indicated he would at his deposition, I think it might be worthwhile for us to subpoena the police department file at some point so that we can get a legible copy of the whole file. I am enclosing a statement for our copying costs in this matter.'"

"Now that's from the Prudential lawyer. Right?"

"Roger Johnson. True."

"And that's August 25, 1982. Correct?"

"True."

"Nine years after the crime. Nine years after he became Mr. Wartnick's lawyer."

"True."

"Mr. Gainsley's affidavit stated that he got them twice, once from Prudential and once subpoenaed for trial. Right?"

Sheran studied the paper in his hand. "Ya."

"This is where he gets them from Prudential, isn't it?"

"Ya."

"It's 1982, isn't it?"

"Yes."

Friedberg paused, then softly said, "Tardy?"

"What's the question, please?" Mason barked.

"Wait a minute," Friedberg objected.

"Could you ask a question, please, Mr. Friedberg." The Court spoke from the bench.

Friedberg complied. "This is one of the two times that he gets them—with this letter. Correct?"

"This is repetitious and argumentative," Mason hammered.

"Question, please," from Judge Stanoch.

"There's no need for him to—" Mason continued.

"We've gone through this twice," Judge Stanoch warned. "Please ask a question."

"All right," Friedberg acknowledged and turned again to the witness. "Were they legible or illegible when he first received them in 1982?"

"Object to the form of the question." Mason again. "It suggests that's when he first received them."

Friedberg's focus remained on Sheran. "Do you have *any* evidence that Mr. Gainsley *ever* got them before August 25th of 1982? Are you aware of *any*?"

"I am assuming," Sheran said, still with pages in hand, "that Mr. Gainsley had knowledge of the contents of that report before this date. How he came to get it, that I don't know."

"I think, Mr. Sheran, what I want to know is do you have any evidence anywhere that shows us he had them prior to August 25, 1982?"

"My answer is, I'm not in a position to prove it but I'm assuming he had access to the police report. Whether that assumption is justified or not depends on facts that are not in my possession."

Friedberg took a step closer to the witness. "In order for him to have had them before August of 1982, isn't it true that his affidavit would have to be wrong?"

"Well, I'm not sure about that."

"Take your time." Another step closer. "Explain to me how his affidavit could be correct if he had them before he got them from Prudential."

"I'm just not in a position to explain that except as I've undertaken to do."

"All right," Friedberg turned swiftly toward counsel's table to retrieve another document; he extended it to the witness. "Now let me show you Plaintiff's Exhibit Seventy-Three. You've seen these. We've all seen lots of those. What is that, for the jury?"

"This is a subpoena."

"And what is its date?"

"April 17, 1986."

"When is that subpoena returnable?"

"April 21st."

"Is that the first day of the trial?"

"If you tell me that, I accept it. I don't carry that date in my head."

"So the subpoena asks for the police file. Correct?"

"Yes."

"It's returnable on the first day of the trial. Correct?"

"Yes."

"The prior time, in 1982, Roger Johnson is sending them to Phil Gainsley with a cover letter that says they're not legible and you probably should subpoena them. Correct?"

"Okay."

"Does it then seem, from a comparison of these three exhibits—the affidavit of Gainsley, the subpoena by Gainsley, the letter in Gainsley's file from Roger Johnson—that until April 21 of 1986, he did not have a legible copy of the police reports?"

Sheran studied the three exhibits, his hands quivered as he glanced from one to the next. "That doesn't make sense to me, what you're talking about."

"Well, can you concede that if the man didn't have a legible copy of the police reports until the first day of trial, that would be very bad?"

"Yes. I think that."

"That would be negligent beyond belief, wouldn't it?"

Sheran finally glanced up to Friedberg. "Well, depending on the circumstances. But your suggestion that he didn't have the police report simply because he hadn't subpoenaed it before, to me that's just off the wall."

"Can you think of any other way to rationalize his sworn affidavit that he'd only received them twice—once from Prudential and once by subpoena—the letter from Prudential that says 'here they are but they're not legible'? In 1982?"

"Object to the characterization of the letter as being from Prudential," Mason said.

"Sustained. Members of the jury, why don't you talk amongst yourselves for a minute. Counsel, I'd like to see you in chambers."

Judge Stanoch, Jack Mason, and Joe Friedberg emerged through the door at the front of the courtroom. The judge resumed his seat behind the bench. Mason returned to his place at counsel's table. Friedberg stood in front of counsel's table and awaited the judge's nod—"Mr. Friedberg."—and faced the witness.

"I have one more question for you, Mr. Sheran. Your testimony concerning the failure or lack of investigation is based on the assumption that Mr. Gainsley had the entire police file at a timely time?"

"Whether he had access or didn't have access to it doesn't change the fact that all of the depositions that have been taken in this case, of all of the witnesses of whom those depositions have been taken, have produced nothing, in my judgment, except hearsay, gossip, and innuendo—none of which would have been adequate to dispel the strong case based on uncontroverted facts which existed against Mr. Wartnick."

"Do you agree that in this type of case, a whodunit, that casting suspicion on someone else is about the only way you can defend it. Correct?"

"Well, the way you phrase it is not quite accurate." There was the chin jut again. "It's not permissible to be casting suspicion on other people, either ethically or practically, unless you've got a basis in evidence for doing so."

"So, in your opinion, for a person to have presented to a jury the fact that there was a get-together the night before where drugs were taken and alcohol was consumed and two people discussed stealing, robbing, or burglarizing the deceased the next morning; *and* where a person overheard that, repeated it, and took the Fifth Amendment in response to part of it; *and* where one of the people discussing it may have left town forever or may have stayed in town and hid from the police; *and* where one of the people, at least, at that party had a strong dislike if not hatred for his father—your belief is there is nothing there a jury could've made any use of. Correct?"

"Depending on the source of that information. If the witness who provides that information is a reliable, credible witness, the answer is, Of course. But if the person who gives you that information is Dennis Kreuser, then I say, No. And, as a matter of fact, I don't think it would even be prudent to put that man on the witness stand."

"How about if he gives the same information years later, then years after that gives information very similar to it in a trial?"

"Well, the basic problem remains the same. You're dealing with an unreliable individual giving statements under highly questionable circumstances. That just doesn't get the job done."

Friedberg paused then faced Justice Sheran. "Who determines credibility in a trial?"

"The jury."

"They," Friedberg motioned to the jurors, "they determine whether information is credible, believable—enough to raise things to the level of suspicion or belief. Correct?"

"Well, in the end they do, yes. But somewhere along the line an attorney has a responsibility of not bringing witnesses into court to give information to jurors if the person providing that information is inherently incredible, prejudiced, and unreliable. Dennis Kreuser fits that description."

"Mr. Sheran, does it frequently occur that rotten no-goods provide evidence that *convicts* people in criminal cases?"

"I think that's true."

"Doesn't every prosecutor in the world apologize for witnesses by saying 'You don't find swans in the sewer'?"

"Well, I know that it's done."

"You have heard it?"

"Oh, of course."

"Now, do you find it at all suspicious that Roger Nordstrom, a known user of guns, vanished immediately after this?"

"Well, as Detective Krueger said, he's a missing link."

"What do judges instruct juries about people who disappear after crimes?"

"Well, there's a principle that flight is evidence of guilt."

"Thank you," Friedberg nodded. "No further question."

Mason was ready for his redirect examination. He stood and said, "The letter being waved around by Mr. Friedberg in his histrionics—is that a letter from Prudential to Mr. Gainsley transmitting the illegible copy?"

"I don't have that in front of me, but my recollection is that it's a letter from Roger Johnson, and Johnson is an attorney, and I took it he was representing Prudential."

After a thorough rehash of Sheran's review of thousands of transcripts and a lengthy discussion regarding what constitutes circumstantial evidence, Mason turned to that evidence.

"The deposition of Bobby Nachtsheim and Debra Feist were taken in this matter," Mason said. "Those depositions were shown by videotape to that original jury. In those depositions, Mr. Nachtsheim, Bobby, testified that he was at home sleeping in bed with his wife at the time of this murder. His wife, Debbie, testified that she had dragged him to bed at three in the morning where they slept together until the phone rang and they learned, for the first time, of the murder.

"She further testified," Mason continued, "that she'd been engaged to Bobby from March to August of 1973. In August they had broken off, but she was pregnant with Bobby's child. Russ Krueger had come back to her and attempted to get her to change her story and testify she was not with Bobby, but she reaffirmed the alibi that Bobby had, even at a time when he had jilted her and left her with his baby.

"Would that sort of evidence," Mason concluded, "be the kind that a lawyer representing Mr. Wartnick, a lawyer who wanted to point the finger at Bobby, would be concerned about and would risk getting if he took Bobby's deposition?"

"You would be concerned about it and for good reason. In this case, Bobby Nachtsheim has got a tested alibi. Mr. Wartnick has no alibi. That was bad news."

CHAPTER 48

TUESDAY, OCTOBER 18, 1994 – TRIAL DAY 16

"Mr. Snider, this is a serious matter that you could expect to have sanctions against you as a lawyer." Judge Stanoch addressed attorneys in chambers. "Given the fact you elicited testimony on direct examination of Mr. Meshbesher and in light of my ruling granting a motion *in limine* which reads: 'Defendants' motion to exclude any reference to advice given to plaintiff in the bathroom prior to his 1979 deposition....'"

"You shouldn't, because it was me, I believe," Friedberg interrupted.

"Well, the issue here," Judge Stanoch said, "is why shouldn't I strike this given the fact I ruled it should not be admissible. [Mr. Mason's made] a motion to strike, basically. What we'd have to do is strike all testimony related to where the advice was given and when."

Friedberg shook his head. "Wartnick's entitled to say when the advice was given. What you precluded was the geographical location."

"The issue we're considering," Mason said, "is one of the points we raised in our motion *in limine*. We don't think there's any question but that this was a deliberate act on the part of plaintiff's counsel. We think the jury must be instructed not just that this testimony is to be stricken but that the reason it's stricken is there was an order *in limine*, that the motion *in limine* was made and heard and decided, and counsel for the plaintiff violated that order."

"Frankly," Friedberg said, "I don't know that it makes any difference at all where he told him, be it the hallway, outside the bathroom, inside the bathroom, in his office. It's harmless."

"This court's order has been expressly violated," Mason countered. "And in the context of a case where Gainsley has been alleged to have committed malpractice because he *should* have somehow protected himself by a motion *in limine*, it's particularly egregious."

"All right," said Judge Stanoch. "I'm not at this time going to order the testimony stricken or rebuke the attorneys in front of the jury. I'll decide prior to conclusion of testimony what I'm going to do."

During the next two days, Judge Stanoch ruled against plaintiff on several issues. He stated Friedberg and Snider had "vastly expanded the scope of information presented to the jury," so he narrowed what the jury would be able to use in their consideration of Gainsley's liability. That included striking large sections of F. Lee Bailey's testimony on whether or not Gainsley's Fifth Amendment advice was appropriate.

Stanoch also ruled the jury could not consider it a failure on Gainsley's part to have not raised the issue of Meshbesher's requesting punitive damages in his unjust enrichment claim.

The judge eliminated testimony given by witnesses who had no direct knowledge of the events, including of the party and Larry Strehlow's death, as well as testimony which could not have been heard by the jury in the underlying trial, such as Nordstrom being willing to kill someone for two hundred dollars.

During another chambers session they dealt with the issue of alternative theories and suspects. Stanoch opened the discussion with "Mr. Mason, if I'm understanding correctly, you've brought up throughout the course of this trial that all the discussion about alternative suspects being presented here is something that Judge Davis granted summary judgment on and ought not be part of the failure to investigate claim."

Mason nodded. "For that reason and for the additional reason that their Answer to Interrogatory No. 9 says Roger Nordstrom done it, Bobby assisted—and at a minimum, if the court doesn't agree with us on the alternative suspects argument, we'd urge at least to limit the plaintiffs to Bobby and Nordstrom."

"Plaintiffs." Stanoch glanced to Friedberg and Snider.

Snider shook his head. "I don't understand the argument, Your Honor."

"Well, the argument is this," Stanoch said, "Attorney Gainsley's decision not to present alternative theories as to who killed Mr. Nachtsheim was a judgmental decision within the discretion of the trial attorney. So, as it relates to this trial, this person might have had a motive, that person might have had a motive, this person did it, that person did it. Anybody—first of all, anyone; secondly, anyone beyond the empty chair of Bobby at trial; third, anyone beyond Nordstrom and Bobby which you identified in your answers to interrogatories can't be an alternative theory that you bring up here to this jury because—"

"That is the theory," Friedberg interrupted. "I mean, you want to restrict us to a combination of Bobby and Nordstrom? We're not arguing anybody else and we don't intend to, so we agree."

Snider, though, wanted clarification. "I don't understand what the import is of what Jack is asking, Your Honor. Is he asking to go back and to strike some more evidence and ask the court to reconsider some of this? What is the net effect of this? I don't understand."

"It's a predicate for striking all sorts of evidence," Mason admitted. "To the extent that evidence doesn't support your theory of the case, how in the world can it be admissible—even if it were admissible evidence in other respects—because it would be irrelevant."

Friedberg slapped the arm of his chair. "It's in the case!"

"That gets away entirely from what the Supreme Court says we're trying, Your Honor," Snider said. "It's the failure to interview and depose key suspects."

"Well, this is an issue we'll have to join again when it comes to jury instructions because that's where it's going to come up," Stanoch concluded. "But, by the way of example here, if your theory of the case is that Nordstrom did it and Bobby was an accomplice, then I'm having trouble understanding why I admitted and allowed testimony in this trial regarding, for example, Krueger talking to these guys in prison or somewhere. Somebody said that at one point he had to know about it. What does that have to do with anything?"

Snider leaned toward the judge. "To interview and depose, Your Honor. Nobody has told me until now, and Jack is doing it by implication, that we have to solve this murder. Our claim is there were leads out there, that's what our experts testified to, and Gainsley should have pursued them and didn't."

"Are you taking the position that if there's information out there that wouldn't have been admissible at the trial, that Mr. Gainsley can be held negligent for failing to interview and depose those individuals?"

"The standard is whether or not it's likely to *lead to* the discovery of admissible evidence," Snider's blue eyes blazed with determination, "and the answer is Yes."

Mason leaned back, grimaced, and nodded. "Yes, that's their position."

"And we have to show what admissible evidence it would lead to," Friedberg added. "That's our burden. And that's not a problem."

CHAPTER 49

"We're gonna show 'em, Norm," Friedberg placed a hand on Wartnick's shoulder. "Bad attorneys hurt justice."

Wartnick leaned back in his seat on the row behind Snider and Webber. He nodded his appreciation to Friedberg and shivered. The gray wool sport jacket was not quite enough against the crisp Autumn air that crept into the room.

That morning Mason had given his fervid closing plea on behalf of his client. Mr. Gainsley was a victim of 'hindsight is 20/20,' he said. In every civil litigation one party will lose, and attorneys who face Ron Meshbesher have often been on the losing side. Every attorney must use his best judgment on behalf of his client and that is what Phil Gainsley did. He made the best judgment call he could make at the time, and Wartnick was enough satisfied with Mr. Gainsley's representation that he asked Mr. Gainsley to take his case to the appeals court. And, as former Chief Justice Robert Sheran explained to you, Norm Wartnick was considered by the Minneapolis Police Department's homicide investigators as the most likely suspect for having caused the murder of Bob Nachtsheim. Phil Gainsley's representation of Mr. Wartnick met the standards of the legal community and gave Wartnick, the most likely suspect in the murder of Bob Nachtsheim, the best opportunity to defend himself against the claims of the Nachtsheim family.

Now it was Friedberg's turn. Mason, his assistant Ed Magarian, and Judge Stanoch filled their seats and the jury was summoned.

Friedberg stood behind a small, wooden lectern at the front of the room, placed to face the six women seated in the jury box. "May it please the court, counsel, Norm," Friedberg nodded to each in turn. For this occasion he had actually made notes, indeed had filled pages of a yellow legal pad. "I've never said thank you to a jury for their time and attention in a case and I don't intend to start. I've known a lot of people who've fought and shed blood and died for your right and privilege to sit here.

"Jurors don't ordinarily get specific questions answered here, but a question was asked by the juror, Ms. Little-Mark, at the end of the proceedings yesterday about, 'Why do we got to wait to hear this until tomorrow morning? Why can't we do it now?' I'm going to give you my answer. When we got done with court yesterday, I had more notes than I do here. If we hadn't taken the night, you might've had to listen to an awful lot you don't need to listen to. When given the time before his final argument, a lawyer continues to take things out so what you have left is what we believe we really ought to tell the jury.

"In his closing argument, Mr. Mason talked about the fact I referred to Mr. Gainsley's conduct in this case as lazy, stupid, and arrogant. That was not a denouncement of Mr. Gainsley's career, but it is a sincere denouncement of what passed as the practice of law in this underlying case.

"Now I stand here defending a murder case because the man who was given the sacred trust of showing six people on a jury that someone else was likely to have murdered Mr. Nachtsheim, the man who testified under oath in his own deposition saying, 'I believed him to be innocent . . . he never said anything incriminating to me,' that man now sits in front of you and calls his former client a murderer.

"But this is not a criminal case." Friedberg moved to the side of the lectern. "Granted, it has criminal ramifications, but this really is not a criminal case, and I'm asking that this justice system, through you and through this judge, do something affirmative for my client."

Friedberg moved back behind the lectern and ripped the top sheet of notes from the legal pad. "Before he came to me, Norm Wartnick had gone to four or five lawyers. Lawyers do not easily sue other lawyers. *I've* never been in a case like this one." As he spoke, Friedberg realized there was no shelf on the lectern to hold his used pages. "There was a time when doctors would not cooperate against other doctors in medical malpractice cases; it was the old-boy network where a doctor would be ostracized if he testified against another doctor." What was he going to do with the pages? "That has faded away and now doctors will, quite honestly, testify for both sides. Lawyers have been slower at this. There's still a self-protectiveness in the legal community; so Norm had to go to four or five places. Then when he came to me, I told him he was going to have to take a polygraph test."

Friedberg wadded up the page and tossed it the ten feet that separated him from Snider. Snider instinctively caught it. One of the jurors giggled. With an expression of startled amusement, Snider selected the top of counsel's table as repository.

"Remember," Friedberg continued without a glance toward co-counsel, "he took two polygraph tests. Now, everybody agrees polygraph tests are not admissible in court, yet you've heard [about] them and seen the results here in this trial. They're not admissible because they're not scientifically reliable. As [defense expert] Ted Collins says, they're witchcraft. At times, some lawyers have been tempted to ask a polygraph examiner if they also read tea leaves. Be that as it may, the tests are probably right more than fifty percent of the time, so they're helpful—but they universally don't get admitted into trials except for a new doctrine that was carved out in this case, and you're entitled to know why.

332

"When we started thinking about this case, it came to our attention, Wait a minute. The first jury was prejudiced against Norm by the fact he didn't take one and other people had. If we can't show this jury that he took one and that he passed, he'll suffer the same prejudice in front of this jury. So, as the judge has told you, polygraph evidence was admitted for this limited purpose. But in the mean time, and in the normal course of business, Mr. Shaw had destroyed the polygrams but kept his report. Well, that wasn't good enough. So Norm was polygraphed again with the same result: He passed. Those polygrams were retained and you saw them.

"But they must have worried the heck out of the side that wants to prove my client is a murderer, because they hired a guy to be their polygraph expert who the state of Minnesota's Court of Appeals has essentially determined is a bigot and whose conduct is reprehensible. Three years ago this defense expert tested a client of mine who was denying he had committed a murder and this expert passed him, then the client testified that he *had* committed the murder. Now you've got to be awfully worried to want to hire somebody like that. ...

"But Norm Wartnick is not innocent simply because he passed a polygraph test. He's stone cold innocent for a lot of other reasons. What is it that Norm Wartnick did?"

The second page was ripped from the tablet, wadded up, and tossed to Snider. It was caught and placed next to the first.

"He purchased an insurance policy in 1970 called a key-man policy, but it wasn't the ordinary type of key-man policy—it was a policy with a dual purpose. If you're going to get as much insurance as you can for the money, or get it as cheaply as possible, you buy term insurance that builds up no cash value. So he probably could have gotten one-hundred thousand dollars worth of term insurance on Bob Nachtsheim for a lot less money—a lot less than the two thousand five hundred-a-year premium.

"The only reasons you would have bought permanent insurance was so it could build up cash value. Mr. Nachtsheim understood that. He was involved. He had to have a physical, he had to sign the papers. He knew that if he died, one hundred thousand dollars would replace the business Midwest would lose over the next five years. But if he lived and stayed with that company, they'd hand over the insurance policy to him when he retired. And there were two others in the company, Mr. Stoller and I forget who else, who had the same type of policy. It was a type of retirement program.

"When Bob left in August of 1972, the policy had recently been paid for the next year. If you cash-in insurance policies or terminate them in the first few years, you don't get anything back because, as most of you probably know, most of the money goes to the premium and the premium goes for the salesman's commission. So when the year had gone by, Midwest Floral had two choices, just two choices. They could leave the hundred-thousand life insurance policy in effect for the next six or seven months for free and give up the retirement benefit part of it, then after six or seven months it would be all over. If they did that, they'd simply be insuring the life of Bob Nachtsheim for that hundred-thousand as cheaply as possible. That was choice A, the cheap way. And if the man was a murderer, he would've left that policy the way it was and not called attention to himself; he would've had six or seven months to murder Mr. Nachtsheim and walk off with a hundred grand. That's how the policy beneficiaries would have done it if they were murderers.

"Now, choice number two was to leave the policy in effect for twelve months rather than seven and so keep the retirement benefit, all for an outlay of one thousand dollars. As Norm said, that benefit wouldn't be enough to get Bob Nachtsheim back if his business was going okay, but if the business failed, well, the man was a flower salesman and he was going to work for somebody. Fact is, the retirement benefit would still be available. And that thousand dollars was cheaper than buying a new policy four or five years later when Bob was older. So, for a thousand dollars, if Mr. Nachtsheim's business failed, Norm had a competitive advantage over the rest of the industry in getting Bob back. So Norm chose B.

"If he was going to murder Bob, Norm didn't *need* to pay a thousand dollars to keep the retirement benefit in the policy—it says there in the policy it continues for seven months. If he was thinking of murder, Norm wouldn't have paid the thousand dollars; he'd just let the policy stay there and nobody would have ever come to see him.

"That insurance policy should have been explained to that first jury. It should have been explained to that jury just like I explained it to you. Paying that premium was not the action of a man who intended to commit murder. Exactly the opposite.

"That's why people should've been called. Norm saw his wife and children that morning. They should've been called. Norm went to work and was called by Tom Whalen in front of a whole bunch of people. He was told help was needed, he went over, pitched in, told them if they needed any more help to call him. Those are not the actions of a murderer.

"Norm granted Krueger an interview when Krueger asked him, talked to him for an hour. He told Krueger he intended to give a significant part of the insurance dollars to the family, and he agreed to take a polygraph."

Another yellow wad flew in Snider's direction.

"Now, everything I just ran through with you are things Norm did that make it appear *not* that he's guilty but that he had nothing to do with this thing. Everything Norm's done up to the point of hiring a lawyer is consistent with being innocent. Then Mr. Gainsley was retained, and after hiring a lawyer, this is what happened. Now I'm not saying these early things are negligent, but this is how the view of Norm from the outside world changed after he got a lawyer.

334

"First, he refused to talk further with Lieutenant Krueger because of his lawyer's advice, after having already talked to him for an hour. He'd already told Krueger he'd take a polygraph test. Now he refused the polygraph because his lawyer told him not to take it.

"He was told by his lawyer he didn't have the authority to give any of those insurance dollars to the Nachtsheim family. With Mr. Gainsley in the saddle, Norm aggressively pursues the hundred-thousand dollars—of which Mr. Gainsley is trying to sign on for a contingency fee. Now Prudential had to pay that insurance policy to somebody, but why in the world should a lawyer get a contingency fee from it? So Norm gets sued for one-hundred-thousand dollars, which he'd wanted to share in the first place.

"Norm takes the Fifth Amendment when he's deposed because his lawyer tells him to, even though he's never told his lawyer anything but the truth, which that lawyer says was not incriminating. In his deposition, Mr. Gainsley states: 'Norm had not told me anything that would incriminate him,' but that sure makes him look guilty, and we're going to discuss that.

"Norm gets sued for wrongful death. Things have gone from bad to worse since he got a lawyer. The jury hears about the insurance policy and they hear that when Norm's asked if he killed the man he said: 'I refuse to answer on the grounds it might tend to incriminate me.'

"The first jury hears about the polygraph when his lawyer says: 'After he talked to me, I advised him not to take the polygraph.' The whole case is tried and the first jury never hears that there is a possible suspect anywhere else in the world. Norm's life is destroyed."

Another yellow page was added to the collection.

"Now, to add insult to injury, his lawyer, who said Norm's innocent, comes into this courtroom and blames Norm for the murder. Our expert, Mr. Earl Gray, told you about belief, and client, and about dedication to purpose. It's what separates a lawyer from an attorney.

"But I'm not done with how it began to look bad for Norm, because then Betty Nachtsheim developed a three million dollar motive. These are the things she says that you just don't have any backup for except her:

"'Bob Nachtsheim quit Midwest Floral because Norm was shipping pornography.' No complaints were coming from anybody and Bob left because he wanted to start his own business, but you blacken Norm by saying 'Oh, my. He's a porno dealer now.' Juries don't like porn dealers. Betty invented that as a reason Bob left, invented it with a three million dollar motive.

"Betty says, 'Bob told me Norm was parked outside.' That's all Betty. Nobody else in the world says that and it's just not true.

"This business about the only reason orchids would be out of the cooler was because Bob was going to sell them to another wholesaler. The only person in the world who says it is Betty Nachtsheim. In the police reports and in his own testimony, Alan Mentes says Bob's normal practice was to take the orchids out of the cooler every morning, let them warm up because they're fragile and make sure they're fresh enough to use. Tom Whalen testified that's what the whole industry did with orchids, but Betty Nachtsheim, who knows it's not true, sticks that into the case. Norm told you, 'I told Gainsley that's b.s.,' but Gainsley never did anything about it. It was in the police report from Alan Mentes's testimony, and Gainsley never raised it.

"So now we've got information in the first trial that only comes through Betty Nachtsheim that Norm was a porno dealer who was stalking the victim and who went into B and B the morning of the murder to buy a whole flat of orchids—when Norm had a business five times bigger in the first place. But that's only from Betty with her three-million dollar motive. Nobody else says it.

"And now comes the final blow. Betty inculcates into her own children—and you heard the testimony—that Norm is the only person Bob would let near him with a shotgun because he knew Norm wouldn't have the guts to kill him. That's the testimony. That's Betty Nachtsheim talking. I don't know if you believe that even for a little while, but, first of all, this was a sawed-off shotgun that killed the man. Not much bigger than a pistol and the worst looking weapon in the world. You go to prison for ten years just for possessing one, much less using it. It's a sawed-off that people carry in bank robberies. They're owned and carried by felons. You think you can just walk into a gun store and say, 'I'd like to purchase a sawed-off shotgun'? That's nonsense.

"And Norm is the only person that Bob would have let in with a shotgun? Can you imagine that? Standing there in the street with a shotgun, knocking on the door in the morning to come in? Yeah, sure. That's ridiculous, and Betty invented it. First, so she could narrow in on Norm because that was who she was suing; and second, so she could get in a little dig, a swipe at Norm that he wouldn't have the guts to kill Bob, as if that was really a jab.

"But even that wasn't enough. Remember that before he got a lawyer, everything made Norm look innocent. Norm hired a lawyer and it began to look bad. Betty Nachtsheim throws dirt all over him with these silly statements, and now here's where we get into the reasons for this trial. His own lawyer, rather than defending the case and saying, 'I did a workmanlike job,' instead makes him look guilty."

Snider added another yellow ball to the pile growing on counsel's table.

"The Fifth Amendment issue. Every expert on both sides of this trial said Norm's taking the Fifth Amendment was damaging. *You* know it was worse than damaging. To sit in a trial and have a man ask, 'Did you kill Bob Nachtsheim?' and have to *read*, 'I refuse to answer on the grounds that it may tend to incriminate me'"—it's inconceivable you could dream up any worse evidence against him. In fact, according to Judge McCarr's order, which is in evidence, this case would *never* have even been given to a jury—it would have been dismissed—*except* for that taking of the Fifth Amendment. Hugely damaging.

"Now our question today is, if Mr. Gainsley could have done something about it and didn't, then his case is over. He loses. He was negligent and it caused the original verdict.

"What was it that Mr. Gainsley should have done? All right. Step One. Remember Mr. Gainsley wrote a letter to Mr. Meshbesher. The wrongful death case was a year old and he wrote Mr. Meshbesher and said: Dear Ron, I was thinking about having my client waive his Fifth Amendment right and you can take his deposition if you forget that I instructed him to take the Fifth and that he took it. Mr. Meshbesher came into this courtroom and testified that, Yes, he remembers receiving that letter; but, he said, that letter wasn't worthy of a response.

"So, Step One is to write Mr. Meshbesher and do it early before the judge can say you're sandbagging. Mr. Gainsley's letter was written late, after the case had been pending for a year. You should write to Mr. Meshbesher and say: 'Dear Ron, My client is ready, willing, and able to be deposed, so you may do so at your earliest convenience. Phil Gainsley.' No conditions on it.

"It doesn't matter what Meshbesher does at that point. If he takes the deposition, then when you get in front of the judge a week later you say, 'Judge, I need an order from you laying the ground rules here. Meshbesher just took my client's deposition; we have an old deposition in another case, stakes aren't the same, I instructed him to do it. It's not fair. We're not blocking discovery. Meshbesher's found out everything he can. Please keep the first deposition out of this trial.' Very logical position if Meshbesher takes the deposition.

"The reason the Fifth comes in and the adverse inference can be drawn in the first place is that Phil Gainsley blocked Meshbesher's ability to take an informed deposition so the jury heard what Ron was able to get. But now, right at the beginning of the case, if Mr. Gainsley offered Mr. Meshbesher the unconditional deposition and Ron takes it, there's no prejudice. Now a judge doesn't have to rule the way the earlier judge did.

"Or Meshbesher's other choice is that he does *not* take a new deposition. If he doesn't write back then, Step Two, you call him and say, 'Are you going to take his deposition? I'm offering it.' And he says, 'No, I'm not going to take his deposition.' Then you can say, 'Then, Ron, don't be arguing that you didn't have a chance to take my client's deposition, because I'm making a memo of this, and we're going to go in front of the judge and you're not going to be able to claim that you can't depose my client so you've got to use that Fifth Amendment deposition.'

"Either way, as the experts said, you can go in front of the judge and say, 'Judge, he's got an old Fifth Amendment claim here. It was in another case. It's got nothing to do with this. The fair way to rule is to tell Meshbesher to use the new deposition he took or he'd better take one because he's not going to be able to make this claim anymore.'

"Now, let's suppose the judge says, 'No, he took it once. I don't care whose fault it is. I don't care if you instructed him.' Then and only then does the *good* lawyer say, 'I can't let this happen to my client. I can't let this jury hear he claimed the Fifth Amendment without standing up in front of them and testifying he never wanted to do that. I told him to do it; he never told me anything incriminating. I made him do it.' Then another lawyer would have to try the case so Mr. Gainsley could have gotten up on the witness stand and taken the blame. Then the effect is blunted. The jury no longer assumes Norm is guilty just because he took the Fifth.

"This is something Mr. Wartnick should never, never, never have been saddled with. Norm spoke freely to Lieutenant Krueger before his lawyer got involved. Norm wanted to tell his story. It's in his correspondence to Gainsley that's in evidence. And Mr. Gainsley said, 'Take the Fifth.' And you know, if Mr. Gainsley had withdrawn himself from the case so he could testify, the polygraph issue that he raised in his opening statement would have been gone, too.

"Members of the jury," Friedberg wadded another page and sent it flying. The jury seemed to enjoy watching the mound grow.

"Earl Grey said in his expert testimony here: 'I've tried two hundred cases, ordinarily involving people accused of wrongdoing. There is no doubt in my mind, there isn't a judge in this state that wouldn't declare a mistrial.' Ron Meshbesher testified he would not dare refer to a polygraph in his opening statement, then Mr. Gainsley says, 'I was afraid Ron was going to slip the polygraph issue in on me.' But that's not why Mr. Gainsley did it. No, 'he made a mistake.' Prior to the trial they'd been discussing the polygraph issue and the judge said it doesn't come into the trial. But Mr. Gainsley says, 'I made a mistake.'

"I used to watch Willie Mays play baseball. If he dropped a fly ball, a big 'E' would light up in center field. If you make an error, you're expected to step up and admit it.

"But let's talk about the real sin. Mr. Gainsley was essentially hired to defend a murder case. As lawyers, Mr. Gray said—and remember, he has defended a whole lot of them—you know if you don't show the jury that someone else might have done it, you're stuck with the fact that somebody murdered the victim and you leave the jury no alternative suspect. You're creating the impression there's no one else in the world who could even have conceived of doing such a thing.

"The failure to investigate, to depose and marshal evidence really goes to the heart of this case. The simplest thing revealed by the lack of investigation is the fact that Mr. Gainsley never spoke to Mr. Mentes, who could have told him Mr. Nachtsheim habitually took those orchids out of the cooler first thing every morning. It was in the police report, but he never caught it.

"If Mr. Gainsley had taken a *reasonable* deposition of Betty Nachtsheim, she would have had to admit she told her psychic that she believed her son committed the murder. That's called an admission of a party opponent. That's admissible evidence.

"Ron Meshbesher, in that original case, argued that the May 1973 incident clearly was not a robbery because the assailant never took Bob's wallet out of his back pocket. Now, in this trial, Lieutenant Krueger was an expert witness. We asked him if this was an aborted robbery—robbers don't plan to kill people, they plan to threaten them. There's no more threatening weapon than a sawed-off shotgun. Bob Nachtsheim was the type of personality that would have told them, 'Get out of here,' and if the gun was fired accidentally, what would the robber do? He would flee. His plan's gone astray. It's an aborted robbery and the guy was looking at life in prison.

"Now then, let's talk about whether or not this was readily available from the police report. Roger Nordstrom—you remember Nordstrom? He's down in Texas, wore sunglasses during his deposition. He's an ex-convict. Scary guy. Roger Nordstrom has now testified under oath that he cannot recall what he was doing the night before his best friend's father was murdered, despite the fact that three people testified he was there when they were discussing at least some type of plan to steal from the man who was murdered the next morning.

"Now what do you expect him to do? Say, 'Yeah, I did it'? No! You subpoena him, he shows up, and his testimony is as revealing as any you've ever heard. Bobby Nachtsheim is his best friend. A couple of hours after this get-together at Bobby's apartment, when Roger is drunk and loaded, his best friend's father is murdered. We know he was discussing stealing from him and now he can't recall where he was that evening. If you believe that, I have a bridge to sell. Of course he remembers where he was. Just how many parties do you think he's been to where the next morning his best friend's father was murdered?

"When a jury hears that, they've got to get suspicious. Ask yourself, 'Why would he lie?' There's only one reason.

"Two weeks earlier, Bob Nachtsheim had gone to his son's apartment where Roger Nordstrom and Debra Feist were present, and guess what Bob Nachtsheim brought? Mr. Nachtsheim went to get back his car from his son while Roger Nordstrom was present, and Mr. Nachtsheim brought a policeman with him. How do we know that? Debra Feist-Nachtsheim told us. I'm reading from her deposition: '"I seen the officer. I didn't see the squad car 'cause I don't—" Question, "Did you see one officer or two officers?" Answer, "One." Question, "Do you know why Bob Nachtsheim felt compelled to come to the door to pick up his car with a police officer shortly before the murder?" Answer, "No, I don't."'

"Nice lady, Debbie, but let me ask you something. Do you believe she doesn't know why Bob brought a cop with him to his own son's apartment to get his own car back? Well, of course she knows. Have you ever heard of another father going to his son's apartment and feeling like he had to take a cop with him? There's only one reason: fear.

"Which just adds credibility to Mr. Evers's statement. Tom Evers testified Bob told him he'd been threatened by Roger Nordstrom with a shotgun. That's a terrible experience, and Tom Evers sat in that witness seat and recounted Bob saying to him, 'The guy threatened me with a shotgun.' No wonder he took a cop with him. You think under those circumstances the first jury would've been able to say there were no other possibilities for who committed the murder?

"Now add a few more things to that, and this is all admissible evidence. Bobby hated his father, we know that. We know he needed money. He couldn't pay for the car. We know he used drugs, and don't for a minute believe it was just pot. In Dennis Kreuser's deal it was cocaine, and Kreuser testified they used cocaine. And remember all this took place back in 1973 when using cocaine was not cool, not avant-garde like it is today. These aren't just guys lying around smoking a joint. They're guys, all of whom have committed crimes, two have been to prison and the other guy is one hateful sucker.

"The party or whatever you want to call it took place late evening of May 23rd, early morning hours of the 24th. Bobby discussed with Roger Nordstrom about robbing Bob at the florist shop. Kreuser [sic] testifies to that. I had Kreuser [sic]* up here on the stand and I said, 'Explain to the jury the difference between robbery and burglary.' He used the words *force* and *violence*. The defense wants you to believe this nonsense about sticking a pole in the window and lifting somebody's pants. That's right out of Huck Finn. But how do we know it's not true? How do we *know*?

"First, Kreuser says they weren't talking about some prank. They were talking about a robbery in the florist shop. That's Kreuser's testimony. Made him so uncomfortable he left the party, not because he had any moral compunctions at that point in his life about crime, but because he didn't want to be involved in doing it to Bob, the man who'd helped him get out of prison.

"You forget about something? Mr. Mason apparently did. Terry Nachtsheim-Peters, the same woman who testified she is convinced it must be Norm Wartnick because he's the only person her father would let into his florist shop with a shotgun—and I think she does believe that, she's gotten it from her mother and she's come to believe it over the years. But Ms. Nachtsheim-Peters was questioned right here in front of you all. 'Did it come to your attention that your brother drew a sketch of the florist shop for one of the party participants by the name of Nordstrom?' Her Answer: 'I think I heard at some point there was a sketch drawn. I don't think I ever knew who drew it.'

"Well, now who could have drawn it? A sketch was drawn at that party of the florist shop. Is this a casual rumor, speculation, innuendo? People intend

* - It was actually Sheran who make these statements on the witness stand.

the natural consequences of their acts. These people were at, not a party, but a get-together consuming pot, at best, cocaine at worst, and booze. There's a synergistic effect to those when you do them together. These guys, an ex-con and a son who hated his father, discuss robbing that father at his florist shop. A sketch is drawn of the florist shop. The evidence is here. It's admissible.

"Originally Bobby and Debbie conflicted when they talked to Lieutenant Krueger about who went where with whom, but ultimately they got their stories linked up and said they slept together—which gave Bobby an alibi.

"Somehow, some way, Nordstrom walks into the store, still drunk, still loaded, with his shotgun, having looked at the diagram of the florist shop. Bob tells him to screw off, the gun is fired, and Nordstrom runs. That, ladies and gentlemen of the jury, is what happened.

"When Lieutenant Krueger looks for Nordstrom all over town, he can't find him; and Bobby Nachtsheim tells you, 'Well, I think he's around. I'm not really sure. I think maybe he lived—no, he's either hiding out or he did split.' But when Krueger, the Fox, looks for somebody, he tends to find him, and this guy was gone.

"Bobby goes to B and B and, get this—it's in the transcript, I'm not making it up—Detective Quinn testified in the first trial where the jury never heard of a party, Detective Quinn does not know there's a man named Nordstrom somewhere in the world, does not know anything about a crime being planned, doesn't know that Bobby hates his father, knows zero, nothing. And Detective Quinn is questioned about trying to interview Bobby. His father's just been carried out; there's still blood there. Question: 'Do your notes reflect whether or not you asked him to come give a statement?' Answer: 'Yes, I did ask him.' Question: 'Did you ask him to be interviewed extensively regarding information that might be helpful in resolving the case with the homicide of his father?' Answer: 'Yes, I did.' Question: 'What did he say to you?' Answer: 'He said he was too busy, he'd have to stay at the business and work and perhaps later we could talk.'

"Wait a minute! This is Officer Quinn, first detective that has the case. Bobby, your father's in the hospital; he's dying. I'd like to talk to you about this. Meet me; let's talk.

"'I'm too busy. I can't go with you. No, I have work to do.'

"You know what he's saying? Inside he's saying, 'Oh, oh. Last night I told Nordstrom my father had money, talked about robbing the place. I drew him a map. Last time I saw him, he was flying. Now my dad's been shot. I can't talk to this cop, I've got to get hold of Nordstrom. I've got to find out what's going on. We've got to get our stories together.' That's the only conceivable reason that when a detective asks you to talk to him about why your father is dying, you say I don't have time. That's an insight into why Betty Nachtsheim believed her son was involved—until she saw three million bucks floating around.

"That's why it took Terry Nachtsheim-Peters twenty-one years, by her own testimony, to get up the courage to ask whether Bobby did it.

"And the most amazing thing of all is that the jury in that original trial did *not* know any of this, yet one person on that jury *still* did not think Norm did it.

"Ladies of the jury, there's no way in the world that, knowing this, a person could still believe the most likely person to have murdered Bob Nachtsheim is Norm Wartnick, a guy who didn't even appear to be guilty until his lawyer started advising him.

"If Mr. Gainsley relied on the police reports and did not do any further investigation himself, then our experts have said that reliance on the police report in a murder where there is circumstantial evidence, that is inexcusable. It is negligence. And it's what caused the jury to find that Norm Wartnick did it: because they did not have any other possibility.

"Earl Gray said it's a disgrace to rely on the cops, not that they're dishonest but because they point their investigation. So how could Gainsley testify under oath that he didn't trust Krueger and then rely on Krueger's investigation? That's a sin.

"But, you know that just isn't what really happened. Mr. Gainsley did not have the police reports. He just flat out did not have them, and we can prove it. Follow this chronology with me:

"October 13, 1976—the unjust enrichment complaint was filed.

"February 16th of 1979—Wartnick and Betty Nachtsheim were deposed. No questions were asked by Mr. Gainsley about any alternative suspects. An accusation is being made against Norm Wartnick. Gainsley knows there's furor in the Nachtsheim family. Gainsley asks no questions about alternative suspects.

"March 9th of 1979—Gainsley files a summary judgment memorandum. No reference to alternative suspects.

"April 17, 1979—Gainsley's petition for discretionary review is denied by the Minnesota Supreme Court. He mentions nothing about any alternative suspects.

"April 28, 1981—Lieutenant Krueger is deposed. He's the guy who put these reports together. There's not a single question about alternative suspects.

"August 25, 1982—A letter from Prudential to Mr. Gainsley enclosing an illegible police report where they suggest he subpoena the police file to get a legible copy. Ya just can't get out from under Plaintiff's Exhibit Forty-Two, that illegible copy of the report.

"May 2nd of 1984—the wrongful death lawsuit is served.

"November 12, 1985—Gainsley directs interrogatories to Meshbesher's law firm to say 'give me the answers to anything I want to know.' But no references to alternative suspects because he doesn't have the police reports. He doesn't know about a party, doesn't know about Nordstrom and Bobby and a shotgun threat, and the father who comes with a cop, and the son who hates his father.

"December 1985—Second Memorandum for Summary Judgment. No reference to alternative suspects. He still has not hired an investigator.

"Gainsley serves Wartnick's statement of the case and tells Meshbesher he's going to call one witness, Roger Walker, an economist who'll say Bob Nachtsheim wasn't worth much money. For crying out loud, members of the jury, you want to argue your client didn't murder someone and the only witness you list is somebody who's going to come in and testify the deceased wasn't worth that much while he was alive?

"Hey! What's this? By golly, here's a subpoena. The subpoena Roger Johnson suggested back in 1982. It's directed to the Minneapolis Police Department custodian of records and issued on the 17th day of April, 1986, and says give me the police reports on the first day of the trial. Thirteen years after the crime Mr. Gainsley subpoenas the police reports for trial. Why? Because he still didn't have them.

"Ladies of the jury, he never investigated, he never ever, ever got the police file until the first day of trial. Now Mr. Mason wants to say I'm impolite for calling Mr. Gainsley lazy."

The pile of wadded, yellow balls became hard to control. Snider enjoyed seeing the jurors chuckle as they watched.

"You heard Mr. Gainsley state, 'My job was not to show who did it. My job was to stop him from proving Norm did.' That's how he defined his role.

"The Fifth Amendment killed Norm Wartnick, and the man who has testified repeatedly, 'I had the right to rely on the police files' never had them.

"So, April 21st to 25th—Time after time after time during that trial, Gainsley repeatedly and unsuccessfully attempts to introduce the police reports into the trial. But the law says you can't put police reports into evidence. You must have live witnesses.

"Everybody, even his own expert witnesses, say if he didn't have the reports, that's negligent. No wonder the first jury never heard about Roger Nordstrom. But let's go on. More proof.

"After the trial, Gainsley argues for a judgment n.o.v.—he says I want a new judgment, there was a mistake made here—that's what a motion of judgment n.o.v. is. Gainsley now argues for the very first time in a memorandum, our Exhibit Ninety-Six, that others are implicated in Nachtsheim's death. He's never said anything about that up until his attempts during the trial and afterwards. In his brief to the Minnesota Supreme Court, Gainsley quotes at length from the police report for the first time.

"We asked Jane Lerner, 'Did you ever see the police report? Her Answer: 'No. I think Phil might have got it but no, I never saw it.' She never saw it because it wasn't there."

Friedberg paused and took a deep breath to allow the tension in the room to settle a bit. When he spoke again, his volume had lowered.

"Betty Nachtsheim's sitting in intensive care by her dying husband's bed and she gets a phone call. It's Bobby. What does he say? 'Mom, don't believe what people are saying about me.' A day-and-a-half after Bob's shot? You think maybe a good lawyer would have wanted to ask, 'Bobby, what was it people were saying about you?' Was it because people knew what had gone on? That he drew a map of the shop? That somehow Nordstrom had gotten loose? And Betty believed that Bobby did it, as she's testified.

"You had an opportunity to listen to Norm Wartnick testify, to tell you his life has been totally destroyed and he did nothing wrong. What he did was bank on a lawyer who, at the beginning of this litigation, said that he, Phil Gainsley, was Norm's friend; but now Gainsley testifies he doesn't even know what that means. In his original deposition he testified, 'I believed him.' Now he testifies, when it's in his own interest, 'I was just doing my job.' Well, he didn't.

"Members of the jury, it was never adequately explained to the first jury that Norm Wartnick had two choices back on May 10th of 1973—that both of those choices would have resulted in the insurance continuing for months and that he chose the route that'd make it least likely he was planning a murder.

"Pleading the Fifth Amendment made him look guilty, and it's the only thing that got the case to that first jury. The man—all he had was his own story, his own ability to say that despite having taken the Fifth Amendment and there being no other suspects, the only thing Norm Wartnick had was himself to say, 'I didn't do it.' And his first lawyer in the opening statement says, 'He told me his story and I told him not to take that polygraph test.'

"Here is the special verdict form. You've seen it before. It's my suggestion that the most orderly way to look at it is to start with the Fifth Amendment question and find that he was negligent in not mitigating the Fifth amendment problem and finding, as everybody agrees, that it damaged Mr. Wartnick, that it proximately caused the original verdict, and that *but for it* there would not have been a case and would not have been a verdict against Norm Wartnick.

"Then you can go to the investigation part of the verdict form because it logically follows. And you should find the same way because there wasn't any investigation. Even his own experts, when we catch him without the police reports, say that is negligent, it was the proximate cause, and except for it the jury would not have reached that verdict.

"And then the polygraph question is the icing on the cake. He set the whole trial when he stood up in his opening statement and keyed the jury into the fact that 'the man talked to me and I told him not to take the lie detector test,' when no one else in the world could have gotten that issue into the trial.

"Then the last question is, 'What sum of money will fairly and adequately compensate Wartnick for his damages in this case?'

"There really isn't any sum of money that would fairly and adequately compensate a man for going through life with this handle on him, suffering scorn and ridicule in the community. You cannot compensate him for those things—the law does not allow it. There's only one thing you can do. You can take the judgment off his back so that he can keep what he earns; so that when he goes out and referees a Little League game, he gets to keep the whole check.

"The current judgment against him is $3,444,369.37—it's written right there. If that amount of money is deposited into the court, then that relieves him of that judgment. It's paid. Then, in addition to that, he has already paid $95,241.13 and he is entitled to get that back."

Friedberg pushed aside his notepad and stepped from behind the lectern so nothing separated him from the jury. "Mr. Mason brought up something in this case that I suppose he brought up because he thought it might affect you. He brought it up through Mr. Meshbesher. There are a lot of lawyers' fees in this case. But you cannot compensate Mr. Wartnick for his lawyers' fees, whatever they may be. That's his problem and you can't award money for it. You can only award money to liquidate the judgment.

"Mr. Wartnick, after it was brought up, told you what he believes is going to happen in this case. Any amount of money that's awarded is going to be deposited into the bankruptcy court when he files bankruptcy; and the bankruptcy court, without a jury, will determine 'Do lawyers get anything?' and, if so, how much and who gets what?

"But the most important thing to him now, and has always been, that the world understand he is not a murderer. That doesn't make up for twenty years of pain and suffering, but it does give him back the name he had and that's all we want you to do."

CHAPTER 50

Once again Wartnick waited in the war room at Faegre. Once again he readjusted himself in a chair and watched the second-hand tick around the face of the clock on the wall.

"There's the argument you planned to give," Friedberg said. He stole a sip of coffee. "—the argument you gave, and the argument you wish you gave." He glanced at Wartnick. "Since closing all I can think of is what I wish I'd said. But," he shrugged, "it is what it is."

"Judging by the reactions of the judge and jury, I don't think your closing will be forgotten, Joe." Snider swallowed the last drops in his cup and set it on the tray to be picked up at the end of the day. "But not very good planning on your part." He chuckled.

"Well who would've thought there wouldn't be a shelf!" Friedberg grinned. "But I have to say, Chuck, what I'll never forget is the look on your face in chambers."

During Friedberg's closing argument another skirmish had been mounted by Mason. Judge Stanoch had taken them all into chambers. Mason made his objection, then Stanoch turned to Friedberg, who had grinned and turned to Snider, who had grinned and turned to Webber—proof things do roll downhill.

"For crying out loud, what was Mason in a wad over?" Webber said. "So you read from the *Rules of Evidence* during closing. Big deal! I still don't see what all the excitement was about—though a little warning would've been nice. Next time at least give me the few minutes walking to chambers to figure out what I might say."

The phone rang. Webber answered. "Faegre. Webber speaking. Okay, we'll be right over." He turned to Snider and nodded. "Jury's in," He put a hand on Wartnick's shoulder and smiled. "Here we go."

From his chair on the front row behind counsel's table, Wartnick saw the Nachtsheims take their customary seats behind Gainsley, the pucker on Betty's face more well-defined than he expected.

"Norm." Snider's voice penetrated the ringing in Wartnick's ears and the noise in the room. "Norm, did you hear what I said?"

Wartnick shook his head, more to clear his thoughts than in answer.

"Joe and I, when we were coming up just now, were stopped by two of the alternate jurors—you know, the ladies who were sitting to the side over there. They wanted to tell us that, if it was up to them, we'd win hands down."

Wartnick looked confused, as though he could not comprehend the statement.

"Just thought you'd like to know," Snider smiled. "I won't tell you to relax because I can imagine how hard this is, but try to anyhow." He dropped a reassuring hand on Wartnick's shoulder.

Webber entered the courtroom behind Mason and made his crazy way to defendant's end of the table—shook Mason's hand, then Magarian's, and finally Gainsley's. To each Webber said, "Good luck" with a smile.

Friedberg entered. He and Snider were seated just as the bailiff sang out, "All rise. The court of the honorable Judge John Stanoch is now in session."

"Let's bring in the jury." Stanoch spoke before he was even seated.

"Madam Foreman, have you reached a verdict?"

"We have, Your Honor."

Stanoch nodded to the bailiff, who crossed to the jury box, retrieved the Verdict Form, and walked it to the bench. The judge unfolded the paper, perused it for technical and legal accuracy, nodded, refolded the Form, and returned it to the bailiff. Once the form was returned to the Foreman's hand, Judge Stanoch said, "Please stand, Mr. Gainsley, for the verdict.

"For Count One: 'Was Mr. Gainsley negligent in what he said concerning polygraphs in his opening statement,' how do you find?"

"For the Plaintiff, Your Honor." Snider heard Wartnick inhale.

"For Count Two, 'Was the jury's finding against Mr. Wartnick proximately caused by what Mr. Gainsley said concerning polygraphs in his opening statement,' how do you find?"

"For the Defendant."

Phil Gainsley exhaled in a rush. Mason looked smug. There was only silence on plaintiff's side of the courtroom.

With Count Two found for the Defendant, Count Three was skipped.

"For Count Four, then," Judge Stanoch said, "'Was Mr. Gainsley negligent concerning interviewing and deposing witnesses and suspects in the Nachtsheim murder,' how do you find?"

"For the Plaintiff, Your Honor."

"For Count Five, then, 'Was the jury's finding against Mr. Wartnick proximately caused by Mr. Gainsley's conduct concerning interviewing and deposing witnesses and suspects in the Nachtsheim murder,' how do you find?"

"For the Plaintiff."

"For Count Six, 'Would Mr. Wartnick have been successful in his defense of the wrongful death action if Mr. Gainsley had interviewed and deposed additional witnesses and suspects in the Nachtsheim murder,' how do you find?"

"For the Plaintiff, Your Honor."

Wartnick's breathing deepened. John Nachtsheim instinctively glanced to his mother to determine if they liked the jury's decision. Betty's jaw was clinched. Terry's arms crossed in front of her like a shield.

"For Count Seven, 'Was Mr. Gainsley negligent concerning the offer for a second deposition,' how do you find?"

"For the Plaintiff, Your Honor."

"For Count Eight, 'Was the jury's finding against Mr. Wartnick proximately caused by Mr. Gainsley's conduct concerning the offer for a second deposition,' how do you find?"

"For the Plaintiff, Your Honor."

From defendant's end of the table, Magarian glanced sideways at Snider and offered a faint smile and near-imperceptible nod. Gainsley gazed into some distant location and tapped his fingers rhythmically against his knee, an indication he was, mentally, no longer with them.

"For Count Nine, 'Would Mr. Wartnick have been successful in his defense of the wrongful death action if Mr. Gainsley's conduct concerning the second deposition had been different,' how do you find?"

"For the Plaintiff, Your Honor."

"For Count Ten, looking at the jury's findings for Questions One, Four, and Seven, 'Was the jury's finding against Mr. Wartnick caused by the cumulative effect of Mr. Gainsley's negligence, if any, as found by you in those answers above?"

"Yes, Your Honor."

"For Count Eleven, 'Would Mr. Wartnick have been successful in his defense of the wrongful death action if Mr. Gainsley's negligence, if any, as found by you in those answers above had not occurred?"

"Yes, Your Honor."

Snider relaxed into his chair. The prophet Amos's words rang in his ears: *Let justice roll down like mighty waters.*

"What sum of money will fairly and adequately compensate Mr. Wartnick for his damages in this case?"

"Four million, forty-five thousand, six hundred and sixteen dollars."

Friedberg panicked. Could the excessive reward be nullified by Stanoch? He glanced to Snider, but Snider beamed and thumped Webber on the back.

"The verdict is received," Stanoch concluded. "Thank you, jury, for your service. Court adjourned."

The gavel fell.

Mason strode immediately up the aisle and out the door, followed closely by Gainsley and Magarian. No customary handshake of congratulations, not even a nod. Betty Nachtsheim and crew almost beat them to the door.

Webber noticed Wartnick was seated; a vacuous expression of disbelief etched his face. As Webber reached out his hand and placed it on Wartnick's shoulder, the weary man began to quietly weep. Justice had come at enormous cost.

CHAPTER 51

FRIDAY EVENING, OCTOBER 28, 1994

The day had been warm for this late in October. Southerly wind gusts whipped up the waters of Christmas Lake and rattled the shutters on the west side of Jerry Snider's home. Babe Wartnick looked out across the lake from that bank of west-facing windows, sipped champagne, and watched the black, leafless fingers of old sugar maples claw at the overcast sky.

Snider studied the thin lines that etched the corners of Babe's eyes and mouth, evidences she had braved a life filled with both great joy and great sorrow. He moved slowly to stand beside her. Together they watched the figures of a family aboard an old runabout on the lake; the family had managed to get in one last outing before winter set in. Their silhouette slowed and bobbed as they circled something in the water.

Wartnick joined them. He, too, quietly watched the scene unfold.

"Many nights I've stood here," Snider's resonant voice rumbled softly, "and let the wind blow away thoughts of the day's struggles. The window at the far end opens, and when the wind's from the west you can hear the waves against the shoreline."

Babe took another sip and concentrated on the little family. They disappeared behind the bulk of a spruce.

"So," Wartnick finished off his champagne with a quick gulp. "How'd the meeting go this afternoon? Betty still stubborn, or was she willing to settle?"

"Well, I was going to wait until Joe got here. He wanted to give you the details."

"I've done enough waiting for two lifetimes." Babe turned from the window. "What did Betty say?"

"More to the point, I think, is what Judge Stanoch said." Snider watched the couple closely. "He informed Meshbesher that if Ron doesn't convince the Nachtsheims to settle, then he may investigate Nachtsheim's murder."

Babe's eyes closed, briefly, in relief. She inhaled deeply, then continued to take small sips at the champagne.

Wartnick just shook his head and tried to decide if he was more relieved or more angry. It had been a long, hard battle and they were all tired of the

Nachtsheim zoo. Betty would end up taking the deal—anything else would be inconsistent with the goal she had been so determined to grasp.

Justice. Snider could read it in Wartnick's eyes. Would there ever, truly be justice in this world?

"Having steak. Right, Jerr?" Friedberg's voice rang from the foyer. "You know I like mine rare."

"Make that moo-ing." A woman's voice called out.

Then the man, himself, strode into the room. He escorted a slender woman his age whose long legs were well suited to the short length of black skirt.

"Carolyn, you've heard me speak of Babe Wartnick," Friedberg said. "Babe, my wife Carolyn. Norm, how ya doing?" The two shook hands with fervor.

"Nice to finally meet you." Babe said.

"I'll be doing a lot better when you two tell us what happened today," Wartnick replied.

The attorneys shook hands with the warmth of mutual respect. "I'm afraid it's not steaks tonight, Joe."

"I was joking. Whatever Kathy fixes will be great. It's the reason for the occasion that's important tonight." Friedberg slapped Wartnick on the back. "Did you tell Jerry your elevator story?"

"Not yet."

"Well, tell him! You waiting on Christmas?"

Kathy Snider escorted the group into the dining room. "Norm, if you would be seated here, and Babe, to Norm's right, there by Jerry. Carolyn, you're welcome to be seated by your husband. Lord knows we don't get to see these guys often enough."

"I was riding down to the parking garage after the verdict—" Wartnick began. "This looks really good, Kathy. I love roasted potatoes.—and one of the ladies from the jury was riding down, too, and she told me they'd have given me more if the judge would have allowed it."

Snider nodded, then lifted his glass. "To Judges Hartigan, Devitt, Davis, Stanoch, and all fair-minded men and women of integrity."

"Hear, hear!" Friedberg agreed as crystal clinked. "There's nothing better than a good cause and an innocent client. That's why you become a lawyer." Then he grinned. "And thank God for Jack Mason." He caught a flitter of confusion cross Babe's face. "You've got to know your jury, what makes them tick, what they're gonna respond to."

"Jack Mason didn't have a clue," Snider explained.

"Or how to pick his expert witnesses," Friedberg said. "With Sheran not remembering his previous rulings—. And if things hadn't already been going against them, the bow-tied bigot would have sunk them." Friedberg glanced toward Snider. "I thought I was gonna hoot when Stanoch said what he did as we were leaving the courtroom that day."

Snider smiled at his wife. "Joe's cross-examination of Mason's polygraph expert, Charles Yeschke." He mimed Stanoch's air of judicial authority. "'Brutal cross.'"

"The judge said that?"

Snider chuckled. "What else could he say?"

Forks clunked against china; salt and pepper were passed; wine was poured.

"Not to be a spoil-sport," Babe said, "but why does Betty get to keep the money? We just proved she shouldn't have gotten it in the first place."

"No, Babe," Snider said. "Unfortunately all we've proven, legally, is that Phil Gainsley contributed negligently to the original verdict. There was only a short time after the original verdict when Norm could have challenged the judgment. Now, it would require winning another trial against Mrs. Nachtsheim-Prokosh—and even then nothing would be guaranteed. It would require significant evidence of fraud on her part, evidence we don't have. She was awarded the judgment, the judgment must be paid. That's what we accomplished."

"I believe in our judicial system," Wartnick said as he took another bite of salad.

The dinner clatter quieted. Wartnick glanced up and around the table to meet their curious, watchful gazes. "I was crushed by the system, but I believe in it. Being in the wrong place at the wrong time—there's a lot of what-ifs—"

"If this system of justice is gonna work," Friedberg barged in, "you can't have it take ten, twelve years to find resolution. You ought to be able, at the end of the day, to get a fair and speedy decision." He raised a piece of tenderloin to his mouth.

"—before a fair and impartial judge," Snider added. "If you do right, then you do well—and we're fortunate that happened here."

Snider saw Wartnick smile at Babe, and she received his smile with gentleness in her eyes. She looked still too weary to smile. She would, though, Snider knew. In time.

❧

EPILOGUE

- Norm and Babe kept their home, the judgment was settled, and their family is closer now than ever. At time of publication, they have seven grandchildren, and the family still meets together for dinner every Friday evening, just like it has done for over forty years.

  o When Babe was asked if she had been able to find any positives through their ordeal, she replied, "When you've been at the bottom, you become more empathetic. ... Out of every ugly thing comes something good. It pushes you to where you need to be." She maintains that each part of life, even the difficult situations, makes you who you need to be for the steps ahead.

- After more court hearings, Betty finally settled. Her children again dispersed to opposite corners of the country, and she spent her last years selling clothes for a major retailer in a suburb of St. Paul. She died in 2002, was buried beside Bob, even though investigators interviewed by the author said that, in their opinion, she never shed a tear over his death.

- Jerry has retired from Faegre [now titled Faegre, Baker, Daniels]. He and his wife, Kathy, are active socially and professionally.

  o Jerry clerked for U. S. Supreme Court Chief Justice Warren Burger and Associate Justice Tom C. Clark. He focuses primarily on the trial and appeals of complex civil cases and has tried numerous cases to jury verdict or court decision. Jerry has been a managing partner of the international law firm of Faegre and Benson and is a Fellow of the American College of Trial Lawyers. At the appellate level, he has argued cases in the Eighth Circuit Court of Appeals, the Federal Circuit Court of Appeals, the Minnesota Court of Appeals, the Minnesota Supreme Court, and the United States Court of Claims. Jerry has taught litigation and trial practice and lectures at various seminars on issues involving professional trial preparation and practice. Jerry's professional recognition includes:
    » Fellow of the American College of Trial Lawyers since 1991
    » Lawdragon's 500 Leading Litigators in America
    » *The Best Lawyers in America*, Commercial Litigation, 2006–2011
    » *Chambers USA: America's Leading Lawyers for Business*, Litigation:

General Commercial, 2004–2011
- » Top 40 Business Litigator, *Minnesota Law & Politics*, 2009–2010
- » *Super Lawyers*, Top 100 (Minnesota), 2008
- » *Super Lawyers*, Business Litigation, 2007–2011
- » Local Litigation Star, *Benchmark: Litigation*, 2008–2011

- Until the late 2000s, Ed Magarian still sent Jerry Snider a Christmas card every year, and once, on crossing paths, he expressed appreciation for how much he had learned from watching Jerry handle the Wartnick case.

- Joe Friedberg and his wife, Carolyn, are favorites at get-togethers for their senses of humor and the stories they tell.

  o Joe has extensive experience in litigating criminal, white-collar criminal, and complex civil cases in state and federal courts across the United States including the United States Supreme Court. The Minnesota Association of Criminal Defense Lawyers honored him with their Distinguished Service Award. He is President of the American Board of Criminal Lawyers and is a member of the American Board of Trial Advocates. Joe is a fellow in the American College of Trial Lawyers. The National Board of Trial Advocacy has certified him as a criminal trial specialist. He is a frequent lecturer at law schools and continuing legal education seminars and is a television and radio commentator. *Minnesota Law & Politics* named him to their Minnesota Legal Hall of Fame as one of the 100 most influential lawyers in the history of the state. Joe is listed in all editions of *The Best Lawyers in America*.

  o Joe says: "I'm sick of people being convicted without being defended aggressively with positive theories. If nothing else I'm going to at least scare the prosecutor."

- Charles F. "Chuck" Webber is a trial lawyer and appellate specialist with Faegre and in October 2010 was selected a Fellow of the American College of Trial Lawyers. Jerry Snider considers him one of the best trial lawyers within the firm, and Chuck is one of the leading appellate specialists in the Twin Cities area. He sits on the Supreme Court Advisory Committee on the Rules of Civil Appellate Procedure and is the immediate past chair of the Appellate Section of the Minnesota State Bar Association. Chuck has been recognized as:

  - » *The Best Lawyers in America*, Commercial Litigation, 2006-12
  - » *Chambers USA: America's Leading Lawyers for Business*, Litigation: General Commercial, 2004–11

» *Super Lawyers*, Business Litigation, 2007–11

- Steven L. Severson is a member of Faegre's ERISA litigation practice. He also concentrates in the areas of franchise and distribution litigation, antitrust litigation, products liability litigation, minority shareholder disputes, and other complex commercial matters. He was recognized by *Super Lawyers* in the Employee Benefits/ERISA area for 2011.

- Ronald I. Meshbesher still practices through his firm, Meshbesher & Spence, in the Minneapolis area. He figures as a character in the Coen Brothers' 2009 film *A Serious Man* (Focus Features).

  o Ron Meshbesher is recognized as a top lawyer by his peers and by the press in nearly every legal publication in the United States; earned Distinguished Service or Lifetime Achievement Awards from the Minnesota Association of Criminal Defense Lawyers, the Minnesota Trial Lawyers Association, and the American College of Trial Lawyers.

  o Ron earned his national reputation in several highly publicized criminal defense cases in Minnesota in the 1970s and 1980s.

  o In the civil courtroom, Ron has set multiple state records for the settlements and verdicts he has won for his clients.

  o "I respect jurors," Meshbesher says. "Some lawyers think they're stupid. I don't. I think the jury system in this country is the most important part of our legal system. To have 12 people from all walks of life, who know nothing about the case, come in and make a decision is the right way to do it" (interviewed in *Minnesota SuperLawyers* by Erik Lundegaard, August 2010).

- Michael J. Davis was appointed by President Clinton to the Minnesota Federal District Court. As of publication, he is Chief Judge of that court.

- John Stanoch retired from the bench shortly after this trial.

- Phil Gainsley still practices law, primarily divorce cases. Throughout 1992 and following, a number of Gainsley's articles were published in a leading, international journal for the music industry in which he was involved. Gainsley occasionally speaks at various regional legal conferences on the topic of courtroom litigation.

- Russ Krueger never advanced the murder investigation; he declared leads too cold to follow. When the author tried to contact him for his input for this manuscript, he declined to participate.

- Terry Nachtsheim Peters was active with victim's rights organizations. She may have been among the forces behind passage of legislation in Minnesota that eliminated an employer from being the recipient of insurance proceeds following the death of a former employee, though no confirmation of this could be found.

- Larry Strehlow's death is further discussed in Rubenstein's *Greed, Rage, and Love Gone Wrong: Murder in Minnesota*—potentially another miscarriage of justice, though we probably will not know for sure until revealed by the final Judge once time is no more.

  o The sisters of Larry Strehlow came to Jerry Snider after the malpractice verdict with a request he look into their brother's bizarre death. After twenty years, there was not enough evidence or information to make further investigation possible.

- In the early 2000s, Wanda Evers injured her back in a motorcycle accident while riding with her husband. Life became overwhelming for Tom and he moved out-of-state. The author would like to tell him thank you for his service to this country.

ACKNOWLEDGEMENTS

Special appreciation goes to:

~ Ken: my second pair of eyes and the granite that keeps my balloon sufficiently grounded, and who helps me to look ever deeper into the important

~ Jerry Snider, Carol Kissner, Becky Reichel, Steve Severson, Chuck Webber, Jerri Lou Holmgren, Linda Faber, and Faegre & Benson for freely sharing source documents, experiences, thoughts, memories, emotions, and enthusiasm

- Joe Friedberg and Ron Meshbesher for not flinching from the truth

~ Nancy Peters, Susan Larson, and Media Relations, for their assistance in understanding behind-the-scenes at the Hennepin County Government Center

- the helpful ladies hard at work in those dank Government Center basement file storage rooms, for always replying graciously to my requests

~ freelance editor and new friend Betsy Gonzalez, for understanding, insight, and enthusiasm

- Charlotte, Diane, Eric, Erin, Ernestine, Ken, Kristi, Jerry, Sam, Sarah, Scott, Traci, and all those who read, criticized, and encouraged and, in the process, made the telling of this story much better than it could otherwise have been

~ Scott and Jeff, sounding boards and adverb police: let's keep getting better

Please visit the website, http://theOrchidMurder.com, for photographs, deleted scenes, author blog, thoughts and explanations from Jerry Snider on various aspects of the case, and additional materials and information, including the complete "Dear Jane" memo and conflicting testimony within the police file, some of which was never investigated.

CPSIA information can be obtained at www.ICGtesting.com
Printed in the USA
LVOW040026091112

306565LV00002B/3/P